Henry James and *The Turn of the Screw*

Archbishop Benson giving Henry James the idea
for *The Turn of the Screw*—according to Max Beerbohm

Henry James
and *The Turn of the Screw*

E. A. Sheppard

Auckland University Press · Oxford University Press

FIRST PUBLISHED 1974

PRINTED IN GREAT BRITAIN
BY RICHARD CLAY (THE CHAUCER PRESS), LTD,
BUNGAY, SUFFOLK

© E. A. SHEPPARD 1974

ISBN 0 19 647810 3

Contents

Prefatory Note

In December 1969 I was honoured by an invitation to deliver the Macmillan Brown Lectures[1] for the following year, and these were duly presented at the University of Auckland on 6, 8, and 14 October 1970. These were public lectures, not designed either in subject or in treatment for an exclusively academic audience, and in preparing them for publication I have kept to the general plan, and as far as possible the informality, of their original presentation. But since my view of the story discussed is not quite in accord with any so far put forward, and since a number of observations relative to it, varying both in scope and in evidential strength, have occurred to me over years of lecturing on the work of Henry James, it seemed desirable to make as full and amply documented a statement of these matters as my resources permitted. A year's refresher leave in 1971 provided the opportunity, and when in December 1971 the book was accepted by the Auckland University Press it was virtually complete, even to the two appendices. At that stage, however, I decided to include Chapter VII and to extend what is now Chapter VIII, the main addition being Section x. But in 1972 I had to resume teaching, and a series of unforeseen difficulties and delays in obtaining reference material further hampered work on these additions; so that it is only now, at the end of May 1973, that a book which is essentially a product of 1971 goes to the printer.

I have taken no account of two studies recently brought to my notice, although these overlap portions of my own work—Michael Egan, *Henry James: the Ibsen Years* (London: Vision, 1972) and Ernest Tuveson, 'The Turn of the Screw: a Palimpsest', *Studies in English Literature 1500–1900*, XII, Autumn, 1972, 783–800. The corresponding portions of my book having been completed some two years before these studies appeared, I note merely that a similarity of interests has produced in the first case views for the most part divergent from my own, and in the second some near parallels with certain of my arguments as these were formulated in my Macmillan Brown Lectures.

My grateful thanks are due to the Librarians and Staff of Auckland University Library and Auckland Public Library respectively for the freedom with which they have made their books and periodicals available. I am especially indebted to the Interloan Department, Auckland University Library, for procuring material not obtainable in Auckland; to Yale University Library; to the National Libraries of Australia and New Zealand; and to all those State, City, and University Libraries, both in Australia and in New Zealand, whose readiness of response through the interloan system is so vital to literary research in this part of the world.

For permission to quote extracts, acknowledgments are due to the following publishers and owners of copyright, or their agents:
Ernest Benn Ltd. (Sir James Crichton-Browne, *The Doctor's Second Thoughts*, 1931 and *The Doctor's After Thoughts*, 1932); E. J. Brill (H. G. Farmer, *Bernard Shaw's Sister and her Friends . . .*, 1959); Éditions Calmann-Lévy (Anatole France, *Histoire contemporaine : L'Orme du mail*, 1897); Criterion Books Inc. (Leslie A. Fiedler, *Love and Death in the American Novel*, 1960); Curtis Brown Ltd. (Janet Dunbar, *Mrs. G. B. S.: A Biographical Portrait of Charlotte Shaw*, 1963); Duke University Press (Francis X. Roellinger, 'Psychical Research and "The Turn of the Screw" ', *American Literature*, XX [1949], 401–12); Granada Publishing Ltd. (Leon Edel, *The Psychological Novel: 1900–1950*, 1955 and Leon Edel, ed., *The Diary of Alice James*, 1965); William Heinemann Ltd. (William Archer, tr., Henrik Ibsen, *Little Eyolf: a play in three acts*, 1894); Alexander R. James (Henry James, ed., *The Letters of William James*, 1920; Ralph Barton Perry, *The Thought and Character of William James*, 1935; letter of Henry James Jr., quoted Leon Edel, *Henry James: The Conquest of London, 1870–1881*, 1962); The Johns Hopkins University Press (Donald P. Costello, 'The Structure of *The Turn of the Screw*', *Modern Language Notes*, LXXV [1960], 312–21); The London School of Economics and Political Science (Beatrice Webb's Diaries, quoted Barbara Drake and Margaret Cole, edd., *Our Partnership by Beatrice Webb*, 1948; Margaret Cole, ed., *Beatrice Webb's Diaries, 1921–1924*, 1952 and *Beatrice Webb's Diaries, 1924–1932*, 1956); Macmillan, London and Basingstoke (A. C. Benson, *The Life of Edward White Benson . . .*, abridged ed., 1901 and Constance Lady Battersea, *Reminiscences*, 1922); Macmillan Publishing Co. Inc., New York (Allan Nevins and Milton H. Thomas, edd., *The Diary of George Templeton Strong*, 1952); William Morris Agency (Leon Edel, ed., *The Ghostly Tales of Henry James*, 1948); W. W. Norton and Co. Inc. (Robert Kimbrough, ed., *Henry James: The Turn of the Screw . . .*, Norton Critical Edition, 1966); Oxford University Press Inc., New York (F. O. Matthiessen and Kenneth B. Murdock, edd., *The Notebooks of Henry James*, 1947); Pemberton Publishing Co. Ltd. (J. M. Robertson, *A History of Freethought in the Nineteenth Century*, 1929); Routledge and Kegan Paul Ltd. (Alan Gauld, *The Founders of Psychical Research*, 1968); The Society of Authors, on behalf of the Bernard Shaw Estate (Dan H. Laurence, ed., *Bernard Shaw, Collected Letters 1874–1897*, 1965; letter quoted in *The Complete Plays of Henry James*, ed. Leon Edel, 1949; Prefaces to *Immaturity* and *The Irrational Knot*, *Our Theatres in the Nineties*, *Music in London 1890–94*, *London Music in 1888–89 . . .*, and *Sixteen Self Sketches*, 1930–1949; 'The Religion of the Pianoforte', *Fortnightly Review*, LV [1894]; 'On Going to Church', *The Savoy*, 1 [1896]; 'Ibsen's New Play', *The Academy*, 16 January 1897 and letter, *The Academy*, 13 November 1897); The Swedenborg Society (Emanuel Swedenborg, *Heaven and its Wonders*

and Hell . . ., rev. trans., 1958 and *Arcana Cœlestia . . .*, Vol. II, 1901); The Theosophical Publishing House (Annie Besant, *Death—and After?*, 7th ed., 1968); University of Texas Press (Thomas M. Cranfill and Robert L. Clark Jr., *An Anatomy of* The Turn of the Screw, 1965); A. P. Watt and Son (Hesketh Pearson, *Bernard Shaw: His Life and Personality*, 1961).

The courtesy of the Society for Psychical Research, in permitting quotation from its *Proceedings*, Volumes I to XII (1882–1897), is gratefully acknowledged. In the case of certain works still presumably in copyright, it has been impossible to trace the present owners: to these, and to all others whose claims to acknowledgment may have been overlooked, apologies are offered.

Illustrations

CHAPTER I

Henry James, Author of Ghostly Tales

The Turn of the Screw is a short fiction—a *nouvelle* of a scant 167 pages in its first, handsomely printed edition[2]—but it has attracted as much critical attention as any of James's major works; and for the general reading public it 'represents' James as inevitably, if not as fairly, as *Hamlet* does Shakespeare. In neither case is the popular allegiance wholly, or even mainly, due to the sensational quality of the ostensible theme: the fascination lies in the unsolved problems that complicate it. *The Turn of the Screw* is a ghost story in which, perhaps, there are no ghosts, yet in which the ghostly suggestions remain both enigmatic and challenging. I want here to take up that challenge; but since I do not believe (as many critics now do) that valid conclusions can be reached, whatever heights of fancy may be attained, by even the closest scrutiny of a work in isolation, I propose to examine *The Turn of the Screw* in its context—the circumstances of its production, the literary tradition in which it was conceived, and the influences that helped to shape it. Within that context the author's expressed intentions and the objective testimony of the text of his story will be my sole guides to interpretation. My first concern, therefore, must be to 'take bearings'—to consider and relate certain indisputable facts of literary and personal history.

In the course of his career Henry James wrote nearly a score of stories, and half-finished one long novel, involving what we may loosely call a supernatural theme. Some of these tales are what we should rather term parapsychological or even merely psychological fantasies than ghost stories. They are stories of morbid obsession, of startling intuitions, of split personality and the like, and several of them (such as 'Nona Vincent', 'The Private Life', 'The Great Good Place', and 'The Jolly Corner') are not concerned with the dead at all; while in others ('Sir Dominick Ferrand', 'The Altar of the Dead', 'Maud Evelyn', and 'The Tone of Time') the antecedent deaths are the mere logical premise to the action, for the oddity of which the living actors are wholly, and patently, responsible.

But some of these tales (such as 'The Romance of Certain Old Clothes' and 'De Grey') postulate the physical intervention of the dead in the affairs of the living; and at least five of them (excluding *The Turn of the Screw*) are ghost stories of the traditional pattern. That is, they deal with 'hauntings'—with *appearances* of the dead to the living, and 'what happened then'. These five are 'Sir Edmund Orme', 'Owen Wingrave', 'The Friends of the Friends', 'The Real Right Thing', and 'The Third Person'. One may note, too, that of all these tales, only one is a hoax—the early story of the 'The Ghostly Rental', and even here James momentarily introduces a real 'haunt' to frighten the hoaxer.

These dealings in the supernatural, or paranormal, belong to the early part of James's career, up to the time of his settlement at the age of thirty-three in London, and to the whole of its latter course, from 1891 (the date of his first venture into theatre) to 1915, the last year of his life. And we must, briefly, examine the significance of this fairly large section of James's work. He has, after all, established himself pre-eminently as the observer of manners and morals in a sophisticated contemporary society—do these tales indicate a streak of primitive superstition in a sophisticated writer, or what?

There is, of course, not to be discounted, the motive of expediency. Henry James, as a professional writer of fiction, was largely dependent on magazine publication. Ghost stories, like any other source of literary 'thrill', from sex to murder, were and are staple magazine fare, the strength of the situation excusing even the highest degree of art. In America they were always in season; in England they were seasonal fare, and magazine editors assembling 'Christmas Numbers' always liked to include one. That is how James's stories 'Sir Edmund Orme' in 1891 and 'Owen Wingrave' in 1892 first appeared, and how, James records in his *Preface* (p. 170),[3] *The Turn of the Screw* was intended to appear. Perhaps it was not finished in time: at any rate it first saw the light in an American magazine, *Collier's Weekly*, from January to April 1898.

For a period of fifteen to sixteen years, spanning the publication of *Daisy Miller* and *The Europeans* in 1878 and that of *The Tragic Muse* in 1890, James composed no new stories in the supernatural vein, although he did reissue two of the earlier ones. These are the years in which he most nearly realized his truly American dream of fortune through literary art, and the years (from 1885–86 and the publication of *The Bostonians* onwards) when he saw the dream gradually receding. In these years he was the committed social realist, and the psychological problems he dealt with were not further complicated by hints of the supernatural. But from 1890 he made his thrust for fortune in a new direction—as a playwright; and it was while he was awaiting the fruits of theatrical success (not, you note, *only* after he had confessed failure—on the production of *Guy Domville* at the beginning of 1895), that he turned to the commercially reliable ghost stories to keep the pot boiling. One must not, as I say, discount these practical considerations; but they are superficial, if obtrusive, and there are others, less obvious but more potent, which we must take into account.

Henry James is not, after all, an isolated phenomenon of literature—a *lusus naturae*. He was, consciously, a writer in a tradition; but the literary tradition in which he worked is a very complex one. It is not solely the 'Great Tradition' of the English novel of manners as described by F. R. Leavis: its many elements include also the American tradition of story-telling and its literary equivalents. Now story-telling is a genuine folk amusement, particularly in isolated, though not necessarily primitive, communities, and more especially those inhabiting the far northern latitudes of long winters and long winter nights. In such circumstances, where the isolating cold and darkness hold real dangers, you find that the story-tellers in self-defence, as it were, hypostatize their fears—concentrate and personalize them in malignant spirits and revengeful ghosts. The Scottish highlands are a wonderful source of ghost stories; and it is hard to equal the realistic horrors of the Scandinavian ghost tales, with their opening graves and menacing 'undead', physically 'real' enough to throttle and dismember men and horses. Similarly, in the early New England communities ghost stories flourished—the audience and the appetite for them were there together. It is that tradition which James invokes, quite deliberately, at the beginning of *The Turn of the Screw*, in the frame of his tale. He gives us a circle of people at Christmas time, exchanging stories by the fireside.

But here there is another point to note. At the very time when an American literature was taking shape, in the late eighteenth century, there arose in Europe a literary vogue for tales of terror, which relied for their effects very largely on supernatural suggestions. Horace Walpole's *The Castle of Otranto* is always taken as initiating the vogue, as the first 'Gothic romance', but Mrs. Ann Radcliffe and 'Monk' Lewis towards the end of the century are the best-known specialists in Gothic terror. In America, the first noteworthy novelist was also a Gothic romancer—Charles Brockden Brown, who published six novels full of horrors between 1798 and 1801; and Edgar Allan Poe's *Tales of Mystery and Imagination* are still popular, even in New Zealand; but much the best and best-known American writer in this genre is Nathaniel Hawthorne, who died in 1864, the year Henry James commenced author.

Most of Hawthorne's *Twice-Told Tales* and *Mosses from an Old Manse* deal with supernatural themes (examples are 'Dr. Heidegger's Experiment' and 'Rappaccini's Daughter'); and many deal with apparitions (such as that masterpiece 'Young Goodman Brown'); but Hawthorne's are not simply 'tales of terror' *or* 'ghost stories'—they are uneasy, very often heavily allegorical, expressions of psychological insights. Many of the Gothic authors, Mrs. Radcliffe among them, are at pains to explain away the supernatural effects they conjure up. Hawthorne makes his reconciliation between life and literary fantasy rather differently. And here I think I can profitably quote a passage from Leslie A. Fiedler's *Love and Death in the American Novel*:

Like other self-protective devices of the gothic, the explained supernatural poses
new problems as it solves old ones, leaving some readers at least with the sense of
having been shamefully hoaxed, betrayed into responding with pity and terror
to a mere bag of tricks. What is the point of horror that is not in some sense real?
Only Hawthorne, of all writers who insist on casting a new light in their final
pages on what they have all along presented in quite another, manages to leave us
satisfied and unashamed; for he developed in his novels and tales a method of
'alternative explanations' that permits us at the end of an action to throw back over
it the interpretation that suits our temperament best. He gives us the choice of
many readings: magical, mechanical, psychological; and even allows us not to make
a choice at all, but like him to endure them all, to emerge from his story not with
some assured insight into the causes of human depravity but only with a confirmed sense of the ambiguity of life.[4]

Now for Henry James the American tradition in literature is represented
by, is summed up in, the work of Hawthorne. It is the disciple of Hawthorne
who writes 'De Grey' and 'The Romance of Certain Old Clothes' in 1868—
two tales of the supernatural; just as it is the admirer and critic of Hawthorne
who uses his symbolical method in 'Mme. De Mauves' of 1874 and *The
Wings of the Dove* in 1902; who repeoples Hawthorne's New England setting
in *The Europeans* of 1878 and who adapts a whole novel of Hawthorne's in
The Bostonians of 1885–86. And to the end of James's career, it is Hawthorne
who continues to provide one model at least for his handling of supernatural,
and particularly of ghostly, themes. Nothing, for instance, could be more
Hawthornesque than *The Sense of the Past*, the novel on which James was
working in 1915.

Of all the multiplicity of literary influences to which Henry James was
subjected, the American story-telling and literary tradition is the one most
clearly operative in his use of the supernatural; but again, it does not provide
all the clues. For *The Turn of the Screw* especially there is another contributory factor which has been strangely neglected or minimized by literary
critics: that factor is religion. I do not, of course, refer to any profession of
religion on the part of Henry James himself. He did not subscribe to any
faith, but neither was he anti-religious—he was simply a quiescent observer,
and sometimes, it seems, a partaker by indirection of the comfort that
religious practices (if time-honoured, dignified, and picturesque) could
afford. Again and again in his books the troubled hero will make his way into
a church 'of the old persuasion', and there in the quiet and the candle-lit
gloom, while others pray or worship, regain (perhaps) his calm. As James says
of one of these, 'it struck him as good that there should be churches'.[5]

No, what I mean is the religion of the father, Henry James Sr., which
provided the ambience, the emotional and intellectual climate, in which the
childish imagination of our Henry James began its development. Leon Edel
refers to the novelist's 'Presbyterian heritage';[6] but this is precisely what it
was not. Henry James Sr. had been brought up in the strictest tenets of

Presbyterian Calvinism; as a young man he began to train for the ministry; but in 1837, while still a theological student, he rebelled against and decisively rejected Presbyterian orthodoxy. During the next six years he was a man in public quest of a theology; for he tried to clarify his ideas as much by lecturing and writing articles about them as by private wrestling with them in his study. But in 1844 (he was now a married man, and his second son, our Henry James, was just one year old) he suffered a psychological 'breakdown', in which, though still sane, he became the prey of intermittent but uncontrollable mental anguish—'depression' is too mild a word for the state he describes. And then after months of misery he was drawn, almost accidentally, into the eager study of a theology which had not before attracted him—and the sun shone again for him, he was 'lifted by a sudden miracle into felt harmony with universal man':[7] he had discovered Swedenborg. He himself said that such relief from such a source (for on the surface the Swedenborgian writings 'repel delight') could follow only on a destruction of spiritual values, a 'vastation', as complete as he himself had experienced. But to the attraction of Swedenborg for the poetic imagination there is ample testimony—William Blake is the example most familiar to the student of English literature. And one need not have been a despairing, merely a diligent and unsatisfied student of the Bible, to experience James's sense of liberation—as Helen Keller touchingly bears witness.[8]

It would be impossible, and it is unnecessary, for me to attempt to characterize Swedenborg's elaborate system of 'pure correspondences' through which he re-interprets the Christian scriptures. It is enough to say that the key-word of his 'message', so often and so variously repeated, is 'Love'. And it is clear that such teaching could only reinforce his new disciple's hatred of repression, whether felt or exerted, and the value he set on 'spontaneity' in the upbringing of children. All of which made for a happy home, a united family, and the untrammelled development of young minds—and this, we are assured from a wealth of evidence, *was* the good fortune of our Henry James and his brothers and sister. There was, our Henry James insists,[9] absolutely no indoctrination, and 'Father's Ideas' early became a matter for affectionate banter in the family circle. Swedenborg was inescapably there, in many battered volumes with black and 'somewhat sinister' titles, but the little boy, obstinately 'incurious' except about 'things and persons, objects and aspects', never peeped into them. His mother and his elder brother each made an approach to the spiritual world of which his father had gained the freedom, but the closest Henry came to a religious impulse was the wish that they might 'keep Sunday' in the more picturesque, social, church-going fashion.

Yet, in a Swedenborgian household, visited even occasionally by members of the New Church and permeated, as James admits, by the influence of Swedenborg's teaching (even if interpreted by such an original as Henry James Sr.), it is incredible that his 'small uneasy mind, bulging and tightening', as he says, 'in the wrong, or at least in unnatural and unexpected places' should have gained no inkling of the doctrine set out so matter-of-factly in one of the volumes he names—Swedenborg's *Heaven and Hell*.[10] It may be summarized, in part, as follows:

Life and personality continue after death—'death is merely transition' (493). Men recently dead not only retain a similar appearance but also lead a life similar to that they had 'in the natural world' (495). But in the 'second state' after death they are drawn irresistibly to their affinities, those whose ruling passion while alive was similar to their own. Thus inevitably the good and the bad congregate, and while the good move upward from the world of spirits into heaven, where they become angels, and pass after instruction into appropriate societies, the bad move downward into hell. And from the spirits of hell flows forth 'a perpetual effort to destroy all that is good and true, combined with anger and a kind of fury at not being able to do so, especially an effort to annihilate and destroy the Divine of the Lord. . . .' (538). They cannot do so, because of the spiritual equilibrium maintained by God between good and evil (or, heaven and hell) so that man 'thinks and wills' in freedom (537). But 'in order that man may be in freedom, for the sake of his being reformed, he is conjoined as to his spirit both with heaven and with hell. For with every man there are spirits from hell and angels from heaven. It is by means of the spirits from hell that man is in his own evil, while it is by means of angels from heaven that man is in good from the Lord. . . .' (599). But no one after death can renounce 'the life of his love' in order to gain the life of heaven 'as a result of immediate mercy' (480, 527): when the life of its love is gone the spirit is destroyed.

What a child might gather from this doctrine, is set out very clearly by James's friend and contemporary, the novelist William Dean Howells, who also grew up in a Swedenborgian household, though in less affluent circumstances than Henry James. I quote from his account, written for children, of his early childhood in Hamilton, Ohio:

[My] grandfather was a fervent Methodist, but [my] father, after many years of scepticism, had become a receiver of the doctrines of Emanuel Swedenborg; and in this faith the children were brought up. It was not only their faith, but their life, and I may say that in this sense they were a very religious household, though they never went to church. . . . They had no service of the New Church, the Swedenborgians were so few in the place, except when some of its ministers stopped with us on their travels. My boy [Howells is speaking of himself] regarded these good men as all personally sacred, and while one of them was in the house he had some relief from the fear in which his days seem mostly to have been passed; as if he were for the time being under the protection of a spiritual lightning-rod. Their religion was not much understood by their neighbors. . . . But the boy once heard his father explain to one of them that the New Church people believed in a hell, which each cast himself into if he loved the evil rather than the good, and that no mercy could keep him out of without destroying him, for a man's love was his very self. It made his blood run cold, and he resolved that rather than cast himself into hell, he would do his poor best to love the good. The children were taught when they teased one another that there was nothing the fiends so much delighted in as teasing. When they were angry and revengeful, they were told that now they were calling evil spirits about them, and that the good angels could not come near them if they wished while they were in that state. . . .

I fancy no child can ever explain just why it is affected in this way or that way by the things that are or are not in the world about it; it is not easy to do this for one's self in after-life. At any rate, it is certain that my boy dwelt most of his time amid shadows that were, perhaps, projected over his narrow out-look from some former state of being, or from the gloomy minds of long-dead ancestors. His home was cheerful and most happy, but he peopled all its nooks and corners with shapes of doom and horror. The other boys were not slow to find this out, and their invention supplied with ready suggestion of officers and prisons any little lack of misery his spectres and goblins left. He often narrowly escaped arrest, or thought so, when they built a fire in the street at night, and suddenly kicked it to pieces, and shouted, 'Run, run! The constable will catch you!' Nothing but flight saved my boy, in these cases, when he was small. He grew bolder, after a while, concerning constables, but never concerning ghosts; they shivered in the autumnal evenings among the tall stalks of the corn-field that stretched, a vast wilderness, behind the house to the next street, and they walked the night everywhere.[11]

Howells, clearly, is a less evasive, more confiding autobiographer than Henry James—whose only acknowledgment of death in his memoirs of childhood is as a romantic enhancement of the bereft and orphaned, and who confesses to no ghostly fears: the often-quoted nightmare of the Galerie d'Apollon which is narrated in these memoirs occurred, he tells us, 'many years later'.[12] But Howells did not, any more than Henry James, grow up to be a visionary, although like James he wrote some supernatural tales. In fact, 'Howells and James' were almost inevitably linked, by the English reading public at least, in a kind of literary partnership:[13] as purveyors of social realism, American brand, artists of the ordinary and sometimes (by Victorian standards) the sordid. I am not suggesting that ghostly fears and childish misconceptions troubled the adult consciousness of either man, and still less am I suggesting, as Quentin Anderson does,[14] that Henry James constructed his works as a kind of Swedenborgian cryptogram. Oddly enough, *The Turn of the Screw* is almost the only work Anderson does not ransack for ciphers.

What I do suggest is that the idea of ghostly accompaniment, of living persons' being attended, dreadfully or not, by visitants from beyond the grave, of the concern of such presences for their living protégés or victims, was one familiar to Henry James from childhood, not as a mere literary fabrication, but as part of the accepted scheme of things—as it might be, a mechanistic detail in the play of forces between the spiritual and the phenomenal world. I am not arguing for active belief, even on the part of the child, only for his imaginative exposure to the idea.

That some connection with the Swedenborgian 'world of spirits' was present to his mind as he wrote *The Turn of the Screw* is indicated (no more than indicated) by a phrase here and there that seems to have floated up from a forgotten residue of impressions. I give just three examples. First, when the governess opens the door of the schoolroom 'to find again, in a flash, [her] eyes unsealed' (pp. 111–12), we are reminded not so much of St. Paul, or of the blind man of the Gospels, or even (directly) of Elisha's servant, as of Swedenborg's description of seeing 'through the eyes of the spirit within him':

[A]s everyone knows, the bodily organ of sight which is the eye is so gross as to be unable even to see, except through magnifying glasses, the smaller things of nature; still less then can it see the things that are above the sphere of nature such as are all things in the spiritual world. But these things may be seen by a man when he is withdrawn from the sight of the body, and the sight of his spirit is opened. This takes place instantly whenever it pleases the Lord that these things should be seen. In that case, the man does not know but that he is seeing them with his bodily eyes.[15]

There may even be a reminiscence of the somewhat gruesome image Swedenborg later employs, of couching a spiritual cataract.[16]

Secondly, when the governess reports this particular visitation to Mrs. Grose, she says:

'I came home, my dear . . . for a talk with Miss Jessel.' . . .
'A talk! Do you mean she spoke?'
'It came to that. . . .' (p. 115)

Again, Swedenborg explains: '. . . the speech of spirits does not enter through the ear, nor by the medium of the air, but by an internal way, into the same organs of the head or brain. . . . [T]he language which is familiar to spirits is not a language of words, but a language of ideas of thought. . . . I have frequently spoken with spirits, thus in their proper tongue, that is, by means of ideas of thought.'[17]

And for a third example, it is interesting to note that Peter Quint's 'white face of damnation' (pp. 162, 167) is a detail vouched for by Swedenborg. The spirits of hell, whom he saw, 'in general' had faces 'void of life like those of corpses'.[18]

But there remains the question, which readers of *The Turn of the Screw* persist in asking, did James personally believe in ghosts? The short answer would be, 'No, I'm sure he didn't, but he never actually says so.' More at length and more helpfully for an understanding of his supernatural stories, especially *The Turn of the Screw*, we may say that Henry James had an imaginative concern, just as his brother William had a scientific concern, with supernatural manifestations, both in their connection with abnormal states of mind—their psychological implications, that is—and in their wider 'psychic' import.

It is necessary to remember here that there was a strain of what used to be called 'nervous instability' in all the Jameses. Their father's 'breakdown' has been mentioned; but a similar psychological collapse occurred in William's case, when he was a young man; and in Alice's case, where it produced a chronic physical incapacity. Henry James escaped until his sixty-seventh year, when, quite possibly as a result of his monumental labours on the New York Edition, from 1907 to 1909, he suffered much the same shattering experience as his father had done, though without the religious complications. All these sufferers remained sane, and intensely curious regarding their own and one another's condition: only the father, one must add, experienced a cure by religious conviction. To this extent, therefore, there is a practical and personal basis for William's and Henry's interest in the paranormal.

William James, from 1885 till his death in 1910, was a patient investigator of mediumistic evidence and 'psychic phenomena' generally, and, although his inclination and training always led him to seek for the psychological rather than the supernatural explanation, he was still, in 1909, content to describe himself as 'baffled, as to spirit-return, and as to many other special problems'. 'I personally am as yet neither a convinced believer in parasitic demons, nor a spiritist, nor a scientist, but still remain a psychical researcher waiting for more facts before concluding.' The conception of 'ghosts' he found to be a 'somewhat idiotic' approach to 'the hypothesis of spirit survival'; but he recognized that ' "bosh" is no more an ultimate element in Nature, or a really explanatory category in human life than "dirt" is in chemistry'. William James felt that the subliminal self, the human 'subconscious', held the key to these mysteries; but he did not exclude the possibility of a disembodied consciousness or a cosmic consciousness which might enter into the question.[19]

These are William James's published statements. Of Henry James it was said that he 'was in love with the next world, or the next state of consciousness; he was always exploring the borderland between the conscious and the super-conscious'.[20]

To a curious symposium on 'The Future Life' conducted in 1910 by *Harper's Bazar*, he contributed an article entitled ' "Is there a Life after Death?" ' His answer seems to be that he wishes so strongly for a continuation of personal consciousness, that his desire has the force of belief; but, much more flatly than his brother William, he denies any evidence for 'survival' in communication from the dead—what we have to bear, on the contrary, he says is 'the grimness of their utter refusal, so far as we know it, of a retrospective personal sign'.[21]

In the *Prefaces* of 1908–09 to his 'supernatural' tales he equates ghost tales with fairy stories, and expressly dissociates his fiction from the 'psychical record of cases of apparitions'. 'Recorded and attested "ghosts" ' he says 'are . . . as little expressive, as little dramatic, above all as little continuous and conscious and responsive, as is consistent with their taking the trouble—

and an immense trouble they find it, we gather—to appear at all' (p. 174). And to return to the article on survival: mediumistic phenomena 'often make, I grant, for attention and wonder and interest—but for interest above all in the medium and the trance'.

All of which seems to say, that, personally, Henry James is inclined to treat ghosts and ghostly communications as William James did the soul— as not *dis*provable merely. As a member of the Reform Club and a house-holder in Rye he doesn't really believe in ghosts, or only with many quali-fications and reservations.

But as a novelist he takes quite a different position. I quote from the *Prefaces* to *The Turn of the Screw* and other of his supernatural tales that he wrote for Volumes XII and XVII of the New York Edition. He has, he says (and he seems to be speaking straight out of the Hawthorne tradition) 'consistently felt . . . the appeal to wonder and terror and curiosity and pity and to the delight of fine recognitions, as well as to the joy, perhaps sharper still, of the mystified state [to be] the very source of wise counsel and the very law of charming effect'. As a novelist 'he has revelled in the creation of alarm and suspense and surprise and relief, in all the arts that practise . . . on the credulous soul of the candid, or, immeasurably better, on the seasoned spirit of the cunning, reader. He has built, rejoicingly, on that blest faculty of wonder . . . as on a strange passion planted in the heart of man for his benefit.' What is to be the subject for this 'excited wonder'? 'The ideal, obviously, on these lines, is the straight fairy-tale . . . and I am prepared with the confession that the "ghost-story", as we for convenience call it, has ever been for me the most possible form of the fairy-tale' (pp. 253–54). He compares *The Turn of the Screw* with 'Cinderella and Blue-Beard and Hop o' my Thumb and Little Red Riding Hood'—like them it is 'an excursion into chaos' (pp. 171–72). Within the story, the ghosts exist—not as products of the seance, but as 'goblins, elves, imps, demons as loosely constructed as those of the old trials for witchcraft; if not, more pleasingly, fairies of the legendary order, wooing their victims forth to see them dance under the moon' (p. 175).

The author's appeal is to the reader's 'wonder'; but 'to begin to wonder' the reader 'must begin to believe', and therefore, James thinks, in tales of the supernatural 'the safest arena for the play of moving accidents and mighty mutations and strange encounters, or whatever odd matters, is the field . . . rather of their second than of their first exhibition'. He feels that he shows them best 'by showing almost exclusively the way they are felt, by recognising as their main interest some impression strongly made by them and intensely received. We but too probably break down, I have ever reasoned, when we attempt the prodigy, the appeal to mystification, in itself; with its "objective" side too emphasised, the report (it is ten to one) will practically run thin. We want it clear, goodness knows, but we also want it thick, and we get the thickness in the human consciousness that entertains and records, that amplifies and interprets it. . . . [P]rodigies . . . keep all their character . . . by looming through some other history—the indispensable history of somebody's *normal* relation to something. . . . The extraordinary is most extraordinary in that it happens to you and me, and it's of value (of value for others) but so far as visibly brought home to us' (pp. 254–57).

So then *The Turn of the Screw* is a story about ghosts, and in order that the reader may be won to temporary belief in them, they are shown as making 'a strong impression intensely received' by a narrator, the governess, 'through' the history of whose 'normal relation' to her pupils these prodigies 'loom'. You may challenge the ghosts if you like—'the critical challenge,' says James, is really only 'the spirit of fine attention', and a writer can't be bothered about meeting a hundred possible objections to his delineation of ghosts. But the percipient's, in this case the governess's, 'mind about them' is a different matter: you can't challenge that without 'stiffening' the 'whole texture' of the story (p. 257). He means, I take it, that the more you refuse to take on trust from the narrator the more you have to account for, awkwardly and with difficulty perhaps, in the reported manifestation, which then becomes either a delusion or a trick in a complicated exhibition of character and motive.

We shall return to the governess presently, but you should note that nowhere in the *Prefaces* is there a suggestion that she is not dealing with maleficent *external* agencies. They are expressly termed 'hovering prowling blighting presences, my pair of abnormal agents. . . . They would be agents in fact; there would be laid on them the dire duty of causing the situation to reek with the air of Evil. Their desire and their ability to do so, visibly measuring meanwhile their effect, together with their observed and described success—this was exactly my central idea. . . . The essence of the matter was the villainy of motive in the evoked predatory creatures' (p. 175). Nowhere a hint of a suggestion that the governess has imagined, has subconsciously invented them. Nor is there any suggestion to this effect in James's first record of the tale in his *Notebooks*.

CHAPTER II

The Turn of the Screw and the Critics

Saturday, 5 January 1895, had been the disastrous opening night of the play *Guy Domville*, on which Henry James had staked all his hopes of theatrical success. During the following week, he spent a couple of days at Addington, the home outside London of the Archbishop of Canterbury, Edward White Benson. The visit had no doubt been arranged by one of the sons, Arthur Christopher Benson, who had first met James in 1884 and had ever since perseveringly cultivated the acquaintance.

On Saturday, 12 January 1895, James made the following entry in his notebook:

Note here the ghost-story told me at Addington (evening of Thursday 10th), by the Archbishop of Canterbury: the mere vague, undetailed, faint sketch of it—being all he had been told (very badly and imperfectly), by a lady who had no art of relation, and no clearness: the story of the young children (indefinite number and age) left to the care of servants in an old country-house, through the death, presumably, of parents. The servants, wicked and depraved, corrupt and deprave the children; the children are bad, full of evil, to a sinister degree. The servants *die* (the story vague about the way of it) and their apparitions, figures, return to haunt the house *and* children, to whom they seem to beckon, whom they invite and solicit, from across dangerous places, the deep ditch of a sunk fence, etc.—so that the children may destroy themselves, lose themselves, by responding, by getting into their power. So long as the children are kept from them, they are not lost; but they try and try and try, these evil presences, to get hold of them. It is a question of the children 'coming over to where they are.' It is all obscure and imperfect, the picture, the story, but there is a suggestion of strangely gruesome effect in it. The story to be told—tolerably obviously—by an outside spectator, observer.[22]

The only further evidence of intention given by the *Notebooks* is *ex post facto*: in some notes of August 1900 relating to a projected novel, *The Sense of the Past*, James writes, 'The ideal is something as simple as *The Turn of the Screw*, only different and less grossly and merely apparitional' (p. 299); and again, the projected novel is to be '*fantasticated*', 'and I know what I mean by it as differentiated from the type, the squeezed sponge, of *The T. of the S.*' (p. 300).

It was the very obscurity and imperfection of the original *donnée* that engaged James's imagination—as he tells us, some twelve years later, in his *Preface*; and it was this which he was anxious to preserve for the reader: 'the tone of suspected and felt trouble, of an inordinate and incalculable sort—the tone of tragic, yet of exquisite mystification' (pp. 172–73). 'To bring the bad dead back to life for a second round of badness is to warrant them as indeed prodigious' he says, so, to avoid all risk of anti-climax by ill-judged specification he decided on a 'process of *adumbration*': 'the haunting pair' must be felt by the reader to be 'capable . . . of exerting, in respect to the children, the very worst action small victims so conditioned might be conceived as subject to'. But there is 'no eligible *absolute* of the wrong'; it remains 'relative' to the reader's own experience. Therefore 'make him *think* the evil, make him think it for himself, and you are released from weak specifications' (pp. 175–76). The *author's* 'values are positively all blanks save so far as an excited horror, a promoted pity, a created expertness . . . proceed to read into them more or less fantastic figures' (p. 177). What sort of evil do you fancy? Diabolism? Sexual perversion? Crime? (Mrs. Grose, whose simplicity has its limitations, thinks of 'stealing' [p. 150].) You can imagine precisely what you choose—and then, says James resignedly, you blame the author for the morbidity or depravity of your own imagination (p. 177).

The tale was not composed until three years after the *Notebook* entry, towards the end of 1897. And immediately on its publication in book form, in the autumn of 1898, it roused an interest and a curiosity which still persist.

It is true that the first audience for the tale was not very much impressed. James's Scottish secretary took it all down from dictation with complete impassivity: after some phrase that James thought blood-curdling he would look up 'and in a dry voice say, "What next?"' [23] And the reviewer in the London *Times* declared he 'could read it unmoved at midnight in a haunted house'.[24] But the interest of the reading public is attested by James's replies (which still survive) to letters of enquiry (which he of course burnt).

Lubbock prints three of these replies in his edition of James's *Letters*. The first is to Dr. Louis Waldstein, a physician and psychologist, who has clearly refused to accept (or dismiss) the tale as a fabricated ghost story. The precise nature of the compliment he has paid James does not emerge from the reply, which is a series of polite disclaimers of any conscious intention beyond the artistic. '*But*, of course, where there *is* life, there's truth, and the truth was at the back of my head. . . . My bogey-tale dealt with things so hideous that I felt that to save it at all it needed some infusion of beauty or prettiness, and the beauty of the pathetic was the only attainable—was indeed inevitable. But ah, the exposure indeed, the helpless plasticity of childhood that isn't dear or sacred to *some*body! That *was* my little tragedy—over which you show a wisdom for which I thank you again.'[25] I take it that Waldstein has remarked what a striking account of children demoralized by suggestion

James has produced; and James, while agreeing that the victimization of the children is indeed the theme of his story, neatly side-steps any mention of *who* is victimizing them.

H. G. Wells's comment was, it seems, mainly directed to the characterization of the governess. James replies,

Of course I had, about my young woman, to take a very sharp line. The grotesque business I had to make her picture and the childish psychology I had to make her trace and present, were, for me at least, a very difficult job, in which absolute lucidity and logic, a singleness of effect, were imperative. Therefore I had to rule out subjective complications of her own—play of tone etc.; and keep her impersonal save for the most obvious and indispensable little note of neatness, firmness and courage—without which she wouldn't have had her data. But the thing is essentially a pot-boiler and a *jeu d'esprit*. (Lubbock, I, 306)

Wells's letter, compliments aside, had questioned not James's moral or scientific intention, but his skill as an artist; and James was evidently irritated by it, because he repeats his defence in one of the *Prefaces* from which I have already quoted. Those critics who find it necessary to discredit the governess have made great play with this defence. What James in his letter seems to be saying, is this: 'I don't believe in ghosts, Wells, any more than you do. It was therefore very difficult for me to assume the attitude of a believer, and the only way to make my rendering plausible was to eliminate all overtones of doubt from my narrator's voice. So that in the tale we have simply the expressed reaction of one seeing malevolent spirits and sensing that these are threatening one's charges. All that I had to establish, for the narrator, was sufficient force of character to see and sense and react without imputation of neurotic unreliability.' I do not see what other interpretation of James's 'neatness, firmness and courage' can justifiably be made.

James's third correspondent, F. W. H. Myers, did believe both in survival after death and in ghostly apparitions, but James has not quite understood, he says, Myers's 'principal question' about the story. He more or less admits what seems to have been a charge of ambiguity, which he excuses on the grounds of his own 'imperfect ingenuity'. And he goes on,

The *T. of the S.* is a very mechanical matter, I honestly think—an inferior, a merely *pictorial*, subject and rather a shameless pot-boiler. The thing that, as I recall it, I most wanted not to fail of doing, under penalty of extreme platitude, was to give the impression of the communication to the children of the most infernal imaginable evil and danger—the condition, on their part, of being as *exposed* as we can humanly conceive children to be. This was my artistic knot to untie, to put any sense or logic into the thing, and if I had known any way of producing *more* the image of their contact and condition I should assuredly have been proportionately eager to resort to it. I evoked the worst I could, and only feel tempted to say, as in French: 'Excusez du peu!' (Lubbock, I, 308)

This seems a clear indication that the threat to the children is from the ghosts. The communicated fears of the most neurotic of *loving* women could scarcely be described as 'the most *infernal* imaginable evil and danger'. Nor would James describe the relationship between the children and their governess as 'their contact and condition', the 'image' of which he has had difficulty in 'producing'; but *contact* between the living and the dead is the central theme, and the writer's problem, in a ghost story.

Nowhere, indeed, in these contemporary comments, does there seem to have been the suggestion that the governess must be inventing the threat to the children—that, however inadequately she may be presented, she is not a truthful witness. That suggestion comes much later, with the popularization of Freud's psychological theories, and I shall take account of it, in relation to these theories, presently. What I want to examine here is the appeal such critics make to James's own comments in the *Prefaces* and letters from which I have quoted.

Almost invariably, I think, these critics misunderstand the terms James uses, and not only that, they fail to seize the emphasis and tone of a passage, especially when James is not 'wholly serious'. A critic of course has much greater freedom of judgment if he merely skims the work under discussion, but unless one reads James with attention and becomes familiar with his idiom and 'cadence', it is possible to be even grossly mistaken over his meaning.

Here is a statement from James's *Preface* to *The Turn of the Screw*, a statement which is often quoted and nearly always misinterpreted. After discussing his artistic intention in the story, James proceeds: 'I need scarcely add after this that it is a piece of ingenuity pure and simple, of cold artistic calculation, an *amusette* to catch those not easily caught (the "fun" of the capture of the merely witless being ever but small), the jaded, the disillusioned, the fastidious' (p. 172). *Amusette*, in a literary application, means 'light diversion', 'entertainment', and James is applying it precisely as Graham Greene applies the word 'entertainment' to his less serious works of fiction, such as *The Ministry of Fear* or *A Gun for Sale*. But in this case it is to be a sophisticated 'entertainment'—not an ordinary ghost story in which the author makes his readers' flesh creep by an accumulation of more or less mechanical 'horrors', but a ghost story which depends for its effect on the communication of *unease*, a horror which will *remain* mysterious and inexplicable to the reader, all the more so as it is conveyed in a precise and delicately artistic narrative. *Amusette*, in short, is merely a rather affectedly depreciatory term: 'pot-boiler' James calls the story elsewhere, and 'a *jeu d'esprit*'. It does not carry the implication that James intends to hoax the reader. But he says 'to *catch* those not easily *caught*'—doesn't this suggest deception? No, merely 'attraction', 'captivation': he wants to 'catch' their interest and attention. The use of 'catch' here recalls James's use of a favourite adjective, 'attaching'. 'A very *attaching* young man' he may say, where we should say 'very attractive'.

Here is another passage from a discussion of the governess in the same *Preface*: '. . . I saw no way, I feebly grant (fighting, at the best too, periodically, for every grudged inch of my space) to exhibit her in relations other than those; one of which, precisely, would have been her relation to her own nature. We have surely as much of her own nature as we can swallow in watching it reflect her anxieties and inductions' (pp. 173–74). Or, as we might paraphrase it, sacrificing elegance but not (I hope) distorting the meaning: 'Here was I writing a young woman's report of her encounter with certain "intense anomalies and obscurities" [James's phrase], and please remember I was writing for a magazine, with its strict limitation on length. How could I spare the space for detailed character analysis, as in other circumstances I should have done? But indeed, so far as that goes, her character seems to me fully enough exhibited as it is.' That word 'swallow' is the trouble here. James was fond of colloquialisms, which he sometimes slightly misapplied, in what began as a stroke of conscious wit, and ended as an unconscious mannerism. It produced many anecdotes: for example, James gives sixpence to a yokel of whom he has asked the way, and says 'There, my man, put that in your pipe and smoke it.'[26] But here, to say 'as much as we can swallow' suggests that James himself finds something repellent, even nauseating, in the nature of the governess as he has exhibited her. Yet the very next sentence makes it clear that there is no depreciatory intention whatever. James goes on: 'It constitutes no little of a character indeed, in such conditions, for a young person, as she says, "privately bred," that she is able to make her particular credible statement of such strange matters. She has "authority," which is a good deal to have given her, and I couldn't have arrived at so much had I clumsily tried for more' (p. 174). You will hardly believe that any critic could interpret 'authority' in this context, not as 'standing with' or 'impressiveness for' the reader, but as 'dominance over' Mrs. Grose and the children, yet it has been done.[27]

To assure ourselves of James's intention, however, we need only consider the frame of his tale. The governess's written narrative is introduced, into a fashionable contemporary circle which includes the author, by a middle-aged Scotsman. His name, I fancy, is primarily intended to suggest, not so much the romanticism noted by Chesterton, as the traditional Scottish 'canniness' (and, of course, expertise in ghosts). At any rate, Douglas[28] vouches for the governess in terms which constitute an impeccable Victorian character reference. 'She was a most charming person. . . . She was the most agreeable woman I've ever known in her position; she would have been worthy of any whatever. . . . [S]he struck me as awfully clever and nice. . . . I liked her extremely and am glad to this day to think she liked me too. If she hadn't she wouldn't have told me [the story, that is]. She had never told anyone. It wasn't simply that she said so, but that I knew she hadn't' (pp. 5–6). That is, some ten years after her shattering experience, which has (for supererogatory emotional heightening) encapsulated a young girl's first 'love dream', the governess is still in employment, neither deranged in mind nor distorted in personality, so 'charming', 'agreeable', 'clever', and 'nice' that a Cambridge undergraduate not only admires and falls in love with her, but is happy to remember that he did so, forty years later.

Isn't it clear what effect James is trying to convey—by brief notation here in the frame, by suggestion in the tale? The narrator (as we might in our slipshod phrasing express it) is 'a thoroughly normal young girl', except for her extra qualifications of prettiness (to which Mrs. Grose testifies), cleverness (as assessed by an undergraduate of Trinity), and attractive personality (which Mrs. Grose, little Miles, and Douglas each in their several ways attest)—a normal young girl placed in a completely abnormal situation. Half the relish of the story, as of all convincing ghost stories, is there—in the intrusion of the supernatural and incredible upon what is established for us as natural and credible. We scarcely need James's editorial affirmation of the fact. To have a madwoman, a psychotic, even a mildly maladjusted neurotic as recorder of a ghostly occurrence, would be to give the game away in advance.

For of course *The Turn of the Screw* is not, primarily, a story about a governess but a story of two children, as the very title implies. We have only to read to the second paragraph to learn that when a ghost story is concerned with a child, the frightening effect is one degree, one turn of the screw, more oppressive than that of a ghost story concerning adults merely. The symbolic screw may be the carpenter's device for securing tension, or the sinister thumb-screw of torture, as you choose.

James in this story is not, primarily, concerned either with the psychological 'how' or with the metaphysical 'why' of the case—evil *revenants* try to communicate with children they have corrupted: that is his *donnée*. The governess is a device of narration, and as such is invented by James *ad hoc*. The psychological 'truths', fruits of James's insight and of his experience, which emerge in the course of the narrative, are elements of some significance in his general 'philosophy of life', but he does not draw particular attention to them here. There is the peculiar freedom to charm, springing from a basic indifference, a lack of 'concern', which the consciousness of secret knowledge, preoccupation with secret vice, any kind of 'double life', can produce even in young and relatively inexperienced personalities. There are the disquieting appearances which even the most innocently motivated solicitude may assume. There is the duality, in fact, for speaker and hearer, actor and observer, of every word uttered and every action performed, whatever the motive may be. There is the general teasing inscrutability of 'others'—little girl, little boy, comfortable housekeeper, fascinating master.

To any unbiased student of the record, it must be clear that James accepts the corruption of the children as antecedent to the whole narration. What he invites speculation about is not the fact, but the nature and enormity, of the corruption. But inevitably, since James depicts the children as near-perfect little human creatures—beautiful, intelligent, talented, charming —many readers and some critics refuse to accept the fact. How can creatures exhibiting such graces have become and be, in actuality, bad? As every theologian knows, *corruptio optimi pessima*, 'the corruption of the best is the worst corruption', or, as Shakespeare more picturesquely expresses it, 'lilies that fester smell far worse than weeds'. But that is not precisely the critics' difficulty here. Lucifer's brightness, they feel, *must* be dimmed by his fall. They find it easier to ignore or minimize the recorded facts (the boy's expulsion from school, his destruction of the letter summoning his uncle, the girl's descent into spoken, or revelation of acted, 'horrors'—Mrs. Grose's report is not clear)[29] and to redirect, as it were, any suspicions (of deceit, of complicity, or forbidden interests)[30] upon the disordered imagination of the governess herself. This, it seems to me, is a simplistic solution, a kind of critical Fundamentalism which is more appropriate to the judgment of a crime novel or a Western than to the interpretation of a work by Henry James. One is reminded of Moses Primrose at the fair. The determination not to be 'done', to spy out the trick, to find the Machiavel or the charlatan, preferably in the character who presents the blandest appearance of virtuous intention, leaves such critics blind to indications which James never bothers to hide. He so often in his fiction presents the rationalizations which cloak the merely unseemly, or the vile and dangerous passions of a psychologically disturbed person (most skilfully and chillingly in 'The Marriages' of 1891, least so in *The Other House* of 1896), and he so admirably succeeds, with 'Cousin Maria' of 1887 for example, or ' "Europe" ' of 1899, in conveying by indirection the destructive ploys of greed or selfishness, that he ought for convenience always to be doing so. When, therefore, in the depiction of a social relationship, he imparts an authentic, solar-plexus-verified thrill, he must, like some hack novelist, be using his regular, proven technique. This, at any rate, seems to be the assumption on which many critics base their interpretation of *The Turn of the Screw*: there must be a villain lurking somewhere in the story—all that is necessary is to unmask her. But that it is possible James's spectrum of virtues and vices is of a different range from their own—that he simply doesn't *accept* either their black or their white, these critics never consider. That we are intended to 'see through' the favour and the prettiness with which James invests the children, is rarely admitted. Yet these, although they add immeasurably to the 'pathetic' effect which is one of his declared aims in the story, are not insurances against either moral disaster or the assaults of fate. The gifts of nature tempt misfortune—they cannot save. Even Chaucer's innkeeper, Harry Bailly, knew that[31]—though, as a Victorian, Henry James would be more likely to quote 'Rose Aylmer' in his defence.

Perhaps these critics are mainly demonstrating that they are above all men of their time, and that since Henry James in so much of his work expresses the spirit of the twentieth century rather than the nineteenth, they are not willing to consider him historically at all, and feel it intolerable that he should deal so often in now-discarded Victorian *clichés*. They are irritated at being asked to concede ghostly intrusion into real life, and with Bernard Shaw feel that 'it is really a damnable sin to draw with such consummate art a houseful of rubbish'.[32] And they feel a revulsion from the theme of the 'child victim' which recurs so often in Victorian literature. Certainly it seemed to hold some attraction for Henry James, who used it in a number of his stories, at all stages of his career, but especially during the nineties—a fact which may (as Edel, especially, contends) be significant.

Taken in isolation, without their circumstantial justifications, the situations in these novels and tales seem bizarre in the extreme. In 'My Friend Bingham' (1867) a man accidentally kills a child and, as a direct result, marries the mother. In 'The Author of *Beltraffio*' (1884) a mother lets her child die in order to remove him from his father's corrupting influence. In 'The Pupil' (1891) a 'delicate' boy dies of the shock produced by the simultaneous humiliation of his self-respect and gratification of his heart's desire. In *The Other House* (1896) an infatuated woman murders the infant child who is the obstacle to her passion. In *What Maisie Knew* (1897) a child is the shuttlecock batted about, in a game of hatred and reprisals, between divorced parents and their lovers—the novel is the child's interpretation of these (to her) baffling performances. In *The Awkward Age* (1898) a young girl's reputation and marriage prospects are destroyed by a group of cynical sophisticates, whose ringleader is her mother.

Clearly, it is the macabre situation that attracts James, and not entirely for mercantile reasons. In some cases the victim is a mere pawn in the game; but in others he or she can react, and it is the agent–patient interplay in a situation sufficiently vital or dangerous to ensure that the outcome is (and will be seen to be) important, but in which one player is fumblingly inexperienced, that James finds challenging and that elicits all his subtleties.

We know that James was 'fond of children' and that, when he didn't terrify them, they liked and trusted him in return.[33] In his fiction he shows that he has observed and listened to them with comprehension and sympathy. Maisie is of course his *tour de force*, but he can bring a child convincingly to life for us with much less expenditure of literary energy: Randolph Miller of 1878 and Geordie and Ferdy Berrington of 1888 are cases in point. Whatever the scale of their portrayal, the children in James's stories are treated as responsibly and as *objectively* as the adult characters, and with similarly varying success. In certain of the tales mentioned, the situation has decreed a heightening of the emotional tone, but I do not on that account conclude that James is 'identifying' with his child victim—with Dolcino or with Morgan Moreen, as the case may be. Yet this is the serious contention of James's biographer, Professor Leon Edel.[34]

He believes that Henry, the younger brother, in childhood overshadowed by the more aggressive William, all his life long tended to identify himself with young and helpless, 'powerless'[35] creatures, and that, shaken by the failure of his play *Guy Domville* in 1895 and by his personally humiliating experience on the first night, he suffered (over the next five years) a regression to childhood attitudes, and saw the world as a conspiracy of evil forces leagued to destroy innocents such as himself. Miles, therefore, in *The Turn of the Screw*, 'stands for' Henry James, and the governess represents all the forces arrayed against him in his drive for normality. Not only that, certain of James's current anxieties are enshrined in the story: 'Bly' in Essex stands for Rye in Sussex, where James, with some misgivings apparently, had just decided to lease a house.

Great as is our debt to Professor Edel, for his labours over forty years in rescuing, from neglect if not oblivion, the mammoth corpus of Henry James's works, and in establishing, with inexhaustible patience, the details of the life record, one must regret his insistence, as a critic, on interpreting almost every fictional work of James as a chapter of autobiography. James did, of course, draw on his own experience and, sometimes rather callously,[36] that of his friends and relatives for use in his books, just as he utilized every observation of his own, or anyone else's,[37] and every scrap of material that came his way from books or newspapers or chance personal encounters—no novelist can possibly do otherwise. And every artist, being also human, whatever the medium of his art may be, uses his art as an escape from or a solution to the problems of his own personality—uses it therapeutically, in fact. But if that is the extent of his urge to create, his output will not be either large or varied. One has only to look at the enormous scope and variety of Henry James's work, with its multifarious extrovert interests—over one hundred short stories and *nouvelles*, over twenty novels, two biographies and two completed volumes of autobiography, some dozen plays, over one hundred 'travel pieces', between three and four hundred critical articles and reviews—one has only to think of that exuberant creativity, to realize that even though such an explanation as Edel's may fit some artists, it will not fit this one. Henry James is not a Proust.

After all, considering the long roll-call of James's characters, are his child victims proportionately more numerous or individually more pathos-laden than those of Dickens? Yet I don't think we are required to see a portrait of the artist, beard and all, in Paul Dombey or Little Nell.

I cannot, to put it shortly, accept an autobiographical intention, nor indeed contemporary autobiographical reference, in *The Turn of the Screw*, and I am doubtful about the kind of effect we can assume the failure of his dramatic gamble to have had on Henry James's writing. It was not, after all, only in the theatre that he had encountered public indifference to his efforts, and stories of disappointed authors precede as well as follow *Guy Domville*. As far as I can tell, from the tone of such of his private notations as survive, and such of his letters as I have read, he responded not with defensive resignation but with determination. And far from flagging, his literary invention seems to make a forward bound, like the proverbial mettled horse at the touch of the spur. *The Other House* is a pot-boiler indeed, but what of *The Spoils of Poynton* and *What Maisie Knew*? All three novels appeared in the same year —from the summer of 1896 to that of 1897. That elements of assimilated experience are present in *The Turn of the Screw* I do accept, and Professor Edel, not so much in his latest volumes of biography as in earlier studies, has made a number of pertinent suggestions to this effect.

In spite of what one may call the 'generally Freudian tone' of his biography, Professor Edel's analysis of the governess is more in line with that of the late Professor Harold Goddard, evolved as early as 1920, or even earlier,[38] without benefit of Freud, and painstakingly documented from the text. What vitiates Goddard's reading of the story is really his *parti pris*. In his childhood home there was a woman servant, who told him stories, including stories of her own visitation by the dead, and who later became mad; and this woman, he thinks, was 'the very moral' (as Mrs. Grose might have said) of the governess. Inevitably, there is some manipulation of the evidence, a slip here and there in reporting, an occasional *non sequitur* in the argument and so on, but on the whole Goddard's remains one of the most reasonable and plausible of the assaults on the governess's 'authority'.

The suggestion that *The Turn of the Screw* is a Freudian fantasy was first made by Ezra Pound in 1918.[39] It was developed, with no very close attention to the text of the story, and in complete disregard of the chronology of Freud's theorizing, by Edmund Wilson in his essay 'The Ambiguity of Henry James', which appeared in 1934. And the Freudian theory has remained central to much criticism of the story ever since.[40]

Now it is barely possible that Henry James read Dr. Sigmund Freud's first publication, in collaboration with Dr. Breuer, of his psychiatric case studies.[41] It appeared in 1895, as *Studien über Hysterie*: 'Studies in Hysteria'. We have to remember that William James was a leading psychologist, in fact a world-renowned authority in his subject, and to remember also the close bond of affection between the brothers. Henry James 'kept up with', read, and admired his brother's work, and it is possible that even if his own reading did not extend to rather recondite psychological publications, William might have 'put him on to' an interesting newcomer to the field. The core of the joint work is a group of case histories of hysteria, and Freud's contribution includes the case of an Englishwoman ('Miss Lucy R.'), governess to two children in a Viennese household, who had fallen in love with her employer, concealed her love, and as a result exhibited substitute physical symptoms. She was restored to health less by surgery than by the cathartic effect of confession to the psychologist. As I have summarized it the case may seem to offer a not too distant parallel to the situation in *The Turn of the Screw*; but in fact the only common details are that the governess is English, and that she has charge of two children.

Nevertheless the existence of this case history, and its possible accessibility to James, obviously raise a question. So too (although it has not been noticed in this connection) does a statement of William James in a lecture he delivered to the Lowell Institute of Boston in 1896: 'Hysteria is obsession, not by demons, but by a fixed idea of the person that has dropt down—Janet's phrase suffices here. . . . [A]lternate personality, the tendency for the self to break up, may, if there be spirit influences, yield them their opportunity . . . and if there were real demons, they might possess only hysterics. . . .'[42] Janet and before him Charcot, under whom William had studied in Paris (1882), were leading exponents of the theory of the *idée fixe* and of the repression or blockage of memory induced by hysteria, as also of the medical use of hypnotism. And quite apart from William's professional concern with these theories, both brothers had a personal reason for interest in and familiarity with them: Alice James's long invalidism had presented some typical hysterical features, and hypnotism had been used for her relief in the cancer from which, in 1892, she had died.

If, therefore, Henry James had wished to construct a fictional hysteric, late nineteenth-century model, he had ample material, both theoretical and clinical, to draw upon. But has he done so? The governess exhibits neither the 'split personality' William James postulates, nor any physical 'conversion' symptom which would ally her either with 'Miss Lucy R.' or with the exceptionally unsentimental and non-visionary Alice James. And from an examination of Freud's own contemporary findings, it would seem that, in the case of the hysteric, while disorders of vision are not uncommon, visual hallucinations as elaborate as the governess's do not occur in isolation (frequently they form the 'aura' or the sequel to a fit), and are never without a deeply significant prior justification in the personal experience of the hysteric.[43] Perhaps in that 'small, smothered' childhood, which so contrasted with the 'space and air and freedom' the governess enjoys at Bly (p. 28), and in the 'eccentric nature' of her father, which, equally with Goody Gosling and the vicarage pony, supplies a fund of anecdote for her pupils (pp. 97–98), we are meant to detect a source of psychological trouble. Perhaps the governess's brief acknowledgment, 'I had more pains than one. I was in receipt in these days of disturbing letters from home, where things were not going well' (p. 38), is meant to suggest a backdrop of *Angst*, of morbid anxiety, for her whole performance. If so, James has most uncharacteristically economized his means and dimmed his effect. He would seem, in short, to have missed a golden opportunity.

But to return to Edmund Wilson and his following. These Freudians suggest that the governess, secretly in love with her employer, is 'a neurotic case of sex repression', and in consequence suffers from hallucinations. The suggestion is untenable, and for the following reasons.

The governess, granted, has 'fallen in love', 'romantically', 'at first sight', with her charming employer; but she does not conceal the fact from herself, or from anybody else. She has not needed to *tell* Douglas of it—indeed,

Victorian propriety would not countenance so bold a disclosure to a recent acquaintance, a youth ten years her junior; but as Douglas says, 'I saw it, and she saw I saw it' (p. 6). And she *has* told him all about the interview in Harley Street, so that Douglas can describe both the charmer, 'a bachelor in the prime of life', 'gallant and splendid' (p. 9), and the feelings he evokes in her. But she has actually confessed these feelings to Mrs. Grose:

'I'm afraid . . . I'm rather easily carried away. I was carried away in London!'
    I can still see Mrs. Grose's broad face as she took this in. 'In Harley Street?'
    'In Harley Street.'
    'Well, Miss, you're not the first—and you won't be the last.'
    'Oh, I've no pretension,' I could laugh, 'to being the only one.' (pp. 17–18)

That is point one against the Freudian interpretation.

Next: the governess wandering in the garden one evening and gratifying herself with a daydream of suddenly encountering her employer, who would smile his approval of her child-management, is startled to observe a figure on a tower. Later she sees the same figure on a staircase. Twice she observes a female figure by a lake, and on one of these occasions the little girl plays at making a boat by fitting a stick into a piece of wood. The tower, the stair, and the lake all have their place in the Freudian scheme of sexual symbolism, and the child's play can be given a phallic interpretation. But even if these correspondences could be taken as unconscious anticipations of Freudian symbolism, why, if the tower has a sexual connotation for the governess, doesn't she see her master on the tower? Why does she see a complete stranger, whom Mrs. Grose later identifies, from the governess's point by point description, as the valet Peter Quint, of whom the governess had never heard and who was then dead? Was he so like his handsome master? If so, why is this extraordinary coincidence never mentioned at this or at any other point in the story? All the other appearances are explicable as the hallucinations of a disturbed mind—even as symbols relating to a sexual obsession of the governess's own (supposing she were so obsessed)—once the governess has heard the story of Quint and Miss Jessel, but not this first apparition. And if the first apparition cannot be explained in terms of the governess's infatuation with her employer, then it is idle to invoke that explanation at all.

If, however, you accept the apparitions, at face value, as genuine 'ghostly' apparitions, then all the details of their appearances are completely appropriate. They were house servants, their place was in the house—in strictly delimited parts of it. One was the governess: she is seen in the schoolroom, her domain. But the valet's domain was his master's dressing-room and bedroom, not a part of the house visited by the governess (except possibly on her first 'conducted tour' with little Flora), and not therefore a place where she could observe him. So, inside the house, the valet's 'ghost' appears only on the stairs, as he might have come and gone in life—and where Miss Jessel can also, appropriately, be seen. Again, throughout the story these 'ghosts' are represented as seeking contact with the children and as frustrated by the presence of the governess. When therefore she sees the ghosts inside the house, it is in the absence of the children; outside the house, she never sees them except at a distance, and by some means shut out—by the height of the tower, by the closed window, by the waters of the lake.

But as soon as she has identified the apparitions, the governess herself tries to close the gap by forcing a confession from one or other of the children: she tries to bring the ghosts within range, as it were, attack and rout them. Her first two attempts, both justified by nocturnal escapades on the children's part, are abortive. Flora, caught at the window, blandly lies: ' "And did you see anyone?" "Ah, *no!*" ' (p. 80); Miles, who is discovered on the moonlit lawn, his sister again at the window, passes the whole incident off as a 'joke' arranged between them (pp. 88–90). On the walk to church one autumn Sunday, Miles, by his demand for release from her tutelage, almost drives the governess into surrender of her post; but that night, when he calls her into his room for a bedside conversation, and she again questions him, he seems on the verge of confession. Yet while her anguished plea, ' "Dear little Miles . . . I just want you to help me to save you!" ' (p. 124), seems to provoke a shock and gust from the storm outside, it elicits no confidence and raises no ghost. She makes her next attempt by daylight, in the company of Mrs. Grose: the two women have surprised Flora by the lake. The governess asks, ' "Where, my pet, is Miss Jessel?" ' (p. 135), and it seems to her as if she has smashed a pane of glass: the child glares, Mrs. Grose shrieks, and the ghost of Miss Jessel appears across the lake. The final encounter is more prolonged. Mrs. Grose has departed with Flora, and the governess is left at Bly with Miles. As Miles stands at the window the governess thinks, 'The frames and squares of the great window were a kind of image, for him [that is, for Miles], of a kind of failure. I felt that I saw him, at any rate, shut in or shut out' (p. 157). She asks him, ' "Tell me . . . if, yesterday afternoon, from the table in the hall, you took, you know, my letter" ' (p. 161), and the ghost of Peter Quint appears outside the window 'like a sentinel before a prison', 'glaring' into the room with his 'white face of damnation' (p. 162). But this time Miles confesses: ' "Yes—I took it. . . . I opened it" ' (p. 163), and the phantom disappears. Then, pressing for a complete confession, the governess asks the reason for Miles's dismissal from his school: ' "What *were* these things [these things you said]?" ' (p. 167), and Quint appears again. This time the governess misjudges: instead of again imposing her will on the boy to confess and free himself, she proves to him that he has lost his familiar—that is, he is left with his burden of guilt (whatever it may be) but without his demonic support. She has spoilt the exorcism, performed the ritual in the wrong order (to use one traditional way of describing the procedure), or, in Swedenborgian terms, she has acted in ignorance of the fact that man's life is 'the life of his love', and the victim dies of shock as a result. And, again in Swedenborgian terms, the irony of that would be that the governess has not only killed the boy, but destroyed his soul as well, for 'no one's life can by any means be changed after death'.[44] We never learn what happens to Flora and her familiar.

Now that is a ghost story with several exceptional features. The majority of ghosts have a local attachment: they 'go with' the haunted house or the haunted room, and anyone who is there at the appointed time may see them. Ghosts of another type have a personal attachment: they haunt certain persons in whatever place they may happen to be—such ghosts have some of the characteristics of the Old Norse *fylgja* or the Irish banshee. Henry James wrote stories of the first type in 'The Third Person' and 'Owen Wingrave', of the second type in 'Sir Edmund Orme' and 'The Friends of the Friends'. But the ghosts of *The Turn of the Screw* haunt certain persons only, at one particular place—the house and grounds of Bly—although both of them died 'off the premises'. Miss Jessel had gone to her distant home to die; Quint was accidentally killed as he was coming home drunk from the village alehouse. Their recall is to Miles and Flora: the governess accidentally intervenes. This, of course, is the crux of the matter; for it is the governess who sees, not, so far as they can be induced to confess it, the children. This is the testing point of the governess's 'credibility', as James has handled it: which is the more convincing, the governess's assertion, or the children's denial? But to resume: Miles, apparently, is not haunted at school—he is 'bad' and expelled at the end of the summer term, because he has been corrupted already. He *might* have been 'bad' from ghostly instigation at his school, since Quint had died during the previous winter, but if so we are not told of it. Flora, apparently, will be safe from Miss Jessel once Mrs. Grose has taken her to London.

Bly, then, harbours ghosts but is not a haunted house; and you note how carefully James emphasizes its ordinariness, its cheerfulness (the white-panelled hall with its red carpet; the wide windows, with their fresh curtains; the comfortable, spacious bedrooms). 'A big, ugly, antique, but convenient house', we are told (p. 19). The governess insists on the normality of the setting, much as Douglas, in the introduction, insists on the normality of the narrator. James, in fact, quite discards the trappings of horror (the vaults, the dark passages—all the chilling suggestions of antiquity; the monstrous shapes, the weird noises, all the terrifying suggestions of inhuman depravity) which the Gothic novelists pile up around their mysteries (if indeed they are not the macabre encasement of a vacuum), except in the midnight scene in Miles's bedroom, where no ghost appears. The built-over vestiges of a still older building, of which the dizzyingly high 'machicolated square tower' is a feature, carry no menace—they merely suggest 'a castle of romance' with the golden-haired blue-eyed Flora as 'a rosy sprite' to inhabit it (p. 19). And if there is irony here, and we are meant to recall a towering castle on the Rhine, with the Lorelei combing her golden hair on the rocks below, there is no more than a breath of such association.

It is on this incongruity, carried through particular after particular, that James relies for his effect of horror: it is the ground on which he builds his suggestion of trouble, free 'from weak specifications'. We are presented with a benevolent guardian—who disowns all but a monetary responsibility for his charges; trusted servants—who corrupt their little master and mistress; a perfectly beautiful and charming little girl—who can look like an old woman and rail like a fishwife; a perfectly beautiful and charming little boy—who has 'covered and concealed' as the governess puts it, otherwise, in Victorian slang, 'played gooseberry in', a sordid intrigue, and is an undesirable influence at his school; a devoted governess—whose care results in the death of one of her pupils. At Bly, nothing is, but all things seem.

The only matching elements in the story are the deepening anxiety and fear of the governess and the lapse of the seasons—from the golden summer of the first eight chapters to the dull November of the last. Such a matching of physical and emotional 'atmospheres' is of course conventional, but here is a story of developing impressions in which time lapse must be accommodated somehow, and this seasonal order has the advantage of initial incongruity and shock: the first evil apparition comes to 'contradict' the beauty and tranquillity of a summer evening.

CHAPTER III

Some Details of Design

At this point it seems appropriate to consider, even if briefly and selectively, the conscious artistry in *The Turn of the Screw*. And we may begin with its simplest manifestation—the name symbolism James employs. It is true that early in his career he ranged himself with Edgar Allan Poe in expressing distrust of the constructed allegory as a literary form (in the hands of the modern novelist at least), and indeed of 'symbols and correspondences' generally, unless their use 'is extremely spontaneous' and 'the analogy presents itself with eager promptitude'.[45] Inevitably and inexhaustibly for Henry James, the most poetical of prose writers, the most Shakespearean of novelists,[46] it did so present itself: the illuminating images crowd to his pen. He does consistently eschew the rigid parallelism of the allegory, but the isolated or recurrent symbol is a feature of his work, particularly in the later novels. And the time-honoured, almost mechanical device of the revealing name, he uses as freely as Dickens himself. In his notebooks he kept lists of possible names, drawn mostly from newspapers: what attracted him (rather regrettably, from the point of view of his English critics) was often their oddity; but here again, he has the sanction of Dickens.

Of the personal names in *The Turn of the Screw*, the only one which occurs in surviving lists is that of Mrs. Grose,[47] where the symbolism is obvious enough. In spite of her goodwill and general loving-kindness to the children and to the governess, her mortal grossness is never sufficiently purged for her to apprehend the presence of airy spirits. In her trustfulness (and why should it be misplaced?) she believes the governess, but she herself never sees the ghosts. She illustrates in the story, the response James desires from his reader: she perceives and enters into the governess's trouble, and so credits the reality of what has caused it.

Is it only by accident that Peter Quint's name also recalls *A Midsummer Night's Dream*[48] and the sport of fairies and elves? Peter Quince, the carpenter, is one of the ignorant artisans self-elected to entertain the nobility— their stage-manager, in fact. Doesn't Peter Quint's rôle rather horribly parody this? He entertains the 'little grandee', the 'little fairy prince' Miles to a dreadful result.

But for Victorian readers the name would, I fancy, start yet another train of suggestion. Sheridan Le Fanu's *Uncle Silas*, first published in 1864, is a classic of 'terror' which ran through several editions in the sixties and seventies, and has been reprinted in every decade since, the 1930s alone excepted. Here we have a guardian uncle, not careless and indifferent, but bent on murdering his adolescent niece, whom he immures in his remote and desolate country-house. There are in fact two country-houses, and Knowl, though comfortable and well-kept, has its share of ghostly associations and sinister visitors; but it is the decaying Bartram-Haugh which is the scene, and almost the inspiration, of violence and crime. There is a corrupt governess, as grotesque as she is menacing, whose appearance on one occasion (Chapter 49) terrifies the niece into thinking she sees a ghost. And the niece's escape from death is largely due to the loyalty and courage of her personal servant, whose name is—Mary Quince. Now there is no substantial resemblance between the two novels either in plot or in characterization, let alone in structure or in style, but James and Le Fanu share an uncommon strength of pictorial imagination,[49] and there are sufficient glancing near-parallels for a reader to link the two works, to give James's story the benefit, as it were, of the darker shades and denser excitements of *Uncle Silas*—once the echo has sounded for him. The name Quince, I think, might ring such a bell.

The naming of Quint's female counterpart is an even more complicated matter. Jessel is a Jewish name, and as such it perhaps fits the dark, mysterious beauty of James's story. Perhaps, too, it recalls Shakespeare's Jessica, who was reminded, in the midst of *her* 'unthrift love', that mortal ears are grossly closed against the music of the spheres. But Jessel had also been the name of an eminent lawyer, a member of the Athenaeum Club, 'fond of the theatre and of society',[50] whom James would almost certainly have met during his early years in London. And Sir George Jessel, as Master of the Rolls, had presided over the last scenes of a Victorian *cause célèbre*[51]—a matrimonial wrangle prolonged through several years in which (as Sir George observed) the real point at issue was the custody of the two children. From the first the father had won custody of the son, who was (by 1879) ten years old, when finally, in a judgment of great length and ill-concealed bias, Sir George deprived the mother of her nine-year-old daughter as well. Whether or not James's readers sympathized with Mrs. Annie Besant,[52] her notoriety, as a lecturer and campaigner, first (with Charles Bradlaugh) for Freethought, then for Socialism, and later (as an adherent of Mme Blavatsky) for Theosophy, would ensure that the name Jessel had a special resonance for them, even in 1898. And the very murmur of 'Besant' and 'Theosophy' would, for such readers, immediately thicken the occult suggestions of James's story: to their view, not merely unquiet dead of the Anglican persuasion, nor Swedenborgian spirits of Hell, but Elementaries from Kāmaloka might confront the governess. In 1893, 'to meet the public demand for a simple exposition of Theosophical teachings' (as she explains in her Preface), Mrs. Besant published a manual entitled *Death—And After?*. Here we read:

Persons who have led an evil life, who have gratified and stimulated their animal passions . . . remain for long, denizens of Kāmaloka ['Desire-land'], and are filled with yearnings for the earth-life they have left, and for the animal delights that they can no longer—in the absence of the physical body—directly taste. . . . Another class of disembodied entities includes those whose lives on earth have been prematurely cut short, by their own act, the act of others, or by accident. . . . These, whether suicides or killed by accident, can communicate with those in earth-life, but much to their own injury. . . . *Unhappy shades,˙if sinful and sensual, they wander about . . . until their* death-*hour comes. . . . They are the Piśāchas, the Incubi and Succubœ of mediœval times; the demons of thirst, gluttony, lust, and avarice—Elementaries of intensified craft, wickedness, and cruelty; provoking their victims to horrid crimes, and revelling in their commission! They not only ruin their victims, but these psychic vampires, borne along by the torrent of their hellish impulses, at last—at the fixed close to their natural period of life—they are carried out of the earth's aura into regions where for ages they endure exquisite suffering and end with entire destruction.*[53]

Miles and Flora, of course, together represent, and Flora by her name suggests, youth in earliest springtime. I fancy, however, that James is interpreting the name Miles not according to its probable etymology, as a familiar by-form of Michael,[54] but as *miles* 'the soldier'. Like Owen Wingrave, Miles dies in a ghostly encounter, 'like a young soldier on a battle-field', though not in this case 'on the gained field'.[55] I am afraid it is purely fortuitous that in Miles and Flora the medievalist hears an echo, out of the twelfth century, from the springtime debate of Phillis and Flora, where *miles*, the poor knight, is defeated in quite another kind of contest.

The most chillingly effective name in the story is that of the house—Bly. James has given the name its usual pronunciation, but not, as a place name, its usual spelling, which is 'Blyth' or 'Blythe'. It means simply 'cheerful', 'merry',[56] as the more normal spelling would undoubtedly have suggested to James. He actually records the spelling 'Blythe' in his *Notebooks* (p. 66), though not specifically as that of a place name, and he does set down, as a possible house name, 'Gaye' (p. 119), which he uses in *Guy Domville*. So Bly is 'a pleasant, happy abode', and indeed it seems so, when the governess first becomes acquainted with it.

The narrator, the governess, is nameless. So are forty-five other narrators who, from 1866 to 1901, present James's stories. Their anonymity, as a rule, has little significance beyond the implication that (notwithstanding the freedom to expatiate and the assurance of direct knowledge which the first person confers) they are themselves of secondary importance. Mostly they are writers or artists, whose profession adequately explains both their involvement and their tireless curiosity: who challenges, or even considers, the narrator of 'Greville Fane', for instance? Where other indications are in keeping, anonymity may confirm a sinister impression—of scheming and duplicity, say, as in *The Aspern Papers*. In *The Turn of the Screw*, withholding the name, where so lively an impression of personality is conveyed, adds an authentic touch of Victorian propriety: it mimics the anonymity which strict etiquette required of any 'lady' who ventured into print. The pseudonymous lady novelists of the period are tacitly rebuked by the hundreds of their sisters who instruct or entertain with no warrant save their gentility.

But the governess, if not onomastically identified, nevertheless has a local relation: her home is a Hampshire vicarage (p. 9). Just why she should come from Hampshire, or why the country-house of her destination should lie in Essex, is not clear, until we learn that one night she stays up over-late reading Fielding's *Amelia*.[57] As a child she had heard certain eighteenth-century novels mentioned in terms which 'appealed' to her 'unavowed curiosity'; 'a roomful of old books at Bly' allows her to satisfy it (p. 76). Does she identify her own fortunes with those of the unfailingly sweet and faithful wife Amelia, who on one occasion suffers from 'the vapours', or 'the hysterics' (I, 133), who is pursued by one would-be seducer after another, and has from time to time the sole responsibility for her young family? The family, incidentally, at this stage numbers three children (I, 169), not two; but as the narrative progresses Fielding neglects all but the first-born son, 'a good soldier-like Christian' (III, 6), and his young sister. If, however, James has linked his governess with Fielding's impeccable heroine, he has even more obviously provided her with a cautionary reference to the history of Mrs. Bennet in Book VII of the same novel. Mrs. Bennet is 'the younger of two daughters of a clergyman in Essex' (II, 104), who at sixteen lost both her mother and her sister. 'I was now in the nineteenth year of my age, when my father's good fortune removed us from the county of Essex into Hampshire, where a living was conferred on him . . . of twice the value of what he was before possessed of' (II, 109–10). But the vicar marries the youthful widow of the former incumbent; the stepmother turns the father against his daughter; and she has to take refuge with an elderly and cantankerous aunt. She escapes by marrying, for love, an impecunious curate. The young couple seek their fortune in London, where they subsist happily enough until their first child is six months old. But at this stage a Lothario appears, a noble lord who affects friendship for the husband and love for the child: 'I thought he discovered good sense, good-nature, condescension, and other good qualities, by the fondness he shewed to my child. . . . I cannot deny, but that he was the handsomest and genteelest person in the world . . .' (II, 139). In her husband's absence she is persuaded to accept an invitation to a masquerade at Ranelagh, where the noble lord discloses something of his interest in her: 'I will own the truth; I was delighted with perceiving a passion in him, which I was not unwilling to think he had had from the beginning, and to derive his having concealed it so long, from his awe of my virtue, and his respect to my understanding. . . . I fancied . . . that I might indulge my vanity and interest at once, without being guilty of the least injury' (II, 144). But on their return home she is, like Clarissa before her, drugged and raped. After this violent conquest, the noble lord takes no further interest in her, although he

provides her with an annuity on her husband's death. She has 'heard since
. . . that the highest degree of inconstancy is his character; and that few of
his numberless mistresses have ever received a second visit from him'
(II, 156). This is the profligate who lays most determined siege to the
virtuous Amelia. Does he also provide the image for the governess's employer,
'handsome and bold and pleasant, off-hand and gay and kind', as Douglas
pictures him, 'such a figure as had never risen, save in a dream or an old
novel, before a fluttered, anxious girl out of a Hampshire vicarage' (p. 9)?
For Douglas, too, may owe his being to this same 'old novel'. The noble
lord is succeeded in the pursuit of Amelia by her husband's closest friend,
Colonel James, and this gentleman's machinations are accidentally exposed
by another friend, Colonel Bath, devotee of punctilio and the duel, whose
hero, naturally enough, is Hotspur. ' "That Shakespeare," cries the Colonel,
"was a fine fellow. He was a very pretty poet indeed. Was it not Shakespeare
that wrote the play about Hotspur? you must remember these lines. I got
them almost by heart at the play-house; for I never missed that play whenever it was acted, if I was in town" ' (III, 97). The tirade the Colonel mangles
is the rhetorical high-point of the conspiracy scene in *Henry IV Part I*, where
Douglas is ranged in alliance not only with the Percies but also with Owen
Glendower, who 'can call spirits from the vasty deep'. And (very oddly
indeed) Owain ab Gruffydd Glyn Dwr is himself present, incognito, to
judge those described by the governess: the only other member of James's
fireside circle to be named is Griffin, and Griffin is a familiar by-form of the
Welsh Griffith, Owen's patronymic.[58]

What has James achieved by this accumulation of reference? He has, by
the use of some half dozen names and two or three scattered phrases of
description, at once surrounded his governess with intimations of the supernatural, and defined the normality of her own character and interests. The
novel that engrosses her is read (he suggests) as most novels are read, with
application to her own predicament, her own hopes and fears, which are
entirely appropriate to her age and sex. May she not, by devoted service, win
successively approbation, love, and happiness in marriage? Yet isn't her
employer hopelessly indifferent to her, and inconstant, perhaps dangerous, as
well? As the tale proceeds, the supernatural crowds in upon the governess, but
it is, James assures us, an alien invasion.

To one of his correspondents James characterized his subject as 'merely
pictorial': he has certainly exploited its picturesqueness to the full. His visual
impressions were always intense (he was indeed a painter *manqué*), and he
had a truly Wordsworthian sense of the spirit of place; so that his scene
painting is never perfunctory, never a mere conventional setting for the
action, but a vivid 'recall' of some actual scene whose effect he has himself
experienced. The Venice of *The Aspern Papers*, the Paris of *The Ambassadors*
provide superlative examples of such effects. Sometimes it is possible to

check the original recording of the experience against its fictional evocation. Edel, for instance, suggests that the description of the figure on the tower in our story may have its source in an impression of Haddon Hall recorded by James in a travel sketch first published in 1872:

The twilight deepened, the ragged battlements and the low, broad oriels glanced duskily from the foliage, the rooks wheeled and clamored in the glowing sky; and if there had been a ghost on the premises, I certainly ought to have seen it. In fact, I did see it, as we see ghosts nowadays. I felt the incommunicable spirit of the scene with almost painful intensity. The old life, the old manners, the old figures seemed present again.[59]

But, over twenty-five years, the artist's touch has become more assured: this is the scene of the first apparition in *The Turn of the Screw*:

It was as if, while I took in—what I did take in—all the rest of the scene had been stricken with death. I can hear again, as I write, the intense hush in which the sounds of evening dropped. The rooks stopped cawing in the golden sky and the friendly hour lost, for the minute, all its voice. But there was no other change in nature, unless indeed it were a change that I saw with a stranger sharpness. The gold was still in the sky, the clearness in the air, and the man who looked at me over the battlements was as definite as a picture in a frame. (p. 31)

Here, to frame the first appearance of Miss Jessel, is a summer afternoon, conveyed in a single sentence: 'The old trees, the thick shrubbery, made a great and pleasant shade, but it was all suffused with the brightness of the hot, still hour' (pp. 55–56). And here is the early morning appearance of Quint, on the staircase below the 'tall window': 'He knew me as well as I knew him; and so, in the cold, faint twilight, with a glimmer in the high glass and another on the polish of the oak stair below, we faced each other in our common intensity. He was absolutely, on this occasion, a living, detestable, dangerous presence' (p. 77). This is the perfection of descriptive art, and its operation (in the selection of the essential detail and the charged word) is perpetually fascinating for James's readers. But here there is a special ingenuity in its application. We have considered James's use of suggestion, the way he lays the reader's own stock of literary memories under contribution to extend the factual limits of his tale. By contrast, there is no vague penumbra of suggestion, 'no ambiguity' whatever, in the record of things seen. Every detail has the sharp clarity of a colour photograph. We know with certainty what the governess *saw*—her interpretation of it is 'a different matter'.

The construction of the story is equally artful. James in 1895 records his determination to make each short story henceforth 'a complete and perfect little drama', and he congratulates himself that from his 'wasted years' of 'theatrical experiment' he has at least gained 'some such mastery of fundamental statement—of the art and secret of it, of expression, of the sacred mystery of structure'.[60] Most of his stories, from the seventies on, were so long as to require dividing into sections, like chapters of a miniature novel, and one is often conscious of a scenic intention in these divisions. But in *The Turn of the Screw* we have, exceptionally, a sequence of no fewer than twenty-four very brief sections, each clearly constituting a dramatic scene, and many ending with a curtain line: ' "Yes. Mr. Quint is dead" ' (v); ' "It's far worse than I dreamed—they're lost!" ' (vii); ' "Where, my pet, is Miss Jessel?" ' (xix); ' "I'll save you without him!" she cried as she went' (xxi); ' "Well—so we're alone!" ' (xxii); ' "Tell me . . . if, yesterday afternoon, from the table in the hall, you took, you know, my letter" ' (xxiii); ' "Why, the candle's out!" I then cried. "It was I who blew it, dear!" said Miles' (xvii). All of these closing lines have a theatrical (or melodramatic) effectiveness—the last indeed achieves the maximum of sinister suggestion.

Now to construct a story, or even a full-length novel, strictly in terms of theatre—to eschew description (except for stage directions) and present the action solely through dialogue and report—is not an impossible feat. But on this occasion James, mercifully, has not tried to emulate Gyp. He has planned his story for dramatic effect, without sacrificing any of the amenities (though shedding certain of the encumbrances) of orthodox narrative. His narrator's insistent presence and limited view preclude 'omniscience' and exclude the 'intrusive author'; but they permit incidents to be reported and dialogue to be recorded with nearly the immediacy of drama, while the accompanying or interposed commentary (however 'difficult' its content may be) has the spontaneity and also the chronological orderliness of the private journal. But the whole presentation is rigorously contained, as we are never allowed to forget,[61] in a sustained act of retrospect and recollection; and from this opposition ('immediacy' instantly countered by 'distancing') there is contrived, by purely formal means, an effect of tightly-controlled excitement. Here, indeed, is a 'little firm fantasy', as James in his *Preface* is willing to admit (p. 173). The narrative pattern which results is one of the most intricate he ever devised. At each stage of her experience at Bly—and analysis has revealed thirteen such stages[62]—the governess first adumbrates, then presents, then interprets some disturbing incident (and Mrs. Grose's revelations, Miles's rebellion, the children's complicity are motivating 'shocks' as powerful as the presumed 'ghostly' visitations). And in every instance, except for the last catastrophic scene, she summons her resources to 'cope' with the trouble, only to be overtaken by a new development before her plan can be put into effect. There is thus a continuing, wave-like, sequent toil towards the *dénouement*. The only qualification I would add is that James's elaborate variation of rhythm and tempo ensures that this basic pattern never becomes monotonously obvious. Current action and dialogue alternate with retrospective narration and reflection. Either may be used for increase of excitement and tension—as in Ch. xv which, without a word spoken, carries the governess from the church she cannot bring herself to enter to the sight of Miss Jessel in the schoolroom; or in Ch. xvii, where agitated dialogue and comment lead up to the incident of the candle. And either may be used for delaying, slackening, or suspending the action—as in Ch. xiii, where the governess silently reviews her impressions and hesitant conclusions over a month's lull; or in Ch. xvi, where, after a voluble but sometimes inconsequent discussion with Mrs. Grose, the governess at last decides to 'write' to the children's uncle.

But there is one detail of construction which calls for special notice. The bedside colloquy occupying Ch. xvii has been shown to be an interruption to the structural pattern.[63] More significantly, it foreshadows the climactic scene of Ch. xxiv. Once before (Ch. xi) there has been a midnight colloquy with Miles: on that occasion he succeeded in reducing the governess's anxiety to a 'joke' (p. 90), and no 'ghost' appeared. Now he again laughingly eludes the governess's oblique enquiries and emotional appeal, until, as she is quick to see, one particular question strikes home (p. 124). The passionate entreaty she addresses to him provokes a supernatural but impersonal response, and Miles regains his self-possession. In one's appreciation of its effectiveness, one hardly notices that for this intervention of the supernatural, James has uncharacteristically reverted to old-fashioned, elemental, 'Gothic' terror. The explanation is simple. He is here neatly adapting to his own purposes an incident from an early, and now almost forgotten novel of a favourite author —*The Cock and Anchor* by Sheridan Le Fanu.

On a night of wild storm the wicked Sir Richard Ashwoode's Italian valet hears his master's stick thumping a summons, then hears words of terrified entreaty, and next 'a crash as of some heavy body springing from the bed— then a rush upon the floor—then another crash'. When at last he brings himself to enter the room, he finds his master dead upon the floor. In the account that follows (much too long to quote in full), macabre details and comments of awe and terror from both author and actor in the scene are multiplied.

'*Canchero!* it was ugly death—there was something with him; what was he speaking with?'
Parucci walked to the door leading to the great staircase, but found it bolted as usual. . . .
'What made him speak? nothing was with him—pshaw! nothing could come to him here—no, no, nothing.'
As he thus spoke, the wind swept vehemently upon the windows with a sound as if some great thing had rushed against them, and was pressing for admission, and the gust blew out the candle; the blast died away in a lengthened wail, and then again came rushing and howling up to the windows, as if the very prince of the powers of the air himself were thundering at the casement; then again the blue dazzling lightning glared into the room and gave place to deeper darkness.[64]

This passage, indeed the whole incident as treated by Le Fanu, offers a useful contrast with James's method. Le Fanu's terror is on the grand scale, in which the play of huge natural forces is made to evoke the immensity of satanic evil: he is as much interested in the storm outside as in the wicked baronet dead inside. And so it is throughout his novel: he surrenders wholly to the creative impulse of the moment. James's image in his *Preface* (p. 172) of the stream in flood might have been conceived with Le Fanu in mind; and his own treatment of this particular remembered incident demonstrates the principle he there enunciates—of keeping the story 'on terms with itself'. Ch. xvii opens with the governess trying to write her letter and listening to 'the lash of the rain and the batter of the gusts', for 'a great wind was abroad' (p. 119). But that is our only reminder of the storm, and its phrasing emphasizes the close-locked security that Bly affords. So enclosed, Miles and the governess engage in their battle of wills—the child opposing a defensive reserve to the young woman's anxious insistence, as might any normally 'wicked' child resist any mother; and it is on this human basis that the governess wins 'a small faint quaver of consenting consciousness' (p. 124). The shock that follows destroys at once the sense of security and the hope of communication. Here, for comparison with its original, is the passage in full:

The answer to my appeal was instantaneous, but it came in the form of an extraordinary blast and chill, a gust of frozen air and a shake of the room as great as if, in the wild wind, the casement had crashed in. The boy gave a loud, high shriek which, lost in the rest of the shock of sound, might have seemed, indistinctly, though I was so close to him, a note either of jubilation or of terror. I jumped to my feet again and was conscious of darkness. So for a moment we remained, while I stared about me and saw that the drawn curtains were unstirred and the window tight. 'Why, the candle's out!' I then cried.

'It was I who blew it, dear!' said Miles. (pp. 124–25)

One notes that both the child's shriek and the governess's ability to see in the dark imply a memory of Le Fanu's scene: in the second instance, James has retained a mental impression of the lightning flash, which he forgets, or neglects, to mention. But thematically, this passage has a dual importance, which is underlined by its variation from James's norm. It is a kalends of change: from now on the pace of the story, the movement towards disaster, accelerates; and it is the first and only straight acknowledgment that supernatural forces are at work—the only manifestation to which anyone other than the governess testifies. And Miles (convincingly, it seems, for the governess makes no further allusion to the incident) at once denies its import—terror is reduced to scale.

CHAPTER IV

The Influence of Ibsen

It may be asked at this point: 'Is there nothing in all this preoccupation with structure and dramatic effect which suggests the influence of Ibsen?'

We know that throughout the years (1895–97) during which *The Turn of the Screw* was conceived and written, James, in his pursuit of 'dramatic' method, was still very much the student of Ibsen. But in spite of this assiduity and the rather strained enthusiasm with which he writes of individual plays and performances, what impresses one most in his criticism is the reluctance with which he concedes Ibsen's importance. He resents 'the hard compulsion of [Ibsen's] strangely inscrutable art', but he resents even more, it seems, his own inability to analyse and possess its secret. The comments of Archer and Shaw remind us how deformed by inadequate staging and histrionic extravagances these early performances must often have been, but it is still puzzling that James, so discerning in criticism and so accessible, it has always seemed, to every literary influence, should go to Ibsen to learn and yet learn so little. He is struck by the openness of Ibsen's character delineation and the easement this affords the actor, yet he appears to regard it, not as the painfully indecisive outcome of much troubled thinking on specific problems of human character and destiny, but as a device, a policy of keeping the audience (or the reader) guessing, used for a calculated effect. He recognizes that Ibsen presents 'the picture not of an action but of a condition', yet not, it seems, what is central to Ibsen's method—the working back, from a moment of crisis, to the revelation of ultimate motive. It is questionable, indeed, if the method in its strictness could be applied with any effect of naturalness to a full-length novel. What in fact had James to learn from Ibsen that could be so applied? The disciple of Hawthorne had, from the beginning, known the thematic usefulness of the symbol, and the value of the open situation. From the beginning he had known how to exploit the ambiguity of dialogue —the half-spoken intimations and the incoherences of normal conversation and the scope they offer for misunderstanding, whether wilful or unintentional. What could he learn from Ibsen's 'admirable economy' that he had been unable to learn from Maupassant's, in his own medium, and in the Gallic idiom so congenial to him? The whole bent of his imagination, his wit, his irresistible urge to expatiate, to verbalize, tend to an effect quite other than the laconic strength, the 'meagreness' as James calls it, if also the 'intensity', of Ibsen. How characteristic (and how reminiscent of his own practice in *The Turn of the Screw*) is his complaint against *The Lady from the Sea*: 'One feels that the subject should have been tinted and distanced.'[65]

James, then, never produced the complete Ibsenite novel, nor does he ever, to any noticeable degree, achieve an Ibsenite effect; but he does from time to time draw on Ibsen's resources for the creation of effects quite his own. The process is not necessarily one of straightforward borrowing. In *The Other House*, for instance, the central situation bears a vague general resemblance to that of *Rosmersholm*, and certain details (the significance attached to the use of Christian names, for example) and certain properties (notably a bridge over a stream, fitter for suicide than for murder) are imported from *Rosmersholm* to strengthen that impression. But actually the central situation is that of James's own early story 'The Romance of Certain Old Clothes' (where, strangely, the 'bad heroine' also has unpleasantly light grey eyes), and its complication with reminiscences of *Little Eyolf* (in the drowned child Effie-Eyolf and the persistent suitor Vidal-Borgheim) serves only to ally the novel more closely to Victorian melodrama. In *The Turn of the Screw* the debt to Ibsen is an even more complicated affair. Two plays, *The Lady from the Sea* and *Little Eyolf*, are directly related by theme to James's story. In the first, a mysterious Stranger, a self-condemned murderer, has established a hypnotic dominance over the wife and tries to lure her across the sea, away from her husband; in the second, an uncanny being, the Rat Wife, a kind of female Pied Piper, lures little Eyolf to his death in the fiord. In each case the evil agent is a living person, but with such convincingly supernatural attributes and powers that we must suppose ourselves confronted with a troll. Finmark, the mountains, the fiord and the deep sea are all invoked as realms of the supernatural, where the human and the non-human meet and blend: the Norse Ibsen, unlike James, has no difficulty in accepting either materialized spirits or demonic human beings.

By the time he acquired his *donnée* for *The Turn of the Screw* (on 10 January 1895) James was familiar with the text of both plays: the first two acts of *Little Eyolf* (which he did not see performed till November 1896) he thought 'a masterpiece and a marvel'.[66] Even the record of his *donnée* may, therefore, include hints from Ibsen as well as those details imparted by Archbishop Benson. And when, in September 1897,[67] James begins to write his story, he obviously decides to adapt what he conceives to be the Ibsen manner to its narration. The retrospect which frames each stage of the action is his own addition, and provides the distancing which he felt the lack of in Ibsen's *The Lady from the Sea*; but the successive revelations through which the governess becomes acquainted with past happenings at Bly recall those which by degrees acquaint Dr. Wangel and Allmers with the realities of their situation. There are, however, certain important qualifications to be noted. The interlocutors in both plays are painstakingly, if sometimes clumsily, intent on communicating—ultimately there will be an *éclaircissement*, they will achieve enlightenment. Again, the Stranger in the one case, and the Rat Wife and even the child himself in the other, merely project symbolically the problems of human sexuality in which the couples are really involved. There is no such real problem in *The Turn of the Screw*. James has persuaded us to accept instead a speculative corruption of the children as concomitant of Quint's and Miss Jessel's own guilty liaison—a superfluity of naughtiness which does indeed, as Wilde observed, recall (even in shadow show) the more lurid excesses of Elizabethan tragedy.[68] Moreover the Ibsen model James seems to have chosen for his narrator is not Ellida nor Rita nor Asta (women who, in their deepest trouble and perplexity, never fail of candour), but the enigmatic Rebecca West of *Rosmersholm*, so that the record of the governess's 'mystification' inevitably becomes tinged with suggestions of 'her own mystery'. There is, for instance, the crucial moment at which she is overtaken by self-doubt: 'I seemed to float not into clearness, but into a darker obscure, and within a minute there had come to me out of my very pity the appalling alarm of his being perhaps innocent. It was for the instant confounding and bottomless, for if he *were* innocent, what then on earth was *I*?' (p. 166). The governess faces the possibility that she has been mistaken: if the child has not been corrupted, Quint has not corrupted him, and the apparitions (the report of which we have, by every art James can command, been induced to accept as veridical) must therefore bear a different interpretation from the one she has placed on them. But she has acted on her supposition, so as to disrupt a hitherto peaceful household and to blacken the character of both the children. She may well exclaim in horror at the possibility; but why is she alarmed? And why, instead of the instinctive 'What had I *done*?' does she ask, 'What *was* I?', as if, in the 'bottomless' abysses revealed to her, she sees madness or a guilt inviting punishment? Such a question is appropriate enough for Rebecca (with a background of illegitimacy, incest, and, possibly, murder by suggestion) but here it merely implements the policy of bafflement which is so elaborately justified for us, *ex post facto*, in James's *Prefaces*. He has stolen Ibsen's thunder, as it were, but (again) he has ignored the lightning flash.

Method apart, the two plays have left their impress in several details of description and setting. *Little Eyolf* seems to have provided James with a number of indications for the portrayal of Miles. The crippled child's beauty of eye and the irrational fear it inspires in his mother; his desire for boyish pursuits and the prospect of a soldier's life (he is actually dressed as a soldier, and the Rat Wife calls him 'my little wounded warrior'); his father's neglect; the unnaturally close childhood relationship between his father and his aunt, who is not really his aunt, who is nicknamed 'Eyolf' and devotes herself in turn to 'little' Eyolf—all seem to have contributed, if only in a minor degree, towards James's delineation. At one point the play illuminates an area of motivation which, because of his refusal to compromise the children and his adherence to the sole narrator and the single point of view, James in his story has had to leave dark—the mingled fear and fascination which work on the child's imagination to draw him both to the satanic familiar ('I think he has the horriblest—aspect I ever saw. . . . But he's lovely—lovely all the same'), and to the relief it promises from the alienation of his crippled state ('And there it's all as still, and soft, and dark as their hearts can desire, the lovely little things. Down there they sleep a long, sweet sleep, with no one to hate them or persecute them any more').[69] What the Stranger promises Ellida, on the contrary, is not restful death, but a full and passionate life in the freedom of the unknown, a prospect not open to Quint or Miss Jessel. *The Lady from the Sea*, however, offers a number of hints on the literary presentation of phantoms. 'Every now and then,' declares Ellida, 'I suddenly see him stand bodily before me, or rather a little to one side. He never looks at me; he is only there. . . . I see his scarf-pin most distinctly of all, with a large, bluish-white pearl in it. That pearl is like a dead fish's eye. And it seems to glare at me.'[70] And again, when the Stranger makes his first bodily appearance on the scene, Ellida, expecting her husband, cries out, 'Oh my dear —have you come at last!', but then, looking at him, astonished and apprehensive, 'Who are you? Are you looking for some one here?', only to shriek, as he turns his gaze full on her, 'The eyes!—The eyes! . . . Don't look at me like that!' (III, pp. 178–79). While the Stranger climbs over the fence and comes into the garden, she stands as if paralysed with fear against a tree-trunk near the pond, but when she hears her husband's voice, rushes to him and cries, 'Save me, Wangel! Don't you see him? There he stands!' (III, p. 181). Dr. Wangel, who has the double advantage of being in his wife's confidence and of confronting a live adversary, at times utters sentiments which seem to find an echo in those expressed by the governess. 'The children! The children——!' he urges his wife, 'Let us at least spare them— for the present' (IV, p. 213). And finally, reaching a decision rather like that of the governess in Miles's case: 'I see it well, Ellida! Step by step you are gliding away from me. Your craving for the vast and infinite—and for the unattainable—will drive your mind out into the darkness at last. . . . It shall not come to that. There is no other way of deliverance for you; at least I see none. And therefore—therefore I—I cancel our bargain on the spot. So now you can choose your own path—in full—full freedom' (V, pp. 235–36). There is a significant remark passed by a minor character: 'It's great fun here just now; everybody goes in couples; always two and two together' (V, p. 229). And again, 'Just look,—don't she and father look like an engaged couple!' (V, p. 239).

But the most curious parallel, it seems to me, is one of setting. There is a lake at Bly, which the governess sometimes refers to as a 'pond' (pp. 55, 63, 132) or as a 'pool' (pp. 131, 132, 140); and this lake, in Ch. vi of James's story, is the scene of Miss Jessel's first appearance. Here, in part, is the stage setting for Act III of *The Lady from the Sea*:

A remote part of Dr. Wangel's garden. The place is damp, marshy, and over-shadowed by large old trees. To the right is seen the edge of a stagnant pond. A low open fence divides the garden from the footpath and fiord in the background. In the furthest distance, beyond the fiord, mountain ranges rising into peaks. It is late afternoon, almost evening.

Boletta sits sewing upon a stone seat to the left. On the seat lie some books and a work-basket. (p. 169)

Of the books, we learn 'Oh, one's a botanical book, and the other is a geography' (p. 170). Act V has the same setting, with the additional detail that 'the children' and their two male companions 'in a boat on the fiord, are shoving from the left along the shore' (p. 216). One might, of course, argue that the 'ornamental water' is sufficiently characteristic of English landscape art, and that James himself was familiar enough with English country-houses, to make any such prompting from Ibsen unnecessary, yet the similarity in detail—the pond, the old trees, the stone bench, the 'work', the geography game together setting the scene for a ghostly intrusion—can hardly be accidental. But when in Ch. xix the governess and Mrs. Grose have to go right round this lake in their search for Flora, the shadow of Ibsen seems to deepen. The governess's toilsome course is described in convincingly appropriate detail, but since Miss Jessel again appears 'on the opposite bank', that is, the side the governess has just left, one wonders what really has been the point of the exercise. Why in the first place had Flora crossed the lake at all? I suggest that what has operated here is the memory of a passage in Act III of *Little Eyolf*. Allmers is recounting his 'night of terror' in the mountains:

I came to a wide, dreary mountain lake; and that lake I had to cross. But I could not —for there was neither a boat nor any one there. . . . Then I went without any guidance into a side valley. I thought that by that way I could push on over the heights and between the peaks—and then down again on the other side of the lake. . . . I mistook the direction—for there was no path or track. . . . I dragged myself along among the precipices—and rejoiced in the peace and luxury of death . . . . all of a sudden I found myself where I wanted to be—on the other side of the lake. (pp. 166–68)

For Allmers, his experience has meant a recall, without the exaltation of love or hope, to human obligations—in the first place to the individual child, and, the child lost, to his kind. The play ends with a joint resolve of husband and wife: in an emotional desert they will make their life flower into use, and it may be that peace (and communion with spirits) will be added unto them. Can James himself intend, or hope his readers will apprehend, such a por-tentous moral loading of this episode in his story? The excitement of 1891 had died down, but in 1897 Ibsen was still a fashionably advanced and controversial playwright, so that it is possible the 'fastidious' and 'jaded' readers, to suit whose taste James designed his 'fairy-tale', may have been alert to Ibsenite echoes: for them the search for the child by the lake may have acquired this extra dimension of meaning. But the possibility is a very faint one. For most readers, the scenes from Norway, so happily 'acclimatized', as Ibsen's Ballested might say, in the Essex of *The Turn of the Screw*, would be an indistinguishable part of the general picturesque. To be sure of profiting by the associations of a borrowed effect James would, like an eighteenth-century poet, have been obliged to quote his source in a footnote. The significant names we have dealt with fall into quite a different category: they are merely signposts directing to a meaning which the reader has to reach for himself; and their use must therefore be a calculated one. But the presence of a demonstrably borrowed effect is no assurance that the author is aware of his indebtedness. The 'source' may have become so completely a part of his own imaginative experience that he is no longer conscious of prior rights in it. Nor does it follow that, once appropriated, the incident or description will retain its original significance: high seriousness can dwindle into mere literary decoration. I think it has done so here.

In sum, the example of Ibsen has not deeply affected James's handling of *The Turn of the Screw*. Later, it will play its part in the formation of the celebrated 'third manner'—not in its verbal profuseness, but in 'the method of narration by interminable elaboration of suggestive reference' which William James found so irksome.[71] For in the occasional evasiveness of Ibsen's stage dialogue James (so he seems to think) has discovered a formula for treating the crudest of facts and the most awkward of situations without embarrassment or offence: by talking round and round a point he can produce an illusion of magnitude—he will no longer present but 'adumbrate' narrative details and characters alike. In 1897, however, this method is still experimental, still selectively applied, and in *The Turn of the Screw* is subordinated to a predetermined style and form, as I hope to show. But to do so, it is necessary first to discuss the characters of James's story.

CHAPTER V

Jane Eyre and *The Turn of the Screw*

When we turn to the question of characterization, we come to the field of James's greatest triumphs. In this branch of the novelist's art he is an acknowledged master, and our least expectation from him is of characters sharply realized and consistently described. But *The Turn of the Screw* held peculiar difficulties for him: he had to convey an expert's familiarity with details of child behaviour and child management. His male ignorance betrays him, I think, only in his presentation of the little girl. She is, we are told, eight years old (p. 58); she is capable, but perhaps not unaided, of moving and mooring a heavy rowboat (p. 134); under the governess's instruction she 'begins' geography (with the Sea of Azof) (p. 55); but Miles calls her 'a baby girl' (p. 107); and she is first introduced (one would say) as a three-year-old, eating her bread and milk 'in a high chair and a bib' and looking from one to the other of the cooing grown-ups 'with placid heavenly eyes that contained nothing to check us' (p. 17).

The only other technical imperfections, that I can see, are occasional verbal incongruities. The characters in *The Turn of the Screw* are born out of the story—out of the logic of the plot; the story is not (as it often is for James) a crystallization of incident round character. And these coldly-evoked characters sometimes express themselves in phrases which, given their individual wholeness of personality, they could never have uttered. The sometimes unchildlike children may pass—they are precocious, and such children often express themselves with adult pomposity and condescension. ' "I want a new field," ' says the boy of ten; and then, kindly, ' "Well, old lady?" ' (p. 123). Mrs. Grose, for all the effective terms in which she is described to us (for example, 'She offered her mind to my disclosures as . . . she would have held out a large clean saucepan' [p. 86]), Mrs. Grose expresses herself like the stock faithful housekeeper or devoted nurse of Victorian melodrama. The part of her that is not out of an early Victorian novel, is, one feels, straight off the boards. But the governess, on whose aptness of expression and description rests the whole credibility of the story as it unfolds, speaks with many voices which don't all harmonize. If she came fresh from the schoolroom and Mrs. Marcet's *Conversations*,[72] she might talk to Mrs. Grose as magistrally, as didactically as this: ' "you might perfectly have made the claim for him if you had not, as it happened, seen an exception to take. What was your exception, and to what passage in your personal observation of him did you refer?" ' (p. 67); or as this: ' "His having lied and been impudent are, I confess, less engaging specimens than I had hoped to have from you of the outbreak in him of the little natural man" ' (p. 70). And again, if she were fresh from reading Mrs. Radcliffe, she might refer to Quint as 'a base menial' (p. 68); but would she characterize him as 'a hound' (p. 62)? That term belongs to the brother or the virtuous suitor of the persecuted heroine, not to the lady herself. And if she might, in the privacy of thought, enquire with masculine freedom 'how the deuce' Miles or she was to behave (p. 87), or suppose a look of Mrs. Grose's to mean ' "I'll be hanged if *I'll* speak!" ' (p. 135), she would not (in defiance of chronology) use a colloquialism of James's own day, as when she says to Mrs. Grose, ' "I appreciate the great decency of your not having hitherto spoken" ' (p. 62). Nor could she have used the metaphorical elaboration, beautiful and effective as it is, of this passage in Ch. xiii: 'The summer had turned, the summer had gone; the autumn had dropped upon Bly and had blown out half our lights. The place, with its grey sky and withered garlands, its bared spaces and scattered dead leaves, was like a theatre after the performance—all strewn with crumpled playbills' (p. 98). How many theatres had the vicar's daughter from Hampshire seen? None, of course, as she tells us, earlier in the story, during the identification of Quint. ' "He gives me a sort of sense of looking like an actor." "An actor!" It was impossible to resemble one less, at least, than Mrs. Grose at that moment. "I've never seen one, but so I suppose them" ' (p. 46).

Here we are coming to a partial explanation of the reader's involuntary questioning of this story as a ghost story, and of the governess as a reliable witness and narrator. In *The Turn of the Screw* James was, on the evidence of the text, attempting a double *tour de force*—not merely to write a convincing story of the supernatural, but also to compose a period pastiche, or quasi-historical fiction, written from the inside, after the manner of Thackeray's *Henry Esmond*.

He had attempted a similar feat, dramatically, in *Guy Domville*, and failed. There he was confessedly trying to exploit the popular appeal of the costume play in general and of Sheridan in particular. But it is difficult to think of any production which less succeeds in capturing the eighteenth-century tone. Guy Domville grotesquely parodies Charles Surface, but with an intention, alas, wholly serious. In fact both the hero and his problem belong not to the eighteenth century, but to the nineteenth, with its crises of conscience and its colourful series of 'perverts' to Rome and celibacy. One might plausibly surmise that, reset and repeopled contemporarily, the play might have had as resounding a success as Mrs. Humphry Ward's novel *Robert Elsmere* had won seven years before: it is pleasant, at any rate, to imagine Mr. Gladstone's reaction.

But with *The Turn of the Screw* James didn't fail. He chose for his period the less remote, the 'visitable' past, the earlier nineteenth century in which he always felt, historically, most at home; and he chose as his direct model Charlotte Brontë's *Jane Eyre*. I think I can explain exactly why he did so.

Whenever Frederic Harrison appears, as he does constantly, in Victorian memoirs, it is with the sobriquet of 'the Positivist', and, as a follower of Auguste Comte, he was of course not only opposed to all traditional varieties of religious faith, but an ardent social reformer as well. He was a typical Victorian muscular intellectual. In his profession of lawyer he served on innumerable committees, and lent his pen and his platform presence to innumerable causes, but he also found surplus energy to devote to the study of history and of literature, which became the major interest of his retirement. Henry James first met Harrison, already making a name for himself, on his 1869 visit to London: 'What must have seemed to me of a fine international mixture . . . was my thrilling opportunity to sit one morning, beside Mrs. Charles Norton's tea-urn, . . . opposite to Frederic Harrison, eminent to me at the moment as one of the subjects of Matthew Arnold's early fine banter, one of his too confidently roaring "young lions" of the periodical press.' At their second encounter, some ten years later, Harrison proved 'very good company';[73] and the two men remained on terms of friendly acquaintanceship till James's death. Harrison's vigour and his courage were both admirable in James's eyes, as the *Letters* testify.[74] When, therefore, in 1895, Frederic Harrison published a collection of *Studies in Early Victorian Literature*,[75] James would be certain to read it, if only out of curiosity. A curiosity, it may be, sharpened by pique; for in his opening chapter, not to seem neglectful of contemporary genius, Harrison exalts Hardy over Trollope, equates Kipling with Dickens, Stevenson with Defoe, Mrs. Henry Wood with George Eliot, and goes on: 'If any man choose to maintain . . . that Howells and Besant, Ouida and Rhoda Broughton, Henry James and Mrs. Burnett, are as good reading as we need, . . . I do not dispute it' (p. 29).

Harrison's subjects included Charlotte Brontë; and he devoted much of his space to demonstrating that she was precisely the kind of author Henry James was not—that she wrote exclusively out of her own narrow experience of life and the world. The only book of Charlotte Brontë's which Harrison analyses is *Jane Eyre*, and these are some of the observations he makes:

The plain little governess dominates the whole book and fills every page. Everything and every one appear, not as we see them and know them in the world, but as they look to a keen-eyed girl who had hardly ever left her native village. Had the whole book been cast into the form of impersonal narration, this limitation, this huge ignorance of life, this amateur's attempt to construct a romance by the light of nature instead of observation and study of persons, would have been a failure. As the autobiography of Jane Eyre—let us say at once of Charlotte Brontë—it is consummate art. It produces the illusion we feel in reading *Robinson Crusoe*. In the whole range of modern fiction there are few characters whom we feel that we know so intimately as we do Jane Eyre. . . . Much more than this. Not only do we feel an intimate knowledge of Jane Eyre, but we see every one by the eyes of Jane Eyre only. Edward Rochester has not a few touches of the melodramatic villain; and no man would ever draw a man with such conventional and Byronic extravagances. If Edward Rochester had been described in impersonal narrative with all his brutalities, his stage villain frowns, and his Grand Turk whims, it would have spoiled the book. But Edward Rochester, the 'master' of the little governess, as seen by the eyes of a passionate, romantic, but utterly unsophisticated girl, is a powerful character; and all the inconsistencies, the affectation, the savageries we might detect in him, become the natural love-dream of a most imaginative and most ignorant young woman. (pp. 151–52)

Harrison notes as her most conspicuous literary quality Charlotte Brontë's power of vivid scenic description. She had, he says, 'in the highest degree, that which Ruskin has called the "pathetic fallacy," the eye which beholds nature coloured by the light of the inner soul. In this quality she really reaches the level of fine poetry. . . . From first to last, the correspondence between the local scene and the human drama is a distinctive mark in *Jane Eyre*' (pp. 154–56). He refers to a number of scenes in illustration of his point, but he quotes only one passage *in extenso*. This is the passage in which Jane, unaware that a fateful meeting is in store, sets out on a long winter's walk through a landscape where 'if a breath of air stirred, it made no sound', and looks down on Thornfield: 'the gray and battlemented hall was the principal object in the vale below me; its woods and dark rookery rose against the west. I lingered till the sun went down amongst the trees, and sank crimson and clear behind them' (pp. 154–55).

Harrison returns to his consideration of the male characters, and of their 'unreality'. 'But,' he says, 'the intensity of the vision, the realism of every scene, the fierce yet self-governed passion of Jane herself, pouring out, as in a secret diary, her agonies of love, of scorn, of pride, of abandonment,—all this produces an illusion on us: we are no longer reading a novel of society; but we are admitted to the wild musings of a girl's soul' (pp. 158–59). St. John Rivers, given his imputed character, could not behave as he does. Rochester, taken 'simply as a cultured and travelled country gentleman, who was a magnate and great *parti* in his county, is barely within the range of possibility' (p. 159). And as for the plot!—it is 'the very essence of "sensationalism," which means a succession of thrilling surprises constructed out of situations that are practically impossible' (p. 160). But, he concludes,

Jane Eyre's ignorances and simplicities, the improbabilities of her men, the violence of the plot, the weird romance about her own life, are all made acceptable to us by being shown to us only through the secret visions of a passionate and romantic girl. As the autobiography of a brave and original woman, who bares to us her whole heart without reserve and without fear, *Jane Eyre* stands forth as a great book of the nineteenth century . . . one of the most creative influences of the Victorian literature, one of the most poetic pieces of English romance, and among the most vivid masterpieces in the rare order of literary 'Confessions.' (pp. 161–62)

I should perhaps add that Harrison opens his discussion with the impression produced by Charlotte Brontë on her contemporaries, particularly on Thackeray, from whose tribute, 'after forty years . . . too seldom read' (p. 146), he quotes at length. Two sentences he takes from Thackeray are worth noting: 'She gave me the impression of being a very pure, and lofty, and high-minded person. A great and holy reverence of right and truth seemed to be with her always' (p. 147).

Here, from the very vanguard of the Philistines, is a rousing flourish indeed. Not only is it a reminder of the kind of novel that in 1895, after nearly fifty years as a best-seller, could still win critical approval, and, even more important, still 'catch' the reading public; it also pairs James's own best efforts with such productions as *A Fair Barbarian* or *Little Lord Fauntleroy*. What more natural than that, like many another artist so belittled, he should answer the disparagement by producing a duplicate 'masterpiece', a *Jane Eyre* of his own? I have no direct evidence that James read Harrison's essay or did so react; but we are confronted with the fact of the pastiche, and, of course, a good technical reason for its existence: in January of 1895 James had found a *donnée* which attracted him, and which demanded, 'tolerably obviously', narration by 'an outside spectator, observer'.

Something, at any rate, caused James, between 13 May and 4 June 1895, to re-read or at least reconsider *Jane Eyre*; for he then pulls out from an earlier notebook (of 1893) the *donnée* for what ultimately became *The Spoils of Poynton*. The working stages of that novel are very fully documented for us, and this first notation ends, abruptly: 'The horrible, the atrocious conflagration—which may at any rate, I think, serve as my working hypothesis for a denouement.' I grant that this solution (arrived at, as it were by sudden inspiration, in the course of James's first 'dramatic' plotting of his story) may plausibly be referred to the burning of Mrs. Alving's orphanage, in the last act of Ibsen's *Ghosts*. But, if so, in the process of composition another picture has been superimposed—that of the heroine's coming upon the fire-blackened ruins of Thornfield, in Ch. xxxvi of *Jane Eyre*. By 13 February 1896 James triumphantly, if prematurely, underlines: 'LAST CHAPTER.—Fleda goes down to rescue the Maltese Cross and finds the house in flames—or already burnt to the ground.'[76] One may concede, too, that the actual and symbolic contrast between Poynton and Ricks distantly recalls that between the orphanage and Engstrand's projected seamen's home in *Ghosts*; and there is a possible, if remote, kinship between 'the passionate mother and the insolent maid'[77] of Ibsen's play and the equally passionate Mrs. Gereth and the rather more woodenly insolent Mona of *The Spoils of Poynton*. Again, Asta's rejection of Borgheim in *Little Eyolf* may have contributed something to James's handling of the situation between

Fleda and Owen; but Ibsen's slim, dark-haired Asta is of a different calibre from James's slim, dark-haired Fleda, as her final realistic acceptance of Borgheim confirms. I do not underrate the influence of Ibsen here, but I think it may easily be misinterpreted. Ibsen might be regarded as the demi-urge in the planning of *The Spoils of Poynton*: Waterbath and all it stands for (a contrast not implicit in James's original *donnée*) is the expression of James's shuddering antipathy to the material coarseness, the ugly deprivations of suburban life, nowhere (not even at Fox Warren) more grimly displayed, to James's sense, than in Ibsen's domestic settings.[78] But whatever Ibsenite traits and touches may have been envisaged in the initial planning, these seem to have been overlaid as the story was worked out. From the beginning, James had postulated 'exquisite tastes' in his heroine, but, as he develops his story, she assumes the very physical presence as well as the mental and moral attributes of Jane Eyre. In Fleda Vetch's 'fineness', in her 'sacrificial exal-tation'[79] and the scruples which lead her to give up Owen Gereth, it is impossible not to recognize Jane Eyre, moralistically compelled to renounce her passion for Edward Rochester—it is even possible to see something of the materialistic coarseness of both Georgiana Reed and Blanche Ingram in her rival. The motivation (in Fleda's case) has become aesthetic rather than religious and social, and with this sacrifice of the obvious justifications, seems oddly attenuated; but there she is—Jane Eyre, if a little greenery-yallery.

From the beginning of 1897, however, there is direct and incontrovertible evidence of James's preoccupation with Charlotte Brontë and her work. *The Spoils of Poynton* had its first serial publication from April to October 1896, and its composition overlapped that of *The Other House*, which was published in the *Illustrated London News* (then under the editorship of Clement Shorter) from July to September of the same year. Clement Shorter, during a long career of journalism, edited and anthologized the work of many poets and novelists, but he was first and foremost a 'Brontë expert'. In 1896 he published *Charlotte Brontë and her Circle*, and this book was commented on by James in his London letter, dated 15 January 1897, for *Harper's Weekly*. From a discussion of Ibsen's *John Gabriel Borkman* James passes, by way of Lord Roberts's *Forty-one Years in India*, Gibbon's auto-biography, and Meredith's *Evan Harrington*, to 'a graceful trio with which I have just been engaged. . . . These books are not so much of yesterday as of the day before. The day before, let me say once for all, is my highest modern-ity.' In order of 'ascending interest' he deals with Mrs. Ridley's *Story of Aline*, Mrs. Meynell's *The Children*, and *Charlotte Brontë and her Circle*. His remarks on Shorter's work are somewhat darkly oracular in tone. I sum-marize, and interpret, as follows: There is much left to tell of the Brontë story, but what has so far been revealed should be a warning (to critics such as Harrison, perhaps) not to confuse pity (for the personal tragedy) with admiration (for the works produced under stress of it)—a confusion which,

James believes, has been the main source of the Brontë fame; in Charlotte's case especially it might be better if the rest of the story remained untold.[80] This conclusion, one assumes, is prompted not so much by a nervously defensive regard for propriety, as by James's abiding sense of outrage at the invasion of privacy. The significance of the passage as a whole, however, lies in the implied critical judgment on the Brontë novels: psychological interest, yes; literary excellence, no. This judgment cannot have been reached through a perusal of Shorter's book alone—in all its five hundred odd pages there are no more than passing references to any of the novels. It is someone else's over-estimate of the Brontë achievement that James is objecting to, and the tone of his remarks suggests that he is not relying on long-stored impressions, but has recently made a critical appraisal of at least one of the novels in question.

Still, Shorter's book in its own right may have helped to shape *The Turn of the Screw*. Three separate references to Thackeray's *Esmond* (including a reproduction of Thackeray's inscription in the copy he presented to Charlotte Brontë) may have suggested the practicability of an early-nineteenth-century pastiche. Shorter's appreciative mention of the Rev. Patrick Brontë's story *The Maid of Killarney; or, Albion and Flora* may be responsible for James's naming of one of the children; while the boy's name appears in two quite unconnected passages. In 1828 a Rev. Oddy Miles was among the 'gentry and clergy' resident at Haworth; and in 1890 Charlotte's friend Mary Taylor at long last published her novel: *Miss Miles, or a Tale of Yorkshire Life Sixty Years Ago*. Again, Charlotte's evocation, in a letter to W. S. Williams, of 'fertile, flowery Essex' in contrast to the 'mute and sombre' Yorkshire moors may have had some part in James's choice of locality for Bly. But more striking than any of these correspondences are certain of Charlotte's references to her dour Scots suitor, James Taylor. They have almost certainly influenced the portrayal of Quint: not in his total aspect, nor in the details of his physique (for Taylor, according to Shorter, although red-haired was 'small . . . thickset, well-bearded'), but in the impression he produces on the governess. Charlotte mentions the subject repeatedly in her letters to Ellen Nussey:

He is not ugly, but very peculiar; the lines in his face show an inflexibility, and, I must add, a hardness of character which do not attract. As he stood near me, as he looked at me in his keen way, it was all I could do to stand my ground tranquilly and steadily, and not to recoil as before. . . . Friendship—gratitude—esteem I have, but each moment he came near me, and that I could see his eyes fastened on me, my veins ran ice. . . . Dear Nell, I looked for something of the gentleman—something I mean of the *natural* gentleman; you know I can dispense with acquired polish, and for looks, I know myself too well to think that I have any right to be exacting on that point. I could not find one gleam, I could not see one passing glimpse of true good-breeding. It is hard to say, but it is true. In mind too, though clever, he is second-rate—thoroughly second-rate. One does not like to say these things, but one had better be honest.[81]

And that, months later, Charlotte Brontë and her undeserved fame continued to occupy James's mind is shown by the report of Mrs. Humphry Ward. Some time in April or May 1897 James was her guest at Levens Hall, Westmorland; and during an excursion to Grange-over-Sands he so decried the Brontë cult in general, and so remorselessly criticized Charlotte's novels in particular, that Mrs. Ward (as a letter to Charles Eliot Norton explains) felt it necessary to take account of his strictures in her own (1899) introduction to *Jane Eyre* for the Haworth Edition. Months later again, an incidental reference of his own shows James still mindful, if not resentful, of Charlotte Brontë. He begins his London letter of 1 July 1897 with an apology: he has spent June in an escape (from the preparations for Queen Victoria's Jubilee) to 'a fictive world'. One's taste in novels, he says, is variously conditioned: for example, in many cases interest 'vibrates only to "adventure"; in many only to Charlotte Brontë; in various groups, according to affinity, only to Jane Austen, to old Dumas, to Miss Corelli, to Dostoievsky, or to whomever it may be'. The impression of 'sincerity' in an author makes a fairly general appeal; but, in his own case, the 'quantity of art' in any novel is what compels his interest and alone provides relief from the actual. 'I knocked, in this way, at a dozen doors; I read a succession of novels; with the effect perhaps of feeling more than ever before my individual liability in our great general debt to the novelists.' One may be excused for detecting a special proleptic force in this confession of indebtedness; for when, in the autumn of 1897, James comes to write *The Turn of the Screw*, it is Jane Eyre, *in period*, who serves as the model for his youthful, inexperienced, but sensitive and scrupulously honest narrator.[82]

The evidence, as I have said, is in the text. The introduction tells us that the events narrated by the governess occurred some fifty years before Douglas read her story to the assembled company, and that this reading long antedated the author's transcription and publication of the manuscript in 1898.[83] As in *Jane Eyre*, all the travelling in the story is done by coach: the governess comes from London, to Bly in Essex, by coach. But from early in 1843 the Eastern Counties Railway linked London and Colchester; by mid 1846 the connection extended to Ipswich; and by the end of 1849, with the amalgamation of rival companies, to Norwich.[84] And while, during the twenties and thirties, the governess would have had a choice of coaches by which to travel to Colchester or intermediate points, by the mid forties she could not even be sure of being met by a coach at whatever railway station she chose to alight.[85] The days when Mr. Pickwick and Mr. Magnus coached all the way from the Bull Inn, Whitechapel to the Great White Horse in Ipswich were long past.

And there is another clear indication of date which is always misinterpreted, with inductions sometimes grotesque. The guardian of Miles and Flora interviews the governess in a house in Harley Street: the location is mentioned by Douglas, and later by the governess and by Mrs. Grose. Now why should a young man 'of high fashion', with unlimited means, who can maintain simultaneously, fully staffed, both a town and a country house, choose to establish himself, when in London, in the stronghold of physicians and surgeons, in the very ante-room of death? The answer, of course, is that he does nothing of the kind: the 'big' house he owns, 'filled with the spoils of travel and the trophies of the chase' (p. 9), is in one of the most fashionable streets of London. The borough of Marylebone, the ancient manor of Tyburn, was central to the grandiose scheme of urban development planned by Nash and sponsored by the Prince Regent; Harley Street, leading into Cavendish Square, had been part of an earlier development (aimed at aristocratic profit) of the Portland estate.[86] In the latter decades of the nineteenth century 'high fashion' gradually withdrew from the district,[87] to concentrate in Mayfair and Belgravia; but, until the 1850s at least, a Harley Street address remained a warrant of acceptability in the very best of fashionable society—an assurance of impeccable breeding, magnificently and impregnably sustained by immense wealth. That, of course, is the only reason why Dickens's swindling financier, Mr. Merdle, has a 'mansion' there, in a street where the occupants at dinner seem the incarnation of their own houses, 'drawn up on opposite sides . . . in the shade of their own loftiness'.[88] It is also one reason why those professional adventurers, the 'specialists' in medicine and surgery, from the late fifties on invaded Harley Street in ever-increasing numbers. *Little Dorrit*, a novel of strictly contemporary reference, was published in 1857. In 1858, according to the first (1859) issue of the *Medical Register*, there were nineteen doctors resident in Harley Street; by 1900 there were one hundred and fifty-six.[89] James, therefore, in domiciling the governess's employer where he does, is merely confirming what her mode of travel and Douglas's count of the years also indicate to us—the events narrated took place in the early 1840s.

In spite of James's own childhood experience of a succession of French governesses, one can assume that he had very little first-hand knowledge of how English governesses might be expected to behave, or how an English nursery or schoolroom would be conducted in the nineties. But here, in *Jane Eyre*, were a governess and her setting ready-made for him. Very little adaptation was required. The troublesome 'master', Mr. Rochester, and the love affair he entails, are removed to the periphery of the action. The genteel housekeeper, Mrs. Fairfax, is blended with the more buxom and plebeian Bessie to make the comfortable, kindly Mrs. Grose. The 'master's' little ward Adèle, no longer French but still, we learn, suffering the effects of former evil communications, is retained as Flora; a little boy Miles is added to the *dramatis personae*, and the cast of living characters is complete. The blood-curdling laugh and occasional homicidal sorties of the imperfectly guarded madwoman are transformed, 'spiritualized', into two malevolent ghostly presences, one of whom exhibits the sinister Grace Poole's red hair and the other the dark beauty of Jane's rival, Blanche Ingram.[90] Their liaison and their evil influence while living are projected, in monstrous enlargement, from the 'immoral tendency' of the Ingrams' tutor and governess, who 'took the liberty of falling in love with each other', and the consequent 'danger of bad example to innocence of childhood'.[91] There is one, probably deliberate, simplification: the nurse, indispensable in real life, has disappeared, and James's governess, conveniently for the story, takes on her functions—has charge of Flora by night as well as by day, for instance—a blurring of the social grades which, in Jane Eyre's case, would have required elaborate justification.[92]

But in the new setting, among the familiar characters transformed, Jane Eyre comports herself virtually unchanged. Our governess has the same impulsive disposition, the same lively sympathies, controlled by the same demanding conception of personal responsibility and duty as her original. 'I now saw that I had been asked for a service admirable and difficult; . . . I was there to protect and defend the little creatures in the world the most bereaved and the most loveable, the appeal of whose helplessness had suddenly become only too explicit, a deep, constant ache of one's own committed heart' (pp. 53–54): it might be Jane Eyre herself, professing her determination to befriend the 'forsaken' and 'disowned' Adèle (xv, 171). There is the same unsparing self-criticism, a little more rueful and less caustic perhaps, the same promptness to deflate her own romantic expectations:

It was a pleasure at these moments to feel myself tranquil and justified; doubtless, perhaps, also to reflect that by my discretion, my quiet good sense and general high propriety, I was giving pleasure—if he ever thought of it!—to the person to whose pressure I had responded. . . . I dare say I fancied myself, in short, a remarkable young woman and took comfort in the faith that this would more publicly appear. Well, I needed to be remarkable to offer a front to the remarkable things that presently gave their first sign. (p. 29)

This seems to echo even the phrasing of Jane Eyre's self-reproof: 'The confidence he had thought fit to repose in me seemed a tribute to my discretion: I regarded and accepted it as such. . . . [But later:] "*You*," I said, "a favourite with Mr. Rochester? *You* gifted with the power of pleasing him? *You* of importance to him in any way? Go! your folly sickens me."' (xv, 172; xvi, 189). Examples of such correspondence in attitude and reaction might be multiplied,[93] but James's governess is nothing so pallid and mechanical as a copy. She is, one might say, a new creation in the image of Jane Eyre, and she feels and acts as Jane Eyre might have been expected to do if given obviously different credentials for a subtly different role. Jane Eyre is an experienced and competent teacher, and knows it; our governess is painfully aware of her own inadequacy: 'I found it simple, in my ignorance, my confusion, and perhaps my conceit, to assume that I could deal with a boy whose education for the world was all on the point of beginning' (p. 28). Here, however, she echoes not Jane Eyre, but the scorn of governesses vented by the unsympathetic Blanche Ingram and her brother: ' "and then we sermonised her on the presumption of attempting to teach such clever blades as we were, when she was herself so ignorant" ' (xvii, 211). Again, our governess has led a sheltered life, 'privately bred' (p. 31), so that she cannot apply to herself the orphaned Jane Eyre's grim rationalization of her childhood sufferings (ii, 11–12); but she *does* apply it, with a new infusion of pathos, to Miles:

My conclusion bloomed there with the real rose-flush of his innocence: he was only too fine and fair for the little horrid, unclean school-world, and he had paid a price for it. I reflected acutely that the sense of such differences, such superiorities of quality, always, on the part of the majority—which could include even stupid, sordid head-masters—turns infallibly to the vindictive. (p. 37)

I note in passing that the whole suggestion of Miles's school career, and his very name, may come from Jane Eyre's recollection of her childhood tormentor, the gross John Reed, who even in his years at school (where his master was named Miles) exhibited some of the vices which would later destroy him (i, 4).

Throughout, it is clear that something more than the temperate affection Jane displays for little Adèle inspires our governess's passionate concern for Miles and Flora; but that is because the emotional emphasis of the story has shifted. Here the children, not the shadowy 'master', occupy the centre of the stage—are threatened and endangered, exact by turns protective devotion and tears of pity and despair. And since it is the governess's display of emotion, particularly in relation to the children, which is most frequently alleged as evidence of her disturbed personality or diseased mind, we need to understand exactly what it implies. Her emotional expansiveness, her hugging of the children and embracing of Mrs. Grose,[94] are in part extensions of Jane Eyre's attitudes to Adèle and Mrs. Fairfax, but in part also they reflect the sentimental effusiveness of the Victorian family circle, when it was not suppressed by the rigours of Evangelical Christianity, say, or the sternness of paternal authority. Loving mothers devoured their children with kisses (no one had yet whispered about the dangers of 'complexes'); sisters, female cousins, and friends kissed and embraced one another in transports of innocent affection; fathers kissed their sons and wept over them; rejected lovers shed tears of mortification. In short, the uninhibited surrender to emotion, whether joyful or despairing, and particularly the demonstration of tenderness to children, were as characteristic of good and kindly Victorians as their belief in progress, of which one hears rather more. In part this effusion of tender feeling in the presence of young and helpless creatures was a surrender to the sentiment of pathos: Victorian children *were* exposed to real, physical dangers—they died so terribly easily of diseases now no longer terrible. In part it was a revulsion from the strictness of certain brands of

Christian discipline currently applied to children in certain devout house-
holds. Both attitudes (the severity and the tenderness) are exhibited fictionally
in the 'autobiography' of Jane Eyre; we have them drawn from the life in the
reminiscences of Augustus Hare—not only his tearfully affectionate relationship with 'Mamma', but also his sufferings at the hands of his ferociously
inhuman Aunt Esther.[95]

When, therefore, in Ch. xx of *The Turn of the Screw* the governess throws
herself down on the damp ground and for 'a quarter of an hour' gives way to
'a wildness of grief'—'I must have lain there long and cried and sobbed, for
when I raised my head the day was almost done' (pp. 140–41)—we are not
to suppose that James intends this behaviour to mark her as hysterical or
neurotic. He is first of all echoing a 'set piece' of despair by Charlotte
Brontë: Jane's reaction to the revelation that a bigamous marriage has
been prepared for her. The passage is a long one, and I quote it only in
part:

My eyes were covered and closed: eddying darkness seemed to swim round me,
and reflection came in as black and confused a flow. . . . I lay faint, longing to be
dead. . . . The whole consciousness of my life lorn, my love lost, my hope quenched,
my faith death-struck, swayed full and mighty above me in one sullen mass. . . .
Some time in the afternoon I raised my head, and looking round and seeing the
western sun gilding the sign of its decline on the wall, I asked, 'What am I to do?'
(xxvi–xxvii, 356–57)

And he is recalling, too, how Jane Eyre, 'weeping wildly' as she fled from
Thornfield, fell exhausted and 'lay on the ground some minutes, pressing
[her] face to the wet turf' (xxvii, 387–88).

Again, when the governess leaps to conclusions, when, for instance, with
growing 'exaltation' she announces to Mrs. Grose that she 'knows' the
spectral Quint 'was looking for little Miles' (p. 49) and the spectral Miss
Jessel was bent on 'get[ting] hold of' Flora (p. 61), she is not lying or demented, but merely expressing, with all the force and vividness at her command, the final stage of the process by which she has 'thought it all out'
(p. 59)—in other words, intuitively grasped her solution. She is displaying,
in fact, the kind of 'acumen' which Jane Eyre and Mr. Rochester (xiv, 159;
xxii, 294) or Jane Eyre and St. John Rivers (xxxii, 448) frequently manifest
in their interchanges, and which is indeed natural and common enough. The
governess does not 'prompt' Mrs. Grose, or put words in her mouth; but
she does, by her excitement, kindle Mrs. Grose's slower mind to interpret
facts already in her possession. Often, indeed, the two women stimulate one
another antiphonally to conclusions which seem to require amplifying by
voice and gesture to yield their full import, as if James were writing stage
dialogue.[96] Conversations with Miles, also, tend to be elliptical, in the mode
of the newer drama; and a histrionic quality is often noticeable in the governess's speech: ' "No, no—there are depths, depths! The more I go over it,

the more I see in it, and the more I see in it the more I fear. I don't know what I *don't* see—what I *don't* fear!" ' (p. 60). On the other hand, the governess's use of what one may call an excited phraseology (' "Died?" I almost shrieked' [p. 47], or ' "Them—that creature?" I had to smother a kind of howl' [p. 52].) need not always be modelled on the style either of tragedy queens or of lady novelists. James himself has a somewhat excited notation for human utterance: if so many young men 'wail', why shouldn't a young woman 'howl' or 'shriek' on occasion?

But our general conclusion must be that, in his governess, James is simply representing, on indications supplied by Charlotte Brontë, an early Victorian young woman in a state of excitement and alarm, and that to readers of, say, *The Old Curiosity Shop*, the portrait would not seem overdrawn.

It is not, however, only as the expression of emotion that the governess's language is noteworthy. Unlike Jane Eyre, she is an ignorant young woman who has read little—one of the amenities of Bly is that its 'roomful of old books' enables her to fill certain gaps in her knowledge. Nevertheless, like her prototype, she has a highly developed aesthetic sense, witness the incidental descriptions of her surroundings and her constant references to the children's beauty. She cannot, like Jane Eyre, quote poetry and multiply literary references,[97] though it is perhaps a little surprising that her memory supplies so few religious associations (and those mainly pictorial),[98] and that in the whole course of the story she makes only one explicit scriptural allusion.[99] But in place of the literary display we have a more subtle manifestation of literary instinct: her sentences are enlivened with imagery to a degree matched, in James's fiction of this date, only by *The Spoils of Poynton* —where again the reflecting consciousness is that of a sensitive, Brontëan heroine. The images in *The Turn of the Screw* are not always carefully adjusted to the governess's presumed mental range: one would not, for instance, expect her to picture Miles and herself as a pair of circling bruisers (p. 160), or herself as lassoing an answer to her problem—'What if . . . I should throw across the rest of the mystery the long halter of my boldness?' (p. 83). But for the most part the kind of imagination they presuppose is entirely appropriate in an early Victorian narrator modelled on Jane Eyre. The fairy-tale and rose images (pp. 19, 37, 65, 89, 104) limn the children for us with all the pretty sentiment of Richard Doyle, just as the image of the 'wistful patient in a children's hospital' (pp. 120–21) strikes the true note of Victorian pathos, already sounded in *Jane Eyre* at the child Helen's death-bed.[100] And James's favourite metaphor for constructive intellectual effort, that of stitching or weaving—'the brightest thread in the pensive embroidery' (p. 74), 'a view of the back of the tapestry' (p. 86)—seems made for a young woman who invariably, at moments of stress, feels a 'steadying' influence in her 'work' (pp. 56, 156). On the other hand we find, just as much in evidence, the more powerful, sometimes sinister play of fancy which is also characteristic of James's model. The governess evokes the pacing sentinel before a prison (p. 162), the prison itself (p. 49), the prowling beast (p. 163), its spring (p. 29), the noisome flitting bat (p. 66), curtains muffling (p. 67) and doors enclosing (p. 97) nightmare terrors; and, most effective of all, images of water, of the great deep and its abysses, of ships in peril, such as constantly occupy the imagination of Jane Eyre.[101] Often the governess, conscious of her responsibility and lack of guidance, sees herself at the helm of a ship (pp. 19, 151); Mrs. Grose and she take soundings (p. 149), and to arrive, through Miles's confession, at the heart of the mystery, seems to her like reaching port (p. 159). The commerce of which she suspects the children is tacitly denied by 'their sociability and their tenderness, in just the crystal depths of which—like the flash of a fish in a stream—the mockery of their advantage peeped up' (p. 100). And there is one eerie, subaqueous glimpse of little Miles, staring upwards like the drowned Eyolf: 'He might have been standing at the bottom of the sea and raising his eyes to some faint green twilight' (p. 165). This profusion of imagery is James's concession, as it were, to the rather self-consciously literary (but all the more typically youthful) eloquence of his original.

Yet the general stylistic effect is not appreciably lightened by this modification. For the *Times* reviewer, and probably for most readers of 1898, here was Henry James speaking in his contemporary, still noticeably American, voice.[102] And James's highly personal idiom, by 1897 already polysyllabic and involuted, already tending to the billowy amplitude of his 'major phase', is not as well fitted as Charlotte Brontë's for conveying the impression of youthful impetuosity and ardour. Charlotte Brontë's vehement, often florid, sometimes inelegant, but always direct and rapid style seems an exact expression of the character she has conceived. By the mere trick of style James adds, as it were, years to his narrator's age, and while this 'ageing' is to some extent allowed for by the method of retrospect he has adopted, it nevertheless takes from the desired effect—of urgency, for instance. A passage such as the following has the ponderous, clogged awkwardness of movement in a nightmare:

This had become thoroughly her attitude by the time that, in my recital of the events of the night, I reached the point of what Miles had said to me when, after seeing him, at such a monstrous hour, almost on the very spot where he happened now to be, I had gone down to bring him in; choosing then, at the window, with a concentrated need of not alarming the house, rather that method than a signal more resonant. I had left her meanwhile in little doubt of my small hope of representing with success even to her actual sympathy my sense of the real splendour of the little inspiration with which, after I had got him into the house, the boy met my final articulate challenge. (pp. 86–87)

And, perhaps more seriously, it qualifies our persuasion of the narrator's candour. The style, one might say, is too knowing for the professions it conveys: hesitancy takes on the air of evasiveness, emotion seems factitious, extravagance of statement or conjecture not the spontaneous result of excitement but a calculated misrepresentation:

There was an alien object in view—a figure whose right of presence I instantly, passionately questioned. I recollect counting over perfectly the possibilities, reminding myself that nothing was more natural, for instance, than the appearance of one of the men about the place, or even of a messenger, a postman or a tradesman's boy, from the village. That reminder had as little effect on my practical certitude as I was conscious—still even without looking—of its having upon the character and attitude of our visitor. Nothing was more natural than that these things should be the other things that they absolutely were not. (p. 56)

Then again James's fondness for the unexpected term (the colloquial, it may be, juxtaposed with the pedantic, or the violent with the sedate), which in most of his work we accept as a stimulating or amusing zest, has a disconcerting effect in a context such as this:

[My inductions] harassed me so that sometimes, at odd moments, I shut myself up audibly to rehearse—it was at once a fantastic relief and a renewed despair—the manner in which I might come to the point. I approached it from one side and the other while, in my room, I flung myself about, but I always broke down in the monstrous utterance of names. (p. 100)

For some readers at least, 'I flung myself about' carries the suggestion of a maniac in a padded cell; yet all the governess has done (as she tries, agitatedly, to think of a suitable way to frame her question) is to walk rapidly up and down her room. Jane Eyre did just the same, to the concern of St. John Rivers, while she turned over all the possibilities opened by her newly acquired wealth and status (xxxiii, 466).

But there is one habitual feature of the governess's style which is almost a provocation to misunderstanding. She is, admittedly, writing years after her experience at Bly, and naturally enough she displays the attitude of half-amused, half-impatient sympathy with her own more youthful self which is characteristic of all personal retrospect. And, as we have already noted, like her prototype Jane Eyre she is by disposition (not to mention religious training) highly self-critical. But while in *Jane Eyre* this criticism is expressed as the immediate reaction of the young girl, in *The Turn of the Screw* it is unmistakably that of the older woman passing judgment on the younger. Jane Rochester is, of course, writing out of ultimate joy and triumph, whereas the governess writes in all the bitterness of failure as well as grief. Jane can afford to luxuriate in the memory of past trials and narrow escapes, or at least to contemplate without attenuating them, but the governess flinches from the analysis of her past terrors and mistakes even as she engages in it. Now in the expression of this subtlety James has only limited help from Jane Eyre, not in his view an altogether typical Victorian female;

and he therefore falls back on a mannerism he has observed rather in women's conversation than in their literary practice. It is the habit of deprecating, especially to a masculine audience, any imputation of self-importance or conceit, and to this end describing their own actions and feelings in terms of mock-horror and mock-reprobation, or, as the context may demand, of transparently exaggerated complacency and self-esteem. When the governess talks of 'my dreadful liability to impressions' (p. 48), 'my own horrid note' (p. 87), and 'my mere infernal imagination' (p. 96), she is no more to be taken literally than when she says 'I preternaturally listened' (p. 83) or that her deliberation 'must have seemed magnificent' (p. 76). In her case, however, this would-be disarming feminine irony is complicated by the need to describe an 'ordeal' literally 'monstrous' (p. 153), an 'image' literally 'awful' (p. 112), a catastrophe in truth 'dreadful' (p. 104).

And here James encounters a certain difficulty. He must, obviously, keep his governess's range of expression consonant with ladylike decorum, yet this straitens the picturesqueness which the occasion demands, so that her inevitable sallies from these verbal confines, while never infringing propriety, are marked by some bravado and eccentricity in the choice of terms. The one error she seems resolved to avoid is the failure to impress, and she therefore habitually uses the more forcible in preference to the milder turn of phrase: 'in my delusion [not 'mistakenly']' (p. 66); 'in my torment [not 'in my perplexity']' (p. 69); 'my unnatural composure [not 'my unusual freedom from concern']' (p. 74); 'my inexorable, my perpetual society [not 'my constant presence']' (p. 103); 'drive desperately off [not 'give up and drive away']' (p. 110); 'paraded [not 'went about']' (p. 152). The colloquialisms may be regarded as a more lively manifestation of the same tendency; for this governess is not humourless—she can even find the spirit for a joke or two in the course of her narrative. And in all this verbal experimentation we can most readily see, not the unbalanced neurotic, but the unpractised writer, earnestly yet uncertainly trying to convey intimations so startlingly received and so anomalous. It is a touch of nature correctly observed and painstakingly applied.

But as James in his *Preface* wryly observed, there are readers 'capable evidently . . . of some attention, but not quite capable of enough' (p. 173). The variation in tone added to the abrupt changes of key—from the intricately literary or the pedantic to the stagy or the flippantly colloquial—puts considerable strain on the most attentive, the most docile of readers.[103] To discredit his narrator was, I am convinced, no part of James's intention, but by making her contribute, even intermittently, an artificial obscurity of diction to impressions themselves questionable in a situation of its nature mysterious, he has gone some way towards achieving this effect. If this story had been written ten or even five years earlier, it might or it might not have been a more attractive composition, but it would assuredly have provoked far less discussion.

One wonders also whether, the mask of style removed, the identity of James's governess would not have been instantly apparent, and if so, what the critical reaction would have been. For the detailed correspondences (of description and of action) between *The Turn of the Screw* and *Jane Eyre* are so many and so pointless in themselves as to be inexplicable except on the basis of comprehensive utilization—a process not so much of systematic imitation as of total imaginative recall. Thornfield, with its backdrop of tall trees, from which the rooks circle over the lawns, with its encompassing park, and, beyond the park gates on the road to the village, its church; Thornfield, with its crenellated parapet, its long, windowed front, its gallery, its great oak staircase with high latticed window, its luxurious rooms tended but unused, its older, mysterious recesses—Thornfield 'looms through' Bly.[104] The governess's 'sense of the liberality with which [she is] treated' on arrival (p. 15); the long mirrors in which she sees herself 'from head to foot' (p. 15); her tour of the house and ascent of the tower (p. 19); her easy introduction of Flora to regular lessons (pp. 18–19); her repeated impression of 'something undefineably astir' by night at Bly (pp. 16, 76); her 'circling about the place' after Quint's first appearance until 'darkness had quite closed in' (p. 34); her speculation regarding some 'secret' at Bly (p. 34); Mrs. Grose's evasion of questioning (pp. 24, 25); the governess's enquiries (p. 44); Bly's freedom from ghostly legend (p. 51); the precautions against servants' gossip (p. 85); both children's efforts to please and divert the governess (p. 73); dreary weather and desolate scene as objective correlative for trouble of mind (pp. 40, 141, 156); the icy slope, on which, one winter's night, Quint slips and is killed (p. 53); the governess's decision to leave Bly without warning: 'Were I to get off quickly, this way, I should get off without a scene, without a word' (p. 111)—these details, and a host of others as meaningful or inconsequent, are reproduced from *Jane Eyre*.[105] They are differently ordered, differently combined and emphasized, but their origin is unmistakable. James must have known this curious novel 'backwards', as we say.

An analysis of two examples will illustrate the freedom with which he may use (or abuse) his recollections. 'Before tea' on that Sunday which has been marked both by Miles's rebellion and by the appearance of Miss Jessel's ghost in the schoolroom, the governess seeks out Mrs. Grose: 'I secured five minutes with her in the housekeeper's room, where, in the twilight, amid a smell of lately-baked bread, but with the place all swept and garnished, I found her sitting in pained placidity before the fire' (p. 114). Bly is an establishment of considerable wealth and stateliness, yet in the sanctum of its housekeeper, and on a Sunday evening, of all times, the 'smell of lately-baked bread' is perceptible. This is an absurdity which only recourse to James's original can explain. Jane Eyre has escaped from Thornfield, to wander destitute on the Peakland moors, until, on the verge of collapse, she is given shelter (in their unpretentious home) by the parson of the neighbouring village and his sisters. When she is able to rise from her bed, she makes her way to the kitchen—a typical North Country kitchen, with sanded floor, walnut dresser, and scrubbed deal table, the domain of the one family servant: 'It was full of the fragrance of new bread and the warmth of a generous fire. Hannah was baking' (xxviii, 400; xxix, 411). James has abstracted one detail, from a description in which all the details cohere to make a strictly local truth of setting, and has used it as a mere decorative flourish, without any regard for what in real terms it implies.

My second example is a recurrent motif, which James has employed with a new, ironical twist. Early in his story we are told that 'the musical sense in each of the children was of the quickest, but the elder in especial had a marvellous knack of catching and repeating. The schoolroom piano broke into [i.e interrupted] all gruesome fancies [on the governess's part]' (p. 75). The day following his rebellion Miles, anxious to placate the governess, suggests that he play the piano to her for half an hour, and so he does, playing 'as he had never played'. 'David playing to Saul,' reflects the governess, bitterly, 'could never have shown a finer sense of the occasion' (p. 127); but the reader reflects that if, in reversal of the scriptural text, the evil spirit haunts the musician, the listener also is undeniably troubled, and neither is refreshed. The piano-playing motif, like the schoolroom piano itself, is taken from *Jane Eyre*, where it more than once, in literal fact, provides the background music for the drama of love and jealousy;[106] and so is the scriptural allusion, but from a later context, where there is no musical accompaniment. Jane has returned to the maimed and blinded Rochester: ' "You mocking changeling—fairy-born and human-bred! You make me feel as I have not felt these twelve months. If Saul could have had you for his David, the evil spirit would have been exorcised without the aid of the harp" ' (xxxvii, 531). Piano-playing, like water-colour painting (another indispensable 'accomplishment'), features as a matter of course in *Jane Eyre*; and for Charlotte Brontë music, unlike painting, has no more than the conventional appeal. Nevertheless two points are clear: she is fully aware of its affective potency, and she finds nothing unnatural in such emotional release, although she is aware of its dangers.[107] Not so James, or at least his governess, in *The Turn of the Screw*. Miles's precocious skill as a pianist is not, as we might carelessly suppose, one indication the more that he is an exceptionally 'gifted' child, but an audible proof that he is 'under some influence operating in his small intellectual life as a tremendous incitement' (p. 74)—'if there are those who think he had better have been kicking a football I can only say that I wholly agree with them' (p. 127). Mrs. Meynell (whose 'exquisite notes' on childhood won James's praise in his London letter of 15 January 1897) is similarly emphatic in her denunciation of piano-playing as 'most unnatural' to children, in that it directs 'specific violence' upon their characteristic 'unreadiness'.[108] This strange theory is no doubt partly responsible for James's use of the piano as an instrument and emblem of childish corruption; for Mrs. Meynell's essays (so often devoted, through the nineties, to the scrutiny of childish traits) would appear to have suggested not a few of the characteristics with which he endows Miles and Flora. The impression, in the case of the boy, of rather febrile cleverness combined with delicate beauty; Flora's instinct for the diversionary gesture (pp. 57, 134); both children's delight in the mere repetition of not very exciting tales (pp. 97–98); their dramatic sense which, with the childish 'apprehension . . . of things far off' and 'things far apart' (as Mrs. Meynell expresses it), leads them continually to 'pop out at' the governess in various assumed characters (pp. 73–74); their impulse to adventurous naughtiness in the hours of darkness (pp. 89–90)—in all these matters James seems to be speaking by the book, not, in this case, *Jane Eyre*.[109] One might say that while his governess is identifiably early Victorian, his children by some lights are recognizably *fin de siècle*.

But the point I wish to establish here is that in *The Turn of the Screw* music, and the passions with which it is allied, belong not to virtue and the governess, but to Quint and evil. It will have been noted also that while the governess is consistently equated with Jane Eyre, Mr. Rochester, who as the object of Jane's devotion is represented by the governess's employer, is, in at least a couple of significant instances, linked with Peter Quint. And this brings me to perhaps the most curious single feature of *The Turn of the Screw*.

CHAPTER VI

The Real Peter Quint

i

Jane Eyre, like her author, is a close student of physiognomy: not only Mr. Rochester and St. John Rivers, but a succession of minor characters (Mrs. Reed, Miss Temple, Lady Ingram, and Rosamund Oliver) are drawn and coloured for us with the fine detail of the contemporary miniature. Such literary portraits—elaborate descriptions of outward appearance as an index of personality—are part of the nineteenth-century novelist's stock-in-trade, and James himself in his earlier work produces some notable examples. But by the time he comes to write *The Turn of the Screw* he has quite given up the detailed portrayal in favour of subtler, more telling evocations. When, therefore, among glancing impressions of Flora's blue eyes and rosy cheeks and Miss Jessel's dark and haggard beauty, we are given an old-fashioned 'portrait' of Quint with every facial detail inventoried, the effect is startling: so startling, indeed, that the governess has been accused of wilful fabrication here. But James has been careful in preparation of his effect. Like Jane Eyre's first encounter with Mr. Rochester, the governess's first view of Quint is in the open air, by evening light; but, like Jane Eyre, she has the chance to amplify her first impressions. She sees Quint again, by afternoon light, peering in through a window, and it is this second 'close-up' which she reports to Mrs. Grose:

'He has red hair, very red, close-curling, and a pale face, long in shape, with straight, good features and little, rather queer whiskers that are as red as his hair. His eyebrows are, somehow, darker; they look particularly arched and as if they might move a good deal. His eyes are sharp, strange—awfully; but I only know clearly that they're rather small and very fixed. His mouth's wide, and his lips are thin, and except for his little whiskers he's quite clean-shaven. He gives me a sort of sense of looking like an actor.'

'An actor!' It was impossible to resemble one less, at least, than Mrs. Grose at that moment.

'I've never seen one, but so I suppose them. He's tall, active, erect,' I continued, 'but never—no, never!—a gentleman.' (pp. 45–46)

Who is he? Mrs. Grose answers, 'Peter Quint'; some modern critics suggest, 'The Devil'; but in contemporary, realistic terms there can be only one answer to the question: 'He is George Bernard Shaw.'

Before I am accused of a fabrication wilder than any of the governess's, let me set out the evidence.

We are given a few supplementary indications regarding Quint. The governess assents to Mrs. Grose's suggestion that he is 'handsome', and adds that his clothes are 'smart, but they're not his own' (p. 46). Mrs. Grose tells us that he liked women 'young and pretty' (p. 24), and that he was 'so clever', 'so deep' that she was 'afraid' of 'things that man could do' (p. 52). It is surmised also that there had been in his life, 'strange passages and perils, secret disorders, vices more than suspected' (p. 53). In particular, to Mrs. Grose's knowledge, he had had an affair with the former governess, a young and beautiful woman, 'dark as midnight' (p. 112), whose name as we have seen connects her with Mrs. Annie Besant.

To consider first of all the 'likeness'. Here is a description, from the *Workman's Times*, of Shaw, the Socialist orator, in 1894: 'a tall, lean, icy man, white faced, with a hard, clear, fleshless voice, restless grey-blue eyes, neatly-parted fair hair, big feet, and a reddish, untamed beard.' This is very much the impression he made, in 1890 it seems, on Frank Harris, who adds the details of 'a long, bony face' and 'straight eyebrows tending a little upwards at the outside and thus adding a touch of the familiar Mephistophelean sarcasm to the alert, keen expression'. Whether or not, with these features, he was considered 'handsome' seems to have depended on the disposition and sex of the beholder. Beatrice Webb, in a diary entry of 17 September 1893, describes him as 'six feet in height with a lithe, broad-chested figure and laughing blue eyes'; and Bertha Newcombe's portrait of 1893 makes credible his reputed charm for feminine audiences. On the other hand Shaw in 1896 confesses himself to be 'disagreeably cruel looking', with a 'nasty expression about the corners of the mouth'; and Wilfrid Scawen Blunt, meeting him for the first time in 1906, reports: 'He is an ugly fellow, too, his face a pasty white, with a red nose and a rusty red beard, and little slatey-blue eyes.' Photographs of Shaw in his late twenties and his thirties make hair and beard equally dark, and emphasize the 'Mephistophelean' slant of the eyebrows and twist of the moustaches.[110] Allowing for a need on James's part not to be too libellously exact, and for a somewhat laboured exactitude on the part of his governess, Quint's portrait in most of its details is strikingly reminiscent of the living Shaw. These matching particulars are too curiously assorted to be the result of chance selection, and the few discrepancies may be plausibly accounted for. To the observer at the stump or in the lecture hall for example, Shaw's glance seemed 'restless', moving from one to another in his audience. To the governess, the sole object of his regard, Quint's 'sharp' gaze seems 'very fixed'—although here one perceives the intrusive ghost of James Taylor, whose basilisk stare made Charlotte Brontë's veins run ice. Again, Quint seems less hirsute or more neatly barbered than the 'platform spell-binder', but by Victorian standards Shaw's beard may well have seemed inadequate, and, to judge by his photographs, in his early twenties at least the effect was precisely that described by the governess.

Would James have been familiar with Shaw in this earlier aspect? In later years they met socially (on Shaw's own testimony) and also, as we have seen, corresponded.[111] But there are some indications that, at least as early as 1884, when he was gathering impressions for his new novel, James had observed Shaw, the young Socialist, in action—at open-air meetings, and at public lectures. Paul Muniment in *The Princess Casamassima* is a composite character, in whom, for instance, traits of James's brother William have been recognized. Obviously someone other than Shaw has suggested the young North-countryman's 'ploughboy' complexion, but the steady blue eyes and the tall broad-shouldered figure, no less than the big shoes, belong to a young man of abstemious habits, who is 'cool' and 'easy' when faced by an audience, who 'plays' with it, remaining good-humoured in the heat of debate, who with a 'fresh, cheerful, reasonable manner' can put the case for 'the swindled classes' in the most forcible terms, and of whose future his associates have 'the greatest expectations'[112]—a young man, in short, who has not a little in common with the young Fabian, George Bernard Shaw.

But *The Princess Casamassima* was written in 1885–86, *The Turn of the Screw* in 1897: in the interval Shaw, while still tireless in the Fabian cause, had gained a wider notoriety, and a popular legend was taking shape. It is to this stratum of impressions that the detail of Quint's 'smart' clothes, which are not his own, must be referred. The Jaeger suits, which Shaw began wearing in 1885, are part of the legend: Frank Harris, for example, records that at the first performance, in 1892, of *Widowers' Houses* Shaw answered the call for 'Author!' wearing a knitted suit of 'dazzling silver grey', and the knickerbocker cycling suits, the yellow tweeds, and the red tie were almost equally conspicuous and unconventional. 'You have all seen him,' declared the *Workman's Times* in 1894. A well-dressed man? You might take him for 'a fairly respectable plasterer'—so (in November 1896) his Chicago 'interviewer' suggested. But readers of the *Saturday Review* on 15 February 1896 already knew that Shaw's 'main reason for adopting literature as a profession' was that an author 'need not dress respectably', since 'literature is the only genteel profession that has no livery'. This critique ('The Tailor and the Stage') is perhaps Shaw's most thorough-going denunciation of 'the black and white ideal of purity'; elsewhere, for instance in his 1905 preface to *The Irrational Knot*, he concedes a degree of usefulness to evening dress, 'that blessed shield of literary shabbiness'; but he never modifies his detestation of the only 'correct' day-time wear for a gentleman 'in town'—the morning suit. Harris (prompted by Shaw) recalls the incident of R. B. Haldane's dinner-party, to which, before a group of notables in immaculate evening dress, Shaw was misled into wearing a specially purchased morning suit, and had in his own defence to behave with arrogant self-confidence. But the most pertinent expression of his views occurs among the notices he wrote as 'Corno di Bassetto', music critic for *The Star*. On 11 April 1890 Shaw disputed the right of theatrical managers (as distinct from operatic impresarios) to demand the wearing of evening dress 'in stalls, dress circle, and private boxes': 'I object to be forced into the uniform of any class—most of all that of the class of gentlemen to which I do not belong, and should be ashamed to belong.'[113]

Here we see the point of James's allusion—over which, again, there flickers the ghost of that 'Taylor' who was no gentleman. For to James conformity in dress, as in other usages of polite society, was necessary and important—not least because of the protective coloration, the 'blessed shield', it offered to the stranger. His careful elegance on all appropriate, and some inappropriate, occasions, is part of the James legend. Far from rejoicing, as an author, in his emancipation, he wore the livery of the morning suit even at Rye, even in the privacy of his study. In 1876 London had accepted him as a social entity, a gentleman—clubman, diner-out, country-house guest—and that character, with whatever sacrifice of the artist's time and convenience, he had sustained now for over twenty years. In one sense, then, Henry James himself was an 'actor', but he had so grown into his rôle, it had become so much a part of his artistic as well as his social experience, that its conventions were now second nature to him.

When therefore Shaw proclaimed himself 'no gentleman', James would readily accept this self-classification, and noting with distaste Shaw's love of publicity and his flamboyant showmanship, might well term him, in addition, 'an actor'—if not, more sharply, a *cabotin*, a mountebank. For here again, in the description of Quint, there is a barbed allusion. An actor is traditionally clean-shaven (as Quint with his insufficiency of whisker *almost* appears to the governess), but he is also an assumer of many rôles and of costumes not his own, and in 1897, despite Henry Irving's knighthood, he was still of dubious gentility. Actors and actresses were no longer classed with rogues and vagabonds, but 'the profession' still seriously disqualified them as gentlemen and ladies: Henry James, in *The Tragic Muse*, is very clear on this point. And 'to cap the globe', as Jane Eyre would say, Shaw had more than once appeared in stage productions and been billed as an actor. The various Socialist groups frequently called on the talents of their members and friends for the staging of an 'entertainment' to aid some worthy cause, and Shaw, at the behest of Eleanor Marx or May Morris, would take his part— sometimes (as on 21 November 1884) in piano duets, sometimes in a play. Thus on 30 January 1885 he was cast as Stratton Strawless in Simpson and Merivale's *Alone*, and on 14 April 1888 as Mr. I. Roscius Garrick in a sketch entitled *The Appointment*. These were public performances, and it is conceivable that James, in search of local colour for his novel, might have wandered into one of them; but the Bloomsbury 'social gathering' referred to by Paul Muniment carries no hint of such an experience. The probability is that James knew nothing of these histrionic exploits, any more than of the private theatricals in the Marx-Aveling drawing-room on 15 February 1886, when Shaw read the part of Ibsen's Krogstad, or of the copyright performance, at the Novelty Theatre on 6 November that year, of Edward Rose's *Odd, to Say the Least of It*, for which Shaw, in full costume, played Chubb Dumpleton. These episodes (unimaginable in the case of Henry James) are highly characteristic of Shaw, and no doubt for a future dramatic critic and dramatist they had their uses—teaching him to 'finger the stage', as Shaw put it, more expertly than any mere theatre-goer could learn to do. But they were obscure, unimportant, and not in themselves of a nature to excite gossip, so that one is inclined to regard them rather as one does the Greenwich Park bomb incident of 1894 in relation to *The Princess Casamassima*, and to decide that 'actor' as a gibe, like Greenwich Park as a setting, is used by James with uncanny appropriateness, but without special knowledge. Yet the term has a certain relevance to the Shaw of 1897—as the London theatre world, if not society at large, knew him. Four of his plays had by now been produced: he had conducted the London rehearsals with a force and an authority quite beyond any that James had (or could have) brought to bear on the casts of *The American* or *Guy Domville*; and his procedure had become 'newsworthy'. *The Sketch* of 25 April 1894 carried a full-page illustration of Shaw rehearsing *Arms and the Man*—an actor by proxy, as it were, in his own play.[114]

These are trivialities, however, and something much more sinister is required to link Shaw with James's predatory 'demon-spirit', Quint. It is more than adequately provided by his contemporary reputation—that of a dangerously subversive political agitator, who in private life was an equally dangerous seducer of women. As he himself said, in a letter of 26 September 1890, there clung about him a 'faint but unmistakeable flavor of brimstone'. One has to remember that until 1888 at least Shaw was 'better known to the public as a Socialist than as a writer'. He preached the standard doctrines of Fabian Socialism—denouncing *laissez-faire* capitalism, advocating municipal and state ownership of land, nationalization of industry and all public utilities —but with such a freshness of approach and such persuasive logic that he was everywhere in demand as a speaker. From 1884, 'for about twelve years', he spoke all over the country, wherever he was invited—'a street corner, a public-house parlor, a market place, the economic section of the British Association, the City Temple, a cellar or a drawing room'—to audiences of tens or thousands, and on an average three times a fortnight. So Shaw, in his old age, recalled his fighting days; but his letters at the time reveal that the pace was frequently harder: a lecture tour of September 1890 involved the delivery of thirteen lectures in as many days. As a challenge to the established order these activities were serious enough, but in addition, during years when political assassinations and bomb outrages were more than threatened, Shaw, despite his denials, was repeatedly charged with being an Anarchist, which in popular misconception meant a Dynamitard. It is true that, like many other Socialists, he was on friendly terms with Kropotkin and Stepniak, undoubted revolutionaries, and that on occasion he spoke at Anarchist gatherings—including that Autonomie Club which in 1894 really did harbour a dynamiter, if an ineffectual one—but he did not subscribe to their views. On the contrary, in a paper written in 1887, delivered to the Fabian Society in 1891, and published in 1893, he exposed 'the impossibilities of Anarchism' whether 'individualist' or 'communist'. Unfortunately neither he nor the Society had always been so prudent: as he admitted in his 1892 review of its history, 'the Fabian Society was warlike in its origin', and in its early days 'a sort of influenza of Anarchism' spread among its members. For one of these, the Anarchist Charlotte Wilson, Shaw set out his 'idea of the line an anarchist paper should take in England', and this article, which appeared over his signature in the first (March 1885) number of *The Anarchist*, was reprinted without his authority both in America (April 1885) and in England (1889 and 1896). Not surprisingly, a fear 'of things that man could do' persisted.[115]

So did the gossip regarding his sexual adventures. Most of it was due to his own calculated indiscretion: there never can have been a less surreptitious philanderer. But the more freely the contemporary diaries are opened, and the more outspoken his biographers become, the more plainly they reveal that philanderer (with whatever qualification of callous, cynical, egocentric, or unscrupulous the commentator's own high standards may suggest), not profligate or libertine, is the right designation for a man whom, even more clearly than the young Paul Overt, 'Nature dedicated . . . to intellectual, not to personal passion'. As he confessed to Ellen Terry in 1897, 'My pockets are always full of the small change of love-making; but it is magic money, not real money. Mrs. Webb, who is a remarkably shrewd woman, explains her freedom from the fascination to which she sees all the others succumb, by saying "You cannot fall in love with a *sprite*; and Shaw is a sprite in such matters, not a real person." . . . It is certainly true: I am fond of women (or one in a thousand, say); but I am in earnest about quite other things.' Mrs. Webb, incidentally, seems to have thought that 'sprite' was the *mot juste* to apply to Shaw, for she repeats it again and again in her diaries; and a term so relished by both of them may well have gained wider currency.[116]

Nevertheless the roll-call of courted and enamoured ladies—almost all of them dark-haired ladies—is a long one: in 1888 for instance, six of these affairs were in progress simultaneously. Such of these women friends as did not, even intermittently, attend Socialist lectures, or take their part as members of the Fabian Society, were actresses on the London stage, so that two inexhaustible reservoirs of London gossip were fed by their own and Shaw's ill-judged disclosures. There is therefore no question whether James 'could possibly know of' Shaw's connection with Mrs. Patterson, Mrs. Besant, Florence Farr, Janet Achurch, Eleanor Marx, Mrs. Bland ('Edith Nesbit'), May Morris, or Bertha Newcombe—to name the most conspicuous examples between 1885 and 1897. James, with his personal as well as professional appetite for gossip, his wide circle of London acquaintance, and (from 1890) his close connection with the theatre and its personalities, could not have avoided such knowledge. Moreover Shaw, as if challenging slander, turned his affairs to dramatic account. Mrs. Patterson and her supplanter, Florence Farr, between them supplied the model for Blanche Sartorius in *Widowers' Houses*—a rôle played by Florence Farr and witnessed, on the opening night, by Mrs. Patterson; and it was Jenny Patterson's unladylike violence (as reflected in Blanche), even more than the play's attack on slum landlords, which incensed the critics. *The Philanderer* of 1893 was even more offensive: it presented the two ladies and Shaw himself (all personally identifiable, if the author's stage directions of 1898 were followed) in their real-life involvement and rivalry; and again Julia-Jenny's wrath was shown exploding into violence. *Candida* of 1894 was evolved from Shaw's idealization of Janet Achurch, who first, on tour in 1897, played the heroine. In rôle and mentality Mrs. Clandon of *You Never Can Tell* (1896) was to some extent reminiscent of Mrs. Besant. It is true that, of these four plays, only *Widowers' Houses* was known to Londoners in general before 1898, but all Shaw's plays (and by the close of 1897 he had written eight) were many times read to and by friends and actor-managers he hoped to interest in their production; so that the characters and situations of real life so thinly disguised in *The Philanderer*, for example, must have delighted the scandalmongers long before they shocked the critics. None of Shaw's ladies, on or off the stage, suffered the fate of Quint's Miss Jessel, though several are alleged to have been temporarily heart-broken at the conclusion of the affair—the artist, Bertha Newcombe, for instance, as described by Beatrice Webb, and May Morris in the report of Shaw's sister. As Lucy Shaw remembered her, the one-time beauty of *The Golden Stairs* might have served as the model for Miss Jessel:

The worst of it was, she always wore her heart on her sleeve, and everyone knew about her madness for G[eorge]. I shall never forget the picture she presented the last time I saw her, in perfectly straight down clinging black garments, her black hair divided in the middle and combed low over her ears, . . . and the extraordinary sadness and gloom of her face, which never was at any time subject to lights and shades of expression, her tall figure of willowing [*sic*] slenderness, and the listless droop of her carriage, all went to make up a most pitiful personification of grief.[117]

But in fact it is Mrs. Besant who is singled out by James, and not primarily because of her liaison with Shaw. This (ironically enough, and piano duets notwithstanding) seems to have been, as Strether would have phrased it, an entirely virtuous attachment. The special relevance of Mrs. Besant's case to James's story has already been discussed, but there are other considerations which may have influenced him. As *The Bostonians* makes very clear, James abominated female demagogues, platform advocates of 'causes', from women's rights to eccentric cults; and Mrs. Besant, aided by great beauty, a magnificent contralto voice, and inexhaustible zeal for whatever cause had temporarily won her devotion, was the most renowned woman orator of her day. St. John Ervine has testified to the emotional effect, like 'a flaming fire', of her eloquence, which left the hearer as if beaten with brands, but without a single rational trace of her argument. This oratorical power, which, in a somewhat different kind, and with a more conscious gauging of audience reaction, Shaw himself delighted to wield, was completely lacking in James: he shrank from public appearances; stump oratory, as he told Shaw, would have been impossible for him. A temperamental antipathy, then, to demagogues in general and female crusaders in particular, must count for something in James's choice of evil agents. But it is by no means the full explanation. James himself could not have subscribed to the popular fallacy which identified lack of faith, in God or government, with lack of morals. It is true also that by the century's end the fierce Anglican logic of Charlotte Brontë's 'Who can trust the word, or rely on the judgment, of an avowed atheist?' was no longer applied in courts of law or Parliament, but it still held good in popular opinion, along with its corollary, that since ill-regulated thoughts meant ill-regulated lives, a man and a woman united as political agitators must inevitably be coupled in illicit sex. And since this bogy still had credence with his readers, James has not scrupled to invoke it. He may have felt, too, that Mrs. Besant's notoriety was already so black as to be impervious to further stain. For several months of 1895 *The Notorious Mrs. Ebbsmith* had exhibited her, glamourized by Mrs. Patrick Campbell, in a travesty of her real character and career. Suicide to avoid the shame of bearing an illegitimate child—which, Mrs. Grose hints, was Miss Jessel's end (p. 63)—might seem no more, in the way of remorse, than was to be expected of a heroine who could plunge her arm into a red-hot stove to rescue the Bible she had spurned.[118]

ii

But while one may grant the topical piquancy of the Shaw–Besant allusion, provided any of James's readers were alert and malicious enough to seize it, there still remains the question: what inspired the covert attack on Shaw? In 1885–86 (if indeed Shaw contributed to the portrayal of Muniment) James had already noted, without condemnation, his opportunism and his essential ruthlessness: Muniment is by no means a villainous, or even an unsympathetic character. But Quint in 1897 is the mere ghost of a vulgar seducer and corrupter of youth: whatever the enormity of his offences, he survives only as a pernicious influence on the imaginations of the living. What has occasioned this change in James's attitude—why, in 1897, should he wish symbolically to obliterate Shaw?

A glance at their London history provides a clue. In the autumn of 1897 Shaw was forty-one years old; James was fifty-four. Both of them had descended on London in the same year—1876. But whereas from Bolton Street Piccadilly, James with his irreproachable connections, his assured if modest means, and his writer's reputation at once gained the freedom of literary and social London, from Victoria Grove Fulham (and its Euston equivalents later), Shaw, without standing or means or experience, had to force his way to recognition—had to 'capture the castle' by whatever method (of frontal assault, mine, or subterfuge) his patient and resourceful ambition could devise. Over the following twenty years James had steadily pursued a literary career—not (after 1879 and *Daisy Miller*) with a resounding popular success, but to a secure position of esteem in the world of letters; Shaw by contrast had assumed a bewildering variety of rôles. He had begun as a diligent apprentice to the craft of fiction: by 1884 he had produced five novels, all but the first of which appeared, unremuneratively, in Socialist magazines. The fourth, *Cashel Byron's Profession*, in 1886 and the fifth, *An Unsocial Socialist*, in 1887 achieved independent publication, and *Cashel Byron's Profession*, being favourably reviewed, was republished in 1889. There is, by the way, no evidence that James read it, and, if he had done so, he would hardly have shared Stevenson's pleasure in it. But five years' unprofitable labour had convinced Shaw that novel-writing was not the way to fortune: his alternative resource was journalism. From his earliest years in London he had done occasional journalistic work, but in 1885 he became a regular book-reviewer for the *Pall Mall Gazette*. He was art critic for *The World* (1886–89), music critic successively for the *Dramatic Review* (1885–86), for *The Star* (1888–90), and for *The World* (1890–94), and from the beginning of 1895 dramatic critic for the *Saturday Review*—a post which he filled until May 1898. In addition to his regular weekly notices he wrote articles and reviews, on subjects of his choice in any of these fields, for periodicals such as the *Fortnightly Review*, the *English Illustrated Magazine*, and the *Illustrated London News*. Meanwhile, in the Fabian cause, he had not only acted as stylist in ordinary for whatever literary enterprise his friends might have under way, but also composed numerous articles and pamphlets on his own account. The volume of *Fabian Essays* (1889) which he had edited and in part written was still a best-seller among readers who had never heard of Henry James. And as a by-product of his combined Fabian and journalistic activities he had published two major critical essays—*The Quintessence of Ibsenism* (1891) and *The Sanity of Art* (1895). For if in musical circles he was known as the indefatigable champion of Wagner, in the theatre world he was, not the only, but certainly the most vociferous, champion of Ibsen.

And when, in 1892, he turned dramatist—so achieving the fusion of all his talents—it was as an Ibsenite, in studied revolt from 'Sardoodledom', that he completed his first 'realist' or, as he himself termed it, 'didactic realistic' play. Since then he had written *The Philanderer* and *Mrs. Warren's Profession* (in 1893), *Arms and the Man* and *Candida* (in 1894), *The Man of Destiny* (in 1895), *You Never Can Tell* and *The Devil's Disciple* (in 1896). And if only four of these plays had so far been staged in England, *Arms and the Man* had at least been well received, and in New York, where *Arms and the Man* was only moderately popular, *The Devil's Disciple* in 1897 gave Shaw his first box-office success. All this against a background of ceaseless political activity, which from 1897 included conscientious application to the details of local government: in April 1897 he was elected to the St. Pancras Vestry (later Borough Council) and continued in this civic duty for the next six years.[119]

Such a career of strenuous and persistent effort, always in ideological conflict with authority and convention (in every field, from art to politics), yet always in forced contact with the unglamorous realities of living (whether economic or emotional), pursued always under scrutiny, with a minimum of privacy and of the peace and quiet most creative artists find essential—such a career not only demanded a special constitution of mind and spirit, but also conditioned its artistic product in ways equally striking and characteristic. Shaw himself thought that his immersion in practical affairs had been wholly beneficial to him as a writer. 'I am a politician,' he explained, in a letter of 1894, 'because life only realises itself by functioning energetically in all directions. . . . My passion, like that of all artists, is for efficiency, which means intensity of life and breadth and variety of experience; and already I find, as a dramatist, that I can go at one stroke to the centre of matters that reduce the purely literary man to colorless platitudes.' He omits to mention what, for a self-acclaimed 'genius', must have been even more salutary—the constant interplay, in an equality of youth and friendship, with minds as active as his own. The Webbs, Olivier, and Wallas, for instance, received his confidences, read his work, disputed or approved his arguments without constraint or flattery. And to protect him from the atrophy of sensibility, the Philistinism in one word, which normally afflicts the devotee of practical affairs (and which he likewise omits to mention), Shaw possessed effective safeguards. His education had been imperfect, but he had, by way of compensation, enjoyed from childhood two special extensions of aesthetic experience. He had discovered pictorial art for himself in the National Gallery of Ireland, and ever since had followed his own course of direct, practical self-instruction in art appreciation and art history. More importantly, in a household of singers he had been immersed in the experience of music; and if his powers as an executant were limited, and his theoretical knowledge unsystematic, he had nevertheless a wide, practical acquaintance with works of music, especially opera, and a genuine and keen appreciation of musical effects. It is strange that notwithstanding this aural sensitivity he was no linguist—he had taught himself to read French, but had great difficulty in following it when spoken: the nonchalance with which, in his reviews, he owned to this handicap was more than equalled by the arrogance with which he displayed his musical competence. But indeed, whatever the mitigations he enjoyed, the truth is that of all creative talents Shaw's was least likely to be damaged by untoward circumstances. 'During all these years,' he wrote in 1896, 'I have acquired a certain power of work, and hardened myself to stand unscraped by many knife edges that cut ordinary folk.' His very limitations were a defence. His self-conceit made him proof against flattery (as Beatrice Webb noted); he had lost, or never possessed, the capacity either for reverence or for sentiment; he had acuity and vigour of intellect without profundity; he was essentially a dialectician, and it is in the rebuttal of any argument, even one he has himself advanced, that his wit is sharpest and most spontaneous; he was accessible only to logic but quite unterrified by novelty, so that in all his works (from tracts and critiques to novels and plays) he presents the spectacle of a writer who is 'advanced' and 'daring' in his 'open-mindedness' but at the same time confidently dogmatic; he was, it seems, incapable of sustained intellectual growth—he acquired knowledge and skill without matching development of creative imagination or sympathy, so that (for instance) to the last, in his most celebrated plays as in his early novels, his characters remain incompletely realized, demonstrations of ideas in situations contrived to exhibit them. Such a writer (and he is the nearest approach to Voltaire yet enshrined in the English pantheon of letters) early attains his maximum force, and Shaw had got his strength by 1894 at latest.[120]

He had also evolved and fixed his method of work and his literary standards. He was neither scholar nor scientist, but he shared with both their respect for and reliance on attested fact. 'Get your facts right first:' he told a literary aspirant in 1894, 'that is the foundation of all style, because style is the expression of yourself; and you cannot express yourself genuinely except on a basis of precise reality.' The acquisition of facts, in however dry and repellent a form, never daunted him—the British Museum reading room was his familiar haunt; but he also had the journalist's instinct for the direct, personal source. If he read Marbot, Wolseley, and Porter for 'the truth about' nineteenth-century warfare, and Burgoyne's correspondence (in Fonblanque) for details of the American War of Independence, he also went to a refugee 'Bulgarian admiral' for local colour in a Balkans setting, and the private report of 'an officer who served in the Franco-Prussian war' for the description of a cavalry charge, just as (when planning, aged twenty-four, to introduce a death from alcoholism into his current novel) he had drawn up a list of medical points for a doctor friend to check. But a proviso is necessary. Shaw's aim is not really accuracy (in the plodding scholar's sense) or ultimate truth (in the scientist's or the philosopher's or the visionary's sense) but factual density and colour (as a journalistic or artistic resource) and the acquisition of a defensive or offensive weapon (for service in polemics or in criticism). Next to facts, he valued clarity—the first lesson his speech-making had taught him was the necessity for straightforward, forcible communication. It had also taught him that the easiest way to gain attention was to startle (the unexpected stroke of wit, invariably termed paradox by his hearers, the blunt vulgarism, and the challenging over-statement were equally useful), and that the shrewdest home thrust would be approved (by all but the victim and, possibly, the victim's friends) if delivered with a jest. Of course the jester's immunity entailed certain disadvantages: few could believe in the simple truth, the literal accuracy of statements made by a writer so irresistibly given to levity and posturing. But those who laughed might later understand and accept, which could count as success in a Fabian manœuvre. And Shaw had also learned to play directly to the gallery—to take the audience, or the reader, into his confidence with the kind of personal revelation beloved of the popular press. It might be only an aside in a Fabian lecture, it might be a whole factitious 'interview', but it established Shaw as a personality in the eyes of the world. Publicity, in short, of the very type from which James recoiled with loathing, was Shaw's chosen element.[121]

But in almost every respect—in native endowment, in circumstances, in acquired competence, in literary techniques and standards—James differed from Shaw. He was a cosmopolite, with an easy mastery of three languages beside his own. He therefore enjoyed both direct access to three foreign literatures, and the ability to participate, at certain levels, in the life they interpreted. He was 'at home' in France and in Italy, and to revisit either meant almost unfailingly a deep refreshment. James took pride in his linguistic skill and valued the privileges it conferred on him: there was more than a touch of snobbery in his attitude. From the scorn with which, on Mrs. Wharton's testimony as offender, he greeted spurious proficiency in the written language, one can measure the irritation he would feel when a confessed ignoramus should not only declare the city of light to be, artist-ically, 'a pedant-ridden failure' 'imposing on American greenhorns and British Philistines', and denounce the traditions of the Comédie-Française as 'equal parts of gag and horseplay', but also commend 'the acting' in a play of which he could not follow the words. And this presumptuous distribution of praise and blame—among actors and actresses judged chiefly as mimes, and playwrights whose words when spoken were incomprehensible—continued throughout Shaw's term as musical and dramatic critic. His ridicule of *La Princesse lointaine*, his commendation of *Pelléas et Mélisande* and later *Peer Gynt* (in the Prozor version) must to an admirer of the art, as distinct from the message, of Rostand, Maeterlinck, and (with qualifications) Ibsen, have seemed effrontery as unendurable as his attacks on the conventions of the French theatre.

Perhaps (wrote Shaw, apropos of Sarah Bernhardt's *Lorenzaccio*, in June 1897) I am a prejudiced critic of French acting, as it seems to me to be simply English acting fifty years out of date, always excepting the geniuses like Coquelin and Réjane, and the bold pioneers like Lugné Poë and his company. The average Parisian actor was quaint and interesting to me at first; and his peculiar mechanical cadence, which he learns as brainlessly as a costermonger learns his street cry, did not drive me mad as it does now. I have even wished that English actors were taught their alphabet as he is taught his. But I have worn off his novelty by this time; and I now perceive that he is quite the worst actor in the world.[122]

And if, in matters where James felt himself competent to judge, Shaw was revealed as an impudent charlatan, how could James take his word on matters to which his own expertise did not reach, and in which his own taste was no guide—such as music? For alert as he was to the cadence of speech, James was incapable of appreciating music. As a social duty he endured innumerable recitals, and his hostess might mistake his absorption in the performance, so expressive of personality, for interest in the sounds emitted. But he was not always so guarded. He would rather (he told Mary Anderson) go to the dentist than listen to Bach in St. Paul's: he disliked the organ 'more than any other musical instrument'. On his own showing, in the *Notebooks*, only his 'want of musical knowledge' deterred him from handling the 'curious, picturesque and distinctly usable' plot offered him by Du Maurier in the spring of 1889. One can faintly imagine that Jamesian *Trilby*, so completely 'written' and so free of sentimental extravagance, and while one can be perfectly sure that it would not have built a theatre or drowned its author in gold, one can be tolerably sure also that its musical theme would have acquired sinister overtones undreamt of by Du Maurier. For James, despite his technical ignorance, will occasionally in his fiction employ a musical motif, and almost invariably the connotations are both sexual and menacing. It is of course on Flaubert's authority, and almost as if calling in support his massive evocation of Donizetti-in-Rouen, that James uses opera as a prelude to seduction. So Isabel, 'excited' by Verdi, is more accessible to the fascination of Gilbert Osmond, and Meyerbeer's *Les Huguenots* provides cover for the elopement in *A London Life*. But the pianist also may be the agent of evil. So (with a lack of decorum which should at once put Isabel and the reader on guard) Madame Merle intrudes upon the hush of mortal illness with a display of pianistic skill. It has never been clear to me why Beethoven should first have been chosen, or why in 1908 Beethoven should have been replaced by Schubert, as a composer appropriate to dark designs; but it is obvious that her musicianship is tactically used by Madame Merle to initiate the beguilement of her victim. And again, in that equivocal story of 1892, 'Collaboration', where James seems to reverse his usual stand on the Franco-Prussian question, it is the piano which is the catalyst—dissolving ties of patriotism, disrupting friendships, and wrecking an engagement, for an unnatural intimacy to flourish in their place. Not that James is alone among Victorian writers in this suspicion of music, the 'universal solvent': the second Mrs. Tanqueray, among her other dubious attractions, plays Schubert to perfection, and Alma Rolfe in Gissing's *The Whirlpool* (read and reviewed by James in 1897) is fatally addicted to the violin, or at least to public appearances as a violinist. When therefore in 1894 Shaw, with his customary forcefulness, declared music and its realization to be a necessity of life, playing an essential part in the 'education of the feeling', when he preached 'the religion of the pianoforte' as a means to that end—'with [the pianoforte] nothing else was needed, except the printed score and a foreknowledge of the power of music to bring romance and poetry to an enchanting intimacy of realization'—most readers of the *Fortnightly* would at once doubt his reliability, in musicianship as in morals. No really erudite critic of music would condone such amateur vulgarization, such cheapening of a difficult art; and advocacy of music as giving a loose to the emotions was typical of the Bohemian Shaw was reputed to be. He was in fact too good a journalist, too amusing and readable, to be credited with the technical knowledge he actually possessed: his musical criticism, as he said himself, was at first regarded as a clever imposture, 'a huge joke'. James certainly would not have been a 'constant reader' of the 'Musical Mems' in *The Star* or the weekly column in *The World*, but an occasional article, such as that cited from the *Fortnightly*, might engage his attention, to confirm his adverse opinion of Shaw.[123]

And sometimes even a present-day reader is inclined to endorse such a verdict. I am thinking in particular of Shaw's article 'On Going to Church', which was given pride of place in the first (January 1896) number of *The Savoy*, and which James must surely have seen. Here Shaw, as a substitute for the drugs and stimulants contemporarily ruining London life and letters, advocates church-going, provided first that the building itself meets Shaw's own requirements of architectural fitness, and secondly that it is empty of any religious service. He proceeds, 'My own faith is clear: I am a resolute Protestant'—in proof of which he offers his own secularized version of the Apostles' Creed (substituting the Immaculate Conception for the Virgin Birth) and denounces the Book of Common Prayer as 'quite rotten with the pessimism of the age which produced it'. He concludes on a note of elevated sentiment: instead of the drinking-shop or the conventicle 'with its brimstone-flavoured hot gospel' we must for 'refreshment and recreation' frequent the church—'going in without thought or belief or prayer or any other vanity, so that the soul, freed from all that crushing lumber, may open all its avenues of life to the holy air of the true Catholic Church'. What degree of seriousness there may be in this astonishing performance I should not care to guess, but there are three points which deserve notice. One is that some, at least, of Shaw's contemporaries gave it full and respectful credence: Elbert Hubbard reprinted it twice. Secondly, the display of learned familiarity with Italian churches, both in their architectural and in their religious aspects, is based on five weeks' experience of Italy (gained on two conducted tours, in 1891 and 1894, with the Art Workers' Guild). James could not, as the present-day reader may, check the article against Shaw's extempory record, hot with the frustrations of the English-speaking tourist—'Italy seems to me a humbug'—but he might very well detect the hollowness of Shaw's pretensions. And finally, the central theme reads like an extravagant parody of one James had almost made his own—that of the church as a haven of spiritual quiet even for the unbeliever. But James, although (as Graham Greene has shown) his 'Altar of the Dead' reveals some strange misconceptions, is never so illogical as to desire the banishment from a sacred edifice of the rites for which it was consecrated, and to the tradition of which the special effect he values is mainly due.[124]

iii

Any moderately fastidious, pedantic, or humourless reader of the nineties would have found much to deplore, on general grounds, in Shaw's writings; but those exposed to his criticism had their particular reasons for fearing him: 'I wish,' wrote one critic of *Arms and the Man*, 'to run no risk of incurring the hatred of such a dangerous man as Mr. Shaw.' His ear was keen, his eye was alert for any failure or ineptitude on stage or concert platform, and the next issue of *The Star*, *The World*, or the *Saturday Review* would hold the offender up to ridicule—it might be Sir Augustus Harris or 'the newest American soprano', Sir Henry Irving's Richard III or Mrs. Patrick Campbell's Rita; it might be the composer or the playwright himself. An inflated reputation, a false standard of propriety, a presumptuous or an unintelligent neglect of the author's intention—these always required censure. Take the case of Emma Eames, that 'newest American soprano' with whom James declared he 'fell in love' at her 1889 appearance in Paris: as Mireille, in 1891, Shaw found her to be 'never . . . more emphatically that very attractive and ladylike person Miss Eames', and of her Charlotte three years later, he wrote, 'Never, since Miss Mary Anderson shed a cold radiance on the rebuked stage, have virtue and comeliness seemed more awful than they do at Covent Garden on Werther nights.' And as for Mary Anderson, also American and James's friend, when in 1896 as Madame de Navarro she published her reminiscences, Shaw noted that these merely confirmed what she had already demonstrated on the stage: 'Mary Anderson was no actress. In no page of these Memories can you find any trace of the actress's temperament.' Shaw's long review contains nothing either unjust or offensive: even an American and an old friend should not have resented his strictures—indeed, in the author of *The Tragic Muse* they should have touched a responsive chord.[125]

The case of Miss Elizabeth Robins is somewhat different. Here was a young and beautiful American actress, with dramatic powers of extraordinary intensity if of limited range, with intelligence and literary taste, who from 1891 to 1899, by a combination of enthusiasm and organizing ability, brought play after play of Ibsen's to the London stage, and who by her own distinctive performances in many rôles (notably those of Hedda Gabler and Hilda Wangel) established herself as a leading exponent of Ibsen in England. Henry James, it appears, first saw her act in January 1891—as Mrs. Linden in *A Doll's House*. He had already made her acquaintance socially, and by the time she came to play the heroine in the London run of *The American*, from September to December 1891, James and Miss Robins had become friends, meeting frequently and exchanging letters. They remained on these familiar terms throughout the nineties—as long, in fact, as her serious commitment to the theatre persisted. It really does not matter (in this connection at any rate) that Elizabeth Robins was a young woman of secretive disposition and unfocused ambitions, that she turned to writing bad novels and fighting for women's rights, or that she had led and continued leading a private life of which James had no knowledge. That he had an avuncular concern for her personally, and took a keen interest in her stage career, is beyond question: he would not otherwise have spent 'evening after evening' of 1895 and 1896 in revising, for her benefit, someone else's clumsy translation of Echegaray's *Mariana*. What is more to the point is her contribution to James's appreciation of Ibsen. He had, through his friend Edmund Gosse, access both to the cult and to the sacred texts: he manifested no curiosity about either till 1889, and when Gosse obligingly sent him translations remained obstinately unimpressed. But Elizabeth Robins, by her 'slightly uncanny' interpretations, realized for him something at least of Ibsen's authority and artistry. It is doubtful whether, lacking this stimulus, James would have been at such pains to keep abreast of Ibsen in the text and on the stage, or been moved to formulate his Ibsen criticisms—all of which were written either on the occasion of some performance by Miss Robins, or in anticipation of one of her productions.[126]

Shaw's relations both with Ibsen and with Elizabeth Robins were on an entirely different footing. He also had a friend who was a Norwegian scholar and an Ibsen expert—the critic William Archer; and although his Socialist connections had early made him aware of Ibsen (he read the part of Krogstad, for instance, from Henrietta Lord's 1882 version of *A Doll's House*), Shaw freely acknowledged Archer as his mentor: 'I concerned myself very little about Ibsen until, later on, William Archer translated Peer Gynt to me *viva voce*, when the magic of the great poet opened my eyes in a flash to the importance of the social philosopher.' For it was as the 'social philosopher', the 'great teacher' isolating and exposing the hypocrisies and injustices (particularly as regards women) of a capitalist society, that Shaw venerated Ibsen the dramatist. From 1888 at least he was actively concerned to promote a vogue for Ibsen in England, even going so far as to meditate an 'assisted' verse translation of *Peer Gynt*. When in June 1889 the Charringtons successfully produced *A Doll's House*, Shaw, deputizing for Archer, wrote a review and also drew attention to the enterprise in his musical criticism. In a Fabian lecture of July 1890 he discussed all the available works of Ibsen, from *Brand* onwards, so as to elucidate their collective message; and after the excitements of 1891—*A Doll's House* in January, *Rosmersholm* in February, *Ghosts* (reviled by most critics) in March, and *Hedda Gabler* in April—he revised and amplified this paper and threw it into the ensuing controversy as *The Quintessence of Ibsenism*. The very title is provocative: Gosse, in his *Northern Studies* of 1890, had published a similar conspectus of Ibsen's works, but for all his special knowledge Gosse is content with a literary appraisal of individual works, more than once confessing himself baffled by their multiplicity of suggestion: he does not attempt to extract a gospel of 'Ibsenism' or assume the rôle of evangelist. Henry James, in his critique of June 1891 'on the occasion of *Hedda Gabler*', even more pointedly eschews 'moral' considerations: Ibsen is a dramatist, to be judged in terms of the form he has chosen. Shaw, however, claims that in Ibsen's plays he has discovered a 'perfectly definite thesis': Ibsen is consistently the anti-idealist, who repudiates the ideal in all its evocations—public or domestic, romantic or ethical, whether termed respectability, political loyalty, self-sacrifice, wifely submission, or womanly duty—and asserts in its stead the natural law of self-fulfilment. Shaw examines twelve of Ibsen's plays in the light of his thesis; but he also applies it, in a prefatory discussion, to various situations of contemporary life, and he concludes his essay by reviewing the state of the English stage in 1891 and estimating what it implies for Ibsen and the drama of the future. Purely literary considerations he disregards—they are not of the essence. As usual, Shaw's directness and pragmatism make the rival commentaries seem both confused and superficial. This impression is not altogether just: it has not escaped Gosse, for instance, that an 'emphatic defence of individuality' links the plays, and many of his observations are in Shaw's own vein of practical shrewdness; James, alone of the three, notes the 'absurd' foreshortening in *Ghosts*: 'he makes his "heredity" too short and his consequences too long'. But it cannot be denied that in his *Hedda Gabler* essay James is at his most precious and his most pontifical, and that throughout he condescends to his subject. One remembers that only a month before he had made exalted claims for literary criticism (as a difficult rite of empathy) and for the critic (as its dedicated celebrant). Here, perhaps, he expects that leniency of judgment for which he begged 'if the picture, even when the aim has really been to penetrate, is sometimes confused, for there are baffling and there are thankless subjects'. Enlightened readers of Shaw's persuasion would no doubt feel that James's difficulties were of his own, not Ibsen's, manufacture. On the other hand, forceful and persuasive as he is, to many readers (Ibsen enthusiasts included) Shaw's confident logic must have seemed less impressive than presumptuous. Even William Archer was repelled. James's opinion is not recorded, but he is unlikely to have approved a defence of Ibsen which so resolutely ignored the paramount question of art. He would, however, be certain to discuss Shaw's essay: his friendship with Gosse and Miss Robins would alone ensure that it came to his notice.[127]

For by mid 1891 Elizabeth Robins was very well aware of Shaw. He had seen her in July 1889 playing Martha Bernick and 'suffus[ing] that part . . . with emotion'; he saw her in the January 1891 revival of *A Doll's House*, the feebleness of which not even her 'sympathetic' portrayal of Mrs. Linden could redeem; and after the opening matinée of *Hedda Gabler* he wrote her a characteristic letter, full, not of compliments, but of suggestions for improving the performance. Later, at any rate, she was aware of the value of Shaw's critical support: 'beyond any critic of his day', she wrote in 1928, 'Mr. Shaw was master of the power to make reputations'. During 1891 she seems to have invited his help and advice—as she did James's—in the matter of *Denise*, the acting rights of which she hoped to secure. But what Shaw called her 'frightful and quite undeserved mistrust' of him seems to have impeded their acquaintance, even before two ludicrous incidents of 1893— an 'interview' during which Miss Robins threatened to shoot him, and a passage in a hansom cab from which she summarily ejected him—brought their correspondence temporarily to a close. Miss Robins, it is easy to believe, resented certain 'familiarities' on Shaw's part, for which not all his clever excuses nor his handsome tributes to her acting and production could make amends. When his letters are resumed in 1896 they are more businesslike and more distant in tone: one of December 1896 ends, significantly, 'You must play Hedda again in any case. Asta is ladylike—the last weakness of your Americanism. Who would pay any attention to me if I were a *gentleman*?' Is it possible that James gained no inkling of Elizabeth Robins's aversion to Shaw, and the grounds for it, real or fancied? Miss Robins had a very close friend and confidante in Mrs. Hugh Bell, who was also a close friend of Henry James. It is true that both these ladies could keep a secret: witness *Alan's Wife*, and the long-preserved mystery of their joint authorship. But in the unlikely event that neither of them breathed a word to James concerning Shaw's misdemeanours, there were still, from the beginning of 1895, Shaw's weekly dramatic criticisms, which, whenever Miss Robins was their subject, contained at their most laudatory some acute but unflattering observation. On 8 May 1897, for instance, in his criticism of *John Gabriel Borkman*, Shaw devotes much space to analysing Miss Robins's failure as Ella Rentheim: it was wholly consistent with her earlier successes, as Martha Bernick, as Mariana, as Hilda Wangel. In the latter part, indeed, 'she has succeeded heart and soul, rather by being the character than by understanding it'. As Alan's Wife and Mrs. Lessingham 'she has set up the infection of agony in the theatre with lacerating intensity by the vividness of her reproduction of its symptoms'. But 'in sympathetic parts properly so called' she achieves only 'an affectation of sentiment; . . . there is no reality, no sincerity in it'. In fact, she is 'too young and too ferociously individualistic' to play such parts successfully. It had been precisely this defect of temperament which had marred Miss Robins's interpretation of Claire de Cintré, so that, privately, James no doubt held the same opinion as Shaw; but he might nevertheless resent Shaw's expression of it, especially in such professionally damaging terms.[128]

He might, indeed, have been moved by fellow-feeling: as a playwright he also had experienced Shaw's critical attentions. One of Shaw's first assignments as dramatic critic had been to report on the production of *Guy Domville*. The week before, incidentally, he had expressed to Archer not merely Alexander's fear, but his own certitude also, that the play would fail. Professor Edel notes that James, in his *post mortem* letter to his brother, makes no reference to Shaw's critique, although he mentions with approval those of Archer and Scott, 'the only two dramatic critics who count'. The explanation may lie in a passage Edel omits from his résumé of Shaw's notice. Shaw is scrupulously polite throughout—stresses every discernible merit, indicates as briefly as possible the flaws of construction and faults of interpretation which spoiled the second act; but he makes it quite clear that this is fair dealing from an adversary, not a tribute from a supporter:

There is no reason why life as we find it in Mr James's novels—life, that is, in which passion is subordinate to intellect and to fastidious artistic taste—should not be represented on the stage. . . . As it happens, I am not myself in Mr James's camp: in all the life that has energy enough to be interesting to me, subjective volition, passion, will, make intellect the merest tool. But there is in the centre of that cyclone a certain calm spot where cultivated ladies and gentlemen live on independent incomes or by pleasant artistic occupations. It is there that Mr James's art touches life, selecting whatever is graceful, exquisite, or dignified in its serenity. It is not life as imagined by the pit or gallery, or even by the stalls: it is, let us say, the ideal of the balcony. . . .

All of James's work, one notes, not merely *Guy Domville*, is here glanced at with an easy tolerance in which there is more than a flash of contempt—an effete art, Shaw implies, but its right to exist, however vapidly and tediously, must be defended. And Shaw (one must note also) is not content with this veiled censure. In his final review of the season, on 27 July 1895, he deals again with James and his play. The past months have been disappointing, for audiences and managers alike: 'the public', Shaw argues, 'are getting tired of the old-fashioned plays faster than the actors are learning to make the new ones effective'. An English version of Sudermann's *Heimat* would have been more successful than Henry Arthur Jones's *Triumph of the Philistines*:

All this, however, is wisdom after the event. At the beginning of the season Suder-mann was an unknown quantity; and everything pointed to the expediency of producing The Triumph of the Philistines. Besides, Mr Alexander had already made a heroic contribution to the cause of art by venturing on Mr Henry James's Guy Domville, and producing it with great care and unstinted liberality, though the result was one for which he could hardly have been quite unprepared. The play, delicately written and admirably performed, was too fine for the audience; and the gallery first-nighters behaved very badly. . . . The production of Guy Domville was an attempt to conquer new territory by a *coup de main*; and that sort of enter-prise needs a heavier weapon than Mr Henry James forges. Then, too, Mr Henry James's intellectual fastidiousness remains untouched by the resurgent energy and wilfulness of the new spirit. It takes us back to the exhausted atmosphere of George Eliot, Huxley, and Tyndall, instead of thrusting us forward into the invigorating strife raised by Wagner, Ibsen, and Sudermann. That verdant dupe of the lunacy specialists, Dr Max Nordau, would hardly recognize in Mr Henry James 'the stigmata of degeneration,' which no dramatist at present can afford to be without. Mr Alexander should have struck his blow with the arm of Ibsen or Sudermann, or else kept to the old ground.

Tyndall and Huxley (invoked, presumably, as former leaders of rationalist scientific enquiry) figure rather oddly in an attack on the semi-traditional drama of Henry James, whose interest in Science and its popularizers was minimal: the unsigned 1871 review of Tyndall's *Hours of Exercise in the Alps*, in which he quotes also from *Fragments of Science for Unscientific People*, seems to be James's only published acknowledgment of such interest. But the reference to George Eliot is a home thrust. Henry James, then, is some twenty years out of date? In their moral assumptions, their analysis of motive and presentation of behaviour his plays and his novels recall *Middlemarch* and *Daniel Deronda*? That 'complete world George Eliot builds up', so 'full of the world' in the 1870s, is still Henry James's world of imagination? Such a suggestion, to a writer who had always prided himself, not only on the close observation of contemporary manners, but also on a Gallic enlargement from the restrictions of Victorian literature—a writer whom critics had always agreed to praise or to censure as 'advanced', must have been at least disconcerting. For nearly ten years past (since the publi-cation of *The Bostonians*, in fact) dwindling sales had made James aware of his unpopularity; but it is one thing to be in advance of popular taste and quite another (although the effect on sales may be the same) to have fallen behind it, to be not imperfectly but too well understood, the bore at the intellectual party. This, precisely, is what Shaw's next thrust insinuates: among practitioners of the arts, it is consistently the innovators, the original geniuses, who furnish Nordau's examples of degeneracy; Henry James is therefore in no danger of being so pilloried—he is blamelessly conventional. Shaw had of course intimated as much, rather more politely, in his January review: Henry James's play differed from the general run only in its ele-gance, of diction and of sentiment, and in modifying, if not rejecting outright, the standard theme of love triumphant. The 'new territory' Alexander might hope to conquer by producing *Guy Domville* lay in the realm of refinement, not of ideas.[129]

One cannot help wondering what effect, beyond passing irritation or lingering resentment, such acridities might have on a writer of James's temperament. 1895 is a watershed in James's development as a novelist; and while a number of factors, including the failure of *Guy Domville*, must contribute to the changes that from 1896 manifest themselves in his novels, a conscious decision to meet the charge of obsolescence would go far to explain them. From *The Portrait of a Lady* to *The Tragic Muse* the example of George Eliot has dominated James's handling of the long novel: her many-angled presentation, with parallel and interwoven story-lines, with undisguised authorial intervention, and with, in sum, 'a vast amount of life' to compensate for any looseness of form, is the model he naturally follows. His manner indeed is lighter and more dry, his construction (particularly in *The Tragic Muse*) more neatly symmetrical, but as Shaw perceived, more than fifty years before Dr. Leavis, the literary descent is obvious. Now the disciple has broken away: the influence of George Eliot is no longer apparent. From *The Spoils of Poynton* onwards, the choice of an observer, a reflecting consciousness, becomes a major consideration; themes and characters are reduced in number; action is circumscribed in order that all the implications of the chosen subject may be exhaustively analysed (in meditation or discussion) within the fictional frame. The effect at times is oddly suggestive, a rarified echo as it were, of the voluble dialectic in Shaw's 'new drama'. Of course, what James has actually done in these late novels is to apply, not so much a recently acquired dramatic method, as the technique he has long perfected through many short stories and some *nouvelles*, with their single observer and their necessarily limited action. To this extent he has carried out the intention he announced to Howells in January 1895: 'I shall never again write a *long* novel; but I hope to write six immortal short ones—and some tales of the same quality.' If, in his last great novels, he has wilfully broken these self-imposed bounds, it is fair to note that all three were originally plotted on the smaller scale: 'the little story', 'a little 3-act play'; 'a *sujet de nouvelle*'; 'a little tale'. But the modernization (if that is what it is) of James's novels after 1895 is not limited to form: the subjects he now chooses are for the most part uncharacteristically *louches*, and this impression is deepened by the fascinated repulsion with which they are treated. The commercially motivated 'daring' writer, the consciously emancipated pioneering writer, the denunciatory moral-pointing writer, have each a distinctive tone for the discussion of unorthodox sexual relationships. Henry James resembles none of these. Like his own Strether he seems to be wandering, with still-untouched fastidiousness and aloof curiosity, but with an ever-present sense of danger, in the darkness of the human jungle. And at every turn he finds, pitifully mangled, victims of *les grands fauves*. Has he perhaps undertaken, a little in the spirit of Dumas the Younger, 'to carry a particular, an aesthetic form of investigation as far as it will stretch—to study, and study thoroughly, the bad cases?' If so, carefully as he refrains from moralizing ('Woe, in the aesthetic line, to any example that requires the escort of precept'), he might seem to be turning the tables on critics (Shaw, for instance) who at once ridicule his prudishness and exalt the beneficent effects of sexual freedom. And to carry speculation a little further, the beginnings of such an intention might seem to be taking shape in the long essay 'On the Death of Dumas the Younger' which James published in the March 1896 issue of the *New Review*. At a number of points James's criticism of Dumas might be applied with equal justice to Shaw: 'What shines in [Dumas's pamphlets] most is the appetite for a discussion, or rather the appetite for a conclusion, and the passion for a sort of simplified and vindictive justice. . . . Our author's prefaces and treatises show a mistrust of disinterested art.' And Dumas's intellectual force and technical competence have prolonged the effect of his moral dogmatism: 'The energy that went forth blooming as Dumas has come back grizzled as Ibsen.' But an apostle of Ibsenism, ignorant of the French theatre, would probably not admit any connection, let alone any debt, and James disdains to specify.[130]

iv

Guy Domville was the only play of James's to reach the boards during Shaw's term as Saturday reviewer, so that he was spared further analysis of his deficiencies as dramatist. The weekly reviews continued, with their some-times annoying references to friends of James, their constant disparagement of the French theatre, their laudation of Ibsen, and their quips at American manners and institutions generally. And to these accumulated irritations there was added, in 1897, the tension of virtual rivalry—on Shaw's own journalistic ground. Once before, from November 1875 to August 1876, Henry James had engaged in regular, commissioned journalism—supplying a fortnightly Paris letter to the New York *Tribune*. He now undertook to write a series of London letters for *Harper's Weekly*. Ten of these were printed at irregular intervals from January to September 1897, when the engagement was abruptly terminated, after very nearly the same length of tolerance on the editor's part and for much the same reasons as the first had been. In June 1897 Queen Victoria was to celebrate her Diamond Jubilee, and it was certainly because of this fact and the resulting concentration of interest on London that James had been asked to supply his letters. Yet he ostentatiously absented himself from London on the great day, and his only notices of the event were expressions of intense personal distaste. In a premonitory jeremiad he deplores the 'gross defacement' of the city with 'miles of unsightly scaffolding' and 'screaming advertisements', and shrugs at the ignoble exhibition of the British instinct for trade, the real support of the monarchy, as revealed by 'the uproarious traffic in seats'—they order this matter better in Paris; and in a brief, melancholy postscript he describes London as 'a huge, dusty, cabless confusion of timber already tottering, of decorations already stale, of *badauds* already bored'. In lieu of the Jubilee he offers his readers Paul Bourget's Oxford lecture on Flaubert—or rather his own reflections on attending it; his final, August letter transports them as arbitrarily to Suffolk, in a blend of literary associations and leisurely traveller's impressions. For the rest he discusses his own reactions to books he has read, to plays he has seen, to exhibitions of paintings he has visited.

His choice of books for review testifies more to his own catholicity of taste than to any consideration for the tastes of his American readers. One might suppose they would be interested in a book about the Brontës, and possibly in the announcement of new works by Loti and Anatole France; but who among them would care whether or no Gissing was an 'authority' on 'the lowest middle-class' in England? A pious tribute to Mrs. Oliphant was in order; but some sixteen novels had followed *Kirsteen*, the only title James mentions. And who, outside England, could possibly be suspected of an interest in narratives of British India? Yet almost the whole of James's March letter is devoted to these—to Lord Roberts's memoirs, to an account of the Thackeray family in India, and to Mrs. Steel's 1896 novel of the Mutiny. And for all the space he gives to books, James only once particularizes, only once illustrates from the text (it happens to be Lord Roberts's) the generalizations he makes upon any of these authors. It is literary discussion at its most blandly, remotely authoritarian—at once opinionated and uninformative.[131]

There is, on the whole, more vivacity in James's discussion of painting. Yet in his January and February letters he begins on much the same note of bored condescension. Three major exhibitions (of peculiar interest to a connoisseur of art who, like James, was also a student of Victorian *mores*) were in progress simultaneously during the winter of 1896–97. For the first time the critic could view the assembled works of G. F. Watts and Ford Madox Brown; and at Burlington House a contrast in values was supplied by the exhibition commemorating Lord Leighton. No one to this day would quarrel with James's summary damnation of the latter, 'one of the happy celebrities who take it out . . . in life'; nor, essentially, with his verdict that Watts succeeded only as a portrait painter, nor with his choice of the Walter Crane portrait in illustration of that success. One might perhaps take exception to certain accents in the general disparagement ('If women could paint they would paint, I surmise, very like Mr. Watts'), and to James's curious limitation of the portrait painter's advantage—not, it appears, that of

a sharpened insight into character, but the 'vicarious thrill' of near-partici-
pation in 'so much definitely distinguished life'. But there is an obvious failure
of sympathy in his treatment of Madox Brown, which the conscientious
notice of two very minor successes hardly glosses over: Madox Brown, as
the rejected genius posthumously vindicated, is 'not quite up to his part';
there are so many canvases 'which have a little of everything, including
beauty, but which are so crammed with independent meanings as rather to be
particolored maps than pictures of his subject'. And then, without warning,
in his letter devoted to the May exhibitions, he takes a long half-paragraph
'to make amends to the name of Madox Brown for not having mentioned . . .
his "Farewell to England," valuable perhaps supremely as an example of his
queer, hard, ugly, but rich and full sincerity'. There follows a skilfully
evocative description—a minor art in itself, and one at which James is an
adept. What, one might ask, has produced this change of mood—or rather,
what has stimulated him to this display of expertise? It might be suggested
that genuine pleasure and excitement at his friend Sargent's triumph—the
portrait of 'Mrs. Carl Meyer and her Children' was the 1897 Academy
'sensation', and James's description of it here is almost as remarkable in its
vividness as the picture itself—have overflowed to enliven the writer's whole
approach to his journalistic task. For Millais as well as Madox Brown is a
beneficiary of James's new alertness, and, it seems, every American represented in the Academy exhibition, including those (such as James Shannon
and G. H. Boughton) whose American origins were almost forgotten, receives
a friendly notice: Abbey, indeed, might be thought to benefit unduly from a
friend's regard.

But there is also the possibility that James was goaded into a demonstration
of his critical perceptiveness by Shaw's unintentional exposure of his
omissions. In the *Saturday Review* for 13 March 1897, Shaw (brandishing
James's favourite maxim 'There is only one art') had drawn the attention of
theatre-lovers to the significance of the three current exhibitions—'the life-
work of the most dramatic of all painters, Ford Madox Brown, who was a
realist; . . . that of Mr G. F. Watts, who is an idealist; and . . . that of
Leighton, who was a mere gentleman draughtsman'. What follows, if not
exactly art-talk for the million, is vigorously plain-spoken; and Shaw's
illustrations and comparisons—of Madox Brown and Rembrandt, for instance—are boldly seized rather than nicely calculated. But the argument is
generously framed: there is no attempt to enhance the claims of 'the realist',
Madox Brown, by depreciating 'the idealist', Watts; and although the trund-
ling of the hobby-horse is audible throughout, Shaw's critical 'moral' is
effectively brought home.

Have you never been struck with the similarity between the familiar paroxysms
of Anti-Ibsenism and the . . . invincible misunderstanding provoked by Madox
Brown? Does it not occur to you that the same effect has been produced by the
same cause—that what Ibsen has done is to take for his theme, not youth, beauty,

The author of *The Turn of the Screw*

*in a portrait of 1897, a caricature of 1898, and
a snapshot photograph of 1899*

Shaw in 1879

Shaw in the early nineties

Mrs. Annie Besant in 1885

*Miss Elizabeth Robins
as Hilda Wangel in 1893*

George Bernard Shaw and two of his acquaintances

morality, gentility, and propriety as conceived by Mr Smith of Brixton and Bays-
water, but real life . . . ? Have you forgotten that Ibsen was once an Idealist like
Mr Watts, and that you can read The Vikings, or The Pretenders, or Brand, or
Emperor and Galilean in the New Gallery as suitably as you can hang Madox
Brown's Parisina or Death of Harold in the Diploma Gallery at the Royal Academy?

And as for Leighton, the mere gentleman, 'there are less handsome things in
the world' than his art, with 'its refined resolution to take the smooth without
the rough, Mayfair without Hoxton, Melbury Road without Saffron Hill.
All very nice, gentlemen and ladies; but much too negative for a principle of
dramatic art.' There is an echo here of Shaw's criticism of *Guy Domville*;
and it is associated, one notes, both with his championship of Ibsen and with
yet another denunciation of gentility: 'I doubt if it was ever worth while
being a gentleman, even before the thing had become the pet fashion of the
lower-middle class; but today, happily, it is no longer tolerated among
capable people, except from a few old Palmerstonians who do not take it too
seriously.' But the stimulus of Shaw's intrusion into art criticism, if one
concedes that it operated on James in May, had almost ceased to do so by
June; for in his notice of dramatic and other portraits on view that month
James, despite the opportunities afforded him by Whistler's 'Irving' and
Sargent's 'Ellen Terry' and 'Coventry Patmore', relapsed for the most part
into critical generalizations. He also saw fit to make Whistler's 'Irving'
the text for a diatribe on contemporary standards of taste: 'how *should* a
stupid generation, liking so much that it does like, and with a faculty trained
to coarser motions, recognize in Mr. Whistler's work one of the finest of all
distillations of the artistic intelligence?' Perhaps this was intended to appeal
to his readers' sympathy for an ill-used fellow-American; but the tone of
bored superiority was unlikely to conciliate Americans of the Gilded Age.[132]

A similar lack of journalistic flair is obvious throughout James's theatrical
notices, and here in every case he invites direct comparison with Shaw.
Irving's December production of *Richard III* and Miss Robins's *Little Eyolf*
of November had already been reviewed by Shaw when James dealt with
them in his first letter; the day after James dated (and presumably dispatched)
his second letter, with its pronouncements on Ibsen and the text of *John
Gabriel Borkman*, Shaw's article on the same play appeared in *The Academy*;
and Shaw's review of Henry Arthur Jones's *The Physician* and Pinero's
The Princess and the Butterfly was published three weeks in advance of
James's, dated the same Saturday. Shakespeare, Ibsen, and Jones-Pinero
between them provide a fair test of critical adaptability, as well as insight;
and it is interesting to note that James deals more acutely and responsibly
with Jones (Pinero is dismissed in two sentences) than he does with either
Shakespeare or Ibsen. James, unlike Shaw, is concerned almost exclusively
with the merits and defects of the plays themselves: their current theatrical
realization and the success or otherwise of individual impersonations he very
largely ignores. In fact Irving's Richard III is the only performance he

singles out, and that, no doubt, because he is able from personal recollection to compare the Richards of 1896 and 1877. But having noted Irving's characteristic ability to devise 'for the setting, a big, brave general picture', and the effective combination for his own part of 'the sinister-sardonic' and 'the elegant-grotesque', he decides that the play itself is 'a loose, violent, straddling romance' impossible 'to make real or even plausible', and more sweepingly that 'the represented Shakespeare is simply no longer to be borne'—indeed 'there is absolutely no representing him'. He takes as a case in point 'Richard's wooing of Lady Anne': no actress could possibly 'give a touch of truth' to the woman's part in that scene. One's reluctant conclusion is that if, over twenty years, Irving the actor had progressed, Henry James the dramatic critic had not: in his comments of 1897 only the verbiage and the total rejection of Shakespeare are new. And there, rather cruelly, was Bernard Shaw—to recall (with a quite un-Jamesian stridency of tone) something of the crisp outspokenness, the freshness of judgment, and the literary appetite of Henry James Jr. There is nothing wrong, Shaw tells us, with Shakespeare's *Richard III* or with Irving's edition of the text, but in Irving's production there was a great deal wrong both with the casting of subsidiary rôles (Why give an actor whose 'delicacy' would have been 'perfect' for Henry VI the part of 'the strong ruffian of the York family', Edward IV?), and with Irving's own performance. Take, as a case in point, his playing in the scene with Lady Anne. Here he gave 'a flat contradiction, not only of the letter of the lines, but of their spirit and feeling as conveyed unmistakeably by their cadence'.

But if we are not to have the tears, the passion, the tenderness, the transport of dissimulation which alone can make the upshot credible—if the woman is to be openly teased and insulted, mocked, and disgusted, all through the scene as well as in the first 'keen encounter of their wits,' why not have Lady Anne presented as a weak, childish-witted, mesmerized creature, instead of as that most awful embodiment of virtue and decorum, the intellectual American lady?

The actress did her best; 'but how could she play to a Richard who would not utter a single tone to which any woman's heart could respond?' Irving conducted himself 'as if he were a Houndsditch salesman cheating a factory girl over a pair of second-hand stockings'. The actor might well be indignant at such rough handling, but what the reader today finds curious is that Shaw understands the vagaries of sexual fascination and that Gilbert Osmond's creator apparently does not. Or is James's scorn really directed not against Shakespeare's want of artistry but against Shaw's vulgarity—is his criticism in effect a rebuttal of Shaw's? This is the only piece of dramatic criticism in the *Harper's* series which, from its date, might have been so intended; and it is amusing that James here takes the wind out of Shaw's sails by proclaiming Ibsen a better dramatist than Shakespeare. He is indeed so absolute in his repudiation of Shakespeare and so unctuous in his approval of Ibsen that one is tempted to query the sincerity of both judgments—as if, on this occasion, James were actuated rather by contrariety than by zeal for truth.[133]

More than a quarter of his space in this first letter is given up to 'the wonderful old man of Christiania', but the only critical points that emerge are first, that Ibsen suits the contemporary taste for realism, and secondly, that Ibsen's drama constitutes a little world in itself, the 'spell' of which in performance James is unable to resist. There is of course a contradiction here, and there is even a hint, in James's phrasing, that Ibsen is a Lear character whose microcosm is a world of nonsense. *Little Eyolf* and its production are dealt with in one sentence—its place 'is not of the highest' and 'even in London' Ibsen 'has had more acting': for the detailed explication of Ibsen's 'mysterious force' James and the reader must wait till Miss Robins produces *John Gabriel Borkman*. James's reticence over *Little Eyolf* is understandable: not only had Shaw twice discussed the production (giving, in his first notice, a very forthright analysis of this 'suburban' marriage drama), but the change in management and changes in casting which provoked his second, mercilessly satirical review had not been effected without 'unpleasantness'. Moreover Miss Robins's Asta had not been wholly successful—Shaw declared it to be 'an urbanely pictorial recommendation' of a part which Miss Robins's temperament disqualified her from acting. *John Gabriel Borkman*, however, as yet untouched by Shaw and unspoilt by deficient presentation, offered a fresh critical prospect. A fortnight later, therefore, still in advance of the production, James dilates upon Ibsen (now 'the sturdy old symbolist') and his new play for almost a column's length. This time the critical points (whether in sympathy or in emulation) are festooned with picturesque imagery, but their application is still neglected. Ibsen, perhaps because he is a Norwegian, has no sense of comedy; his plays are really moralities in which the conflict of wills is powerfully exhibited; for Ibsen respects the unities: his plays have an almost classical strictness of form; and the contrast between this formal elegance and their bleak and graceless provincialism is a main source of their effect. In *John Gabriel Borkman* 'a great span of tragedy is taken between three or four persons—a trio of the grim and grizzled—in the two or three hours of a winter's evening'; 'the whole thing' is immensely actable and Ella Rentheim is the 'most touching' of Ibsen's heroines. The nature of the moral problems involved, the relationship of the characters, every indication of what the play is 'about' James keeps as dark as if he were writing a chapter of a mystery novel: the reader must wait for the performance. Meanwhile, it seems, he is invited to admire the brilliance, the sensibility, the generous enthusiasm (for after all the playwright is seventy and a barbarian, *quoi?*) of the critic himself. Shaw's article of the next day, hurriedly composed and with no stylistic pretensions whatever, is not only better journalism but also more discerning criticism. He notes the refusal of Ibsen's characters to romanticize emotion, and, in particular, the truth within the pathos of Ella Rentheim's situation, the complementary disappointments of the two sisters, the mutual dependence of Foldal and Borkman, the optimism of the young man's inevitable rebellion— 'the whole play is a wonderful chapter on the illusions of youth and the illusions of age'. When in the first week of May the long-heralded production took place, Shaw duly commented on its inadequacies (among them Miss Robins's own performance) and amplified some of his earlier critical observations; James (possibly from unwillingness to find fault with Miss Robins either as manager or as actress) completely ignored it.[134]

The topics he chose for his April letter were all theatrical; and in this letter, consciously or not, he followed a pattern reminiscent of many of Shaw's articles: first a general discussion of some misconception or abuse affecting the theatre, and then, ingeniously linked, a detailed review of the latest production. So, for more than half his space, James discusses 'the blight of the drama' in England: the causes are two—interest in the player to the neglect of the play, and the irrationality of popular favour—as exemplified by the theatrical fortunes of Mrs. Patrick Campbell. Again, there is immense public curiosity regarding Mr. Tree's new theatre, but none whatever about his new repertory. The theme is not of itself one to attract the general reader (although Shaw has managed to enliven much less promising subjects); James's argument is confused; and worst of all, his newly acquired dictation style is both obscure and prolix. It is, besides, not at first clear why he has chosen to introduce a review of Jones's *The Physician* with these morose reflections. But one remembers that Alexander had produced *Guy Domville* immediately after the May–December run of Jones's *The Masqueraders*, and that James at the time had been unwilling to concede any merit to the latter: its success was due entirely to a vitiated public taste—audiences demanded only 'a roaring actuality, simplified to a few big *familiar* effects'. So here again a play by Jones suggests the culpability of audiences, and having again obliquely justified himself by assailing them, James proceeds (with considerable relish it seems) to dissect another ill-made 'play of modern life'. His criteria, obviously, are those of Dumas the Younger, not to mention Sardou. First he 'tells the story'—that of a great London doctor in love at first sight with a young woman who consults him about her *fiancé*, an apostle of Temperance, smitten with a malady which only the doctor realizes to be secret alcoholism:

This situation is the doctor's predicament, his dilemma. . . . He is so mad to possess the girl that an easy way stares him in the face: he has only to reveal to her the private turpitude of her lover and she will infallibly fall into his arms. She does so, of course, in the last act, but by ways remarkably devious.

But Jones's chief offence is that, having elected to treat theatrically a subject of 'gradual growth', he fails altogether to demonstrate the relations which are central to it—those of the doctor with the heroine and with his rival: dramatically, therefore, the hero is in relation only to himself, and remains—

Mr. Wyndham. Jones (obviously) has supplied the plot, and James (possibly) has supplied the title for Shaw's *The Doctor's Dilemma* of 1906, and one turns with some curiosity to his review of *The Physician*. Unlike James, Shaw takes the 'dilemma' for granted. What strikes him, apart from the morbid persuasion of both Jones and Pinero that death begins at fifty (or forty), and the physician's lack of science, is that both dramatists consider extreme disparity in age to be no impediment to romance—an error which he is at pains to rectify in his own adaptation of the theme. He compares the realism of Jones's characterization with the artificiality of Pinero's, notes the latter's faults of construction, and gives his remaining space to the players. It is typical of their approach to literature that James should here be concerned only with technique, with the manipulation of the fictional *donnée*, Shaw chiefly with its plausibility, measured by the standards of real life. And since the common reader invariably judges literature by its 'truth to life', James's failure in journalism was as predictable as Shaw's success.[135]

It may here be objected that the journalistic venture of 1897 was even less important in James's career than the first had been, and that to dwell (as I have done) on the contrasts inevitably set up, between an amateur and a professional handling of similar *feuilleton* material, is not only to be unjust to both parties, but also to give disproportionate emphasis to a very minor episode. In the first place, however, I am not attempting to 'rank' two very different geniuses—to assess James in terms of Shaw, and *vice versa*—I am simply trying to focus Shaw from James's standpoint: to decide what general impression derived from the contemporary 'image' of Shaw, and what particular reactions to individual statements in Shaw's writings may have inspired the portrait of Quint. An artist such as James (of a ruminant, reflective habit of mind, and a critical faculty much stronger in imaginative empathy than in objective analysis) might have confronted the phenomenon of Shaw with, shall we say, appreciative disapproval—even though it was embodied in a fellow Irishman. But not only were there marked antipathies, there were certain definite areas of conflict where these could be displayed; and in this respect alone the *Harper's* letters are important for my enquiry. They are even more significant, perhaps, in what they reveal of James's own developing tendencies as a writer.

The best of these letters ('Old Suffolk') and the best parts of others are as effective, in description or in criticism, as anything we have from James's pen; at their worst they are both dull and difficult. But none of them is calculated for its immediate purpose; and James's contempt for his task, for many of his subjects, and for his readers, comes through only too palpably. He seems to have felt that his reputation as an artist was imperilled by his acceptance of a journalistic commission, and that therefore he must be extraordinarily vigilant about the figure he himself presented: it must be that of the cool, experienced citizen of the world, the authoritative critic of literature and the drama, the connoisseur of painting, who is unquestionably his readers' superior, and who will not bate one jot of that advantage. It is even a matter of principle. ' "Life consists of the personal experiments of each of us. . . . People . . . may not like you, but there's a chance they'll come round; and the only way to court the chance is to keep it up—always to keep it up." ' So says Gabriel Nash in *The Tragic Muse*; and in the long run, and over the wider field, James's posthumous success may be held to have justified this contention; but neither the journalist nor his public can afford to wait, and what is read running must above all be written plain. The obscurity of style which is the most tiresome feature of the letters had been 'growing on' James for some time: dictation accelerated the process, of which, it seems, he was quite unaware. More than anything else, this change in style betrays James's intellectual isolation. He had a numerous acquaintance and a few close friends in England; but there had never been anyone with whom (after Shaw's fashion) he discussed his work while it was in progress: he communed with himself over it in his private notebooks, he did not write about it in his letters. And there was no one now who could utter a word of informal, privileged criticism: the sharp-tongued Alice, and the long-absent Stevenson were both dead; the imperfectly sympathetic William and the faithful Howells were at letter's length away. None of James's surviving friends—neither his contemporaries nor the young men who were now beginning to cluster about him—would dare to make a habit of criticism. Fullerton (in 1897) suggested that dictation might be hazardous for style; Gosse (in 1906) deplored the revision of *Roderick Hudson*: neither comment was well received.[136] And if neither young admirers nor old and trusted friends could safely question James's style, how would he take public ridicule of it— from Shaw?

The Academy for 6 November 1897 carried a proposal for the establishment of an 'Academy of Letters', and invited the opinion of readers on a list of forty names, among which that of Henry James appeared as the thirty-fifth. One of the readers who immediately accepted this invitation was Bernard Shaw, tongue in cheek. An Academy of Letters, he declared, should consist only of men of letters: 'that is to say, men who write for the sake of writing, and not men who use the pen solely in order to convey information or spread ideas'. Swinburne, who is 'incapable of receiving ideas from life, and writes only what he has read', is therefore eligible, and so is the 'virtuoso' Meredith. 'Mr. Henry James is also a stylist: his recent essay on Du Maurier was written with such extraordinary literary preciosity that its most critical sentences were quite unintelligible, though their emotional inspiration was touchingly sincere.' Further, 'Mr. Pinero and Mr. Gilbert are no more men of letters than I am. The only dramatist, besides Mr. Henry James, whose nomination could be justified is Mr. Oscar Wilde.' George Du Maurier, a close friend for nearly twenty years, had died the previous October, and James, in *Harper's New Monthly Magazine* for September 1897, had offered a deeply felt but ponderously written tribute to his memory; Wilde, who had been released from prison in May, was now in exile and his plays were banished from the stage. Shaw, therefore, had not only delivered a wounding stroke at a point where James was least tolerant of criticism—his style—but also coupled it on the one hand with an impertinent allusion to James's private feelings, and on the other with a comparison which James, given both his contempt for Wilde's plays and his own sexual bent, might take as insulting or as sinister, at his choice. If he had not before decided that Shaw's offences against good taste cried out for rebuke, here was provocation enough; but by 13 November (unless it were inserted during a late revision, of which there is no sign) the portrait of Quint must already have been completed.[137]

v

The final letter to *Harper's Weekly*, dated 31 August 1897, was written during James's summer holiday, and it is probable that almost immediately after his return to London, in early September, he began work on *The Turn of the Screw*. The story was completed by 1 December 1897, but only, it would seem, after a number of interruptions and delays: James's mention of it (apparently in answer to an enquiry) indicates as much—'I *have*, at last, finished my little book—that is *a* little book, and so have two or three mornings of breathing-time before I begin another.' Business connected with the lease and renovation of Lamb House encroached on his time; and barely a month after his return he was absent for 'four to five days' on a country visit, returning to London on 7 October. This visit, to Ford Castle in Northumberland, allows us to date the course of composition a little more precisely. Bly, as we have seen, reproduces the fictional Thornfield pretty closely, but James has made one significant alteration: Bly has not, like Thornfield, a mere crenellated parapet fronting the leads; it possesses, among 'a few features of a building still older, half replaced and half utilised', 'an old machicolated square tower' (p. 19). This tower, we are told later,

was one of a pair—square, incongruous, crenelated structures—that were distinguished, for some reason, though I could see little difference, as the new and the old. They flanked opposite ends of the house and were probably architectural absurdities, redeemed in a measure indeed by not being wholly disengaged nor of a height too pretentious, dating, in their gingerbread antiquity, from a romantic revival that was already a respectable past. (p. 30)

Suggestions of gingerbread apart, we might be looking at the north front of Ford Castle. Now Ford was a 'genuine' medieval Border castle, but, although continuously occupied, it had been twice destroyed and four times rebuilt since the battle of Flodden, to which it mainly owes its historical and romantic fame. The nineteenth-century restoration, carried out with loving care over many years by its chatelaine, Lady Waterford, had won the approval of her friend Augustus Hare, but failed to please Henry James: oh, for someone 'to dis-restore both room and house! There *is* work cut out here for an architect!' James had been assigned the 'King's room' in one of the two surviving medieval towers, the north-west, known as King James's Tower—as high and square and crenellated as any perambulating ghost could desire. In this tower also, on the floor below the King's room, but still 'high above the gardens' and the wide lawn it overlooks, is 'Lady Heron's room'; and it was this, no doubt, which served as model for that 'large, square chamber, arranged with some state as a bedroom' (p. 84), to which the governess resorts in her nocturnal search for Miles and Quint. These architectural details, and perhaps the general impression of 'restoration', seem to be all that Ford Castle has contributed to James's description of Bly. A point of interest here is that James, although what in fact he evokes is the late nineteenth-century aspect of the castle (with Lady Waterford's 'new' tower to balance the one his ghost frequents), suggests that Bly is a product of eighteenth-century, Strawberry Hill antiquarianism—and borrows Augustus Hare's term 'gingerbread' for the purpose. Hare, unlike James, had seen the castle before the alterations of the 1860s, and this small discrepancy in James's account indicates once again his choice of an early Victorian setting for *The Turn of the Screw*. But to revert to the process of its composition: Bly's ancient tower appears in the first chapter of the story proper, so that no great progress can have been made until at least a month after James's return from Suffolk.[138]

Nevertheless, it seems reasonable to assume that when *The Turn of the Screw* was plotted and its composition begun, James's grievance over his treatment by Harper's was still fresh in his mind. And considering his reaction in 1895 to the success of Jones's play, one might, at this latest rebuff, expect him again to minimize his failure by depreciating his nearest and most obtrusive competitor. Besides, it is probable that James had more than once been reminded of Shaw during his Suffolk holiday. From 1 August to 17 September 1896 the Webbs' Fabian house party had occupied the Stratford St. Andrew rectory, about three miles south of Saxmundham. Dunwich, where James was staying (in the same rural district of Blyth), was some eight miles to the east of Saxmundham, through which anyone going north or south by the main road had to pass; and both James and (a year earlier) the Fabians occupied their afternoons in cycling. The odds are that at the inn where he lodged and at those where he stopped for refreshment James would hear a good deal of Shaw and his friends—especially the women friends, in their newfangled cycling dress. Such reminders of actuality would not have been particularly welcome to James in the mood revealed by his August letter. He was luxuriating in nostalgia—for the historical past, for the literature of yesterday remembered in its appropriate setting. And far more than Crabbe at Aldeburgh, or Fitzgerald at Woodbridge, Dickens at Blundeston and Yarmouth (which James did not revisit) haunted his imagination. Suffolk, indeed, had from his childhood meant *David Copperfield*, illustrated by 'Phiz'.

The opening lines of David's history offered in this particular an easy perch to my young imagination; and to recall them to-day, though with a memory long unrefreshed, is to wonder once more at the depth to which early impressions strike down. . . . Dickens took his Rookery exactly where he found it, and simply fixed it forever; he left the cradle of the Copperfields the benefit of its delightful name; or I should say better, perhaps, left the delightful name and the obscure nook the benefit of an association ineffaceable. . . .[139]

It is interesting, with *The Turn of the Screw* in mind, to look again at those opening chapters. David Copperfield, one notes, was born 'to see ghosts and spirits' but did not, and a strange visitation preceded, indeed precipitated, his birth:

My mother . . . lifting her eyes as she dried them, to the window opposite . . . saw a strange lady coming up the garden.

My mother had a sure foreboding at the second glance, that it was Miss Betsey. The setting sun was glowing on the strange lady, over the garden-fence, . . . and now, instead of ringing the bell, she came and looked in at that identical window. . . .

My mother had left her chair in her agitation, and gone behind it in the corner. Miss Betsey, looking round the room, slowly and inquiringly, began on the other side, and carried her eyes on, like a Saracen's Head in a Dutch clock, until they reached my mother. (i, 3–4)

One remembers Quint, 'looking straight in' through the window at Bly: 'His face', says the governess, 'was close to the glass, . . . his stare into my face, through the glass and across the room . . . quitted me for a moment during which I could still watch it, see it fix successively several other things. . . . He had come for someone else' (p. 39). Then there is the first visit to Yarmouth. How old was David by this time? Very small, very charming as drawn by 'Phiz', very intelligent and very sensitive as evoked by Dickens, he seems younger than the ten years suggested by the history of the caul (i, 1–2). But on this first visit he met little Em'ly, round whom ('that baby', 'that blue-eyed mite of a child') his 'fancy raised up something . . . which etherealised, and made a very angel of her' (iii, 37). The two children, one already orphaned, the other soon to be so, became inseparable playmates, and their first ramble on the beach together was marked by a curious omen:

She started from my side, and ran along a jagged timber which protruded from the place we stood upon, and overhung the deep water at some height, without the least defence. The incident is so impressed on my remembrance, that if I were a draughtsman I could draw its form here, I dare say, accurately as it was that day, and little Em'ly springing forward to her destruction (as it appeared to me), with a look that I have never forgotten, directed far out to sea.

The light, bold, fluttering little figure turned and came back safe to me, and I soon laughed at my fears. . . . But . . . I have thought, Is it possible, among the possibilities of hidden things, that in the sudden rashness of the child and her wild look so far off, there was any merciful attraction of her into danger, any tempting her towards him permitted on the part of her dead father, that her life might have a chance of ending that day? (iii, 36)

For there in the wings, of course, waiting his cue, was the villain of the melodrama, the irresistible charmer, that 'dangerous friend' Steerforth (xxv, 367), who would delude and betray both children, and, even so, after his death retain David's hero-worshipping affection. It is the memory of this childhood reading ('long unrefreshed' as James tells us) which has supplied, in *The Turn of the Screw*, certain vital elements not accountable to *Jane Eyre*. First and foremost there is little Miles himself. David Copperfield, with his intelligence, grace, and pathos, has simply walked out of Blunderstone into a new setting, and carried with him more than a trace of the passionate, grieving emotion Dickens lavished on his own youthful image— carried with him, in fact, all the self-identifying thrill of pity with which every child reads *David Copperfield*. It is this emotional charge which Professor Edel has detected in *The Turn of the Screw*, and which (I think) he misinterprets as referable to James's own life experience. *The Turn of the Screw* does, it is true, enshrine a *souvenir d'enfance*, but it is to the childhood of the literary imagination that the memory belongs. And its influence is not limited to the conception of Miles. There is David's mother, the former nursery-governess, 'not yet twenty' at her marriage, whose tenderly affectionate relationship with her son restores to its natural proportions that of the governess with little Miles; there is Peggotty, a heartier, more demonstrative Bessie, to contribute a touch to Mrs. Grose; there is Steerforth's rejected mistress, Rosa Dartle, to add another fictional example to the list of the dark-haired and impassioned; there, to blend with the memory of Steerforth and make corruption base and servile, is Steerforth's evil agent—the smooth, secretive valet Littimer.[140]

And on this Suffolk holiday, where all these literary phantoms were re-evoked, they were mingled with impressions of Shaw: wasn't he, in real life and to scandalous effect, playing the part of Steerforth? One of those 'glimpses' which, James tells us, were 'the constant company of the afternoon "spin" ', beginning at Dunwich and ending 'as far inland as you have time to go', was 'that of the pretty little park gates that you pass to skirt walls and hedges beyond which the great affair, the greatest of all, the deep, still home, sits in the midst of its acres and strikes you all the more for being, precisely, so unrenowned. It is the charming repeated lesson that the amenity of the famous seats in this country is nothing to that of the lost and buried ones.' Did James, one afternoon, enter in this hopeful spirit the long tree-lined drive of Stratford St. Andrew rectory? Hesketh Pearson describes it:

Going towards Ipswich from Saxmundham, the traveller passes through the red-brick hamlet of Stratford St. Andrew, turns up a drive to his right and walks about 150 yards between large trees with a rich meadow on his left. All is leafy and lush, excessively rural and reposeful. He expects to see a rambling Elizabethan mansion when he reaches the top of the drive, or at least an elegant Georgian building. He finds instead an efficient house of greyish brick, built in late Victorian style.

Such a disappointing 'glimpse', allied with his memories of Ford Castle, might perhaps explain James's insistence on Bly's lack of architectural charm—the 'ugly' convenience he superimposes on the image of Thornfield. There at any rate (and in Blyth, too) had been the temporary abode of the inexplicably fascinating, the clever and dangerous Shaw-Steerforth and his questionable associates. And James, by early October in full possession of his data, was ready to compose his new story.[141]

But with all the will and all the excuse in the world to administer a rebuke to Shaw, it is doubtful whether James would have gone so far as to portray him satirically in *The Turn of the Screw*, if it had not been for the example of Anatole France. *L'Orme du mail* had been published in January 1897. James read it, apparently, at the beginning of May ('the last loose flower— as spicily sweet as a clove-pink—of the genius of Anatole France'), and, wandering among 'the acres of canvas' at Burlington House, was driven to compare the public implied by such works and the readers for whom France could dare to produce his book: 'Oh, the adorable people; the intelligent, exquisite, delicious people; oh, the people to commune with, to live with, to work for!' This first volume of *Histoire contemporaine* had been appearing in *feuilletons* from the beginning of 1895; and a chapter of the novel, in its first state, had actually been published in the *Yellow Book* for April that year. It is true that James had not been in Paris during these years, but through his correspondents, his visitors, and his reading he kept in touch with French affairs. He would therefore have had little more hesitation than Anatole France's Parisian readers in identifying M. l'abbé Lantaigne and M. l'abbé Guitrel, M. le préfet Worms-Clavelin and the rest of the provincial worthies. Indeed, from the memory of his *Little Tour* of 1882 he would be ready to give a precise location to Anatole France's *ville de province*, with its elm-shaded *mail* and its *voyante* inspired by Ste Radegonde. Surely this was Poitiers, with its Merovingian patron saint and her church, and, rampart-enclosed above garden plots and winding river, its Promenade de Blossac, 'the most charming thing' in the town. Recent and current scandals of church and state, made familiar by press controversy, were here fictitiously re-enacted by characters teasingly suggestive of the original players. It was all typical, to the last details of the setting, and yet sharply individualized—a most skilful exhibition of the satirist's art, delicately but relentlessly applied. Among the French, it is true, the satirist traditionally enjoyed much greater freedom than in England; but then the English reading public (hadn't James long been of this opinion?) was much more obtuse than the French. If one were subtle enough, one could draw from the life and one's skit would pass unchallenged. So, I fancy, James may have argued. So at any rate he ventured, and so the event proved: like his own Corvick, of 'The Figure in the Carpet', 'he was prepared to out-Herod the metropolitan press; . . . he exquisitely outraged taste. Nobody ever knew it—the taste was all his own.'[142]

Incidentally, on behalf of those who, with Professors Edel and Cargill, take the governess to be a deluded hysteric, or who see a depraved sexuality in her affection for Miles, one must note that *L'Orme du mail* supplies a parallel for each of these morbidities. First there is the report of a miraculous visitation: the eighteen-year-old Mademoiselle Deniseau regularly sees the spirit of Ste Radegonde, by whose instruction she is enabled to prophesy, accurately, the fall of the Ministry, and more dangerously that of the Republic. In the interests of political stability, officials of church and state combine to suppress the prophetess:

L'inspirée de la place Saint-Exupère, désavouée par l'archevêché, abandonnée par le clergé, reniée par *le Libéral*, ne retenait plus auprès d'elle que les deux membres correspondants de l'Académie des sciences psychiques, dont l'un la tenait pour un sujet digne d'étude, et l'autre pour une simulatrice dangereuse.

Secondly, there is the murder in 'la maison de la reine Marguerite', over-heard in the fact by the cronies in the bookshop next door, and discussed by them at length. The aged widow Houssieu, miser and recluse, had been murdered by a young butcher's-boy she had seduced: 'Le crime de la maison de la reine Marguerite est d'un genre connu, classé; je puis dire d'un type classique,' says M. le président Peloux. But beyond assuring us that James was sufficiently well informed of such aberrations to have used them, if he had wished, in his own fiction, the two cases in themselves throw no light on *The Turn of the Screw*. What importance they may have for James's story lies in the way they are treated—not by direct presentation, nor by authenticated report, but in the challenge and counter-challenge of informal discussion. The Grand Guignol effects of the widow Houssieu's case are quite alien to James's scheme, but Mademoiselle Deniseau's comes close enough to that of the governess for James to have noted the method with some care. Between the honest scepticism of M. Bergeret and the equally honest orthodoxy of M. Lantaigne the feasibility of miracles in general and the credibility of miracle-workers, from Joshua to Joan of Arc, are inconclusively debated; between the dishonest pragmatism of M.

Worms-Clavelin and the over-supple diplomacy of M. Guitrel expediency is served and a decision is taken; but the rights and wrongs of Mademoiselle Deniseau's case are never determined: even the psychical experts are divided, and the author remains uncommitted. Have we here the initial suggestion for those colloquies of the governess and Mrs. Grose—those prolonged discussions, so fruitful of speculation and circumstantial detail, so reliant on intuition and so deficient in logic, which multiply scruples and inhibit action? These interlocutors are unsophisticated women, and their problems are those of a nursery world, so that the whole matter is dealt with on a lower intellectual level, more solemnly and more innocently than Anatole France handles the very minor incident of the *voyante* in his pageant of contemporary life. But the device itself is similar, and since the visions here in dispute are of central importance, the mingling of perplexity and (for readers so constituted) of fear which results becomes the prevailing atmosphere of the tale. And where all is in doubt, the credit, the sincerity of the interlocutors themselves seems questionable, whatever precautions to the contrary the author may take. This insidious doubt is not enough to destroy, or even shake, the attentive reader's faith in the narrator, but it does communicate an additional thrill of unease—one might regard it as unearned increment from Anatole France's dialectic method.[143]

But in any case James (I suggest), fortified by example, proceeded to draw his villain in the likeness of Shaw. He might feel that Shaw had himself invited such a portrayal. On Saturday, 26 June 1897, there appeared the notice of Sarah Bernhardt's *Lorenzaccio*, already referred to, and, as it happened, this play had a special, by then nostalgic interest for James: at the age of seventeen he had translated it, 'introduc[ing] some scenes of his own'. Shaw opens his review with a highly characteristic enquiry into the origins and nature of the Romantic movement. The 'great Romancers', he continues, 'were . . . pure enchanters, who conjured up a region where existence touches you delicately to the very heart, and where mysteriously thrilling people, secretly known to you in dreams of your childhood, enact a life in which terrors are as fascinating as delights; so that ghosts and death, agony and sin, become, like love and victory, phases of an unaccountable ecstasy'. And this clamant Ibsenite further admits that his criticism of these 'once dear and beautiful' mirages 'has all along been a pious dialectical fraud'. Why not restore him to his lost dreamland, where, 'spectral' as any character in *Lorenzaccio*, he could enjoy a truly 'unaccountable' esctasy of terror? The part was ready and waiting; it only remained to name the character: what better than to identify him with the actor's ruling passion? In November 1896 a much-abbreviated French version of *Peer Gynt* had been staged by the Lugné Poë company; Shaw had gone to Paris to attend the performance, and reviewed it enthusiastically on 21 November 1896. 'The humiliation of the English stage is now complete. Paris, that belated capital . . . has been beforehand with us in producing Peer Gynt.' But even London will one day see this play: 'Peer Gynt will finally smash anti-Ibsenism in Europe, because Peer is everybody's hero. He has the same effect on the imagination that Hamlet, Faust, and Mozart's Don Juan have had.' James had never seen *Peer Gynt* acted, but as early as 1890 he had read excerpts in Gosse's verse translation, and he would almost certainly have read the complete 'authorised translation' by William and Charles Archer which appeared in 1892. And when Shaw recalled the career of Ibsen's 'clever, vain, greedy, sentimental, rather fascinating braggart and egoist', a reader even moderately familiar with the text might feel that Shaw himself (as his own conduct and written testimony, let alone current gossip, presented him to the world) was in many respects 'the living image' of Peer Gynt. Hero of many amorous encounters, who always escaped untrammelled, 'with honour' as he put it, holding mere lust to be of no account; a self-taught man who had studied nothing methodically, but thought and speculated and read a bit about almost everything; who had assumed the rôle of prophet; who claimed music as his natural sphere; who from first to last courted attention by fantastic behaviour and extravagant statements; whose code was self-sufficiency, but who had never been himself: in short, a responsible human being only in appearance, in secret a would-be destructive force, a 'troll'—these aspects of Ibsen's Peer Gynt, reduced to humdrum prose, might seem to have their trivial counterpart in Ibsen's votary. As Peer Gynt, then, 'a dead man long before he died', let Shaw feature in *The Turn of the Screw*, but under the cloak of an English near-transliteration—the familiar 'Peer' restored to formal completeness as 'Peter', 'Gynt' sharpened into 'Quint'. There is a double appropriateness in this modification of the surname; for Shaw claimed not only to have distilled the 'quintessence' of Ibsen's doctrine, but also to be a musical expert. 'Quint' is the technical term for the interval of a fifth, and the composer's bogy of consecutive fifths was one of Shaw's standard examples of pedantry among musicians. So in Peter Quint the reader was offered a portrait from the life, with the name of the sitter appended—and not a creature recognized it.[144]

The author, whether relieved or disappointed, gave no sign. His references to the story, in his letters, are all depreciatory, as if intended to check rather than satisfy curiosity: it is 'a fantastic fiction', 'that wanton little Tale', 'a very mechanical matter, I honestly think—an inferior, a merely *pictorial*, subject and rather a shameless pot-boiler'. Only to Wells, who had ventured to criticize his treatment of the narrator, does he add a tell-tale phrase: 'the thing is essentially a pot-boiler', of course, but also 'a *jeu d'esprit*'.[145] By the time he comes to write his *Prefaces*, James's critical approval of the story is much less carefully dissembled: 'this perfectly independent and irresponsible little fiction . . . has the small strength . . . of a perfect homogeneity' (p. 169). And he even brings himself cautiously to hint at associations undivulged: in one case at least frankness was impossible—Shaw's position now was very different from what it had been in 1897. 'To have handled again this so full-blown flower of high fancy is to be led back by it to easy and happy recognitions' (p. 169).

Indeed if the artistic value of such an experiment be measured by the intellectual echoes it may again, long after, set in motion, the case would make in favour of this little firm fantasy—which I seem to see draw behind it to-day a train of associations. I ought doubtless to blush for thus confessing them so numerous that I can but pick among them for reference. (p. 173)

The only 'recognition' he explains to the reader is that of the Addington source for his *donnée*; but again the remembrance of Wells's adverse criticism provokes him to a justification of his method, and again the tell-tale word slips out: at that criticism, he recalls, 'one's artistic, one's ironic heart shook for the instant almost to breaking' (p. 173).

vi

What difference does an acceptance of this element of personal satire make to our understanding of *The Turn of the Screw*? It does not of course dispel the mists of surmise in which James forces his readers to grope; it does not make the story less terrifying; but it does somewhat alter the quality of the terror. Critics have remarked that Miles's confession acknowledges only verbal indiscretions: ' "Well—I said things" ' (p. 165). There is no reply to the governess's 'stern' enquiry, ' "What *were* these things?" ' (p. 167). And even though Miles thinks them to have been 'too bad' to be repeated in the letter sent from the school to his uncle, it is as a rule assumed that only typical schoolboy crudities are in question—or, as Edel puts it, 'Miles probably used words he had heard from Peter Quint. In little matters.'[146] But (granted that, out of bravado or under pressure of ragging, a child so fastidiously well-mannered might on occasion retail smut) even at Dr. Strong's, let alone Salem House, this would scarcely have procured Miles's expulsion. Yet if Peter Quint is no more than the combination of two stock characters—the subservient, insinuating valet, who has wormed his way into his master's confidence, and the drunken lecher, the rake in low life, whose flashy attractions have been too much for the virtue of a 'most respectable' governess—what more than the details of vulgar debauch can have been communicated by Miles? Quint is a thief, we are told, but he has not taught Miles to steal. And Quint is not a paederast, nor Miss Jessel a lesbian, so that their physical abuse of the children can hardly be part of the author's intention. The only other possibility, the capabilities of the two evil agents being so defined, is some form of diabolism—which might indeed comprehend practices at all levels of horror, physical or spiritual. There is not a hint, in the story, that anything of the kind has occurred; but then again neither is the possibility ruled out. Once, however, Quint and Miss Jessel are envisaged as fellow conspirators, godless revolutionaries who acknowledge neither divine nor human law, the threat to the children is at once extended and intellectualized: it becomes a matter of indoctrination rather than initiation into evil practices. The 'things said' will not then be mere puerile obscenities, but mockery and denials of authority, of social obligations, of moral and religious sanctions, programmes for disruption and violence—a precocity in error much more alarming than any 'normal' childish wickedness. Miles as boy atheist and anarchist, Flora as infantile 'new woman' would be phenomena as shocking to Victorian teachers and guardians as their presumed commerce with the dead is to the governess.

James himself was, as we say, 'unshockable' by enormities of human conduct, but, as he demonstrates again and again in his novels and stories, he had a very acute sense of fitness in personal relationships: what one might call moral trespass, the failure to respect another's individuality,[147] the exploitation or subjugation, for whatever end, of a personality and an intelligence—this was the ultimate turpitude. But latterly (and his novels of 1885–86, *The Bostonians* and *The Princess Casamassima*, are his first and most comprehensive statements to this effect) he had observed that the neglect of individual rights might be associated with a brutal contempt, masquerading as a desire for reform, of existing institutions. Even if forces so suspect and hands so far from clean could rectify public abuses, would they not in the process destroy those values, moral and artistic, which, gradually evolved and long cherished, alone justified the name of civilization? Were there not, both in life and in literature, already evidences of such destruction? Nordau's crass intolerance, no less than his standards of argument, would have disgusted James (if in 1892–93 he read *Entartung*, or in 1895 *Degeneration*, as so many thousands did); but he would not have thought Nordau's case lacked support. Shaw might rejoice in the sense of impending change, 'in the resurgent energy and wilfulness of the new spirit'; to James (an older man, and of a foreboding disposition, certainly, but with a knowledge of current literary trends much more extensive than Shaw's) it was full of menace. 'If it didn't sound British and Pharisaic I would almost risk saying that, on all the more and more showing, young and old France both seem to me to be in a strange state of moral and intellectual decomposition.' He was writing at the close of 1897, and his reflection was prompted by a novel of Barrès lately published—*Les Déracinés*, 'very curious and serious, but a gruesome picture of young France'.[148] The central theme of the novel is the debauch of young intelligences by a political theorist who, finally, turns out a corruptible politician. The irony of the case was that Barrès himself, secured (like his protagonist Sturel) by *délicatesse* and tradition against the worst effects of pernicious doctrine, nevertheless in his own career demonstrated the ethical inadequacy of *le culte du moi* to which he consecrated so much of his writing. For *L'Ennemi des lois* of 1891, that most refined anarchist, so delicately appreciative of the feelings of others, gave place in 1897–98 to the Anti-Dreyfusard, ready for expedience' sake to deny the most elementary rights of the individual. *The Turn of the Screw*, apparently, was finished some weeks before James read *Les Déracinés*; but in judging it he sums up long-accumulated impressions and assessments, social as well as literary, and his judgment has a bearing, not only on *The Turn of the Screw*, but on all the other studies of youth in the toils which occupied him from 1896 onwards.

This, it seems to me, was not an inward-looking phase, as Edmund Wilson and Professor Edel would have us believe,[149] but one of active social concern. None of these works (any more than the novels of 1885–86, strictly considered) can possibly be described as a *roman à thèse*, but in each, from an unexpected even a disconcerting angle, and with an irony which masks its force, James makes a specific criticism of contemporary society. If any moral principle can be said to emerge, it is the thoroughly Victorian one that the chief duty owed by the adult to the young is to present, in their own conduct, the example of self-discipline and respect for others' rights. Nowhere, to James's view, is this duty more imperative, and nowhere is its dereliction under licence of *le culte du moi* more conspicuous, than in the one matter of universal importance—sex. The puzzled child Maisie, like the serious-minded adolescent Nanda, is trying to discover and to play, to everyone's satisfaction, the rôle appointed for her in life. Neither of them succeeds—or rather, James takes neither beyond the preliminary failure. The reader feels a lively concern for their plight, but on that very account his attention, like their own, is directed beyond them to the actors in the scene—at times not unlike a rout of satyrs. As James himself states in his *Preface* to *What Maisie Knew*, 'The one presented register of the whole complexity would be the play of the child's confused and obscure notation of it, and yet the whole, as I say, should be unmistakeably, should be honourably there, seen through the faint intelligence, or at the least attested by the imponderable presence, and still advertising its sense' (pp. 144–45). And again, of *The Awkward Age*: 'Half the attraction was in the current actuality of the thing' (p. 102).

His specific reference here, of course, is to the intrusive rivalry of the female young; but he does not, in his novel, take the problem to its logical and, in actual fact, its usual conclusion—'the revolt of the daughter'. There is no need for Mr. Longdon's protection: Nanda has been traduced, and she has been disappointed in love, but the whole world is before her and, like the 'new woman' she obviously is, she can make her own way in it. This would have been as plain to Shaw, as to an enlightened mother such as James's friend Mrs. Crackanthorpe, or to James's intelligent and independent-minded young friend among the daughters, Alys Pearsall Smith;[150] but James himself has taken sides with the old-fashioned virtues and the 'womanly woman' of the Victorian ideal. One remembers his instinctive recoil from the indomitable will revealed and the turbulent passions hinted at in the story of Charlotte Brontë: there already, in that devout Anglican and most dutiful of daughters, was the 'new woman'; and her fictional self, Jane Eyre, claims her individual status and equal rights as boldly as any Nora Helmer:

'I tell you I must go!' I retorted, roused to something like passion. 'Do you think I can stay to become nothing to you? Do you think I am an automaton?—a machine without feelings? and can bear to have my morsel of bread snatched from my lips, and my drop of living water dashed from my cup? Do you think, because I am poor, obscure, plain, and little, I am soulless and heartless? You think wrong! —I have as much soul as you,—and full as much heart! And if God had gifted me with some beauty and much wealth, I should have made it as hard for you to leave me, as it is now for me to leave you. I am not talking to you now through the medium of custom, conventionalities, nor even of mortal flesh;—it is my spirit that addresses your spirit; just as if both had passed through the grave, and we stood at God's feet, equal,—as we are!' (xxiii, 303)

It is easy to see why the love affair central to *Jane Eyre* had to be changed both in character and in importance, if James's governess, in a situation belonging to 'the day before yesterday', were to serve as a reliable commentator. For this situation has been caused 'to reek with the air of Evil', but the evil remains mysteriously undefined except in one significant particular—the liaison of Quint and Miss Jessel. Both in *The Turn of the Screw* (for the sake of historical consistency) and, to emphasize the modernity of 'permissiveness', in *The Awkward Age* James needs an observer who can establish an antiquated standard of moral judgment. The governess can do so, correctly and in period as Jane Eyre, provided that young woman's unfeminine boldness is toned down; Mr. Longdon has to be given grandfatherly status to justify both his opinions and his mission of rescue. The latter indeed has an equivocal air; but I fancy that all James had in mind was a sentimentally acceptable conclusion, in a novelistic tradition antedating even *Jane Eyre*—the tradition which enjoins that a Burchell, a Brandon, or a Knightley, mature in years and common sense, first saves (from physical danger, misplaced affection, or misguided notions) and then takes to wife a girl barely half his age. Besides, Mr. Longdon is so obviously and so elaborately devised to spare authorial intervention, that one cannot (with Professor Edel) take him to be the 'idealized self' of Henry James:[151] as the fictional descendant of Mr. Knightley, Longdon married is credible, but not as a surrogate James. For clearly, James's own psychological inhibitions have to be taken into account here—just as they most easily explain his reticence in treating the love affairs and matrimonial problems with which, throughout his career as novelist of manners, he is obliged to deal. This was undoubtedly the more prudent course, since in the novels of the later, 'outspoken' phase, like the deaf man conversing, he often miscalculates the strength of his effects. But granted these psychological limitations, granted also the Victorian over-protectiveness and distrust of youthful impulse to which James subscribes, his view of sexual licence is neither irrational nor, where the young are affected, markedly different from informed opinion today. He notes that the child of a broken home suffers not only deprivation but disorientation; he believes that too early 'exposure' (his own word) to the emotional stress no less than the physical crudities of sex is damaging to the immature personality: modern authorities would agree with him. Dr. Waldstein, it appears, did so in 1898.

But in that gathering of shadows, *The Turn of the Screw*, menace lurks in 'the withheld glimpse' as much as in the clearly 'imputed vice', and I think it not extravagant to suppose that Paul Muniment, 'more or less honourably buried' in *The Princess Casamassima*, is (like the Princess herself) one of those characters who 'revive . . . and "walk" round [the novelist's] house of art like haunting ghosts, feeling for the old doors they knew, fumbling at stiff latches and pressing their pale faces, in the outer dark, to lighted windows.'[152] In his second and more corrupt state, he has pursued the indoctrination of a younger, more vulnerable, if more richly endowed Hyacinth, to rob him, also, of his ideals and indirectly of his life.

CHAPTER VII

Another Model for the Governess?

And it may be that we have not yet taken the full measure of James's con-
jurations in *The Turn of the Screw*. What if his governess also had a prototype in real life—not this time a living acquaintance of the author's, but a
personage contemporary with his fictional model? In short, does the rôle of
James's governess perhaps reflect that of Mlle Henriette Deluzy, *institutrice*
in the household of the ill-fated Duchesse de Praslin?

The suggestion[153] is novel and startling, but not (or not wholly) fantastic.
Quite apart from its gruesomeness and the political repercussions that helped
to make it a *cause célèbre*, the Duc de Praslin's murder of his wife (on 18
August 1847) retained a special interest for Americans, in that the *femme
fatale* its heroine, acquitted of complicity in the crime, had emigrated to the
United States. There, some eighteen months after her arrival, she had
married a scion of one of New England's most respected families—Henry
Martyn Field, almost ten years her junior. The marriage was happy, though
childless, and Mrs. Henry Field, wife of a Presbyterian divine and herself
now a Protestant, became a leading figure in the intellectual and artistic
circles of New York, so that her death in March 1875 was mourned as a
distinct loss to the community.

Among the 'comings and goings' of his years in Boston from 1864 to 1866,
Henry James in his autobiography records 'winter attempts, a little weak, but
still more or less achieved, upon New York'.[154] Again, in the spring of 1872,
he visited and reviewed the exhibition of Dutch and Flemish pictures at the
Metropolitan Museum. It is therefore not impossible that, recommended
both by artistic interests and by literary aspirations, he was on one of these
occasions introduced to Mrs. Field's *salon*, and that he could have recalled
some brief personal experience of her social graces and quality of intellect.
At the time of her death he was himself resident in New York: before his
final emigration to Europe, on 20 October 1875, he spent six journalistically
busy months there, from January to July. By January 1875, indeed, Mrs.
Field was in the last stages of a long illness, and none but old and close
friends would have been admitted to the 'levees' in her sick-room. But
whether or not he ever made her acquaintance, local gossip, supplementing
the obituary notices in the New York press, would have informed him of her
antecedents. Moreover when, three months after her death, Henry Field

published his wife's *Home Sketches in France, and Other Papers*, 'with some notices of her life and character', James reviewed the book: his observations, unsigned, appeared in *The Nation* of 10 June 1875. As an example of journalistic tact, if not as a distant foreshadowing of James's governess, with her 'note of neatness, firmness and courage', the review has an interest of its own.

This little work will have a value to many persons as a memento of a woman of much social eminence—a woman who introduced into quarters where they would otherwise (and regrettably) have been little known, those gifts and graces which we are taught to attribute to the social and conversational play of the French mind. This will be its chief value, for the papers of which it is composed are of a slight and unpretending sort. They are agreeable, however, and indicate the multiplicity of the author's interests. Some of them, at least—the private letters from Europe— were originally written in French, and we are sorry that the editor should have thought it necessary to translate them. Easily, apparently, as Mrs. Field handled English, it is probable that in her own tongue her style had a stronger savor— a savor of which her many friends would have relished a literary memorial. If the letters contributed directly to the press were written by Mrs. Field in the excellent English in which they now appear, this seems to us a remarkable literary feat. But even if they suffered certain corrections, it is perhaps not fanciful to see in them, slight and amateurish as they confess themselves to be, a trace of that natural neatness of style, that instinctive sense of shapeliness, which is perhaps the most characteristic sign of the charming race to which Mrs. Field belonged, and so many of whose virtues (even the incongruous ones) she apparently contrived to reconcile with so many of ours.[155]

Only in the last, discreetly-worded sentence is there a hint that anything beyond a conventional, literary interest attaches to these memorials. Yet if one could assume the persistence over twenty years of a mere second-hand impression of character—regarding the impress of a living personality there would be no question—the eulogies of Mrs. Field, so temperately acknowledged in James's review, *might* seem to be reflected, not in the self-portrayal of his governess's narrative, but in the admiration expressed by Douglas. In the words of the New York *Evening Post*, Mrs. Field was 'one of the most remarkable women we have ever known,—remarkable for natural strength of mind and force of character, for a variety of talents, and especially for power of conversation, for a large generosity of nature, and for an eventful history'.[156] The governess, says Douglas, 'has been dead these twenty years. . . . She was a most charming person. . . . She was the most agreeable person I've ever known in her position; she would have been worthy of any whatever' (pp. 5–6).

By the beginning of September 1847 'the Praslin tragedy' had been widely publicized in the newspapers of many countries,[157] and a series of official reports and of scandal-exploiting redactions and commentaries ministered to curiosity during the rest of the year. The course of public interest, though not its scale or rate of progress, is typified in the reactions of Flaubert. In the space of six weeks Flaubert passed from morbid inquisitiveness over undisclosed details (particularly the alleged 'révélations curieuses de l'institutrice') through a philosophic savouring of the contrasts offered between high life and persistent low instincts, to boredom—tempered, in his case, only by disgust at President Pasquier's literary style.[158] Well before 1875 *l'affaire Praslin* had taken its place in standard works of reference. In 1858, for example, it appeared in the first volume of Armand Fouquier's *Causes célèbres de tous les peuples*; and in 1875 it occupied three and a half columns in M. Pierre Larousse's *Grand dictionnaire universel du XIXe siècle*.[159] It is, therefore, reasonable to suppose that Henry James Jr. in 1875 would be acquainted, not only with the main facts of Henriette Deluzy's career, but also with the assumptions generally made concerning her moral, as distinct from criminal, responsibility in *l'affaire Praslin*. The question is whether Henry James, writing *The Turn of the Screw* in 1897, would be reminded of them.

By that time, certainly, he must have been aware of Hawthorne's allusive use of the story.[160] So insistent is Hawthorne's ambiguous giving-out, that many readers of *The Marble Faun* in its 1860 edition must, at Chapter 47, have pondered over the 'mysterious and terrible event' in whicn Miriam was suspected 'of being at least an accomplice' and must, like the future Dean Stanley, with no great effort have 'remember[ed] her name'. James makes no reference to such an identification, either in his 1879 biography or in his 1897 critical account of Hawthorne.[161] In the latter, apropos of Donatello's ridding Miriam of an 'obscure tormentor', he remarks that 'the obscurity is rather a mistake', but he offers no conjectural enlightenment. Yet even if in 1878, when James consulted him, Julian Hawthorne had not received, or did not communicate, Henry Bright's information regarding *The Marble Faun*, he quoted it in his 1885 biography of his parents; and this James undoubtedly read. At his meeting with Nathaniel Hawthorne in 1860, so Bright reported,

I told him I had heard that his Miriam (it was Arthur Penrhyn Stanley's idea) was Mdlle. de Luzzy, the governess of the Duc de Praslyn. He was much amused. 'Well, I dare say she was,' he said. 'I knew I had some dim recollection of some crime, but I didn't know what.' He added, 'As regards the last chapter of "Transformation" in the second edition, don't read it; it's good for nothing. The story isn't meant to be explained; it's cloudland.'[162]

This last evasion perhaps explains James's reticence on the subject. For Hawthorne to imply of Mrs. Field, still living, that while declared innocent of one murder, she might yet with a 'look' instigate another, would seem a rather wanton abuse of the artist's licence; and the consequential linking of Henry Field (who lived until 1907) with Miriam's champion Donatello would remain extremely awkward even in 1897. If, however, James *did* tacitly accept Stanley's identification, then in 1897 he would be supplied not only with a reminder of Henriette Deluzy but also with a safe and authoritative, if hardly laudable, precedent for his own use of living models to characterize Quint and Miss Jessel.

Even so, this would not explain why James should apply touches suggestive of Miriam's original to his narrator in *The Turn of the Screw*. Has he in fact done so? What are the resemblances, in situation or in conduct, between the Henriette Deluzy of real life and James's fictional governess? First, one might note the enlargement of prospect which the new employment confers on each: relative to our governess's youth and inexperience, Bly is as liberating to her aesthetically as the Château de Vaux-Praslin, 'ce paradis de ma vie', was to Henriette Deluzy. She repeatedly and gratefully acknowledges the contrast with her former narrow circumstances (pp. 15–19, 28–29); Mlle Henriette's letters, from her cramped *pensionnat*, so vividly recalled the 'splendides demeures' from which she was banished, that the examining magistrate found in them ground for suspicion: 'Dans cette correspondance on voit percer des espérances pour l'avenir. Vous rêvez de beaux jours, les ombrages de Praslin, votre demeure chérie, votre maison paternelle, votre paradis et vous sembliez assigner pour le printemps l'époque de votre retour.' Secondly, there is our governess's instant, passionate attachment to the beautiful children placed in her charge: she dedicates herself to their service and protection (pp. 36–38, 53–54), and her devotion never wavers, even when she is tempted to surrender her post (pp. 110–11), and when with Flora's removal half its justification disappears (pp. 140, 150, 153–54). So Mlle Henriette dedicated herself, and her devotion persisted when she was 'under notice' and after her dismissal:

Pendant six ans, jours et nuits, j'ai veillé sur eux avec une sollicitude que ne s'est pas démentie. Ces enfants m'ont aimée avec tout l'entraînement de leur âge, et moi avec toute l'affection que l'on peut ressentir au mien. J'étais sans famille, sans amis; tous mes sentiments se sont concentrés sur des devoirs qui m'étaient faciles.

That in the one case the governess fears the corrupting influence of ghosts, and in the other the importunities of a wife and mother all too real in the violence of her jealousy and resentment, makes no difference to the intensity of their concern. Thirdly, complicating this devotion, there is our governess's romantic fantasy, quite without reciprocal justification, centred on the children's guardian. So, despite six years' propinquity and a shared concern for the children, Mlle Henriette (by her own account, though not in the opinion of her French judges) cherished a merely sentimental attachment to the unresponsive Duc de Praslin:

je ne voudrais pas répondre qu'à force de voir M. de Praslin, si bon pour moi, si généreux, il ne soit pas mêlé à l'affection que j'éprouvais pour ses enfants une tendresse, une vive tendresse pour leur père, mais jamais, jamais je n'ai porté dans cette maison le trouble et l'adultère. . . .

Cette exaltation, ce sentiment de tendresse était donc partagé par M. de Praslin?

Non, M. de Praslin n'avait pour moi aucune tendresse ni exaltation de tendresse. . . .

And again: 'M. de Praslin ne m'a jamais témoigné que de l'amitié et de l'estime, et je proteste, pour dire le mot, qu'il n'a jamais été mon amant.' Fourthly, James's governess, for all her youth and inexperience, is from the outset given entire control of the children and 'supreme authority' at Bly (p. 10). In terms just as explicit Mlle Henriette was on her appointment given complete responsibility for her charges, with an authority overriding that of their mother: 'Il fut alors convenu que . . . les enfants resteraient sous ma tutelle et sous ma direction exclusive.' 'Je reçus,' she noted later, 'des pouvoirs illimités;' as her judges expressed it, 'l'autorité, qui a disparu entièrement entre les mains de Madame de Praslin, est passée dans les vôtres', to be exercised, as the dispossessed mother complained, not in the schoolroom only but 'sur toute la maison': 'Mademoiselle D. règne sans partage.'[163]

It is here that our governess's situation most closely approximates that of Henriette Deluzy; for no necessity of plot, ghostly or material, ruled that a housekeeper of genteel status should not preside in literate authority at Bly—as did Mrs. Fairfax at Thornfield, for instance. And here perhaps we have the answer to our first question. In most respects, 'supreme authority' and unrequited passion excluded, it is the orphaned, the clever and accomplished Jane Eyre, not our governess, who provides the close, the direct correspondence with Henriette Deluzy. And in *Jane Eyre*, too, the obstacle to household peace and romantic felicity is the same as at Vaux-Praslin and the Hôtel Sébastiani: the obstructive wife is even similarly 'foreign', dark-complexioned, obese, and physically powerful, and only more violently and permanently demented.[164]

Yet in all this, fiction was not imitating, but merely keeping pace with and at times simplifying life: the last folio in Charlotte Brontë's fair copy of her manuscript is dated 19 August 1847—the day after the Praslin murder. But that these accidental resemblances made for the immediate notoriety of her book, as well as for the penning of some abusive reviews, there can, I think, be little doubt. Augustus Hare tells us how, in the autumn of 1847, 'the murder of the Duchesse de Praslin had occupied every one, and we boys [at Harrow] used to lie on the floor for hours poring over the horrible map of the murder-room which appeared in the "Illustrated," in which all the pools of blood were indicated'. If it had not been for this lurid French parallel to Jane Eyre's story, and the menace of French example to English moral standards, Miss Rigby (in the *Quarterly*), writing of *Vanity Fair* and *Jane Eyre* with one eye on literature and the other on the financial plight of

English governesses, might not have been so scathing in her denunciation. Jane Eyre, consistently exhibiting 'either her pedantry, stupidity, or gross vulgarity', is (she considers) 'one whom we should not care for as an acquaintance, whom we should not seek as a friend, whom we should not desire for a relation, and whom we should scrupulously avoid for a governess', and the author, if 'a woman at all', must be 'one who has, for some sufficient reason, long forfeited the society of her own sex'. Miss Rigby was familiar with the Praslin case and disapproved of the governess: she notes that both Becky Sharp and Jane Eyre 'rejoice in that peculiarity of feature which Mademoiselle de Luzy has not contributed to render popular, viz., green eyes'. And it is with a shudder at French precedents, social and political alike, that she writes: 'We do not hesitate to say that the tone of mind and thought which has overthrown authority and violated every code human and divine abroad, and fostered Chartism and rebellion at home, is the same which has also written Jane Eyre.'[165]

It is not, however, only in *Jane Eyre* that Charlotte Brontë sounds the same note as Henriette Deluzy. There is in *Villette* (1853) the incident of Lucy Snowe's confession to a Roman Catholic priest—an incident almost exactly reproduced from the author's own experience of ten years before, and in its turn borrowed by Hawthorne for use in *The Marble Faun*. Henriette Deluzy, grief-stricken and despairing after her release, also had recourse to a spiritual adviser—the Protestant divine Frédéric Monod: Lucy-Charlotte's hours of aimless wandering, her random entry of a church, her impulse to confession are exactly paralleled.[166] The similarity of temperament —in which emotional 'exaltation' and repressive conscience were perpetually at odds—is remarkable, and it seems that the Brontë force of will and of intellect was almost as closely matched: the creative 'genius' certainly was not.

It is tempting to assume that Henry James, reading Shorter's book and reconsidering *Jane Eyre*, was also impressed by these resemblances, and whether in a considered heightening of dramatic effect, or merely to simplify the *mise en scène*, borrowed from Henriette Deluzy's true story the 'supreme authority' which made his narrator fully and inescapably responsible for her dealings with Miles and Flora. Is this assumption justifiable? By 1897 the memory of his reading in and before 1875 might have grown faint, but latterly there had been a number of publications to serve as reminders both of *l'affaire Praslin* and of its enigmatic heroine. In 1887, two years after Victor Hugo's death, there appeared the first edition of *Choses vues*,[167] and no one interested in French life and letters could have failed to read this miscellany of direct observations and gossip recorded by the most imposing figure of his age. Hugo had been a member of the *Cour des Pairs*, convoked to try the Duc de Praslin, and he reports various details concerning the governess. For instance, he quotes, apparently verbatim, the estimate of the philosopher Victor Cousin, who took part in her interrogation:

c'est une femme rare. Ses lettres sont des chefs-d'œuvre d'esprit et d'excellent langage. Son interrogatoire est admirable, . . . si vous l'aviez entendue, vous seriez émerveillé. On n'a plus de grâce, plus de tact, plus de raison. Si elle veut bien écrire quelque jour pour nous, nous lui donnerons, pardieu, le prix Montyon. Dominatrice, du reste, et impérieuse; c'est une femme méchante et charmante. (I ,277)

This is not quite the impression made by Mrs. Field in New York; and neither Jane Eyre nor the governess of Douglas's admiration could be described as *méchante*, in any sense of the word. But one thing is certain: a character, *méchante* or not, formed on such a model would be the reverse of an unbalanced neurotic. Among the picturesque details noted by Hugo, there is just one which may be directly reflected in *The Turn of the Screw*. Mlle Deluzy remained for three months in solitary confinement at the Conciergerie:

Elle se promène tous les jours à deux heures dans la cour. Elle porte tantôt une robe de nankin, tantôt une robe de soie à larges raies. Elle sait que beaucoup de regards sont fixés sur elle de toutes les fenêtres. Les gens qui l'ont vue disent qu'elle *prend des poses*. . . . Elle regarde fixement tous ceux qui passent, cherchant à observer et peut-être aussi à fasciner. (I, 278)

Is it this firmly particularized, almost cinematic scene, rather than Jane Eyre's 'rayless dungeon, with one shrinking fear fettered in its depths' (xxxiv, 488), which, after Quint has been identified, inspires the governess's curious illustration of her state of mind? 'It was the idea, the second movement, that led me straight out, as I may say, of the inner chamber of my dread. I could take the air in the court, at least, and there Mrs. Grose could join me' (p. 49). But, of course, James may not have read *Choses vues*.

   He did, however, read the first three volumes of the *Journal des Goncourt*, published the following year: in October 1888 he reviewed them at some length, and with unusual warmth of condemnation, in the *Fortnightly*—'We are confronted afresh with the whole subject of critical discretion, the responsibility of exposure and the strange literary manners of our day.' And of all the betrayals in the *Journal*, none strikes him as more odious than that of the Princess Mathilde: 'On what theory has M. Edmond de Goncourt handed over to publicity the whole record of his relations with the Princess Mathilde? . . . The liberty taken is immense. . . .' In the third volume of these memoirs, there is a passage which James found especially objectionable. Edmond de Goncourt ('or is it his brother?' asks James) grossly insults the Princess, expresses tearful contrition, and with sentimental kindness is forgiven—an incident which only a Goncourt would have made public. Immediately following this passage, but unconnected with it, comes a reminder of *l'affaire Praslin*—a brief but memorable anecdote of the Maréchal Sébastiani's reaction to his daughter's murder: ' "Ah! un moment . . . que cela n'atteigne pas ma santé!" '[168]

It is doubtful whether in 1895 James would have been tempted to read the biography and letters of Victor Cousin, newly published in three volumes. Only in the Newport days, when he and Perry 'fished in various waters', and William acquainted them with his successive enthusiasms, is there a trace of philosophical interests on Henry James's part; and youthful experimenters, attracted by Renan and the 'delightful pessimism' of 'old Schop', would have been repelled by the temporizations of *Du vrai, du beau et du bien*. By the time James himself was introduced to French literary circles, Cousin had been dead eight years and his reputation, as 'chef de l'école éclectique', even longer in decline. James's choice of 'Longueville' to name the hero of *Confidence* scarcely testifies to a familiarity with *Études sur les femmes et la société du XVIIe siècle*, published during the 1850s; and there was nothing besides, in the mass of Cousin's publications or in his political career, to inspire James with curiosity regarding his biography. If, however, James did read it, he must have come upon the letter of 18 March 1850 in which Henriette Deluzy appealed to Cousin, the most sympathetic of her judges, to write and assure Field's relatives of her innocence in *l'affaire Praslin*— especially her innocence of any liaison with the Duke. This letter, so reminiscent of Charlotte Brontë and *Villette*, would inevitably have been recalled to James's memory by his reading of Shorter's book, and would have provided as strong a link as one could desire between Henriette Deluzy and *The Turn of the Screw*. One of the concluding paragraphs is especially suggestive: the words I have italicized might seem to epitomize the story of James's governess.

Monsieur, pouvez-vous, en conscience devant Dieu, me rendre ce témoignage que je n'étais pas l'infâme intrigante qu'on a livrée au mépris du monde? Vous étiez là; vous m'avez interrogée. Vous connaissez ce misérable intérieur; vous avez pu mesurer d'un œil impartial la part que j'ai eue dans *ce sombre drame, où j'ai joué en aveugle ma destinée et celle des êtres qui m'étaient plus chers que la vie*. Vous savez que, ni l'ambition, ni l'amour du pouvoir ne m'ont donné l'influence que j'avais sur mes malheureux élèves. Vous avez vu les lettres à LUI, et vous savez qu'il ne m'aimait pas.

Unfortunately, there is no evidence nor any great likelihood that James read the work in question.[169]

There is much more likelihood that in the winter of 1896–97 he read, or at least sampled, the first, three-volume instalment of Augustus Hare's autobiography. James had made Hare's acquaintance soon after coming to London: Hare twice records meeting him at Lord Houghton's in the early part of 1877. At that time the two were to some extent competitors in the field of travel literature: Hare was already the author of four very successful books on Italy and Spain, two of which, *Days near Rome* (1875) and *Cities of Northern and Central Italy* (1876), James had reviewed for *The Nation*. In both cases, he pronounced Hare thorough but somewhat dull, with an excessive reliance on quoted impressions: 'His own powers of description, though not brilliant, are always agreeable, and he might with advantage more frequently trust to them.' But obviously Hare was 'a compiler rather than a describer', a writer of guide-books in the tradition of Murray rather than the impressionistic literature of travel to which James himself aspired and of which his *Transatlantic Sketches* (1875) had been not unsuccessful examples. It is true that Hare, being a water-colourist of some skill, could enrich these tame descriptions with charming vignettes—a practice he extended even to his biographical works, six of which had appeared, along with fifteen more 'guide-books', before he published *The Story of My Life*. James's early acquaintance with him seems not to have flourished; and although they had some interests and a number of friends in common, it is probable that, as James's country-house visiting decreased over the years, their social encounters became less and less frequent. And there must have been much in Hare's personality and writings that was antipathetic to James. But for all their differences of temperament and background, they were both snobs, active for some thirty years in the same *milieu*, and it would not have been in human nature to ignore the personal record of Mrs. Duncan Stewart's friend and biographer, of Dean Stanley's biographer and cousin, cousin moreover to so many notabilities up and down the British Isles, especially when reviewers united to censure his too-tenacious memory and unbecoming candour. If, as I have suggested, the 'gingerbread antiquity' of the towers at Bly echoes Hare's description of Ford Castle, then we have an assurance that James consulted *The Story of My Life*, Volume III, if only as a guide-book. And in that case he would not have failed to read the 'anecdotes of old times and people' (more especially those of the successive Bourbon monarchies) with which, at Ford Cottage in 1865, Lady Stuart regaled Hare. To any reader in the least familiar with *l'affaire Praslin* her account of the Duchess's supposed vision would forcibly recall the authentic details of the case. Roused from sleep in her 'great velvet bed' at Praslin, the Duchess caught a flash of green, felt a cold touch as of steel, and saw a figure 'recede and vanish'—no ghostly death-warning, as she believed, but the Duke's rehearsal, complete with green mask and dagger, of her murder a few nights later in the Hôtel Sébastiani.[170]

Now Lady Stuart's anecdote was an independent, more picturesque version of one narrated by Edmond comte d'Alton-Shée in his *Souvenirs de 1847 et de 1848*. These had been issued posthumously in 1879, as a supplement to the Count's memoirs published ten years earlier; and the personality and career of the author, a peer of France turned revolutionary, might well have induced James to read the 1879 volume. Alton-Shée gave considerable space to *l'affaire Praslin*: paradoxically enough, as he saw it (for 'aucun crime n'a été plus étranger à la politique'), more than all 'les détournements, vols, concussions qui salissent cette époque' the Duchess's murder was responsible for the downfall of the July Monarchy. His account of the crime itself is a mere summary of information supplied in the official publications; but for the events leading up to it and the motives that inspired it, he seems to have drawn on gossip current among intimates of the Duchess. Thus we read how the governess, 'gagnant la confiance du père, avait réussi à le captiver, puis à le subjuguer absolument', so that she adopted a dry and haughty tone of address to the Duchess, and how the Duke made two abortive attempts at murder (the first by poison) before his final 'acte monstrueux'. But Alton-Shée also knew of Henriette Deluzy's approach to Pastor Monod, and recounts it in sufficient detail to interest any reader of *Villette* or *The Marble Faun*, although the final inaccuracy might amuse a well-informed New Yorker:

Un dimanche, au temple, M. Monod, pasteur orthodoxe, renommé pour son éloquence, est accosté en descendant de la chaire par une jeune femme qui le suit dans le consistoire.

'Monsieur, je suis bien malheureuse; catholique, j'étais entrée dans une église, la parole du prêtre ne m'a porté aucune consolation; je suis venue ici, je vous ai écouté, vous m'avez rendu courage;' puis elle décline son nom et témoigne le désir de se confier à lui.

M. Monod accueille cette âme malade, les visites se répètent. Plus tard, elle a embrassé la religion réformée et est partie missionnaire au cap de Bonne-Espérance.[171]

Such incidental reminders, from such a variety of sources, would, I think, ensure that James in 1897 was alert to the curious parallels between the true and the fictional histories of Henriette Deluzy, Charlotte Brontë, and Jane Eyre. But for his preoccupation with the two latter he would have been unlikely to seize the connection, and still less inclined to associate with his own work a 'topicality' dead and cold for fifty years: to any but elderly readers of 1897 Mlle Deluzy would be as remotely historical as Charlotte Corday. This remote and faded sensationalism, however, was exactly to James's purpose as allusive shading in a pastiche of the 1840s. No one, it is true, would applaud its artfulness, for its use would be even less obtrusive than the fact of the pastiche itself. Indeed, to the slight if positive indications already mentioned, I can add from the text of James's story only one detail which seems directly referable to *l'affaire Praslin* and its heroine—a detail of no obvious importance, but one on which the author insists (pp. 9, 15, 18, 31, 102). That is the choice of Harley Street as the scene of the momentous interviews between the governess and her employer. As we have seen, in London of the 1840s a man of wealth and fashion might quite appropriately live in Harley Street; but allowing the suitability of the district, why not (even more splendidly) in Cavendish Square or Portland Place—and why of necessity in Marylebone at all? Was *Little Dorrit* the sole inspiration here? Or was James recalling the fact (mentioned in all the official accounts, and with picturesque circumstance by Victor Hugo) that Henriette Deluzy, banished from Praslin and the Hôtel Sébastiani, took refuge 'chez une maîtresse de pension de la rue Harlay-au-Marais',[172] and there on 17 August 1847 had her last and possibly fatal meeting with the Duc de Praslin and her charges? The Marais, till the late eighteenth century, had been the aristocratic quarter of Paris; by the mid-nineteenth century it was no longer fashionable, but was far from being the industrial and working-class quarter of the present day. Its urban past, certainly, was much longer and more brilliant and its actuality of the 1840s very much shabbier than Marylebone's, but from the latter also, though not so dramatically, high fashion was soon to retreat. Even the general site of the *rue Harlay*, the 'marsh' anciently bordering the Seine, might, to anyone curious in local antiquities, suggest that of Harley Street, built on 'ground that had formerly been a basin or reservoir of water'.[173]

It may be objected that, all told, the correspondences alleged do not amount to very much, that for the construction of an effective pastiche *Jane Eyre* alone was surely adequate, and, in particular, that to sophisticate fiction with barely-remembered fact was a waste of ingenuity. Measured by the perception of readers such as H. G. Wells the last objection would certainly be valid; but we have James's warning in his *Preface* that this tale *is* 'a piece of ingenuity pure and simple, of cold artistic calculation' in which the 'beauty' aimed at is 'the close, the curious, the deep' (pp. 172, 174). We should not, so warned, dismiss the possibility of reference beyond reference. And to read *The Turn of the Screw* with *l'affaire Praslin* 'at the back of one's head' not only deepens the contrast of horror and beauty which (on his own testimony to Dr. Waldstein) James was at pains to create, but also helps to explain certain disturbing anomalies in the conduct of the tale.

The central figures in James's *donnée* were child-victims of ghostly molestation: no particular *ficelle* was specified, though one was 'obviously' required. The election of a governess to this rôle served both verisimilitude and convenience, and both Jane Eyre and Henriette Deluzy were, so to speak, eligible. Jane Eyre's pupil, too, in a minor degree answers the specification of the *donnée*: Adèle's past associations and tutelage have been unwholesome and their effects need correction, but no shadow from the past, dark as it may lie on the governess herself, falls across her relationship with the child. This is a normal relationship, which (we understand) develops appropriately after the child leaves the schoolroom and the story. But in the reader's impression of the Praslin case, the children's existence seems bounded by the animosities and anxieties for which they are made the pretext. They are perpetually threatened by and to be protected from dangers which are never clearly defined, which apparently remain matters of suggestion, of morbid emotional excitement only, and the sinister implications of which may be discounted or magnified at will. Sudden death and the collapse of their world are in fact imminent, but the agent of destruction is their professed defender. And after the catastrophe, the children on whose behalf so much affection, solicitude, ink, and blood have been expended, simply disappear from view. So far as the contemporary records go—whether of officialdom, of gossip-mongers, or even of the devoted governess herself—they might have no future at all. In a sense, perhaps, they have not. One has observed them, briefly, in their aristocratic preserve—cherished and yet harassed young creatures in a setting of near-royal magnificence and idyllic beauty: what imaginable future, outside their paradise, could such 'little grandees' enjoy?

[Since for them] everything, to be right, would have to be enclosed and protected, the only form that, in my fancy, the after-years could take for them was that of a romantic, a really royal extension of the garden and the park. It may be, of course, above all, that what suddenly broke into this gives the previous time a charm of stillness—that hush in which something gathers or crouches. The change was actually like the spring of a beast. (pp. 28–29)

It might be at Praslin, not Bly, that the governess (with an 'exaltation' worthy of Mlle Deluzy) pictures her charges: Miles and Flora, it seems, have momentarily been replaced by little victims of a greater eminence, upon whose charmed security a brutal violence will irrupt. The transference is excusable, since the indefinably evil harassment to which they are subjected and which provokes such equivocal reactions, has very much the air of an importation from Praslin. And if the assault of ghostly agents is less brutal and less shocking than that of a live duke, it is none the less conclusive. Flora disappears, without a hint of a future; Miles dies, and the rest is discreet, artistic, and characteristically Jamesian silence. Victorian tradition demanded, Charlotte Brontë or George Eliot would infallibly have supplied, an epilogue.

Moreover the evocation of Henriette Deluzy in support of Jane Eyre characterizes our governess herself after a fashion peculiarly Jamesian. 'Est-ce qu'on ne comprend pas qu'on puisse aimer honnêtement?' Henriette Deluzy asked her judges.[174] 'She saw him only twice,' says Douglas. 'Yes,' answers James, 'but that's just the beauty of her passion' (p. 12). Or, as two more crudely realistic interlocutors put the matter, 'Her consciousness . . . *was*, in the last analysis, a kind of shy romance . . . a small, scared, starved, subjective satisfaction that would do her no harm and nobody else any good'; but it is the Lawrentian scoffers, not the object of their pity, whom James presents ironically.[175] *Amour courtois* and the ecstasy of abnegation figure strangely in a Victorian setting; yet, recollecting the long succession of James's heroines, and heroes, who 'go without'—from Ralph Touchett to Lambert Strether, from Catherine Sloper to Milly Theale and Maud Blessingbourne—one has to acknowledge a theory of life and virtue that, however mistaken or anachronistic, was tenaciously maintained. Even in so artificial a 'fantasy' as *The Turn of the Screw* Cinderella must be denied her triumph—Henriette Deluzy refines upon the 'life and character' of Jane Eyre.

CHAPTER VIII

The Turn of the Screw
and the Society for Psychical Research

i

Passion aside, it will, I think, be admitted that Charlotte Brontë's novel was generally useful in the composition of *The Turn of the Screw*, but there is one particular feature which invites special consideration.

Jane Eyre, throughout her story, constantly plays with the idea of the supernatural. As a child, locked in the red-room at Gateshead, she is overcome by frantic fear at the thought of Mr. Reed's ghost. Later, she consciously evokes romantic fancies—of ghosts, of fairies, elves, and goblins, of a spectral hound: the childhood terrors excited by servant chatter and Bessie's repertory of tales and ballads are now supplemented from a well-stocked literary imagination. And she has disturbing dreams, one at least of which (the vision of Thornfield as 'a dreary ruin') is prophetic. But she also has a waking experience of the supernatural: in her moorland refuge she hears her own name called, answers, and is heard two days' journey away in another county.[176] That is, she is both percipient and agent in a reciprocal telepathic communication.

For an author of 1897 dealing in the supernatural, such an episode was powerfully suggestive; but to understand its almost uncanny relevance to the circumstances in which *The Turn of the Screw* was produced, it is necessary to recollect certain facts in the nineteenth-century history of opinion. One tends to forget that this age of scientific investigation and industrial development was also an age obsessed by the supernatural. If the seventeenth century was witch-ridden, the nineteenth was as undeniably, if less dangerously, ghost-haunted. The period note is struck (as so often, to somewhat ludicrous effect) by Augustus Hare, welcomed in London drawing-rooms and in country-houses alike as a *raconteur*—of ghost stories. From the century's 'romantic' beginnings to its 'decadent' close (which is as much as to say, from the dawn to the sunset of 'romanticism'), ghosts crowd the publishers' lists; and if the number of editions is any guide, the accruing profits at any rate must have been substantial. The editors, the phasmatologists— for I am not here considering novelists and their inventions—are a remark-

Two views of Ford Castle

UPPER: *From the lawns—the north front with the 'new' tower (left) balancing the 'old', King James's tower.* LOWER: *King James's tower viewed from the north-west*

Stratford St. Andrew Rectory

ably mixed company. The clergymen come as no surprise: whatever their denomination or their individual bent they had a vested interest in the supernatural, and many, within the Established Church at least, had both means and leisure to pursue the most recondite interests. So, for example, we find the Rev. Henry Christmas, numismatist of repute, translating and editing *The Phantom World* by Augustine Calmet, and the Rev. Frederick George Lee, disputatious ritualist and initiator of a new Order for the Anglican Church, collecting and publishing over two decades 'examples of the supernatural'. Any compulsive writer, lay or clerical, might at some stage of his addiction turn to ghosts for his material, and folklore enthusiasts could not in honesty ignore them. So the Rev. Thomas Thiselton-Dyer among some dozen, and the Rev. Sabine Baring-Gould among near two hundred separate publications offer each a solitary 'ghost book'; and more influentially, Andrew Lang, armchair folklorist, protean journalist, dilettante of almost every branch of scholarship and practitioner of every literary form except the drama, uses his 'beautiful thin facility' on ghosts among the rest. Then again John H. Ingram's devotion both to Edgar Allan Poe and to haunted houses seems a natural coupling of interests; and for Charles Mackay, journalist and song-writer, these same haunted houses furnish a chapter of 'extraordinary popular delusions'. Given her personal history and religious convictions, it seems no unpredictable accident that Mrs. Catherine Crowe, among novels perhaps undeservedly forgotten, should produce the century's most famous ghost book; but that Robert Dale Owen should pass, by way of American politics, from New Harmony to 'the boundary of another world' and there stake a claim in ghosts, is a startling progression indeed.[177]

Among such chroniclers of the supernatural all grades of opinion were represented, from fervent belief to flat scepticism, and the motives that impelled them were almost as diversified. But whatever the point of view, and whether the ulterior aim was cash or converts, the method was invariable— the appeal to precedent by way of 'narrative illustrations'. And it was the material thus presented not, we may be sure, the arguments founded on it, that sold the books. It did not really matter under what sponsorship the drummer of Tedworth or the Lyttelton ghost 'manifested' in print; even the baldest summary could not quite eliminate nor the most florid elaboration enhance the strange urgency of Mr. Williams's assassination dream. It was the reader's 'thrill', not the writer's parade of authorities nor the mundane facts of the case, that 'attested' these stories, traditional or contemporary. And since confirmed sceptics do not read ghost books, nor require the 'truth about' Glamis or Cortachy, we may assume there existed not only an increasing number of firm believers, but also a multitude of the curious and susceptible, 'credulous' or 'open-minded' as one chooses to label them, who accepted the ever-present possibility of supernatural occurrences. As E. B. Tylor, the founder of modern anthropology, declared:

Apparitions have regained the place and meaning which they held from the level of the lower races to that of mediæval Europe. The regular ghost-stories, in which spirits of the dead walk visibly and have intercourse with corporeal men, are now restored and cited with new examples as 'glimpses of the night-side of nature,' nor have these stories changed either their strength to those who are disposed to believe them, or their weakness to those who are not. As of old, men live now in habitual intercourse with the spirits of the dead. Necromancy is a religion, and the Chinese manes-worshipper may see the outer barbarians come back, after a heretical interval of a few centuries, into sympathy with his time-honoured creed.

And as a leading influence on this 'spiritualistic renaissance', Tylor named 'the intensely animistic teaching of Emanuel Swedenborg'.[178]

But potent as this influence might be on those directly exposed to it, it was too narrowly diffused (for Swedenborgians then as now were relatively few) to produce the almost ubiquitous phenomena Tylor is characterizing. In truth, even as new scientific theory weakened the traditional certainties of Christian faith (and in the long run Tylor's own science proved as destructive as any), the new scientific technology, with its palpable but still for the majority inexplicable marvels, reinforced the old superstition. And if psychological experimentation, particularly with the effects of 'Mesmerism', opened the way to new knowledge and new practical benefits in the treatment of physical and mental ills, it also fostered charlatanism and the proliferation of new cults. From 1848 onwards, Spiritualism, which appropriately to the *Zeitgeist* and the land of its origin, made mystery practicable, not to say material, and which, with Christian Science and the more darkly picturesque Theosophy later, was heavily indebted to Mesmerism, swept America like an epidemic disease. In England, during the same period, it ran a less fevered but scarcely less pervasive course.

Women on the whole seem to have been more accessible than men to the seduction of 'media' and the wonders of the seance—a propensity not always to be explained by deficiencies of intellect or education. Mrs. Crowe was a Spiritualist before the fact; but Sophia De Morgan and Mrs. Browning were each convinced by seance manifestations that failed to overcome their husbands' scepticism. Yet Augustus De Morgan, if he reserved judgment on their spirit origin, was greatly impressed both by Mrs. Hayden's divinations and by earlier feats of clairvoyance; and Robert Browning, who interpreted the most remarkable performances of Daniel Dunglas Home as 'Sludge "the Medium's" ' calculated imposture, nevertheless was driven (as if despite himself—'You know I am not superstitious——') both to record his sister-in-law's death-warning and to acknowledge its confirmation five years later: 'Only a coincidence, but noticeable.' The most striking example of such ambivalence, however, is supplied by Charles Dickens. Under his 'conductorship' Spiritualism was denounced in issue after issue of *Household Words* and *All the Year Round*, and was mercilessly ridiculed in a contribution of his own to *The Haunted House*—indeed, the obstinately accurate 'goggle-eyed gentleman' (' "It came to me, Bosh." ') is a memorable addition to his gallery of caricatures. Yet for these same magazines Dickens not only commissioned but wrote, in all seriousness, tales and reports of the super-natural. Part IV of *Mugby Junction* ('No. 1 Branch Line: The Signal-Man') deservedly keeps its place in anthologies of macabre fiction; but as sympto-matic of a prevailing state of mind, an index of the general superstitious un-ease, his editorial confession to a premonitory dream and authentication of the ghost story 'Mrs. M.' are even more significant.[179]

It is unlikely that Edward White Benson in his undergraduate years at Cambridge, from 1848 to 1852, was influenced by the new cult; nevertheless among his 'diversions' at Trinity, as his son tells us, was 'the foundation of a "Ghost" Society . . . for the investigation of the supernatural. Lightfoot, Westcott and Hort were among the members.' And his son adds, 'He was then, as always, more interested in psychical phenomena than he cared to admit.' Now this episode in the career of the future Archbishop of Canter-bury is highly significant. Westcott was Benson's tutor, Lightfoot and Hort were his contemporaries at Trinity College, of which all four in due course became Fellows. All four were ordained clergymen, Lightfoot and Westcott in succession becoming Bishop of Durham; and Westcott, Hort, and Light-foot, to a greater degree than Benson himself established themselves as formidable scholars and theologians, renowned especially for their work on biblical texts. None of these four undergraduates was other than serious-minded and devout, and Benson at least was of untroubled Christian faith: his private diary revealed (so his son testifies) no trace of 'anything of the nature of religious doubt. I do not believe such a thing ever entered his head.' But whatever impulse beyond lively curiosity inspired the other founding members of the Ghost Society, in Benson's case (for whom 'the day was never long enough' and who even at night 'lived in fantastic and fiery dreams') there seems to have been a deeper impulsion.[180]

With Cambridge undergraduates of the next two decades the case was somewhat different: for them Spiritualism seemed to offer a hope of recon-ciling the affirmations of religion and the denials of science, and thus an escape from obsessive doubt. Three of them—who all as it happened won distinction in classics and fellowships at Trinity—became pioneers in the methodical investigation of supernatural phenomena. They were Henry Sidgwick, Frederic William Henry Myers, and Edmund Gurney—all men of great intellectual power and a high sense of duty, although of widely differing temperament. Henry Sidgwick, deeply influenced by his cousin and schoolmaster Edward Benson, as a matter of course joined the Ghost Society, and his letters as an undergraduate from 1855 to 1859 and as Fellow of Trinity till 1869 reveal him not only as a collector of ghostly evidence along traditional lines but also as a well-read and critical experi-menter with Spiritualism. There is no record of Myers's participation in these interests, nor of close friendship with Sidgwick until 1869, when his own formerly enthusiastic faith was also overthrown: then he came to rely on Sidgwick's judgment and guidance and 'resolved to pursue this quest, if it might be, at his side'. Edmund Gurney, youngest of the three (he took his degree in 1871) was not drawn into the search until in 1874, at the instigation of Myers, a new investigating group was formed, chiefly among Trinity men and their friends. The impulse at this time came from acquaintance with the 'sensitive' Stainton Moses, and from the published articles of the physicist William Crookes and the naturalist Alfred Russel Wallace—all, to hindsight, cautionary rather than encouraging examples. Despite their own personal interests and preoccupations, both intellectual and emotional, Sidgwick, Myers, and (his initial reluctance overcome) Gurney during the next six years attended seances with most of the publicized mediums, including the notorious Slade. The results were invariably disappointing. Nevertheless, when early in 1882 the Society for Psychical Research (proposed by W. F. Barrett of Dublin) was formally constituted, Sidgwick became its first president, and both Gurney and Myers members of its council.[181]

ii

It was at this stage that William James became acquainted with the three —Henry's acquaintance was of longer standing. He had met Sidgwick in February 1877, soon after his coming to London: he wrote home that 'About Sidgwick there is something exceptionally pleasant (in spite of a painful stammer). He has read *Roderick Hudson* (!) and asked me to stop with him at Cambridge.' James visited Cambridge at the end of May 1878, dined and slept at Trinity, and was entertained by the Sidgwicks. Possibly it was on this occasion that he first met Myers, with whom he became better acquainted than with Sidgwick. It was as a guest of Myers in Cambridge that he first, in 1884, met Arthur Benson; and Myers is one of the few English correspondents who seem to have read James's novels with critical attention. Given Myers's ruling passion and his natural exuberance, it is therefore fair to assume that Henry James (without any serious interest or commitment on his own part, and with no more than a superficial appreciation of the problems involved) was by 1882 conversant with the broad lines of psychical investigation as pursued by the Cambridge group, and possibly also with some of the theories tentatively evolved by them. It does not, however, appear that any close friendship had developed. That the relationship later became more intimate, and that Henry acquired greater familiarity with psychical questions was due almost entirely to his brother.[182]

William already had an interest in paranormal phenomena—as his biographer Perry expresses it, 'there was a relish for the non-normal which was deeply rooted in James's genius and philosophy'—and 1882 happened to be a year which, on leave from Harvard, he devoted to study in Europe. His support was thus enlisted from the very foundation of the new society. He became a member in 1884 and remained so till his death, being a vice president for eighteen years and president for two (1894-96). In 1884 he was actively concerned with the formation of a branch society in America; and though he did not revisit England until the summer of 1889, in the intervening years he kept up a correspondence with his friends and fellow psychical researchers there, especially with Gurney. The preference is easily accounted for. Of the three Cambridge associates, Sidgwick undoubtedly had the most penetrating intellect, and it was his sober conscientiousness which preserved the new society in many hazardous situations; but he was an academic to the core ('Of all long-winded, copious, flexible-minded, dispassionate cusses, he is the worst,' said William James) and 'pleasant' as he might be he was not easy to know. Myers brought to life and literature the ardent temperament of a romantic poet, and to his psychical research the crusading zeal of a fanatic. The combination was sometimes felt as burdensome ('Myers is the stuff out of which world-renewers are made. What a despot!' said William James) and sometimes roused active suspicion and dislike. But as to Gurney there could be no dispute—he won golden opinions from the most diverse people. An aloofness of manner, a disconcerting play of wit might sometimes mask his very real sympathy, and be misinterpreted, but such impediments dissolved on longer acquaintance. George Eliot first met him in 1873, when she and Lewes visited Cambridge: 'he was so handsome that for some time she thought of nothing else' but 'she afterwards discovered that his mind was as beautiful as his face'. Both Oscar Browning, who reports these comments, and Leslie Stephen thought Gurney was her model for Daniel Deronda. William James in 1882 was equally impressed: he found Gurney to be not only 'a magnificent Adonis, six feet four in height, with an extremely handsome face, voice, and general air of distinction about him, altogether the exact opposite of the classical idea of a philosopher' but also 'one of the first-rate minds of the time'. Gurney and William James were in fact astonishingly similar in temperament (both were 'manic-depressives' in whom periods of strenuous intellectual activity gave place to recurrent lassitude) and in their cast of thought. Both had an unusual range of interests and sympathies, and whatever the limitations of their physical constitution, intellectually they were not squeamish. There is a robustness, a sense of the concrete and practical, which is never absent from their reasoning whatever the theme. Again and again in Gurney's writing one comes on an opinion expressed or an analogy chosen with all James's vigour and quirkish originality. Clearly the author of *The Power of Sound* and the future author of *The Varieties of Religious Experience* could speak to one another, even though to the central passion of Gurney's life, music, James like his brother was completely insensitive and indifferent. Gurney's devotion to music, not to be satisfied, even after years of training and effort, by interpretation or creation (for he never achieved real competence either as pianist or as composer), came to intellectual fruition in *The Power of Sound* (1880)—'the best work on aesthetics ever published', in James's view. Disappointed as musician, Gurney had turned to medicine and, revolted by its clinical details, to law, before channelling all his energies into the investigation of combined philosophical and psychological problems. The essays collected in *Tertium Quid* (1887) reveal something of his range as well as his unconventionality of thought.[183]

On behalf of the Society for Psychical Research (he became honorary secretary in 1883), Gurney with the rest of the Literary Committee busied himself in amassing and classifying records of spontaneously occurring psychic phenomena. Because of the bulk of material forthcoming, it was decided to make separate publication of the evidence for spontaneous and experimental thought transference, or, as Myers in 1882 designated it, telepathy. Myers was a collaborator, but Gurney's main assistant in this work was a Civil Servant, Frank Podmore (an associate this time with an Oxford background), and the results of their labours were the two large volumes of *Phantasms of the Living*, published in 1886. Gurney was simultaneously conducting experiments in what he believed might be the key to the understanding of paranormal phenomena—hypnotism; and a series of articles expounding his views appeared in *Mind* and the *Proceedings* of the Society (1884–88). It is not surprising that as early as August 1883, in a letter to William James, their friend Croom Robertson, the editor of *Mind*, expressed anxiety about Gurney's health: 'would that he might . . . be weaned from the fury of this hunt after ghosts and the like, which is positively wasting him—the very body of him, I mean!' On 22 June 1888 he died alone in a Brighton hotel, and despite the official verdict of accidental death, the suspicion of suicide remained. He was aged forty-one, and he left a young wife and a six-year-old daughter. William James was deeply grieved; as he wrote to his brother,

It seems one of Death's stupidest strokes, for I know of no one whose life-task was begun on a more far-reaching scale, or from whom one expected with greater certainty richer fruit in the ripeness of time. . . . To me it will be a cruel loss; for he recognized me more than anyone, and in all my thoughts of returning to England he was the Englishman from whom I awaited the most nourishing communion. We ran along very similar lines of interest. He was very profound, subtle, and voluminous, and bound for an intellectual synthesis of things much solider and completer than anyone I know, except perhaps Royce.[184]

Henry James had not like William enjoyed a community of interests with Gurney; nevertheless they had had friends in common (the pleasantly hospitable Cyril Flower and his wife, for example), and must frequently have met. And there was no doubt a curiosity, even some degree of jealous interest, regarding this friend whom William valued so highly, which the strangeness of his death and its consequences would tend to foster. In the summer of 1889 William James, as American representative, attended the International Congress of Experimental Psychology, and on his way to Paris spent ten days with his brother in London. In the course of this visit he called on Mrs. Gurney, and afterwards, as he wrote to his wife, went 'to Brighton, where I spent a night at Myers's lodgings, and the evening with him and the Sidgwicks trying thought-transference experiments which, however, on that occasion did not succeed'. It was during this year that Alice James, now settled in Leamington, began to keep her diary; and she makes some interesting observations on William's visit and his reception in Paris. Some of her comments, however, have an interest beyond the obvious. There are references to friendly attentions on the part of Mrs. Sidgwick which Alice characteristically resented as patronizing, and which she retaliated by certain feline strokes in her private record—all details of the most petty triviality, but indirect testimony to the mounting academic 'value' of William James, as well as to the now easy, familial basis of Henry's acquaintanceship with the Sidgwick group. Again, on 5 August, between William's visits to her of 18 July and 14 August on his way to and from Paris, she notes with apparent irrelevance:

They say that there is little doubt that Mr. Edmund Gurney committed suicide. What a pity to hide it, every educated person who kills himself does something towards lessening the superstition. It's bad that it is so untidy, there is no denying that, for one bespatters one's friends morally as well as physically, taking them so much more into one's secret than they want to be taken. But how heroic to be able to suppress one's vanity to the extent of confessing that the game is too hard. . . .

Who were 'they'? The Sidgwick group, no doubt, as reported by William to Henry; and what occasioned their discussion of Gurney is suggested by Alice's entry of 12 December 1889. Henry had just returned from a stay of some weeks in Paris: 'The Archibald Groves he saw in Paris; got rooms for them in his hotel where they stopped on their way to Tangiers. He said "how the drama of life rushes on and how out of it all poor chloroformed Edmund Gurney seemed".' Kate Gurney had waited little more than the obligatory twelve months before marrying her late husband's complete antithesis, the publicist and politician, editor of the successful but not (by the Jameses) highly esteemed *New Review*—Archibald Grove. Croom Robertson, less than three months after Gurney's death, had written to William James: 'It has amazed me that a man of his power and performance should have dropt out of sight so little heeded even to so vain a world.' Now even the domestic image was obliterated—and Henry James seems to have been deeply impressed by the irony of the situation.[185]

The following autumn chance gave him his first and only glimpse of psychical researchers in the mass. During 1885 William had become interested in the phenomena produced by the medium Mrs. Piper, and in 1890 he was asked by the English society, members of which had also been conducting seances with Mrs. Piper, to give them a report of his findings. Myers invited Henry James to read his brother's paper, and Henry, 'though so alien to the whole business', consented. He begged William to 'imagine me at 4 p.m. on that day, performing in your name'. To William this was 'the most comical thing I ever heard of. It shows how first-rate a business man Myers is: he wants to bring variety and *éclat* into the meeting. I will *think of you* on the 31st at about 11 A.M. to make up for difference of longitude.' Henry was able to reply that the occasion had been a great success: 'You were very easy and interesting to read, and were altogether the "feature" of the entertainment. It was a full house and Myers was *rayonnant*.' One notes that the theory of telepathy is familiar to both brothers. Henry uses the term himself in a very similar joke to Arthur Benson, in a letter of 1895, and again in September 1897 when writing to his architect Edward Warren.[186]

One has at this point to remember that for the last ten years and more the subject had been constantly debated, at all levels of seriousness and frivolity, as of credulity and scepticism. This interest was in part a manifestation of the *Zeitgeist*; in part it had been artificially stimulated (the hand of Myers the business man is visible here) as a means of advertising the new society. The systematic collection of evidence in a 'census of hallucinations' was not begun until 1889; but from its inception the Society had invited 'communications from any person' who might be disposed to furnish 'a record of experiences', and to encourage response to this invitation, as well as the flow of new members, interim reports and tentative theories were published not only in the regular *Proceedings* of the Society, but also as articles in most of the leading periodicals—such as the *Nineteenth Century*, the *Fortnightly Review*, and the *National Review*. For example, 'Thought-reading' (1882) advanced recent demonstrations of the 'willing game' as evidence for thought-transference. Apparitions, in an article so entitled (1884), were boldly claimed as instances of spontaneous telepathy for which experiments in thought-transference might yet provide an explanation. Some dozen striking cases of telepathy were cited—one vouched for by no less of an *esprit fort* than Robert Browning; and the reader pauses in some astonishment at the following:

If further proof be needed that we have not to go to weak or hysterical sources for evidence of these vaguer and more emotional sorts of telepathic impression, we may add that our collection includes under this head accounts from two informants who, in very different ways, have obtained the highest reputation as acute and accurate observers—Mr. Henry James and Mr. J. N. Maskelyne.

To have those devil's advocates, a novelist of manners and a conjuror, testifying for the defence was indeed a score for telepathy, but one wishes the accounts had been printed. 'Visible Apparitions' (1884) continued the argument, discussing 'the various *stages of externalisation* of a telepathic impact' up to that of the '*fully externalised* phantasm', 'the orthodox *apparition*', and this time tentatively offering a physiological theory in explanation. The cited cases were as striking as before—unfortunately, in the next month's issue of the same periodical a correspondent demolished the most remarkable of them by a simple appeal to dates and facts. Again, *Phantasms of the Living* in 1886 had been cautiously received, even by friendly and instructed critics, and for the general reading public it was no doubt completely discredited by an article in the *Nineteenth Century* of August 1887. Here a Scottish lawyer asked 'Where are the Letters?' and found that, although the existence of documentary proof was sometimes alleged, in '*not one*' of the hundreds of cases were the 'probative documents' cited: in default of any other solution he concluded that 'this whole class of stories is without real foundation'. Gurney's 'Reply' in October convincingly answered the main charge (ordinary human beings are *not* record-conscious) but, in its candid admission of evidential weaknesses, it probably failed to repair the damage to the Society's credit—as it certainly failed to convince the legally-trained critic himself. No doubt in all this (and my examples indicate only a few heads of a ramifying controversy) there was much to amuse an uncommitted observer such as Henry James, though perhaps the sheer bulk of it would work to stifle rather than stimulate the creative imagination.[187]

But in 1891, it seems, the case was altered. William James's visit of 1889 must have been partly responsible, giving his brother fresh light both on the Sidgwick group and on their pursuits; for it is a reasonable conjecture that Henry's expressed dislike of English academicism, which stood in the way of personal intimacy, would also qualify his attitude to research thus sponsored. But, seen as congenial to William, both the researchers and their enquiries would gain a new significance for Henry. And the once-outstanding member of the group, now so mysteriously removed, Edmund Gurney, seems to have laid hold on his imagination. Now, of all times, his curiosity would be roused by that dauntingly massive work *Phantasms of the Living*, which his scientist-philosopher brother thought might be 'the beginning of a new department of natural history', and which the merest sampling would reveal (this, even its lawyer assailant conceded) as 'the best book of ghost stories in the English language'. Moreover his own brief contact of October 1890 with the Society for Psychical Research had not only given him a closer view of matters currently under investigation, but also, pretty certainly, introduced him to the official record of these. More than twenty years ago Professor Roellinger argued, from indications in his *Prefaces* and in the text of *The Turn of the Screw*, that 'James had read and studied the reports of the Society'. James, it is true, had not joined the Society as member or associate, so that he would not, as of right, receive either its privately circulated *Journal* or its annually published *Proceedings*, by 1897 amounting to twelve volumes. But we know that besides those copies of the *Proceedings* accessible in public libraries or through purchase, complimentary copies were distributed to persons other than members, and James may have enjoyed this privilege. If he did, one may be sure that his use of these volumes (in which the 'narratives' are stuck like plums in a mass of experimental detail, statistical analyses, and wordy theorizing) would be no more than desultory. As a mere artistic amateur of the supernatural, quite without scientific leanings, he would rarely feel the need to supplement the information to be gained as a matter of course in general conversation or from casual reading. No one, free from academic obligation, would willingly 'keep up with' the reports of a society to whose 'whole business' he felt 'alien'—least of all, surely, the author of 'The Great Good Place'. But in October 1890 James had obligingly lent his presence and made a sacrifice of his time for the benefit of the Society for Psychical Research; and in courteous acknowledgment of this service, no less than as a token of friendship, he would early in 1891 receive a copy of the Society's *Proceedings* for 1889–90, Volume VI in the series. Further, in 1893 he would most probably receive a copy of Volume VIII, for this contained a sequel to the reports with which, as William's deputy, he had been briefly concerned. And again (although in this case there was no motivation of personal or family involvement) in 1894 or later curiosity might very well lead him to explore Volume X, some four hundred pages of which were devoted to the Society's much-trumpeted, long-awaited report on its 'census of hallucinations'. There are a number of indications, which to my mind fall just short of proof, that James did in fact consult this volume; but concerning Volumes VI and VIII there can be no dispute. These two volumes he certainly read, in part at least, just as (before September 1897 if not earlier) he read portions of *Phantasms of the Living*: his own works supply the proof.[188]

iii

In 1891, after a lapse of some fifteen years, James turned once more to supernatural themes for his stories, and certain practical reasons for this change and its timing have already been suggested. But we have just seen that by the nineties 'the supernatural' was a much wider category, offering a more sophisticated choice of theme and handling, than had been the case in the seventies. The author was not forced to change his ground, because there had been no *general* change in taste—the traditional ghost story was still popular; but he could if he so chose make his appeal to a new class of readers, expert in levitations and muslin materializations, to whom the ghostly was matter for speculative curiosity rather than terror, or he could in one operation try to enchain both the old and the new 'faculty of wonder'. Before considering James's method in *The Turn of the Screw* it will be directly helpful to examine the half dozen earlier tales, any one of which may offer a *point de repère* (as the psychical researchers are fond of saying) for some underlying assumption, some utilization of sources, some detail of procedure in the later and much more elaborate composition. James's first essay in this new era of the ghostly was 'Sir Edmund Orme' (November 1891), and this story offers such a curious and illuminating parallel to the weighting of mystery with topicalities in *The Turn of the Screw*, that it demands more than a passing reference.

What is one's instinctive action on first receiving the annual report of a newly-encountered Society? One turns to the list of members. Henry James seems to have done just this with Volume VI of the SPR *Proceedings*. He would note that, both in England and in America, a remarkable number of artists, writers, financiers, and society hostesses (many of them personally known to him), as well as the expected scholars and scientists, were helping to promote psychic research. Incidentally, he would note that one of the three Gurneys listed as members was the widow of Russell Gurney, formerly Recorder of London, Edmund Gurney's uncle and guardian, and (with a certain quickening of attention) that she lived at 3 Orme Square, Bayswater. For this was familiar ground to Henry James. Orme Square, fronting Bayswater Road, was little more than the length of the Broad Walk removed from his own flat in De Vere Gardens, and not only (as he tells us in the essay 'London') was it his frequent diversion to take 'a purely rustic walk from Notting Hill to Whitehall . . . a most comprehensive diagonal', but he also had a more intimate, and (it came to be) nostalgic, association with the whole Bayswater street scene. In his memorial essay on George Du Maurier he records that

year after year—with a year sometimes ruefully omitted—[Du Maurier] had, for three months, a house in London, and a Sunday or, as in town it was likely to be, a week-day reunion took the form of an adventure so mild that we needed the whole of a particular matter to make it often, at the same time, so rich: a vague and slow peregrination of that Bayswater region which served as well as any other our turn for speculation and gossip, and about his beguiled attachment to which— with visions of the 'old Bayswater families'—he was always ready to joke. It was a feature of this joking that, as a chapter of experience for a benighted suburban, he made a great circumstance of the spectacle of the Bayswater Road and of finding whenever he could a house that showed him all that passed there.

James would certainly have been aware of the relationship between Edmund and Russell Gurney: failing any other source of information, there was the

Dictionary of National Biography—Volume XXIII 'Gray—Haighton', including Croom Robertson's obituary of Edmund Gurney, had appeared in July 1890. And though Edmund himself had never lived in Orme Square, to any member of the SPR let alone any acquaintance of the family, the name would carry a 'Gurney' association. 'Sir Edmund Orme' therefore constitutes a not-impenetrable pseudonym for 'Edmund Gurney', but one that would not I think have occurred to James without such a reminder as the SPR list of members provided. It is true that this list was reprinted in all the annual volumes, but in other tales of 1891–92, which are not at all ghostly, James makes use of isolated details only the sixth of these volumes could supply. Mr. Offord, in 'Brooksmith' (May 1891), as he lies in bed wearing 'a curious flowered and brocaded *casaque*', his head 'tied up in a handkerchief to match', reminds the narrator of the dying Voltaire. The first article in Volume VI, Myers's 'On Recognised Apparitions occurring More than a Year after Death', contains an account of an experience at the Château de Prangins, in Switzerland: the apparition of 'a tall, thin, old man, in a long flowered dressing-gown', 'seated and writing at the table in the middle of the [bed]room' is identified as Voltaire, who 'in extreme old age, used often to visit this Château'. Again, 'Lord Beauprey' (April–June 1892), in 1893 retitled 'Lord Beaupré', owes the name, not to any of the lists in the *Notebooks*, but to the address of a lady who communicates another narrative given at length in the same article, and who writes from 'St. Anne de Beaupré, Quebec'.[189]

But James's main concern would be the report he had himself delivered: in Volume VI it is appended to a detailed 'Record of Observations of Certain Phenomena of Trance', over two hundred pages long, made during Mrs. Piper's seances in England from November 1889 to January 1890. The spirit whose authentic presence would have been most welcomed by the sitters was that of 'Mr. E.', otherwise Edmund Gurney; but when Mr. E. announced himself, as he did some eight times during these English seances of 1889–90, and several times during sittings in the house of William James earlier, there was (to quote the latter) not 'the slightest inner verisimilitude in the personation'. Even so flatly rendered, however, there were communicated 'facts' so 'private' that although these were known to the sitter, or if unknown to him 'verified through a common friend', no details could be given in the printed record. Two whole seances with Myers and the details of Mr. E.'s 'long conversation' with Lodge were thus suppressed; and for further security, these portions of the record were destroyed. Richard Hodgson, however, William James's close friend and psychical collaborator in America, later indicated that, on the basis of certain facts not generally known, he himself was convinced of Gurney's suicide. Mrs. Sidgwick, who some twenty-five years afterwards discussed the matter with Lodge, ventured no supposition regarding Hodgson's informant; but surely it can have been none other than William James. During his 1889 visit to Europe he had ample opportunity for gaining, at first hand from Myers or Sidgwick, a knowledge not only of their ante-Piper fears and surmises but also of the 'facts' which then seemed to justify them. Alice James's comment is evidence that he did so, and also that he communicated his knowledge to Henry. Moreover in 1890, at the conclusion of the seances with Mrs. Piper, Myers might well disclose to Henry personally, in strict confidence, matters which in writing to William he defined only by negatives: the principal secret revealed (it is to be inferred that there were more than one) was 'nothing about his *death*, nor about his *wife*—but a matter wh. cd. not be guessed at, rightly or wrongly'. Further, it is quite possible that during William's brief visit in September 1891 (to take farewell of his dying sister, and incidentally to attend the London first night of *The American*) the matter was raised once again between the brothers. It may have been on this occasion also that Henry was forewarned of details concerning his own family revealed by Mrs. Piper during her American seances. The reports of these seances were even then being assembled for publication, and would ensure his anxious consultation of SPR *Proceedings*, Volume VIII, some twelve months later. His predictable annoyance at 'the "Kate Walsh" freak' (as William James designated it) and Mrs. Piper's gropings among the 'cousinage', must also have led him, apprehensively, through the further series of 'unpublished' American cases printed by Myers; for there, to happy effect, he encountered the name of a New England mesmerist-healer and seer—Wilson Quint. But for the time being he was concerned with the mystery of Edmund Gurney. Remembering the extreme fear of publicity, or 'mania for secrecy' as Shaw in another connection expressed it, which governed most Victorians, one is reluctant to suppose that any very damaging 'facts', apart from the confirmation of suicide, were suppressed, but the very obvious censorship of the 1890 reports was certainly of a nature to fan suspicion and provoke enquiry. In any case, whatever his warrant, or for that matter his purpose, James in his story covertly hints at an undisclosed motive for Edmund Gurney's suicide.[190]

The story is set in Brighton, and despite James's assertion (*Preface*, p. 261) that 'the old, the mid-Victorian, the Thackerayan Brighton' was intended, his illustrator in 1891 pictured, as every reader's imagination has done since, a Brighton strictly contemporary. Nevertheless the setting emphasized the desired note—'that of the strange and sinister embroidered on the very type of the normal and easy' (ibid.). The ghost of Sir Edmund Orme haunts (whether protectively or menacingly is not quite clear) the twenty-two-year-old daughter of a still beautiful widow of fifty-five. The narrator is in love with the pretty daughter, and because of his feeling for her becomes aware of the ghostly presence, hitherto visible only to the mother. The narrator calls the apparition

a personage, because one felt, indescribably, as if a reigning prince had come into the room. He held himself with a kind of habitual majesty, as if he were different from us. . . . He stood there without speaking—young, pale, handsome, clean-shaven, decorous, with extraordinary light blue eyes and something old-fashioned, like a portrait of years ago, in his head, his manner of wearing his hair. He was in complete mourning (one immediately felt that he was very well dressed), and he carried his hat in his hand. . . . I could see that he had no capacity for embarrassment. One had met people of that sort, but never any one with such a grand indifference.

The ghost appears (correctly dressed for the occasion) at all hours and seasons, and in a variety of settings, indoors and out of doors, and not always in Brighton: when the mother and daughter and the narrator visit Tranton (strongly suggestive of the Flowers' country home Aston Clinton, near Tring) Sir Edmund Orme is a visitor also. It is at Tranton that the lover first sees him and that the mother discloses his history. At the instigation of her family she had consented to marry Sir Edmund Orme, who was in love with her, but whom she did not love, and at the last moment jilted him for Captain Marden. This was a case of love at first sight: 'It wasn't for interest, or money, or position, or anything of that sort. All *those* things were his [Sir Edmund's]. . . . I threw him over, and he took something, some abominable drug or draught that proved fatal. It was dreadful, it was horrible, he was found that way—he died in agony.' Five years later she had made a happy marriage with Captain Marden; but on her husband's death, 'about seven years ago', she began to see the ghostly Sir Edmund accompanying her daughter Charlotte, who had just 'come out'. It is gradually borne in upon the narrator that Sir Edmund desires to protect *him* from heart-break at the hands of a flirt. When, after the three months of silence Charlotte has imposed on him, the narrator again pleads with her and she seems about to refuse him, Sir Edmund appears to the terrified girl herself. Maternal sympathy (or telepathy) communicates a fatal shock to the mother, who before she dies tries to secure her daughter's promise to accept the narrator. At this point Sir Edmund makes a final appearance, and sends the girl shrieking into her lover's arms. Simultaneously the mother dies, and the 'wail' that is heard, an 'articulate sob . . . like a waft from a great tempest', perhaps marks the departure of an 'exorcised and pacified spirit'.[191]

Now it strikes me that as a 'haunt' Sir Edmund Orme is less than convincing, while as an evocation of Edmund Gurney, like Mr. E., he is without 'the slightest inner verisimilitude'. In life, Gurney seems to have been as free from pettiness as a fallible mortal could well be—of a disposition singularly magnanimous and trustful, as well as compassionate. That from such a nature could emerge a persecuting spirit, implacable in resentment of his own wrong, is a supposition either horrifying or ridiculous. Only the identifying 'facts'—the name, the appearance, the 'money' and 'position', the wife's girlhood poverty, the Brighton setting, the death by suicide—link this 'E.' with the Gurney of real life. It has been argued,[192] I think unconvincingly, that Gurney committed suicide because of his discovery that, through the trickery of a collaborator on whom he relied, his labours of the last six years had been invalidated. That trickery occurred, so as at least partially to discredit Gurney's experiments in hypnotism, is a reasonable inference from all the evidence assembled. What has not been demonstrated is that Gurney discovered it. One is tempted to echo the critical Scotsman and ask 'Where is the letter?'; for that on 21 June 1888 Gurney received a letter of any kind from Brighton, catastrophe-heralding or not, depends on the unsupported testimony, recorded over seventy years after the event, of one person, Gurney's daughter, who was little more than six years old at the time, and who had no direct knowledge of the circumstances. 'What Mother said', though no doubt wholly self-justificatory, and possibly sincere, is not evidence. What is interesting, if not perhaps edifying, is that in the story of 'Sir Edmund Orme' we have, expressed by a contemporary, a suspicion perhaps as ill-founded as Mr. Hall's theory—the veiled and carefully distorted suggestion that Kate Gurney was responsible for her husband's suicide.

Very little has been recorded of Kate Gurney, and nothing to her discredit; but there is a tone (whether of reserve or of apology it is hard to decide) in the tributes to her beauty and to her exemplary conduct both before her marriage (when 'she was very poor' and 'worked . . . to help her mother and educate herself') and as a wife (when in spite of 'many dark days, also hours of unavoidable loneliness . . . her devotion to her husband never flagged') that suggests she claimed the approval and sympathy of older women rather too insistently, by unsolicited and rather embarrassing confidences. There is the fact of her remarriage, and another fact—that she made no contribution whatever, as the sorrowing widow usually feels obliged to do, to her late husband's memorial, the 'Edmund Gurney Library' established by the Society for Psychical Research; but the only hint of adverse gossip is that which occurs in Myers's letter to William James. If Henry James really was persuaded that Gurney killed himself 'to oblige', or because he was driven to despair by his wife's transfer of affection, then his own resentment of the 'flirt', which comes out in so many of his stories ('Louisa Pallant' of 1888 is the most striking example), his own sympathy with suffering, and his anger (expressed also in 'Owen Wingrave') at the waste of human potentiality, might find an outlet in such an oblique accusation. It would 'outrage taste', certainly, but it would be explicable on the grounds of strong feeling. If, however, he has used these identifying details merely to give piquancy to a rather trite novelistic situation (barring the ghost, it exactly reproduces that of 'Louisa Pallant', and with the ghost, its essential features were noted for use as early as 1879), then one can only say that as an artist James could at times be both irresponsible and insensitive. At any rate (and this is my chief reason for dealing with it at such length) the personal reference in 'Sir Edmund Orme' should make my identification of Quint more readily acceptable: personally directed satire was not, it appears, such an aberration from James's practice as the single example might allow one to suppose.[193]

Apart from its topical relevance, however, and considered on its merits as a ghost story, 'Sir Edmund Orme' effectively illustrates the difficulty of the genre in its new form. To be psychologically plausible, Sir Edmund's apparition must be explained as the 'externalization' of Mrs. Marden's remorse. It is associated exclusively with her daughter; therefore, still to keep on terms with psychology, the latter must for Mrs. Marden embody the wrong she herself has done Sir Edmund (by defrauding him of the satisfactions of marriage and parenthood), and the ghost therefore must represent her fear of retribution in and through her daughter—by ingratitude, it might be, or estrangement, or death. But this, it seems, is not the case. The daughter is threatened because she has inherited her mother's faults of character: she is a danger to society, as it were, and as soon as her potentialities are realized, she must be frightened out of exercising them. In 'Louisa Pallant' it was the mother who thus analysed and, whether from remorse or out of spite, opposed her daughter; but here the mother is only anxious to protect her 'innocent child'. So, unless Mrs. Marden is at heart inimical to her daughter (an ambiguity which might, perhaps, be carried over from 'Louisa Pallant'), we have in Sir Edmund not a modern, but an old-style, revenging ghost, and one of multiple intention—bent on bringing Mrs. Marden to justice (and so inexorably as to be 'pacified' only by her death), on restraining the daughter, and on protecting the suitor: he is not so much a modern representative of the Eumenides, as a spirit policeman. To what extent dimly apprehended and almost forgotten Swedenborgian theory might account for such a conception, it is impossible to say; but at any rate there is some confusion, which the author does not attempt to resolve, in the motivation of the ghostly appearances. What the author *has* done, with all a conjurer's guile, is to distract the reader's attention from this problem of ghostly logic, first of all to the reassuringly prosaic circumstances of the mystery—a colourless social round in the most cheerful and banal of settings—and then to the *details* of the manifestations. The ghost is at first mistaken for a living person, so materially complete is the impression conveyed; it appears unpredictably, at irregular intervals; its dress varies according to circumstances; it is mobile, entering a room like a living person; its attitudes and gestures vary—it may, for instance, have its back turned to the percipient; it does not slowly dematerialize or dissolve, it merely ceases to be present. The least typical of these features is that the ghost changes its clothes, and yet even this may be paralleled in the growing record of authenticated apparitions. However large the company assembled, only two persons see the ghost, and this limitation of percipience might be called standard in all the literature on the subject, ancient or modern. Here it offers by implication a conveniently up-to-date explanation of the phenomena—telepathy is operating between the mother and the suitor through their common concern for the daughter. The daughter, however, the centre of the psychic storm, perceives nothing until her own emotions are aroused.

'Sir Edmund Orme' thus exhibits the old and the new spirit lore in a kind of rough joinery. Where I think it fails (although this is not the general estimate of critics) is in the extent to which the sacred terror is overborne, smothered, by the too material commonplace of the 'authenticating' circumstances, and in the unacknowledged contradictions of the motives alleged. In 'Owen Wingrave' (November 1892) James has avoided these particular difficulties by keeping his ghost strictly non-apparitional: he has not here the burden of description on two levels, of realism and of terror. And for greater ease, his ghost is the familiar, old-style, haunting ancestor. But James has purposely subtilized this motif: the murdering ancestor, the reputed haunt, was himself the victim of an impersonal, deadly force, still to be encountered in the haunted room. This family ghost, in truth, is nothing but the emanation of the family's homicidal addiction to military glory, and as a mere picturesque symbol it is both superfluous and a falsification of the real substance of the tale. In the young rebel defying tradition, protesting against wilful waste of human life and powers, in the conventionally ferocious parent, and in the still more formidable aunt and sweetheart, serving with insane devotion the altars of their blood cult, James has produced characters of a realistic force that makes his symbolism as unnecessary as a lamp in daylight. One might raise other, minor objections: Spencer Coyle, for example, the socially acceptable London 'crammer' welcomed by a family so haughtily conservative, is one of James's more unlikely 'reflectors'. But the central, the exasperating flaw (as Shaw perceived) is James's refusal to deal realistically with a problem so vital and so solidly introduced. He has taken a short cut through the symbolic to a conclusion which would otherwise have required some labour to reach. His *Notebook* entries plainly confess this: the '*haunting* business' was not part of 'the idea of the *soldier*' as it originally presented itself, but was a device worked in to illustrate and typify a conflict which, if 'psychologically' treated, his magazine readers would have understood 'no more than a donkey understands a violin'.[194]

James wrote four other tales of the supernatural before he composed *The Turn of the Screw*, but in all of these he kept on terms with the new psychical research. In 'Nona Vincent' (February 1892), a tale which rather embarrassingly fictionalizes James's half-success with *The American*, the true, the 'psychological' subject is the competition of his two women friends for possession of the dramatist; but the latter's single hallucinatory experience usefully bridges the gap between the false climax (the disappointing first night) and the real, but delayed climax (the success following Mrs. Alsager's intervention). It is no more than an ingenious device of construction, but it nevertheless meets the new psychical requirements: the dramatist's vision of his embodied heroine coincides with Mrs. Alsager's personal demonstration of this ideal to her younger rival. Like Strauss's Marschallin, Mrs. Alsager gracefully bows out of the contest, but she does so (in 'vague, clear-coloured garments') telepathically.[195]

The next tale in this series, 'The Private Life' (April 1892), treats the supernatural with unusual levity. James produced only one other ghostly tale in a comparably light-hearted vein—'The Third Person', published in 1900, and therefore not strictly within the limits of this enquiry. Here a family ghost of the traditional sort tries to enliven the monotony of the after-life by 'haunting' his two elderly kinswomen into a repetition of the crime of smuggling for which he was hanged. Beyond the use of Rye as a setting, there is no discernible autobiographical reference, and the whole treatment, but especially the *dénouement*, is sedately humorous. 'The Private Life' is, as James described it, 'a rank fantasy' inspired by the observation that a socially impressive figure (such as Lord Leighton) might be a nullity as an artist, and that a great writer (such as Browning) might be personally undistinguished. The piece is an extravaganza on the theme of double personality—as this is discussed, for example, by Myers in his review of Max Dessoir's *Das Doppel-Ich* for Volume VI of the SPR *Proceedings*. James plays with a number of suggestions such as are there advanced. If genius is a function of the subliminal self, or subconscious, and this latter may operate independently of the waking consciousness, and if hallucinations are produced by the creative activity of the subconscious, why may we not have on the one hand a phantasmal Vawdrey/Browning going through the motions of living while the real creative self works undisturbed, and on the other hand a Mellifont/Leighton, a seeming artist who is the mere projection of other people's idea of him, and who has no creative identity at all? The Mellifont pictures, like the man himself, take shape only in company, as the reflection of someone else's imagination.[196]

With 'Sir Dominick Ferrand', originally called 'Jersey Villas' (July 1892), James reverts to serious, if melodramatic, use of the new psychical lore. Here, to carry his favourite theme of 'the *responsibility* of destruction', he provides enough excitements and coincidences to furnish a whole Wilkie Collins novel. Telepathy is conspicuously in operation, and for the first time James introduces, as heroine, a 'sensitive', who is also significantly a musician—a skilled pianist and a composer of songs. But her latent faculty, which seems to be partly clairvoyant, is roused not so much by the hero, as *through* him by the letters compromising her dead father he has just discovered. '[S]he had been seized with an extraordinary, irresistible impulse'—and she comes to the hero's door at the very moment of his discovery: 'Some secret sympathy had made her vibrate—had touched her with the knowledge that he had brought something to light.' And her plea on sight of the mysterious packets (for she never sees the letters nor learns who wrote them) is ' "Burn them up!" ': she feels ' "as if something or other were in peril" '. But, the letters once safely burned, 'The sensibility, the curiosity they had had the queer privilege of exciting in her had lapsed with the event as irresponsibly as they had arisen.' Only the hero, and of course the reader, ever learn that their exercise has been the unconscious performance of a filial duty on the part of Sir Dominick Ferrand's daughter. The case is not, one fears, likely to have been accepted as veridical by the Society for Psychical Research. Myers, especially, might have recognized it as an adaptation of a case he had himself reported, from a Continental source, in Volume VI of the SPR *Proceedings*. There the discovery of a missing will 'in a secret drawer (Fache)' of '*a chest of drawers* (armoire)' coincided with the announcement of its whereabouts, through a spirit manifestation, to a friend of the testator. It is perhaps worth remarking that all the personal names in James's story are taken from *Notebook* lists, except those of the landlady (Mrs. Bundy) and of the hero (Peter Baron). The landlady's surname appears in the list of SPR members; that of the hero may have been suggested by the case just mentioned, where all the participants are of high degree, including no fewer than five separate barons, and the title itself is repeated eighteen times.[197]

In the three stories I have just considered the paranormal experiences recorded do not entail the intervention of the dead—unless the 'horrid' fragrance detected by the heroine in his letters indicates the mortuary presence of Sir Dominick Ferrand himself. But of course what revolts her fine sense is the odour of moral corruption only, and I fancy that in this passage it is the melancholy of Shirley rather than the macabre of Edgar Allan Poe James wishes to suggest. In 'The Way It Came' (May 1896), renamed 'The Friends of the Friends' for the New York Edition, the theme is the apparition of the dead to the living, and it is treated wholly on the basis of telepathy. Indeed the apparatus of verification and explication is so elaborate that the experience itself is thrust into the background. In an introductory section each of the participants is given, as it were, a certificate of proficiency; and each of the test cases is authenticated in a manner to rejoice the heart of a psychical researcher, and to satisfy even a Scottish lawyer. The woman, travelling abroad and visiting an art gallery, had suddenly encountered the figure of her father, which as suddenly vanished: her cry ' "Papa, what *is* it?" ' was heard and her distress witnessed by the 'old custodian' and her companions; and the coincidence of her father's death that morning was established by a telegram received the same day. The man, as an undergraduate at Oxford, had been visited by the phantasm of his mother: 'He wrote to her that night, telling her what had happened; the letter had been carefully preserved. The next morning he heard of her death.' Nothing in the tale which follows has this clarity and precision. The two sensitives constantly hear of one another but never meet: 'It really took some lurking volition to account for anything so absurd.' But at the moment when a meeting seems possible a jealous 'manœuvre' of the narrator, the man's *fiancée*, prevents it; and indeed a meeting at this stage would have been too late, for the woman is already dying. Nevertheless on the very evening of her death, whether 'in the body' or as a willed projection of her desire to see him (the question is debated but never settled), she visits the man. The presence is so lifelike that he can describe minute details of her appearance, although he had never met her previously. The result is that, as inferred by the narrator and admitted by the man (but never, of course, stated by the author), a spiritual love affair, a nightly communion of souls ensues. The narrator in her 'unextinguished jealousy' breaks the engagement, and six years later the man himself dies: 'it was a response to an irresistible call'. Merton Densher does not die, but in other respects the conclusion anticipates that of *The Wings of the Dove*. And it should be emphasized that, jealous as the narrator shows herself to be, this very correspondence (quite apart from the man's verbal admissions) bears out her interpretation of his case. There is, incidentally, nothing to connect her with the governess in *The Turn of the Screw* beyond her unshakeable conviction that her interpretation is correct, and surely, though 'feminine intuition' may seldom be justified by the event, as an adjunct to feminine obstinacy its use is almost as common in fiction as in life.[198]

Only once, therefore, in the six ghostly tales composed between 1890 and September 1897, does James content himself, and then allusively, with a traditional haunt. The apparition in 'Sir Edmund Orme' is a somewhat uneasy compromise between old terrors and new mysteries. Three of the remaining tales deal with these mysteries as complications of living experience; and 'The Way It Came' inferentially extends their operation to discarnate personalities. Indeed, for the space of this one tale James has been willing to envisage a situation in which the recorded phenomena and their speculative interpretation not only mimic the forms of current psychical research, but also mirror the dearest hopes of the researchers: 'The Way It Came' might almost have carried the dedication 'for F. W. H. Myers'. With diffidence (for I am well aware that it is illustration rather than precept to which his visualizing imagination responds), I would as a possible explanation suggest that, before 21 December 1895 and the first notation of his *donnée*, James had consulted the 'Report on the Census of Hallucinations' in *PSPR* Volume X for 1894. Here the new records of experience cannot greatly have impressed him; he would certainly disregard the statistical computations which had been the main purpose of the undertaking; but from the brief, systematic descriptions and analyses of phenomena, and the equally brief and matter-of-fact theoretical discussions (aided not a little perhaps by an elaborate table of contents), he might get not only a clearer view of the subject as a whole, but also a closer grasp of the conditions imposed by investigators. And to correct any impression of their uniform objectivity and caution, here also he would find Myers asserting his individual freedom to theorize (Appendix G, 'A Proposed Scheme of Apparitions', pp. 415–22), and warning the reader against a too-facile dismissal of post-mortem agency:

The dead, for the most part, are beyond coincidences. If a departed spirit appears, he must, I suppose, appear when best he can; he cannot show us his diary and mark his hour; and if we have accustomed ourselves too strictly to attending only to phantasms which bear witness to an immediate fact we may sweep into the limbo of subjective hallucinations certain phenomena which really indicate an extra-terrene source. (p. 416)

Some such reminder, at this date, would most easily account both for the particular quality of 'The Way It Came', and for James's renewed interest, after a lapse of more than two years, in the fictional possibilities of the supernatural.

iv

In any case, whether or no *PSPR* Volume X contributed to the result, a familiarity with the type of evidence being accumulated, a general acquaintance at least with the theories propounded to explain it, and an awareness of the hope within the alleged, scientific purpose have all been acquired well before James writes *The Turn of the Screw*.

But in none of the three tales in which spirit survival is the working postulate, does James make his own position clear: more than this, in no other section of his work does he so multiply the barriers between the experience narrated and himself as author. The treatment is not uniform. In 'Owen Wingrave' ghostly influence is accepted by the actors in the story and by the observer, Spencer Coyle; but these are all involved in the evil which the non-apparitional 'ghost' symbolizes—the observer taking his blood-fees perhaps more culpably than the rest. They are all, as it were, inside the crystal. In 'Sir Edmund Orme' the narrator is already dead when the editor, his executor, 'in a locked drawer' discovers the narrative, itself written 'long after' the event, and possibly not 'a report of real occurrence'. In 'The Way It Came', again, the narrator is already dead, and the executor, in deference to her wishes, offers the record to a publisher as a sample extract from her diaries: 'I've read with the liveliest wonder the statement they so circumstantially make and done my best to swallow the prodigy they leave to be inferred.' Apparitions, it seems, need a frame: *The Turn of the Screw* in this respect conforms to a precedent already established. Here again the editor-executor vouches for the provenance of the story: the exceptional feature is that the story already has a sponsor and an elaborate narrative frame. So much is always noted by the critics; what is usually ignored is that Douglas's expression of trust in the narrator, and the support it is given by his executor's respect for Douglas, are not standard features in

James's handling of the ghostly tale: the earlier sponsors are distinctly sceptical. But what I am concerned to stress here is the author's attitude so revealed: why, in dealing with the supernatural, does James find this circumspection, this withdrawal, necessary? In this matter of personal commitment, especially, it is instructive to compare the handling of the supernatural by two novelists with whom, in the eighties and nineties, James was on the closest terms of friendship, and with whom his interchange of views was freest and most sympathetic—Robert Louis Stevenson and George Du Maurier.[199]

Stevenson, for all his avowed reliance on the subconscious, produced supernatural tales as factually definite, as concrete in their effect as any of his adventure stories. 'Thrawn Janet' (1881) is more elaborately horrifying, more highly wrought in every way than 'The Body Snatcher' (1884), but the essential macabre remains the same: the manse and its terrors are replaced by dissecting-room crudities—the corpse is less lively, but not more corporeal. It may depart in a gig or 'low up like a brunstane spunk an' fall in ashes to the ground', but it is a physically limited horror just the same; and what is likely to stay in the reader's memory is the surrounding 'wet and darkness' in the one case and 'the Dule water seepin' and sabbin' doun the glen' in the other. And in matters occult but not ghostly the same distribution of emphasis appears. In the history of Tod Lapraik (*Catriona*, 1892–93), it is the green-capped Bass itself, with its 'straight crags' and the solans 'skirling and flying', that makes both the victim's danger and the warlock's unholy joy: the warlock himself, at his loom and in his 'dwam', inspires not terror but a physical disgust, 'like creish'. At the other extreme, physically, is that most debonair of reprobates James Durie (*The Master of Ballantrae*, 1888–89); and it is as a villain of romance (a devil something short of the uncanny) that we accept him. His malevolence, where it exceeds humanly justifiable rancour, asks and for the most part gets the verification of external, picturesque terrors: it is supplied, memorably, in the duel fought by candlelight under 'blackness like a roof'. But the intended 'centre-piece', the resuscitation, to accommodate which (so the author tells us) the whole romantic structure was devised, and which was to give symbolic force and unity to the villain's career, remains an unassimilated curiosity, a marvel of the East indeed, but too grossly physiological, too frankly detailed, and too elaborately circumstantiated (not to say refrigerated) for any shading of mystery. Again, it is characteristic of Stevenson to have written of a vampirish degenerate in such a way that the blood-lust is a mere incidental detail of a romance, less impressive by far than the setting of ancient mansion and encompassing mountains. Styrian Carmilla and Transylvanian Dracula could change habitat without loss of a shudder, but the physically horrific element of 'Olalla' (1885) is given its warrant by the convincingly pictured 'Spain' in which it is set. Yet the fact is that quite half this romance, setting and all, is the product of dream, and that the dream creation is indistinguishable from the waking invention. Similarly, in *The Strange Case of Dr. Jekyll and Mr. Hyde* (1886), the most prosaic incident of a singularly matter-of-fact 'excursion into chaos'—the metamorphosis in flesh and fell by chemist's, not magician's potion—was contributed in dream, he tells us, by Stevenson's 'Brownies'. No doubt, since he also tells us this, the primary inspiration for this story came from his 'strong sense of man's double being' —a theme of infinitely mysterious possibilities—but what came out in the writing was a Rue-Morgue-like horror without mystery. Indeed we get more of the thrill of unease from *The Pavilion on the Links* (1880): Northmour's ferocity is more troubling, in its human impurity, by reason of the strange, wild setting, than Hyde's chemically simplified brutality, exercised in featureless streets and buildings of what might be dullest Edinburgh or Glasgow, as easily as London. One might go further and claim that there is more the *effect* of the supernatural properly so-called—more the oppressive sense of inexplicable and uncontrollable forces—in 'The Merry Men' (1882), a tale in which merely human impulses of greed and fear are pitted against the merely natural but tremendous dangers of rocky coast and midsummer storm. We are not told that the Brownies had a hand in this 'fantastic sonata about the sea and wrecks', but whenever it was that Stevenson learned to discipline his subconscious to such practical ends, the literary results make it clear that, dreaming or waking, his imagination worked by the same strong light, with no crepuscular vagueness to blur the outlines. As James put it, his talent was 'for seeing the actual in the marvellous'; as he himself put it, 'My Brownies are somewhat fantastic, like their stories hot and hot, full of passion and the picturesque, alive with animating incident; and they have no prejudice against the supernatural.' Nor, it appears, against its systematic investigation. How closely and for how long Stevenson followed the reports of such labours I cannot say, but for the last two years of his life he was an associate of the Society for Psychical Research.[200]

Du Maurier was a draughtsman by profession and a story-teller by instinct, and he used both skills to produce his three novels, none of which is conceivable without his own pictorial accompaniment to his text—a text that, as James declared, was not written but 'most delightfully and vividly talked'. All of the stories with which over the years Du Maurier entertained his friends seem to have been of the fantastic order, but in these three, the only ones he brought himself to record, the influence of the new psychological and psychical research is clear. There is nothing of the scientific in them—such as, for instance, glances out in Stevenson's fantasy—but a delighted recognition of everything in the narratives of crystal gazing, of spontaneous thought-transference, or of experimentally-induced hypnotic trance that could lend itself to romantic, sentimental amplification. Svengali is a monstrous projection from a controversial but respected figure of the mid-century—Dr. James Braid of Manchester, surgeon and experimental hypnotist. The working girl 'ignorant of the grammar of her own language' who, at Braid's suggestion, matched 'the far-famed Jenny Lind' word for word in any language, note for note in 'the most difficult roulades and cadenzas', yet when aroused 'had no recollection' of any such achievement, was a real-life equivalent of the prodigiously vocalizing Trilby. Married couples, so Gurney and his assistants learned, not infrequently 'dreamed upon the same subject at the same time': Mr. and Mrs. Toy, for instance, both given to vivid dreaming, could report a number of such experiences; Mr. and Mrs. Fielding once, to their astonishment, simultaneously dreamed of a home they had not revisited in seventeen years. But Peter Ibbetson in Pentonville Gaol and his beloved Duchess in her Camden Hill retirement nightly share an instalment of a joint dream-existence prolonged over twenty-five years. The clairvoyant 'Miss A.', among other feats of retrocognition, in Salisbury Cathedral on 23 February 1890 witnessed the 1641 induction of Bishop Brian Duppa; but Gogo Pasquier and Mimsey Seraskier (alias Peter Ibbetson and the Duchess of Towers) not only mingle familiarly with their great-great-grandmother and her contemporaries, but even, with practice, retrogress into prehistory and the company of the mammoth. The dangerous 'time' mechanism invented (1895) by H. G. Wells was quite unnecessary: all that is required is to 'dream true' and so repossess the past. Baron Carl von Reichenbach's 'odic emanations' and the 'magnetic sense' discredited by Professor Barrett and the future Lord Kelvin were feeble imaginings compared with Barty Josselin's ability to 'feel the north'; and the services rendered by Stevenson's Brownies were as nothing beside those which the enamoured Martian every night performs (cryptographically, in two languages) through Barty's subliminal self. For the fictional blend of psychic with cosmic speculation Du Maurier could cite the authority of Camille Flammarion, 'astronome vulgarisateur'; but since, in addition, the circumstances of each tall, handsome, charming, noble hero reflect those of Du Maurier himself at different periods of his life, we seem to be offered three ingenuous displays of rather melancholy narcissism. And this impression is not corrected either by the style, which amplifies rhapsodically the Thackerayan narrative tone of moralizing sentiment, or by the *obbligato* of musical memories: 'It all belongs to the sociable, audible air, the irresponsible, personal pitch of a style so talked and smoked, so drawn, so danced, so played, so whistled and sung, that it never occurs to us even to ask ourselves whether it is written.' But with all deference to James's critical insight, the overwhelming popularity of *Trilby* (1894) is less surprising than the relative failure of *Peter Ibbetson* (1892) and *The Martian* (1897), since all three mix pathos and the sensational in much the same proportion. What is equally surprising in its way is James's indulgent acceptance, from Du Maurier's hand, of a concoction he would not have tolerated from any other author. In the first place, however, Du Maurier was an artist, whose literary efforts could not be judged with rigour; and secondly, all the novels, but especially that 'exquisite production' *Peter Ibbetson*, not only evoked most poignantly the charm of the author's living companionship, but also appealed, however gushingly, to James's own obsessive 'sense of the past'.[201]

Early in their acquaintance Stevenson had noted, apropos of their very different reaction to Dostoievsky's *Crime and Punishment*, James's tendency to withdraw from any intellectual experience which was emotionally searching:

Raskolnikoff is easily the greatest book I have read in ten years. . . . Henry James could not finish it: all I can say is, it nearly finished me. It was like having an illness. James did not care for it because the character of Raskolnikoff was not objective; and at that I divined a great gulf between us, and, on further reflection, the existence of a certain impotence in many minds of to-day, which prevents them from living *in* a book or a character, and keeps them standing afar off, spectators of a puppet show. To such I suppose the book may seem empty in the centre; to the others it is a room, a house of life, into which they themselves enter, and are tortured and purified.

James found relief and pleasure in Du Maurier's easy frankness—'of all familiar friends [he] was quite the least *boutonné*'—which in the three novels mingled reflections and convictions (on matters supernatural among the rest) in an uninhibited stream of personal confidences. He took equal pleasure artistically in the very different phenomenon presented by Stevenson: to read him was 'much the same as to "meet" him. . . . We grew to possess him entire; and the example is the more curious and beautiful, as he neither made a business of "confession" nor cultivated most of those forms through which the *ego* shines.' Yet James could no more have committed himself to the 'Chapter on Dreams' than to the naïvetés of *Peter Ibbetson*: his own fictional approach to the supernatural, so fascinatingly rich in suggestion, but so dangerously accessible to 'uprush' from the subliminal self, was cautious and indirect.[202]

v

But although James, as usual, carefully disowns any responsibility for the supernatural content of *The Turn of the Screw*, his double frame, providing as it were an antechamber to the mystery, allows him discreetly to hint at a personal acquaintance with the sponsor. And what safer, more reassuring authority in such dubious matters than the Primate of all England? Before the publication of the 1908 *Preface*, the general reader was unlikely to interpret the hint: the possibility that Arthur Benson might do so explains the apologetic letter he received from James during the American serialization of *The Turn of the Screw*. Archbishop Benson himself had died in October 1896: otherwise, one supposes, the apology would have been directed to him, rather than to his son. For Douglas *is* Edward White Benson— not in the dignity of his archbishopric, but in his continuing enthralment by the supernatural, and more especially in the image, self-evoked according to James (*Preface*, p. 170), of his youthful susceptibility and enthusiasm as an undergraduate of Trinity College, Cambridge. In the widest sweep of James's reference, the three pioneers of psychical research—Sidgwick, Myers, and Gurney, with their Trinity connection—are also included. But the individual reference is to the founder of the Ghost Society himself; for, as we have seen, the governess's experience at Bly is set in the early forties, her narration of it to Douglas in the early fifties of the century. And, very strangely, a link existed between Cambridge undergraduates of Benson's generation and Charlotte Brontë herself. Mrs. Gaskell, in the *Life*, prints a letter of May 1850 acknowledging an appreciation of *Jane Eyre* and *Shirley* expressed by 'a young man at Cambridge'; and Charlotte Brontë's reply is so closely suggestive of the relationship James postulates between Douglas and his governess that it seems worth quoting in full.

Apologies are indeed unnecessary for a 'reality of feeling, for a genuine unaffected impulse of the spirit,' such as prompted you to write the letter which I now briefly acknowledge.

Certainly it is 'something to me' that what I write should be acceptable to the feeling heart and refined intellect; undoubtedly it is much to me that my creations (such as they are) should find harbourage, appreciation, indulgence, at any friendly hand, or from any generous mind. You are very welcome to take Jane, Caroline, and Shirley for your sisters, and I trust they will often speak to their adopted brother when he is solitary, and soothe him when he is sad. If they cannot make themselves at home in a thoughtful, sympathetic mind, and diffuse through its twilight a cheering, domestic glow, it is their fault; they are not, in that case, so amiable, so benignant, not so *real* as they ought to be. If they *can*, and can find household altars in human hearts, they will fulfil the best design of their creation, in therein maintaining a genial flame, which shall warm but not scorch, light but not dazzle.

What does it matter that part of your pleasure in such beings has its source in the poetry of your own youth rather than in any magic of theirs? What, that perhaps, ten years hence, you may smile to remember your present recollections, and view under another light both 'Currer Bell' and his writings? To me this consideration does not detract from the value of what you now feel. Youth has its romance, and maturity its wisdom, as morning and spring have their freshness, noon and summer their power, night and winter their repose. Each attribute is good in its own season. Your letter gave me pleasure, and I thank you for it.

CURRER BELL.

James is unlikely to have remembered such a passage over a long span of years, and I have no proof that when he read Shorter's book in 1897 he also consulted Mrs. Gaskell's biography, though he may well have done so. The resemblance may thus be a chance one, but it is nevertheless decidedly curious that a mere extrapolation from a fictional conception should so match the influence in real life of Jane Eyre's original.[203]

In the *donnée* sketched by James for his notebook we have, I imagine, something of the simplicity of terror belonging to the original ghost tale. He seems to have recalled as accurately as possible the scanty details imparted by Archbishop Benson, and one of these in effect authenticates his source: the apparitions beckon across 'the deep ditch of a sunk fence'. Now a ha-ha was not among the dangers to children that would spontaneously occur to James's city-bred, American imagination, but a ha-ha *did* form the boundary of young White Benson's earliest childhood paradise—'the pleasant sunny garden' of Brook House, near Droitwich. The story, thus furnished forth with indigenous perils, was not necessarily a Worcestershire product. Benson, it seems, heard it 'as a young man': he may have been at his home in Birmingham, or on a holiday visit to Yorkshire; it may date from his tutorship during the summer of 1848 at Abergeldie Castle; or he may have gathered it as a youthful amateur of ghosts at Cambridge. It was an old story, imperfectly narrated by an 'old converser', James tells us, when it reached Benson's ears; and I am inclined to refer it to one of those 'magic hours' (as the Archbishop remembered them, forty years later) spent with his great-aunt at Skipton Castle. But whatever its origin, it was, by all the signs, a tale of evil spirits as intent as any kelpie or Lorelei on the physical destruction of their victims. The implication no doubt was that, tricked into destroying themselves, the children would be irredeemably lost souls, and the evil domination would be resumed for all eternity. James's governess, explaining to Mrs. Grose her fears for the children, reproduces many of the suggestions of the *donnée*, the unfamiliar ha-ha excepted:

'They can destroy them! . . . They don't know, as yet, quite how—but they're trying hard. They're seen only across, as it were, and beyond—in strange places and on high places, the top of towers, the roof of houses, the outside of windows, the further edge of pools; but there's a deep design, on either side, to shorten the distance and overcome the obstacle; and the success of the tempters is only a question of time. They've only to keep to their suggestions of danger.'
'For the children to come?'
'And perish in the attempt!' (p. 93)

This is close to what we might call the primitive form of the story indicated by the Archbishop; but in the words 'on either side' there is a momentary shift to another category of the occult. Morover the adherence to primitive, acrobatic modes of haunting would seem totally unnecessary if, as the governess claims, earlier in the same discussion, ' "The four, depend upon it, perpetually meet" ' (p. 91). And the governess seems to have forgotten that Miles has already been tempted out of doors, at midnight, without suffering any harm. Perhaps on this occasion her ready intervention saved him from climbing the tower and perishing in the attempt. But this explanation will not serve when later on, in the absence of the governess, Flora actually crosses the lake without misadventure. The truth is that James has retained, for their picturesqueness, certain accessory details of the old story, such as would be entailed by living creatures' 'coming over to' haunted ground, while for the development of his central theme—the attempt of evil *revenants* to communicate with children they have corrupted —he has not only added a number of illustrations after a newer mode, but also, through his narrator, supplied a whole new set of justifications.[204]

To all fictional intents and purposes the governess is Jane Eyre (even if Mlle Deluzy's green eyes may at times be seen peeping over her shoulder); but in her translation from the forties to 1897–98 she has gained some impression of psychical research and its standards. She knows, for example, that strict observation and report are needed to validate any supernatural occurrence, and she has been warned that subjective estimates of time are unreliable. In recording Quint's first appearance on the tower she notes: 'The great question, or one of these, is, afterwards, I know, with regard to certain matters, the question of how long they have lasted. Well, this matter of mine, think what you will of it, lasted while I caught at a dozen possibilities . . .' (p. 32). And recalling her behaviour at Quint's second appearance, she admits: 'I can't speak to the purpose to-day of the duration of these things. That kind of measure must have left me: they couldn't have lasted as they actually appeared to me to last' (p. 40). A like discrepancy is rather more precisely assessed by one of Myers's correspondents: after describing a combined visual and auditory hallucination, a consolatory vision of her dead father, she writes that it 'occupied so short a time that, glancing involuntarily at the window again, I saw the morning dawn and the little bird [on the sill outside] just as they had looked a few minutes before'. In another case the percipient writes: 'The apparition persisted, and I turned my face from it to the wall, by way of exorcism; and a few minutes later, seemingly, though actually perhaps only seconds, found that it had vanished.' In relatively few of the published narratives, however, is an estimate of duration attempted; and the governess seems to be mistaken in thinking this factor to be of prime importance: what the psychical investigators are at pains to ascertain, and their correspondents dutifully to record, is the *point* in time— the date and hour—of the experience. Without this information it would be impossible either to check the corroborative facts alleged or to establish coincidence. But the governess's precognition of SPR requirements is not always faulty. In order to gauge the quality of the experience (and in particular to allow for merely subjective hallucinations) it was necessary to learn, among other personal details, whether the percipient was 'out of health or in grief or anxiety'. So (in almost all the reports, and with monotonous regularity in those submitted for the Census) we find such observations as 'I was in good health and in no sort of anxiety'; 'I was not out of health, but

I was in anxiety on quite a different subject'; 'I was in perfect health; but we had family trouble at the time'; 'I was out of health and in anxiety about family troubles.' The governess is therefore anticipating the rules of psychical enquiry when, introducing her account of Quint's second appearance, she remarks:

Of course I was under the spell [of the children's loveliness], and the wonderful part is that, even at the time, I perfectly knew I was. But I gave myself up to it; it was antidote to any pain, and I had more pains than one. I was in receipt in these days of disturbing letters from home, where things were not going well. But with my children, what things in the world mattered? (p. 38)

We should not, however, read into this statement an intimation by the author of his narrator's unreliability. Since she could forget her worries in the pleasure of her rôle at Bly, the governess's anxiety was clearly not acute; and the Census Committee, while agreeing with 'the general view' that any emotional disturbance might 'tend to produce hallucinations', would not regard these as necessarily so caused, and thereby invalidated. Indeed, the case in which the percipient was not only 'in anxiety about family troubles' but also 'out of health' is described as perhaps 'the most remarkable case in our collection of a phantasm of the dead conveying true information'. As companions in anxiety, so to speak, the governess has over two hundred future participants in the SPR Census—all of them warranted free from 'delirium or insanity or any other morbid condition obviously conducive to hallucinations'.[205]

James, I think, gives us no reason to suppose that the uncanny happenings at Bly were not the governess's first experience of such strange matters; but in her retrospective account of them (had she been studying Mrs. Crowe, perhaps, in the ten years' interval, or was her story written only after her encounter with Douglas-Benson?) she more than once conveys a suggestion of expertise. In that first scene by the lake, she does not need so much as to raise her eyes to be *convinced* (not merely to suspect) that 'there was an alien object in view' (p. 56). More oddly still, during the interval of some seconds when she concentrates upon her sewing, she reaches 'practical certitude' that the object is a supernatural one. She next looks at Flora, to have her conviction 'confirmed' by the child's attitude, and only then, 'after some seconds' more, actually looks across the lake. This is passing strange; but here, to supply a precedent, is part of a signed statement from the visitor to the Château de Prangins already mentioned—'a near connection' of the Bishop of Ripon, no less:

I went to bed and slept soundly. But in the middle of the night I suddenly awoke in a state of terror, not, apparently, from a dream, for I had no impression of having been dreaming, but with a sort of certainty that a tall, thin, old man, in a long flowered dressing-gown, was seated and writing at the table in the middle of the room. I cannot say what gave me this certainty, or this distinct picture, for I did not once turn my eyes to the place where I felt that the intruder was seated. It did not, in fact, occur to me at the time how odd it was that I thus knew of his appearance without seeing him. The room was flooded with brilliant moonlight; but I did not venture to turn my head. My cries awoke my husband, who naturally thought that I had had a nightmare, and could not understand my persistent assertion that an old man in a flowered dressing-grown was in the room. At last he persuaded me to look at the table where I had felt that the old man was sitting; and there was no one there. (*PSPR*, VI, 53)

But, of course, as we have already noted in another connection, the ghost of Voltaire, or (as Myers would term it) his 'veridical after-image', *had* been there.

Again, on several occasions, although she sees and hears nothing, and cannot allege a material cause for her unease, the governess receives intimations of the supernatural. She has already been the percipient of five separate apparitions and as a consequence, no doubt, is in a state of abnormal tension, but perhaps for that very reason her visualizing 'power' seems temporarily to have deserted her.

There were exactly states of the air, conditions of sound and of stillness, unspeakable impressions of the *kind* of ministering moment, that brought back to me, long enough to catch it, the feeling of the medium in which, that June evening out-of-doors, I had had my first sight of Quint. . . . I recognised the signs, the portents—I recognised the moment, the spot. But they remained unaccompanied and empty, and I continued unmolested; if unmolested one could call a young woman whose sensibility had, in the most extraordinary fashion, not declined but deepened. I had said in my talk with Mrs. Grose on that horrid scene of Flora's by the lake . . . that it would from that moment distress me much more to lose my power than to keep it. (pp. 98–99)

After these secret scenes [i.e. solitary deliberations] I chattered more than ever, going on volubly enough till one of our prodigious, palpable hushes occurred—I can call them nothing else—the strange, dizzy lift or swim (I try for terms!) into a stillness, a pause of all life, that had nothing to do with the more or less noise that at the moment we might be engaged in making and that I could hear through any deepened exhilaration or quickened recitation or louder strum of the piano. Then it was that the others, the outsiders, were there. (pp. 100–01)

Experiences such as these (involving a 'sense of presence' without any sensation, of either sight, hearing, or touch) are noted with relative infrequency by correspondents of the SPR, and then mainly by practised observers—perhaps because the impression is seldom of such intensity as to compel attention. The type receives very brief mention in *Phantasms of the Living*, but greatly interested William James, who devotes a long note to it in his *Principles of Psychology*. Part of this note, with James's interpretation of the phenomenon, is quoted in the Census Report, where an attempt is made at classification. No doubt his brother's interest in the matter, added to such personal experience as is indicated by the Louvre dream, is sufficient to account for Henry James's familiarity with this kind of quasi-perception; but his decision to include these experiences in his governess's psychic history may have been more directly inspired by a lengthy 'Record of Telepathic and other Experiences' included in Volume VI of the SPR *Proceedings*.[206]

Its author, 'Miss X.', otherwise Miss Ada Goodrich Freer (later Mrs. Hans Spoer), was a 'sensitive' highly regarded among psychical adepts, and her story provides a number of analogies for the conditions which seem to obtain in the governess's experience of the supernatural. 'I would say,' writes Miss X.,

that such experiences, though sometimes the occasion, are never the cause, of any distress; the message conveyed may be painful, but it has seldom happened that it has been presented in a manner to startle or annoy; it is not followed by physical exhaustion, nor preceded by any special conditions; it is most to be looked for when my health is normal, and my mind at rest. . . . I have often sought for any condition, beyond that of quiet receptiveness, which shall promote such experiences. The result has been mainly negative. The only occasion when I absolutely lost the power for any length of time (about 14 months) was when I was exceptionally anxious for its exercise; after which, having ceased to look for any messages, they returned suddenly, with perhaps greater vividness and frequency than ever before. (p. 362)

Sometimes, especially in the case of a visual impression, there was no premonitory sign; but often, it seems, Miss X. became 'conscious of a presence' (cf. pp. 369, 392) before the actual manifestation occurred. One such incident is reminiscent of the case used by Charlotte Brontë in *Jane Eyre*:

December 9th. [1889] I was sitting alone about 10 minutes ago, it is now 9.50 (p.m.), when I heard steps, and felt a presence, and that someone was wanting me. . . . I was, contrary to custom, very much frightened. Almost immediately after, however, I heard my name called, distinctly twice, and I think faintly again. . . . I cannot say I recognised the voice, which, though clear, seemed a long way off, but I think it may have been H., who at present is at [a place distant about 50 miles]. (p. 389)

H., it was later ascertained, had indeed called her name repeatedly at the time noted. On another occasion the premonitory, enforced 'pause' was reciprocally experienced: Miss X. 'on the night of December 13th, 1887 . . . was seized with so strong an impression' that the friend with whom she was *en rapport* was thinking of her 'and that something was going to happen' that she decided 'to sit up over the fire and await events'. Simultaneously, this friend found her 'thoughts drawn to' Miss X., 'so that all surroundings were lost' to her, and her 'strange absorption' was remarked by her companions. When, 'about 10.15 p.m.', the potentially dangerous accident occurred without harm to Miss X., both ladies were released from their 'preoccupation' (p. 367).

Miss X., it appears, had great psychic versatility, if one may so express it —telepathy, clairvoyance, precognition, spontaneously occurring or experimentally induced with or without the help of a crystal, were all within the compass of her gift; but only one of the varied incidents she details is reflected in a parallel episode of *The Turn of the Screw*. On her first night at Bly, the governess did not sleep well. Several times she rose from her bed, and she was up

to watch, from my open window, the faint summer dawn, to look at such portions of the rest of the house as I could catch, and to listen, while, in the fading dusk, the first birds began to twitter, for the possible recurrence of a sound or two, less natural and not without, but within, that I had fancied I heard. There had been a moment when I believed I recognised, faint and far, the cry of a child; there had been another when I found myself just consciously starting as at the passage, before my door, of a light footstep. (p. 16)

Similarly, 'at four in the morning of Friday, August 19th, 1887' Miss X. 'was awakened by a sudden noise', a rattling of the Venetian blind at the closed window, the repetition of which prevented sleep.

I then drew up the blind, opened the window wide, noted the hour in my diary (4.20), and sat in my easy chair for perhaps 10 or 15 minutes watching the starlings and wondering what it all meant. At length, however, I felt chilly, so shut the window, leaving the blind drawn up, went back to bed and watched. In a very few minutes the noise began again, quite as loud and distinct but different in character, rather as of something being drawn slowly across the glass. . . . (pp. 372–73)

And all the while there was no wind, no rustling ivy, no motion of the telegraph wires to account for the sounds; but a letter received on the Saturday allowed Miss X. to interpret them as the transferred effect of a dying friend's thought of her. A different interpretation is provided for the sounds heard at Bly, but the dawn vigil is retained.

It is rather Miss X.'s attributes as a sensitive than the particular incidents which display them that seem to have impressed James, and two characteristics dwelt upon in her 'Record' are of special interest in relation to *The Turn of the Screw*. One is her ability, from early childhood, to detect instantaneously and without conscious thought a malign quality (if such were present) in strangers whom she encountered. She gives several examples of this instinctive antipathy: 'One such example would prove nothing, but like experiences extending over a life-time, incline me to think, though I say it with diffidence and humility, that, from whatever cause, I may aspire to some such power of discrimination as that possessed by my friend the dog' (p. 360). It is a similar power, one assumes, that enables the governess to pronounce Quint, even before his identification, 'a horror' (p. 44), and Miss Jessel on her first appearance to be of 'quite as unmistakeable horror and evil' (p. 59)—'wonderfully handsome. But infamous' (p. 61).

A second characteristic is associated indirectly with the governess, directly with Miles. Miss X. was an accomplished pianist ('playing on the piano-forte has been, from childhood, one of my greatest pleasures' [p. 359]), and she records numerous instances when she consciously used her music to summon a friend, or compel a friend's attention, from a distance. One such friend testifies, 'Especially I would notice X.'s power to call me by her music, "playing for" me, as I always call it. I am no musician, but as long as I can remember, music has been associated with all I cared for most, and its power over me is a very real though perhaps only sentimental one' (p. 363). It is precisely this kind of spell which Miles as he plays can exert upon the governess—breaking into all her 'gruesome fancies' (p. 75), causing her to forget time and as it were sleep at her post (pp. 127–28). But in Miles's case the governess is not the only auditor, and his music is also a conjuration: it is 'through' the 'strum of the piano' that the governess becomes aware of invisible presences (p. 101), and when this little David plays evil spirits are called up. Miss X., admittedly, is only one source for James's obvious belief that music is a dangerous art; but her example is significant in that it links music with the *exercise* of psychic powers. And a theory of 'Duplex Personality' independently advanced in the same *PSPR* volume might seem to offer a partial explanation of the phenomena. The author illustrates from his own experience as a pianist the operation of both auto-matic and intuitive faculties: like little Miles, he had the gift of musical improvisation, and could declare that 'where this power exists it exhibits the faculty of intuitive passive consciousness in full exercise. The will is entirely inoperative' (p. 92).[207] But (James in his characterization of Miles seems to pose the question) in this abeyance of the will, is it solely his own subconscious that possesses the musician? One remembers also that the ruling passion of Edmund Gurney, psychagogue in chief, had been music, and (although there is no indication that Gurney made use of it in his re-searches) James might well regard it as one of the influences contributing to his destruction.

It is my impression, too, that James has endowed his governess with certain traits, other than the psychic, which link her with Miss X. The latter, in a testimony quoted elsewhere by Myers,[208] vigorously asserts her freedom from 'any morbid condition'. She is country bred, used to 'early rising, systematic mental work, and a walk of from six to twelve miles a day in almost all weathers. I belong to no effete race, but to a family which for physique and longevity might challenge any in the annals of Mr. Francis Galton;—a family which has never lived in cities, and which, for many

generations, has expended its energies and ambitions on horses and hounds.'
The country upbringing and country interests appear in numerous incidental allusions throughout her personal 'Record': the hay-loft refuge from
suspect visitors (p. 360); the blue-bonneted old village woman whose
eidetic image came to trouble hours of fatigue or worry (pp. 366–67); the
cricket field where a brother's image, and Miss X. had five brothers (p. 630),
rose to assist memory (p. 394); the precognized visitors, 'officers from the
barracks near, who had driven over with an invitation to a ball' (p. 374);
perhaps most revealing of all, the diary entry following a night disturbed by
supernatural intimations: 'Just sent for [news]paper. E. and K. S. married.
Nothing else happened as appears yet. No letters, except from Horse's
Home and H. Even the mare is no worse' (p. 373). Obviously there are
county, as well as country, associations in which the vicar's daughter from
Hampshire could not wholly share; but I do not think I am mistaken in the
type of young woman James wished in part to suggest. It is a type even
more familiar in plays and novels than that of Jane Eyre, with whom she is
not altogether congruously blended in *The Turn of the Screw*—the country
miss, the hoyden or tomboy, whose freedom of speech and manner, not to
be confused with ill-breeding, is the temporary despair of nursery and
schoolroom. Such an element in her composition, implied by her references
to the slavish idolatry lavished on elder brothers (p. 75), and to the desirability of outdoor sports for little boys (p. 127), most adequately explains
the recurrent, sometimes ill-judged colloquialisms (they hardly amount to
'slanginess') of the governess's narrative style. And James, I believe, has
taken his warrant for the blend of Brontëan intensity and sensitivity with
'wholesome' rural simplicity from some such mixed character as is presented
by Miss X. It is a way both of rendering the pastiche less obvious, and of
bringing the supernatural into relation with mundane affairs, without
lessening its mystery. It is also (though James would scarcely have recognized the necessity for this) one more certificate of mental health for his
narrator.

I do not suggest that James's governess is in any degree a portrait of Miss
Goodrich Freer: 'Miss X.' leads, as it were, a life of her own in *PSPR*
Volume VI, which, during the nineties, James seems to have treated as a
useful compendium of psychic effects and psychical information generally.
Miss X.'s 'Record', for example, could also be used in 'Sir Edmund Orme',
where it probably suggested both Sir Edmund's appearance at church, and
Mrs. Marden's haunt-induced fainting-fit at the party.[209] And this 'Record'
is not the only portion of Volume VI on which James may have drawn for his
presentation of the governess. Of all the latter's actions, perhaps the most
reprehensible in the eyes of modern critics is her repeated catechizing of the
children, especially Miles. Such catechizing takes its general sanction from
the darker side of Victorian child management, in which 'breaking the spirit'
constituted a solemn duty. But it may have been directly suggested by one

of the narratives quoted in Myers's paper 'On Recognised Apparitions occurring More than a Year after Death' (Case X, pp. 43–45).

This is an account, written on 23 February 1878, '30 years, at least, after the occurrence', by a French governess, Mlle Julie Marchand, placed as a young woman in charge of two little girls in an aristocratic German household, but subsequently 'for 22 years' governess to an English family, and still, in 1889, alive to vouch for her experience. The young governess slept in the same large room as her two charges, and she had the habit of reading for an hour and more each night by the light of a lamp on her bedside table. One night, when the children were peacefully sleeping ('les deux enfans dormant paisiblement'), 'j'éprouvai un sentiment comme celui qu'on éprouve en sentant une personne près de soi'. She looked up to see the form of a man wearing a broad-brimmed hat. She assumed it to be 'une illusion de ma vue', and finally, the apparition still visible, put out the light and went to sleep. The same thing happened several nights in succession, but for fear of being laughed at she told nobody. One night, however, when she came up from supper, the children having already been in bed for some hours, she heard 'des cris d'angoisse terrible', and found the elder, more timid child Nette out of bed and trying to rouse her sister.

Lorsque l'enfant me vit elle courut se coucher. Je lui dis simplement, 'J'espère que tu ne feras plus un tel tapage.' Le lendemain l'enfant paraissait si misérable qu'elle m'inquiéta un peu. Je lui demandai si elle était malade ou non; elle me répondit, 'Non, je suis bien.' L'idée me vint de la questionner sur le sujet de sa frayeur de hier au soir, car j'étais sûre que son état d'être provenait de sa frayeur de hier au soir. Je la pris dans une chambre seule pour la questionner. Pendant longtemps je ne pus rien lui faire avouer; enfin, après lui avoir promis qu'elle ne serait pas grondée, qu'elle pourrait me dire quelle absurdité elle voudrait, que je désirais savoir la cause de sa peur afin de lui parler là-dessus, enfin, après bien des hésitations elle me dit, 'Je sais que ce n'est pas vrai, mais cela cependant m'effraye.' Elle me dit: 'Dès que vous descendez on frappe à la porte de la chambre d'étude, et au pied de mon lit je vois un homme.' Cela me frappa. Je lui dis, 'Je voudrais bien savoir comment ton imagination effrayée te le représente.' Elle me dit, 'Je sais que ce n'est pas vrai,' mais enfin elle me dit il porte un long manteau, avec un long col, un chapeau avec la tête basse, avec une large aile. J'eus presque peur que l'enfant ne vit mon étonnement, car c'était exactement la même figure que j'avais vu plusieurs fois auparavant. . . .

Thereupon the governess, sure her mistress would laugh at her, reported the matter to her master, the Baron, who to her surprise treated it with great seriousness. 'Il me dit, "Je viendrai ce soir dans la chambre d'étude et nous parlerons de choses indifférentes," car je savais que N. ne dormirait pas jusqu'à ce que je fusse au lit.' But although they waited till nearly eleven o'clock, nothing uncanny happened, except that the governess's name was heard 'aussi distinctement que possible, provenant d'un coin de la chambre. J'allai dans la chambre à coucher; je demandai à N. si elle m'avait appelé. Elle était tout à fait réveillée et elle me dit non.' The upshot was that new quarters were found for the governess and her charges, and it was then revealed that in making the cupboards for the schoolroom, next to the children's bedroom, 'on a trouvé une squelette dans le mur'. There were, however, no further manifestations, and Mlle Marchand herself never experienced another hallucination.

Now there are a number of points in Mlle Marchand's testimony which, to the reader of James's story, have a familiar air. Here, as in *The Turn of the Screw*, we meet a governess who is the first percipient of an apparition which she requires some convincing is supernatural, which at first she does not speak of, and which she continues reluctant to bring to her employer's notice; a governess who reads late while, like Flora, her charges in the same room enjoy 'the perfection of childish rest' (p. 76), but in whom the late hour and the apparition combined produce 'no terror' (p. 77); a governess who, when she finds a child disturbed from sleep at once suspects ghostly influence. But it is in Mlle Marchand's questioning of Nette that we have the closest parallel to the behaviour of James's governess. The latter does not achieve the dry severity of tone and ruthless imposition of authority that (despite her own, professional solicitude and the child's innocence of wrong-doing) mark the Frenchwoman's inquisition: instead, James has not unsuccessfully conveyed the awkward English compromise between a desire to be kind and a need to be 'firm'. Characteristically, Mlle Marchand secures her calculated end—she gets an unequivocal confession, which is more than James's governess, for all her tenderly hesitant, blundering insistence, ever manages to do. But his governess's failure, of course, makes the tragedy and perhaps the irony of James's story. For it is to be observed that Mlle Marchand, the Baron, and apparently Myers himself, are satisfied that she has been, not the victim of an optical illusion, hysterically or otherwise occasioned, but the percipient of a veridical apparition of the dead. Wisely, none of the three attempts to establish a logical connection between the displaced skeleton and the 'haunt'.

To the example of Mlle Marchand and to the multiform psychic capacity of Miss X., James is, in my view, directly indebted for certain exceptional features of his governess's case. But many details of situation and behaviour reported by her are commonplaces of psychical experience, and as such frequently recur in the narratives acknowledged by the Society for Psychical Research. There is, first of all, the matter of age. Though testimonies from persons under twenty-one were not included in the Census, the experiences narrated might have occurred at any age: young adults, between twenty and thirty, proved to be the most susceptible age-group. We find that James's governess was at least thirty when she wrote her story, but only twenty when she saw her ghosts. Then the uneasiness she felt on accepting her post (p. 14) and the inexplicable sounds that disturbed her first night at Bly (p. 16) combined with the letter from Miles's school (p. 20) to produce in her the state of 'expectancy' noted by the Census Committee as favouring hallucinations: 'One evening—with nothing to lead up or to prepare it—I felt the cold touch of the impression that had breathed on me the night of my arrival and which, much lighter then, . . . I should probably have made little of in memory had my subsequent sojourn been less agitated' (p. 76). But the states of mind most favourable to hallucinatory experiences, veridical or otherwise, were proved by SPR statistics to be those not of tension and anxiety but of abstraction and repose. Conformably, before each of the first four manifestations the governess relaxed into enjoyment—she found 'grievous fancies' and 'odious memories' were alike given 'a kind of brush of the sponge', so that she could still have 'hours of peace' (pp. 72–73). After the fourth manifestation, however (the first *within* the house, and so, on her interpretation, a warning that material defences had been penetrated), 'the general complexion' of her nights was altered (pp. 81–82): it was from this point that, so far as the demands of her youth and health for sleep could be resisted, she began to keep nightly vigil. And, again conformably to expert opinion (such as Miss X.'s), her psychic powers diminished: she no longer saw what her anxiety assured her she ought to have seen. Psychical investigators would regret her conduct as impeding the flow of evidence, rather than as prejudicing the veridicality of her phantasms. And in James's pastiche, of course, it has an obvious justification—it keeps up, exactly on the lines of *Jane Eyre*, the suspense which no feminine narrator in the Gothic vein could (or can) possibly forgo. Again, James's governess on one occasion (p. 76) had, like Mlle Marchand, been reading when the 'fully externalized phantasm' rose before her; but one should not suppose (as critics of *The Turn of the Screw* are inclined to do) that what she read had abnormally excited her and so produced a subjective hallucination. At that rate one would have to pair Cicero on old age and Kingsley on chalk streams as unduly stimulating, and discover a hallucinating effect in *The Adventures of Mr. Verdant Green*. One might more plausibly assume that 'the hypnogenic tendency of prolonged reading', so unhappily familiar to students, had begun to affect both governesses; or that concentration on the printed page had resulted in a state of abstraction similar to the crystalgazer's, and equally productive of hallucinations not necessarily 'falsidical'. And yet again, the fact that so often the governess is by herself when her ghosts appear is no cause for suspicion: the SPR Census revealed that '62 per cent. of the visual hallucinations occurred when the percipient was alone or practically alone'. In James's story the proportion is five to three. All these correspondences are certainly not accidental: the only question is whether James arrived at them empirically, as it were, through his reading of SPR case histories, or consulted *PSPR* Volume X and applied, wherever they seemed appropriate, the rules of psychical experience there formulated. Perhaps he did both.[210]

vi

James's percipient, the governess, is thus a creation from many diverse elements, and he has been similarly eclectic in constructing the apparitions that obsess her. Here the range of possible sources is very wide, but on the other hand the available effects fall into well-defined categories, which make identification easier. In *The Turn of the Screw*, excluding those occasions of incomplete percipience when the governess merely senses a presence, and excluding also her auditory impressions during the first night at Bly, the eight visitations (four involving Quint, and four Miss Jessel) are all of 'fully externalized phantasms', to use Gurney's phrase again. No word is uttered, but to the sight, James's phantasms present all the indications of life and sentience. We do not read that they cast a shadow, or interrupt the normal view of objects in the scene (details sometimes emphasized in such narratives); but they look directly and intently at the percipient, they move naturally, and they may even eschew supernatural modes of appearance and disappearance. Mobility is particularly noticeable in the case of Quint, who passes along the tower top and at last turns away in sight of the governess (pp. 32–33); who comes up the stair, stops short on the landing, and finally, as the governess watches, turns and goes down the stair into the darkness of the next bend (pp. 77–78); and who at the last encounter 'comes into view' on the terrace before he reaches the window, where he moves and wheels like a sentinel or a baffled beast of prey (pp. 162–63). It is only in the schoolroom scene that Miss Jessel changes posture in view of the governess—on the other occasions, whether standing by the lake or seated on the stair, she presents a fixed tableau of despair. Again, Quint does not suddenly manifest himself, but is already on the tower when the governess comes 'into view of the house' (p. 30); and at his second appearance, like any corporeal intruder, he is discovered peering in through the window as the governess enters the dining-room (p. 39). Miss Jessel is once discovered crouching, her back turned to the governess, on the stair (p. 82), once found sitting at the schoolroom table (p. 112), but twice, at the lakeside, she suddenly 'appears' (pp. 59, 136), and on all four occasions she vanishes (or must be assumed to do so) in spectral fashion. Quint, on the other hand, except at the last confrontation, always gives the impression of going away or (when the governess rushes into the garden in vain pursuit) of having gone away as a living person might do. At this stage of the second manifestation, it is true, there is a slight ambivalence in the narrative. The governess's action at the time, like her subsequent discussion of it with Mrs. Grose, shows that she has taken the intruder to be a real person; but her description, with the benefit of hindsight, assumes his insubstantiality: 'my visitor had vanished. . . . He was there or was not there: not there if I didn't see him' (p. 40).

The discussion in the Census Report of the 'form and development of hallucinations' shows that in the management of his phantasms James has been attentive to precedent:

Most visual hallucinations represent human beings, and most of these resemble human beings of the present day in all respects. . . . When they move, which . . . happens more often than not, the movement is almost always such as we are accustomed to see. The phantom stands on the ground and appears to walk along the ground, and seems to leave the field of vision as a human being would, by walking out of an open door or passing behind some obstacle. A position impossible for real persons,—such as being up in the air,—when the figure is otherwise realistic, is very rare. . . . Even when a phantom is stationary, it does not usually either suddenly appear out of empty space, or similarly vanish before the percipient's eyes, but is generally seen by the percipient on turning his eyes that way, and vanishes, he does not know how, or when he is looking away. There are, however, instances of sudden appearance and disappearance in free space. (pp. 113–14)

From his first appearance, Quint presents a disconcertingly realistic figure: the impression is so concretely shocking that his physical aspect, as we have seen, can be detailed feature by feature. It is, from James's point of view, a happy accident of physiognomy that has given him, and his model in real life, the Judas-coloured hair appropriate to vampires. Miss Jessel, however, is on no occasion more clearly presented than when in the schoolroom she rises from her seat 'with an indescribable grand melancholy of indifference and detachment. . . . Dark as midnight in her black dress, her haggard beauty and her unutterable woe' (p. 112). Of Quint, therefore, we have an individual portrait, of Miss Jessel we have merely a specific impression; but in both cases the clothes of the apparition—items as essential to psychical as to police descriptions—are negatively dealt with. What did Quint wear? Well, he wore no hat, and he wore his master's clothes. And what were *they* like? Mrs. Grose and the governess know, but not even the colour of a waistcoat is divulged to the reader. This is a very adroit piece of legerdemain on James's part; for any detail of the master's clothing must belong to the 1840s, whereas any particularity in Quint-Shaw's would at once relate him both to the nineties and to his living model. Miss Jessel (as we are told, belatedly, in Ch. xviii) is also invariably hatless. With regard to her dress, however, we are vouchsafed two details, dramatically suggestive but safely non-committal as to period: she is 'in black', 'in mourning—rather poor, almost shabby' (p. 61), and these two 'strokes' help Mrs. Grose to her identification. Now Jane Eyre habitually wore black, but not 'mourning', and if the word is used here in its strict sense, it raises a very nice point. For whom is Miss Jessel in mourning? Quint's death occurred in winter, which might mean any time from November to February; Miss Jessel went home 'at the end of the year' (p. 25): has she had the effrontery to assume the garb of a *de facto* widow before leaving

Bly, or is James merely indicating, and Mrs. Grose recognizing, the customary disguise of the Victorian unmarried mother? No doubt to James's readers of 1898 such hints were both less obscure and more sinister than they appear today; but of course it is two contemporaries of little Em'ly and Ruth Hilton, not two *fin de siècle* moralists, who brand Miss Jessel as 'infamous', and their judgment is merely conventional, like the stereotype of the fallen woman to which it is applied.

Not unfittingly, therefore, Miss Jessel's apparitional style is divided between the realistic-normal (psychically speaking) and the traditional-fantastic. Seen within the house, she is the nineteenth-century governess in disgrace; but there is a faint suggestion of the haunting water-spirit, a black instead of a White Lady perhaps, or even of the banshee, in her persistent stance on the *further* side of the lake. True, her predilection for the waterside may be intended to suggest the mode of her death—presumptively, suicide by drowning—but it can only be tradition that keeps her always on the opposite bank. This is a detail which James has added to the lake settings derived in part, if my interpretation is correct, from Ibsen. And probably even James himself could not recover the source in folklore or legend from which he drew it—perhaps some fairy story read in childhood, perhaps some memory of Richard Doyle's pictured fantasies,[211] perhaps some tale of the banshee (a spirit not always vocal) recounted to him by an Irish narrator in 1891 or 1895. One such narrative is recorded, under the date 1874, by Augustus Hare:

[Mrs. Hungerford] was in her room in the evening in her beautiful house, which looks out upon a lake, beyond which rise hills wooded with fir-trees. Suddenly, on the opposite side of the lake, she saw a form which seemed—with sweeping garments—to move forward upon the water. It was gigantic. Mrs. Hungerford screamed, and her sister . . . and the nurse came to her from the inner nursery. The three remained at the window for some time, but retreated as the figure advanced, and at length—being then so tall that it reached to the second floor—looked in at the window, and disclosed the most awful face of a hideous old woman.

It was a Banshee, and one of the family died immediately afterwards.[212]

No fatal linkage of the events is divined by our governess, but so, within twenty-four hours of the second lakeside haunting, does little Miles.

If all its implications are considered, Miss Jessel's lakeside station is indeed a bizarre feature of James's story; but such a combination appears less arbitrary when in Volume X of the SPR *Proceedings* we find a narrative which, in an Irish setting, unites suicide by drowning, a wraith, a lake, and a meditative lady reminiscent of our governess. This account, submitted by the lady in April 1892, deals with an experience of June 1889 in Castleblayney, where she had gone to meet her sister:

I expected her at 3 o'clock, but as she did not come with that train, I . . . went for a walk in the demesne. The day was very warm and bright, and I wandered on under the shade of the trees to the side of a lake, which is in the demesne. Being at length tired, I sat down to rest upon a rock, at the edge of the water. My attention was quite taken up with the extreme beauty of the scene before me. There was not a sound or movement, except the soft ripple of the water on the sand at my feet. Presently I felt a cold chill creep through me, and a curious stiffness of my limbs, as if I *could* not move, though wishing to do so. I felt frightened, yet chained to the spot, and as if impelled to stare at the water straight in front of me. Gradually a black cloud seemed to rise, and in the midst of it I saw a tall man, in a suit of tweed, jump into the water and sink.

In a moment the darkness was gone, and I again became sensible of the heat and sunshine, but I was awed and felt 'eerie,'—it was then about 4 o'clock or so—I cannot remember either the exact time or date.

On 3 July 1889, as reported in the local newspaper of 6 July, a man drowned himself in the lake described; and the apparition is classified among those 'which have perhaps a *primâ facie* claim to be regarded as prescient or premonitory'.[213] Whatever may have been her psychic powers, the narrator undoubtedly had a sense of 'atmosphere', and whether or not James read this passage, one is struck by its similarity in *effect* to that in which the governess describes the setting of her first encounter with Miss Jessel— 'The old trees, the thick shrubbery, made a great and pleasant shade, but it was all suffused with the brightness of the hot, still hour' (pp. 55–56). The impression of bright heat and stillness, of mid afternoon in high summer, which seems so essential to James's effect, is the one touch lacking in Ibsen's picture.

Most present-day readers, as distinct from most critics, of James's story do not consciously analyse the supernatural ingredients of the mystery they enjoy; but many, if not most, readers of 1898 would have been reassured to find that the elements detectable in the blend were, so to speak, 'guaranteed genuine and reliable' psychic effects. Indeed the only motifs for which contemporary and 'veridical' psychic precedents are not immediately forthcoming, are Quint's perambulation of the embattled tower—for which the ghost in *Hamlet* may be thought to offer a distant parallel[214]—and Miss Jessel's immobile haunting of the lakeside. All the rest may be found, many times repeated, accommodated to a variety of personalities and circumstances, in a host of methodical reports and learned discussions, as well as in the more popular, but still seriously intended and responsible accounts of haunting spirits and haunted houses. How familiar James was with this latter variety of sub-literature, I cannot say. If he read Ingram, for example, or Lang,[215] his reading has left no identifiable traces on his own ghostly tales. Curiosity (one might suppose) would lead him to make trial of works as frequently referred to as *The Night Side of Nature*, *Footfalls on the Boundary of Another World*, and *The Debatable Land between This World and the Next*. Both Mrs. Crowe (with a suggestion of eighteenth-century formality) and Robert Dale Owen (with a show of scientific modernity) attempt, so far as their will to believe allows, a rational assessment of the evidence, and they succeed at any rate in giving an individual cast to their material. The singularity of Owen's career, too, might have been expected to attract James's attention. Yet the only trace of such interest discernible in his fiction is, possibly, the naming of his young ghost-challenger, Owen Wingrave; and he gives not the slightest hint of an acquaintance with Mrs. Crowe or the marvels she relates.

There is, however, one broad distinction to be drawn between the authenticated narratives and the majority of either traditional or invented ghost stories. Despite popular belief and the persuasion of Gothic novelists, external conditions seem to be of little importance: a veridical phantasm may with equal propriety manifest itself in broad noonday or at dead of night, within doors or out of doors. That these manifestations usually occur during the hours of darkness and sleep is best explained by the percipient's greater receptivity in such circumstances. It is therefore noteworthy that every appearance of Quint or Miss Jessel actually witnessed by the governess belongs to the daylight hours (to evening and earliest dawn, it is true, as well as the afternoon), when she is up and about, wide awake, clothed and, inferentially, in her right mind. James twice sets the stage, as it were, for a midnight visitation, but on the first occasion only little Miles appears, on the second nothing at all. Whether this is psychically calculated patterning, or mere artistic variation, the effect is both to minimize any suspicion of delusion on the narrator's part, and to associate the story with the veracious reports rather than the 'lying tales'. Incidentally, there are two qualifications of medium or circumstance often attested in the former, which have gained fictional currency also: the apparition may be a source or a centre of light in a dark room, or the percipient may become aware of a sudden chill, felt perhaps as a draught of cold air.[216] Neither of these features is associated with Quint or Miss Jessel, but at her second midnight questioning of Miles, when no ghost appears, the governess feels 'a gust of frozen air'—a detail added to those which, I suggest, James has taken from Le Fanu.

But it is in the minor particulars of setting and behaviour, somewhat tamely standardized one may think among attested phantasms, that Quint and Miss Jessel most clearly reveal James's orthodox intention. For example, it is not unusual for apparitions (whether wraiths or spectres) to peer in, as Quint does, through closed windows:[217] one might conjecture that the window-glass, always to some extent a reflecting medium, acts like the glass of the crystal-gazer. A staircase is apparently a focus for supernatural activity. Passing or about to pass up or down the stairs, the percipient may meet a phantom similarly in transit (as the governess does Quint) or may catch sight of one, moving or stationary, higher up or lower down (as the governess does Miss Jessel).[218] Without concession to Freud, one might suspect that even by day the change in lighting between the different levels of a staircase would be conducive to the rallying of shadows, 'wicked' or not. Again, the spectral form may have its back turned to the percipient, as happens both with Sir Edmund Orme and with Miss Jessel.[219] Or, more frequently, even though the impression of a bodily presence may be exceptionally vivid, the phantom is seen only 'from the waist up'.[220] A number of merely natural factors may contribute to this effect (including the tendency in any encounter to concentrate attention on the face), but in Quint's case it is secured by his position—on one occasion behind battlements, on others looking in over a window-sill: 'He was . . . seen, this time, as he had been seen before, from the waist up, the window, though the dining-room was on the ground-floor, not going down to the terrace on which he stood' (p. 39). Occasionally, the phantom gives the impression of sidling into view —a head may peep round a door, a hand may grasp its edge.[221] James uses this latter detail to give extra verisimilitude to the picture of Quint on the tower: he had at first 'both hands on the ledge', and as he moved past the battlements the governess could see 'the way his hand, as he went, passed from one of the crenelations to the next' (pp. 32–33).

Moreover, in the sometimes decisive and always difficult matter of ghostly clothing, James's evasions regarding Quint and Miss Jessel do not imply either ignorance or rejection of psychic precedent. The glimmering white shroud is almost obligatory wear for the ghost of popular tradition and of Gothic romance, but veridical apparitions, even of the dead or mortally ill, are quite often fully clothed, and some conspicuous detail of their costume permits identification, even though the percipients may never have seen them when living.[222] The unnamed heroine of 'The Way It Came' thus presents a typical case: alive and 'in the body', 'she wore mourning— no great depths of crape, but simple and scrupulous black. She had in her bonnet three small black feathers. She carried a little muff of astrachan;' and so to the last feather (and letter) of the description she appears, 'out of the body', to her soul's affinity.[223] Whether her spiritual attire ever varied we do not learn: for a ghost to change its clothes, as Sir Edmund Orme does, a little strains credulity;[224] but then repeated appearances of a phantasm are in themselves unusual.[225] James has handled the recurrent apparitions of The Turn of the Screw more circumspectly: Quint, we assume, and Miss Jessel, we are told, preserve the same aspect on each of their four appearances; but in both cases, as we have seen, James has neatly exempted himself from particularizing. So, too, through defect of vision, through somnolence, or through habitual vagueness of observation, may the percipient who attempts to describe a veridical phantasm: often he receives, or recalls, only a general impression, in reporting which he falls back upon cliché. The black-clad, woebegone image of the fallen woman, or the suicide, was for a nineteenth-century reader, apparently, one of the gallery of stereotypes with which the imagination of every person in any age is equipped, and as such it appears not infrequently in psychical reports.[226] The description, as in Quint's case, by comparison (testimony to a similar habit of analogy) is infrequent, but not unexampled.[227]

The hatlessness of James's phantoms, or rather the governess's insistence on it, has troubled some critics; but they have, I think, failed to perceive its range of meaning. Miss Jessel was 'a lady', and was also responsible for the training in deportment of a little girl: it is therefore as an outward symbol of her corrupting influence and contravention of moral laws that her spectre flouts the etiquette of the hat, which (like that of the gloves) Victorian society rigorously imposed on its ladies and gentlemen. James certainly does not intend us to picture his governess as wearing her hat (to lunch, for example) indoors: this was a late Victorian fashionable refinement, consequent on the disappearance of the cap; but she would not normally dispense with it (as her anxious pursuit of Flora impels her to do) when she walked in the grounds of Bly. In Quint's case, however, no consideration of etiquette is involved—a mere glance reveals him as ungenteel. It is simply a question of identifying an unknown intruder, whose 'wearing no hat' is a 'sign of familiarity' (p. 32): ' "He has no hat," ' reports the governess, and in this Mrs. Grose finds 'a touch of picture' (p. 45). He cannot, that is, be a chance visitor, or 'some unscrupulous traveller, curious in old houses' (p. 36), but must be one of the only male members of the household, the indoor menservants at Bly—which one, the governess's description immediately makes clear. This, in James's context, is the whole significance of the missing hat, which is not, if one ponders the matter, essential to the recognition of Quint. But in the supernatural contexts James is imitating, the absence of head-dress, or some peculiarity of the hat or cap worn, is often an indispensable clue to identification.[228] In *The Turn of the Screw* the ghost's bare head is merely an added 'touch of picture', and James weakens its effect, and indeed somewhat confuses the issue, by the subsequent declaration that Quint 'never' wore his master's hat, although he had no conscience about waistcoats (p. 47). Voluntary restraint at this point, implying an acknowledgment of servile status, is not what one would expect from so impudent a scoundrel. I conclude that in this emphasis on a customary feature, as in the matter of timing already referred to, James is more anxious to stress what might be termed the psychical conformity of his narrative, than to ensure the strict relevance of a minor detail.

vii

Indeed, no very extensive knowledge of the subject is required to assure us that James invented little in his governess's encounters with the supernatural—he has authority for almost every touch he introduces. And this in spite of the dissatisfaction he expresses, in his *Preface*, with ghost stories of 'the new type'—'the mere modern "psychical" case, washed clear of all queerness as by exposure to a flowing laboratory tap, and equipped with credentials vouching for this' (p. 169). One point, however, that emerges from the editorial smoke screen is that James is, in fact, well acquainted 'with the to-day so copious psychical record of cases of apparitions' (p. 174): he summarizes, as accurately as it is possible to do in general terms and in two sentences, the observed characteristics of phantasmal appearances—

Different signs and circumstances, in the reports, mark these cases; different things are done—though on the whole very little appears to be—by the persons appearing; the point is, however, that some things are never done at all: this negative quantity is large—certain reserves and properties and immobilities consistently impose themselves. Recorded and attested 'ghosts' are in other words as little expressive, as little dramatic, above all as little continuous and conscious and responsive, as is consistent with their taking the trouble—and an immense trouble they find it, we gather—to appear at all. (p. 174)[229]

Certain percipients (the lady from St. Anne de Beaupré for one) might have objected that while *in general* these strictures were justified, some appearances were expressive and dramatic enough to rouse all 'the dear old sacred terror'; but the discontinuity, the capricious, unpredictable incidence of spontaneous manifestations every observer would willingly admit.

If, therefore, James had gone on to argue that his story required an impression of ghostly pertinacity in *design*, to convey which he had employed the repeated, individual appearances of two phantasms, and that as a result his haunting pair, in death as in life, were somewhat unorthodox in their behaviour, the admission would have been perfectly straightforward and intelligible. The captious reader might still ask why, in that case, being partners in evil, Quint and Miss Jessel do not appear together—an objection which James might have anticipated by noting that a joint manifestation, while it might have helped to suggest complicity, would at once have aligned his ghosts with fictional haunts rather than attested phantasms, among which the simultaneous appearance of a second figure was of 'extreme rarity'.[230] Alternatively, he might have repudiated the necessity for any suggestion of complicity—the 'indifference and detachment' of the spectral Miss Jessel marked her estrangement from the seducer to whom she had yielded; although she had become, perhaps in reality always was, as evil as Quint, there was no common satisfaction in the loveless ends their ghosts pursued.

And here I pause to note, rather uneasily, that Miss Jessel's intermittent personation of a vengeful water-sprite, along with the circumstances of Miles's death, might lend some faint colour to this suggestion of estrangement and enmity. When, in the last chapter, the governess's protective gesture assures him that a spirit he cannot see is at the window, Miles's immediate reaction is to name Miss Jessel, not Quint. The obvious explanation is that, either directly from Flora, or through servants' gossip, Miles has learned of the previous day's scene at the lakeside. But—has Miss Jessel been enlisting Flora's aid against her betrayer, and is the death of Quint's minion a ghost's revenge upon a ghost? The speculation is not supported by James's remarks in the *Notebooks*, let alone the *Prefaces*, and is quite inconsistent with the children's affectionate collusion, *demonstrated* in the story. That so remote and fantastic a possibility could suggest itself, indicates the depth of obscurity in which James's technique of 'adumbration' leaves all questions of motive.

But, blandly oblivious of all such implications, as of the fallacies in his argument, James insists that *The Turn of the Screw* 'was an action, desperately, or it was nothing' (p. 174), and that Quint and Miss Jessel had to be 'agents in fact'—'so that, briefly, I cast my lot with pure romance, the appearances conforming to the true type being so little romantic' (p. 175). The reader can only assume that 'action', 'agent', and 'fact' must here be used in a special Jamesian sense, while the text itself proclaims the author's indebtedness to the 'true type' he disparages. Why does he so equivocate? And why does *The Turn of the Screw* in particular require such an elaborate defence? Proportionately to its length, it occupies more of his critical space in the New York Edition than any other of his works; and exceptionally, it is discussed twice over, for certain of James's observations prefacing Volume XVII (pp. 252–58) are more applicable to it than to the five stories they ostensibly introduce.[231]

The explanation must, I think, be twofold. James's insistence that his story is an 'action' in which Quint and Miss Jessel are 'agents' has nothing to do with their ghostliness: it is really an allusion to James's often-resumed and never-to-be-concluded argument—with Stevenson in 1884 and apropos of Stevenson in 1887 and 1900, with Shaw in 1910 and with Wells in 1915 —regarding the true nature and right exercise of the art of fiction. The relevant portions of James's argument, in its 1884 formulation, may be summarized as follows. A novel must represent experience, but what constitutes experience is not a succession of events but 'an immense sensibility', and the novelist's art consists in the fullness of perfection with which he renders the values so revealed; 'murders, mysteries . . . hairbreadth escapes, miraculous coincidences' or 'the moral consciousness of a child' —it is all one: the treatment makes the excitement as it makes the art.[232] Stevenson retorts that a novel's artistic excellence depends not on 'its resemblances to life' but on the fidelity with which it renders the creative idea; the treatment must therefore vary in accordance with the numerous, valid differences of subject. And of James in particular Stevenson observes that as 'he treats, for the most part, the statics of character' so he instinctively avoids 'the scene of passion' proper to the dramatic novel: the treatment of any of 'the passionate *cruces* of life' must be direct.[233] On the contrary, James in his *Preface* seems to answer, 'moving accidents and mighty mutations and strange encounters' 'when they come straight, come with an effect imperilled' (p. 256). His intermediaries, such as the governess of *The Turn of the Screw* or the hero of 'The Jolly Corner', by their attestation *make* the reader's excitement *and* the story—an 'adventure-story' much more rewarding to the author than any tale of 'detectives or pirates or other splendid desperadoes'; for 'the spirit engaged with the forces of violence interests me most when I can think of it as engaged most deeply, most finely and most "subtly" ' (pp. 257–58). After all (if we may compare a minor with a major work of art), is the liaison of Quint and Miss Jessel, is their corruption of Miles and Flora, so much more shadowy than the *affaire* between Chad and Mme de Vionnet, or their manipulation of the innocent Jeanne? In *The Ambassadors* an army of dissemblers conceals the intrigue, while there is only one such—the master—in *The Turn of the Screw*; for (to digress) could that man of the world possibly believe in Miss Jessel's 'respectability'? Douglas sets the master's comment (pp. 10–11) in what even to an audience at third hand is the key of airy cynicism. The tardiness of Strether's enlightenment therefore has circumstantial justifications which do not exist for the governess, whom the witness of her own eyes precipitates into awareness, for which corroboration is as hastily snatched. But are Strether's elucidations much more realistic in their effect than the governess's intuitions? It seems that for James, once he has decided to treat the selected 'experience' indirectly and allusively, the 'action' may as well be past as present, the 'agents' as well be dead as living.

As for James's denial of the Society for Psychical Research and its veridical phantasms, and his claim that his story is 'pure romance', meaning either traditional or invented fantasy, these, one must assume, are precautionary devices similar to the formula prefixed to many novels: 'All the characters and situations are imaginary, and no reference is intended to any living person.' The portrait of Quint, as I interpret it, adequately if not fully explains James's caution here, as the allusion to Gurney does the evasive introduction to 'Sir Edmund Orme'—set, it is claimed, 'in the old, the mid-Victorian, the Thackerayan Brighton' (p. 261). One must, however, also allow for the changed perspective in which James, writing his *Prefaces* of 1908–09, viewed the founders of psychical research and their pronouncements of the eighties and nineties. There was no longer a personal connection to stimulate interest in, and respect for, the English Society and its researches: both Sidgwick and Myers were now dead; and perhaps more disturbingly, their associate Podmore, whose scepticism had been so reassuring, was now under a cloud, which his mysterious death in 1910 did nothing to dissipate. Moreover the *bona fides* of the psychical pioneers was now being seriously questioned: statements published in the *Westminster Gazette* from November 1907 to January 1908 had alleged fraud in the thought-transference experiments conducted under their supervision, and in the following December and January (1908–09) the weekly *John Bull* substantiated these allegations by publishing the confession of one of the tricksters.[234] This was no time to advertise one's reliance on phantasms so sponsored.

But if the examples already cited are not sufficiently conclusive evidence of James's indebtedness to the Society's records, the following cases offer correspondences with *The Turn of the Screw* so astonishingly close as by themselves to attest his use of the volumes from which they come.

First, a young woman in June 1888 communicates an occurrence of November 1882, 'about five o'clock one afternoon':

Having forgotten some new waltzes I had laid on the music shelf in the back drawing-room, I left the piano, and went dancing gaily along, singing a song as I went, when suddenly there stood before me, preventing me getting the music, the figure of a woman, heavily robed in deepest black from the head to her feet; her face was intensely sad and deadly pale. There she stood, gazing fixedly at me. The song died on my lips; the door, I saw, was firmly closed where she stood, and still I could not speak. At last I exclaimed, 'Oh, auntie, I thought it was you!' believing at the moment she or some strange visitor stood before me, when suddenly she vanished.

Later, from the top of the kitchen stairs, the young woman observed a similar figure walking in the basement. It should be noted that for three weeks before the first visual experience, the family had been troubled by strange noises, which continued to disturb them throughout their tenancy of the house. From November 1887 the house was occupied by new tenants, and among other features of a veritable campaign of ghostly harassment, a child of ten was terrified by the sight of 'a dreadful white face peeping round the door', on which a 'beautiful hand' was laid; and her sister aged nine, passing a room on the stairs, 'saw a man standing by the window staring fixedly; blue eyes, dark brown hair, and freckles'. It was revealed to the second set of tenants that a woman had hanged herself in one of the rooms of the house; and also that the first tenants had had 'a very wicked servant'. A newspaper report of the suicide (from which Podmore quotes) gave the date as 28 March 1879.[235]

Secondly, there is a communication vouched for by a Boston associate of the Society. A professional nurse, watching over a dying woman, early in the morning of 15 April 1890, 'while she was resting on the settee, but wide awake',

happened to look toward the door into the adjoining chamber and saw a man standing exactly in the door-way, the door being kept open all the time. He was middle-sized, broad-shouldered, with shoulders thrown back, had a florid complexion, reddish-brown hair (bare headed) and beard, and wore a brown sack overcoat, which was unbuttoned. His expression was grave, neither stern nor pleasant, and he seemed to look straight at [the nurse], and then at [the dying woman] without moving. [The nurse] supposed, of course, that it was a real man, and tried to think how he could have got into the house.

Then, becoming frightened, she turned her head away and called her daughter, asleep in the same room; when she looked back at the door the apparition had disappeared. Neither the daughter nor, it seemed, the unconscious patient (who died later that day) had been aware of its presence. A neighbour, from the nurse's description, subsequently identified the apparition as that of the patient's first husband, completely unknown to the percipient, and dead for about thirty-five years.[235]

Thirdly, in December 1883 an elderly woman communicates an experience of February 1854, when she 'was about 25 years of age, and had no theory as to ghosts or spirits in general':

My younger brother was in Australia, and had not written to his family for some four or five months, from which my mother had concluded he must be dead. I was sitting with her and my sister in our dining-room one morning, about 11 o'clock. . . . I looked up, . . . when I saw my brother standing on the lawn in front of the window apparently looking at us. I jumped up, saying to my mother, 'Don't be frightened, mother, but there is T. come back all right.' . . . 'Where?' said my mother and sister, 'I don't see him.' 'He is there,' I answered, 'for I saw him; he is gone to the front door,' and we all ran to the door. My father, who was in his library, heard the commotion, and opened his door to ask the cause. I had by this time opened the front door, and not seeing my brother, I thought he was hiding for fun among the shrubs, so I called out, 'Come, T., come in, do not play the fool or you will kill dear mother.' No one answered, and then my mother exclaimed, 'Oh, you did not see him really, he is dead, I know he is dead.' I was mystified, but it did not seem to me the right solution of the mystery. I could not think he was dead, he looked so honestly alive. To tell the truth, I believed for some time that he was in the garden.

Eventually the brother returned, and it was found that his delirious vision of the old home during an illness had coincided with his sister's hallucination. 'I remember,' she adds, 'at the time, that I saw my brother dressed as he usually was when he came home from London, not as he was when he left home, nor as he could be in Australia, nor as I had ever seen him when walking in the garden. He had on a tall hat and a black cloth suit, neither of which he had taken with him.' And regarding her own state of mind and health she asserts, 'I was then young and vigorous; I had no superstitions, never having experienced any exceptional sorrows: those I had gone through were common enough, and more calculated to develop the matter-of-fact side of my character than to induce a morbid or dreamy imagination.'[235]

Fourthly, a lady in July 1884 communicates from memory an occurrence of 'about March 1875', when she lay reading in her drawing-room at Gibraltar 'on a bright sunshiny afternoon':

I suddenly felt that some one was waiting to speak to me. I looked up from my book and saw a man standing beside an arm-chair, which was about 6 feet from me. He was looking most intently at me, with an extraordinary earnest expression in his eyes, but as I walked forward to speak to him, he disappeared.

The room was about 18 feet long, and at the further end of it I saw our servant [Pearson], holding open the door as if he had admitted a visitor. . . . I spoke to him, asking if anyone had called. To which he replied, 'No one, ma'am,' and walked away. . . .

I then thought it over again. I knew the face quite well, but could not say whose it was, but the suit of clothes impressed me strongly as being exactly like one which my husband had given to a servant named Ramsay the previous year. . . . He turned out badly, and I had to send him away before we went to Gibraltar [in February, 1875], but he was taken on as waiter at the Inverness Club, and I had no cause to be anxious about him, as I thought he was well and doing well, and would probably profit by his past experience and keep that situation.

Soon afterwards, it was learned that Ramsay had died in hospital at Inverness, the date of death (ascertained by Gurney) being 9 March 1875. An earlier account of the incident, published in *All the Year Round* on 31 August 1878, contains (as Gurney noted)

a more complete explanation of the non-recognition of the face. As regards the momentary mistaking of the man for a visitor, these words occur: 'I will only remind you that, as far as appearances went, the man was a gentleman. He had gentle birth on one side, was always refined in his manners, and, moreover, was dressed in a suit of clothes of which no gentleman need have been ashamed.'

The servant Pearson, incidentally, gave warning that same March day 'because, he said, "the house was haunted" '; the news of Ramsay's death was received after his departure.[235]

Fifthly, a lady, percipient in a 'transitional' case of experimental thought-transference, writes:

Yesterday, viz., the morning of Nov. 16, 1886, about half-past 3 o'clock, I woke up with a start, and an idea that someone had come into the room. I also heard a curious sound, but fancied it might be the birds in the ivy outside. Next I experienced a strange, restless longing to leave the room and go downstairs. This feeling became so overpowering that at last I rose, and lit a candle, and went down, thinking if I could get some soda-water it might have a quieting effect. On returning to my room, I saw Mr. Godfrey standing under the large window on the staircase. He was dressed in his usual style, and with an expression on his face that I have noticed when he has been looking very earnestly at anything. He stood there, and I held up the candle and gazed at him for 3 or 4 seconds in utter amazement; and then, as I passed up the staircase, he disappeared. The impression left on my mind was so vivid that I fully intended waking a friend who occupied the same room as myself; but remembering I should only be laughed at as romantic and imaginative, refrained from doing so.

I was not frightened at the appearance of Mr. Godfrey, but felt much excited and could not sleep afterwards.

During a subsequent experiment by the same agent, this lady in December 1886 reports having felt 'a cold breath streaming over me . . . and I also distinctly saw a figure leaning over me. . . . The whole time it remained, there was a draught of cold air streaming through the room, as if both door and window were open.'[235]

Sixthly, to be echoed in a single note of unease marking the governess's first night at Bly, there is an experience reported, ten years after the event (of July 1874), by a former nursery governess. One night, while on her summer holiday 'and in perfect health', she 'was awakened suddenly with a cry of distress ringing in [her] ears'. The cry was twice repeated, the last time 'partly suppressed and further away', and she recognized the voice as that of a child between two and three years of age, 'one of several of whom she had been in charge, and whom she had known to be considerably ill-used by the lady who was acting as his guardian'. She 'sprang out of bed and looked out. It was a lovely still night, not a movement nor a sound disturbed the air, and it was so light that [she] could see the time on a small silver watch which was lying on the table. It was 12.45.' On her return to her duties, the governess 'learnt from the servants' that on the night when she had heard the cries the child was kept in his guardian's room, to emerge the next morning with 'marks of cruel ill-usage'. The servants had 'heard cries and moans until they fell asleep, and at midnight were awakened by three successive cries that rang through the house—the last a suppressed echo of the others'.[235] Or, as James's governess 'recognised' it—'faint and far, the cry of a child' (p. 16). The footstep heard during that same restless night at Bly is a commonplace of supernatural experience, and has a more realistic parallel in *Jane Eyre*; but there can have been only one source for that distinctive, and in its new context irrelevant, cry.

The first of these six cases is taken from Volume VI, the second from Volume VIII, of the SPR *Proceedings*; the four others come from *Phantasms of the Living*. *PSPR* Volume VIII seems to have been of limited use to James (though the surname 'Quint' was a notable find); but on the collective evidence presented, both internal and external, direct and indirect, there can be no doubt that Volume VI provided a widely useful source-book for his ghostly tales.

Did he use *Phantasms of the Living* similarly? This would, on the face of it, be unlikely—the two volumes are so large and so selectively indexed as to be unhandy for reference. But James almost certainly drew upon them for *The Turn of the Screw*: apart from the range of standardized 'effects' already mentioned, the demonstrable use of even two exceptional cases (and *The Turn of the Screw* clearly owes 'a touch of picture' in the description of Quint, and pretty well the whole picture of his dawn visitation, to the fourth and

fifth respectively of those just cited) is sufficient to establish as their source
the work in which they both appear. If it were a question of the fifth case
only, one would be faced with an *embarras de choix*. Frank Podmore, to
whom the report containing it had in the first place been addressed, utilized
it in both *Apparitions and Thought Transference* (1894) and *Studies in
Psychical Research* (1897).[236] There was, so far as I am aware, no stimulus of
personal acquaintance with the author, nor (at this date) the fascination of a
tragic enigma, to tempt James into consulting either of these rather drily
written, 'scientific' works—even though the first, a typical handbook, un-
expectedly compliments him with a reference to his story 'The Liar'.[237] By
1894, however, Godfrey and his psychic exploits were familiar to romance-
readers over most of the western world. In 1889 Camille Flammarion had
used them to help ballast his astro-psychic fantasy *Uranie*;[238] and this,
during the next few years, appeared in a string of new editions and translations, all copiously illustrated. In Flammarion's paraphrase, and Ernest
Bieler's more deftly dramatic picturing of it, the staircase encounter loses
little of its suggestive force. But James was not an amateur of nineteenth-
century science fiction; and, in the event, the working principle of economy
of means leads us to the single, common source—*Phantasms of the Living*.
And (if the probable reaction of a reader impatiently 'alien to the whole
business' may be taken into account) the book's very unwieldiness, combined with an accident of publication, may help to explain the degree and
manner of its use in *The Turn of the Screw*. Only one edition of *Phantasms
of the Living* was published, but its printing was delayed, and in November
1886, after a number of copies of the first impression had been issued, the
editors took the opportunity of appending twelve pages of 'Additions and
Corrections' to the original *Introduction*. A note added on the verso of
the title-page to Volume I reads: 'In the later copies of this edition,
a few mistakes which occurred in the earlier copies have been corrected,
and some additions have been made. Of these, by far the most important is
the record which appears on pp. lxxxi-iv of this Volume.' This record,
supplied by the Rev. Clarence Godfrey of Eastbourne, is the one which
includes the fifth case cited above. Since James's interest in the work is not
likely to have antedated Gurney's death in 1888, or even perhaps his own
involvement with the Society's reports of seances in 1890–91, it would
presumably be the volumes of the corrected impression that he consulted—
to be led directly to a most remarkable and, as it proved, useful instance of
the supernatural.

My third and fourth cases are juxtaposed in the final chapter of Volume I,
the subject of which (to be discussed presently) may have attracted James's
attention. For his eye to have lighted on the sixth case, in the midst of well
over three hundred narratives gathered as a 'Supplement' in Volume II,
would argue either a high degree of serendipity, or a more careful reading of
the whole work than I have credited him with. But its position alone, at

the end of Volume II, would ensure the impatient reader's glance at the last narrative of the collection. This is a case on the evidential value of which Gurney laid special emphasis, and which the percipient himself found 'absolutely unique—by far the strangest and most perplexing thing that had ever happened to him'. One remembers that of the audience who listen to Douglas's reading of *The Turn of the Screw* the only member named is Griffin, and that it is Griffin and his wife who remark on Douglas's obvious attachment to the deceased governess, so much his senior (p. 7). The percipient in Gurney's final case was a Mr. Griffin, and the phantasm he perceived was that of 'an old lady friend', who had some years before nursed him through a dangerous illness, and for whom he had 'a warm affection': 'The figure plainly pronounced my name, "Marcus," once, and then gradually disappeared as I watched it.' At that moment the friend was dying: 'a few minutes before her death she said, "Tell Marcus I thought of him"' (II, 703–05).

Not only this—it is with a ghost story told by Griffin that James opens his account, and we are given a summary of Griffin's story:

The case, I may mention, was that of an apparition in just such an old house as had gathered us for the occasion—an appearance, of a dreadful kind, to a little boy sleeping in the room with his mother and waking her up in the terror of it; waking her not to dissipate his dread and soothe him to sleep again, but to encounter also, herself, before she had succeeded in doing so, the same sight that had shaken him. (p. 3)

Several near parallels to Griffin's ghost story are recorded in *Phantasms of the Living* and in the SPR *Proceedings*; for if, as Douglas remarks, a ghost's 'or whatever it was . . . appearing first to the little boy, at so tender an age, adds a particular touch,' one more 'turn of the screw' (p. 4), it is not correct, as another auditor seems to suggest (p. 3), that a child is only exceptionally involved in such occurrences:[239] children feature as percipients in approximately one quarter of Gurney's eighty-odd 'collective cases'. No one of the recorded incidents exactly answers to Griffin's story, which seems to be a memorial combination of a number of more or less typical elements, but the two following examples, both from *PSPR* Volume VIII, are strikingly close.[240] The first is the narrative of a mother, who had been persuaded for one night to leave the bedside of a dying friend: 'About three o'clock that night my eldest son [of nine years old], who was sleeping in my room, woke me with the cry of: "Mamma! there is Mr. Blake!" I started up! It was quite true. He floated through the room about half a foot from the floor, smiling at me as he disappeared through the window.' In this case the apparition could hardly be described as 'of a dreadful kind', and neither mother nor son appears to have been terrified by it; but terror does seem to have entered into the second case, which again concerned a dying friend of the mother's:

The night before she died we were awakened between twelve and one o'clock by a noise like tapping at the window twice. My husband got up and went downstairs, but could see nothing. So we tried to settle to sleep again, when all of a sudden we were alarmed by our little boy, who was not quite two years old, calling out 'Auntie,' by which name he used to call her, and pointing towards the foot of the bed, and there I saw her standing all in white.

Reporting the occurrence some fifteen years later the mother recalled that on sight of the apparition 'she screamed, and frightened her husband so much that he dared not look'. This example, it should be remarked, immediately follows the second of the six cases quoted above.

But (and the point seems usually to be missed) these two narratives, along with the dozens of other tales involving childish percipients which might be cited, are parallels to Griffin's ghost story, not to the governess's. Admittedly, both Griffin's story and Douglas's comment on it prepare the reader for an account of a ghostly visitation in which the percipients will be two children, but James repeatedly and systematically disappoints this expectation. The reminder that neither youth nor innocence exempts children from awareness of the supernatural is given us at the outset, but thereafter we meet only the governess's suppositions of this awareness in Flora or in Miles—until the last scene of all, when even the governess is persuaded that Miles sees no ghost. We are encouraged, every so often, to think both children 'for a change—*bad*!' yet, apart from the governess's suspicions, there is nothing to indicate that this youthful wickedness is supernaturally prompted—nothing, that is, beyond a covert hint or two from the author. The dangerous 'power of sound' and its psychic associations have already been noted; but one must have read, as James seems to have done, reports of seance procedure to gather the psychic connotations of a wafted flower. Miles, we are told, in his 'sweet, high, casual pipe' always 'threw off intonations as if he were tossing roses', and 'there was something in them that always made one "catch" ' (p. 104). So, in the presence of the medium Daniel Home, a flower would be tossed or 'carried deliberately' to a sitter, who might (or might not) believe the motive power to be supernatural.[241] Yet even the roses are ambivalent; for it may be remembered, and James certainly would not forget, that in the final battle for the soul of Faust it is the roses scattered by the angelic host, and searing as they fall, that vanquish Mephistopheles with all his demonic strength and craft.[242]

The Turn of the Screw therefore, whatever it may be, is not a routine ghost story of the new pattern, any more than of the old. There are precedents and parallels galore for almost every circumstantial and contributory detail, but at no stage can the reader fall back on precedent to decide the central question: 'Do Miles and Flora *ever* actually *see* what the governess sees?' Here the reader must 'think for himself', very much as James has invited him to do regarding the nature of the corruption worked by Quint and Miss Jessel. As it happens, in the virtual certainty that James was conversant both with *PSPR* Volumes VI and VIII and with *Phantasms of the Living*, we can with some little confidence estimate his own probable answer to the question.

viii

Phantasms of the Living is of course far from being a mere 'collection of ghost stories'. It marks the first, and so far the only, attempt to collect, sift, classify, and assess the *whole* of the available evidence for paranormal communication between living persons. It therefore presents concerted 'experimental' efforts at 'thought transference', and experimental but unilateral attempts (classed as 'transitional') by an agent to communicate without conscious assistance from the percipient, as well as the much more numerous and extremely varied instances of 'spontaneous' telepathy. In all, seven hundred and two 'transitional' and 'spontaneous' cases are assigned an 'evidential number'; but in fact many more cases, some of which appear to have an evidential value little inferior, are cited and discussed at length and in detail. Most of the narratives recorded deal with 'crisis apparitions' —the appearance to someone at a distance, of a friend or relative shortly before, or at the moment of, or even shortly after, death or grave danger. The impression is not always visual, or purely so: it may be partly or wholly auditory, or tactile, or merely an intuition unaccompanied by sensory phenomena—Gurney, however, notes (II, 22) the great preponderance of visual cases. In an overwhelming majority of the experiences reported (whether 'transitional' or 'spontaneous') a link of emotion or interest existed, however tenuously, between agent and percipient. It is not uncommon, therefore, to find that of a group of people, especially at a gathering more or less public and casual, only one becomes aware of the manifestation. But percipience is not necessarily (though it is usually) shared even when the companions are siblings, mother or father and child, or husband and wife—there are differences in psychic accessibility to be taken into account. And owing, no doubt, to an exceptional degree of such accessibility or sensitivity, but puzzlingly nevertheless, the telepathic impression may be received by one who has no direct personal involvement with the agent. The communication seems to be deflected, as it were, and this third party, accidentally intervening, receives the impression instead of the true or intended percipient. Here is one such example—the communication, from a lady, is dated 30 October 1885:

In the month of August, 1864, about 3 or 4 o'clock in the afternoon, I was sitting reading in the verandah of our house in Barbadoes. My black nurse was driving my little girl, about 18 months or so old, in her perambulator in the garden. I got up after some time to go into the house, not having noticed anything at all—when this black woman said to me, 'Missis, who was that gentleman that was talking to you just now?' 'There was no one talking to me,' I said. 'Oh, yes, dere was, Missis—a very pale gentleman, very tall, and he talked to you, and you was very rude, for you never answered him.' I repeated there was no one, and got rather cross with the woman, and she begged me to write down the day, for she knew she had seen someone. I did, and in a few days I heard of the death of my brother in Tobago. Now, the curious part is this, that *I* did not see him, but she—a stranger to him—did; and she said that he seemed very anxious for me to notice him.

In reply to enquiries, this correspondent answered:

(1) The day of death was the same, for I wrote it down. I think it was the 3rd of August, but I know it was the same.
(2) The description, 'very tall and pale,' was accurate.
(3) I had no idea that he was ill. He was only a few days ill.
(4) The woman had never seen him. She had been with me for about 18 months, and I considered her truthful. She had *no object* in telling me.

Further, the mistress had immediately mentioned what the servant said and the fact that she herself had written down the date to her husband, who gave written corroboration. On checking published records, the investigators found that the day and month of the brother's death had been accurately recalled, but that the year was 1863.[243]

A comparable example of limited percipience is supplied by the second in the group of cases I have noted as specially relevant to *The Turn of the Screw*—the case in which a nurse, unfamiliar with her patient's history, sees a phantasm which concerns the patient, not herself. It was therefore quite in the order of things supernatural for the governess, a stranger to Bly and its household, to become aware of manifestations which were invisible to those whom they presumably concerned. Neither her sanity nor her honesty is impugned by the singularity of her experience—nor is the honesty of her companions. Mrs. Grose and Flora might quite truthfully deny awareness of what was nevertheless there to be seen. One has, of course, to observe that between the Barbados case and the Boston case (a closer analogue to James's fiction) there are important differences. In the first the intended percipient herself identifies the agent and attests her own rôle, while the patient in the second case dies without confirming or denying the speculative interpretation of the phantasm and her relation to it. And the brother's manifestation in Barbados occurred possibly before, certainly not long after his death in Tobago, whereas the husband who appeared in Roslindale had been dead some thirty-five years. Are we then to assume that in these two cases different kinds of psychic operation occurred, and that phantasms of a different kind were manifested? What are we to understand occasions 'phantasms of the living', and what must we accept as the limitations of this category?

In tentative explanation only of matters on which, as they stressed, no final judgment had been reached, Gurney and Myers argued that in the shock and under the impetus, as it were, of crucial anxiety, of physical danger, or of both to some degree combined in the last stages of a mortal illness, there may occur a projection of the personality which will be telepathically received by one or more suitably constituted persons. 'The original of the phantasm', its owner so to speak, is therefore the agent in this telepathic communication. As regards the survivor of a crisis, whatever it might have been, or even a moribund person, the theory (if the hypothesis of telepathy is accepted) is plausible; but difficulties multiply if the alleged 'agent', as happens in so many of these cases, has died before the communication is received. So, not only for reasons 'suggested by actual experience' but from considerations of expedience also—in plain words, to avoid complicating an already 'difficult inquiry' with any whisper of spirit survival—it was decided to ascribe 'phantasms at death to living rather than to dead men' (I, lxv). Now it is true that the actual moment of death might be impossible to establish, and that the awareness of it through an externalized phantasm might be variously delayed; but irreversible physical death, even before the onset of dissolution, surely presents a different psychical problem from that of suspended animation or coma, however prolonged. The theory thus adjusted takes on a very arbitrary air, and its authors, having once permitted themselves Humpty Dumpty's licence, found it easy to allow successive modifications. You were dead, it seemed, and therefore disqualified as an agent, when Gurney and Myers declared you to be so, not before—in *Phantasms of the Living* a mere twelve hours' extension was deemed sufficient (I, 139). But even this period of latency did not cover those manifestations received 'weeks or months' after the accepted moment of death.

By March 1889 therefore, Myers was prepared to acknowledge, as 'the result of some kind of energy exercised by a decedent whose body is unquestionably dead', apparitions perceived up to 'a year after death'. Whether Gurney would have been in agreement with Myers on this point is not clear: in his last, unfinished paper read to the Society he was obviously preparing to deal, on their merits, with cases for which such an explanation would not have been adequate, and in discussing which the question of spirit survival would have to be faced. It is interesting to note Gurney's formulation here of the conditions necessary to establish an apparition of the dead as 'something more than a mere subjective hallucination of the percipient's senses':

Either (1) more persons than one might be independently affected by the phenomenon; or (2) the phantasm might convey information, afterwards discovered to be true, of something which the percipient had never known; or (3) the appearance might be that of a person whom the percipient himself had never seen, and of whose aspect he was ignorant, and yet his description of it might be sufficiently definite for identification.[244]

It is this last requirement with which, on his governess's behalf, James has complied; and he has also observed Myers's time limit: when their phantasms appear to the governess, less than a year has elapsed since the deaths of Quint and Miss Jessel.

In July 1889, however, Myers presented a number of additional cases as illustrations of 'persistent personal energy'—indications 'that some kind of force is being exercised' *more* than a year after death; and he acknowledged his belief that 'in some at least' of these cases 'there has been a real agency of deceased persons'. The phenomena are produced telepathically through the medium of 'a sub-conscious or submerged stratum in both agent and percipient', that is, in both the disembodied and the embodied personality. There are then 'ghosts'? Not exactly; but there may be 'veridical after-images', severally representing a dead man's 'memory or his dream'; and the evidence on the whole 'makes not for haunted men but for haunted *places*'. Realizing, no doubt, that from a co-author of *Phantasms of the Living* such views would be judged at least inconsistent, Myers prefaced them with a bland reversal of his earlier assumptions:

The momentous step, of course, is already taken so soon as we consent to refer any *post-mortem* apparition—dating even from the morrow of the death,—to the continued agency of the decedent. Few readers will question the assumption that in that unknown journey *ce n'est que le premier pas qui coûte*.[245]

But Myers's new theory was not allowed to pass unchallenged. To Podmore it seemed 'that the facts, as so far ascertained, lent themselves quite as readily to what may perhaps be called an agnostic interpretation; and that it would advance the ultimate solution of the problem if both views were fairly represented'. In a lengthy paper, 'Phantasms of the Dead from Another Point of View', he analysed some two hundred cases from the Society's records: these dealt with 'successive' appearances of a phantasm 'to different percipients in the same locality', with 'collective' appearances 'to two or more persons simultaneously', and with experiences of single percipients where 'some corroborating circumstance' proved these to be veridical. Most of the occurrences described could, he found, be attributed to simple hallucination, the origin of which might be 'a morbid tendency on the part of the percipient' or the alarm caused by inexplicable noises. Expectancy alone might ensure that such a hallucination was repeated 'in the experience of the original percipient, or in that of others who shared his alarm', and the universal mythopœic tendency might produce a degree of conformity among the apparitions. Alternatively, in a number of these successive cases, as in collective cases generally, thought-transference might be assumed to operate. And thought-transference, or telepathy, *between living persons* remained the only plausible explanation for all phantasms not merely subjective in origin:

As regards the numerous instances quoted in previous papers read before the Society, of recognition of a phantasm by some marked peculiarity, it is suggested that thought-transference from the minds of persons still living is in almost all cases the explanation more directly suggested by the facts. Moreover, such thought-transference is a cause of whose operation we have independent proof, whilst we have little or no evidence of the action of disembodied intelligences.[246]

In his review of the evidence, Podmore systematically examined most of the narratives quoted by Myers in his papers of March and July 1889, and all of these he found explicable by some form of telepathic communication between living persons. A few cases might be explained by the prolonged latency and subsequent emergence of an impression received before the agent's death. In others the apparition might be the result of a 'collective', or as Podmore on one occasion terms it, 'contagious' hallucination shared between percipients. In yet others, it seemed, the image of an unknown person was 'transferred': in such cases 'we have to suppose the importation into the percipient's consciousness of a phantasmal image already completed, down even to very minute details'. Admittedly the supposition was a difficult one, but it 'could only appear easier for the spirit of a dead man to transmit such images, because we believe ourselves to know something of the limitations of ordinary human faculties, whilst we are free to ascribe to the dead whatever powers our imagination may feign'. For example, rather than assume with Myers that in 1836–37, at the age of eleven or twelve, the future Mme de Gilibert saw the ghost of her great-aunt, Lady Carnarvon, who had died ten years before and whom she had never known, Podmore would infer that the mind of the dying Earl of Egremont was occupied with thoughts of the sister who had predeceased him. Her phantasm was therefore clothed as the brother remembered her—wearing, in particular, a distinctive head-dress with 'lace lappets or strings which, passing under the chin, were tied in a bow on the top of the head'—and was making its way, by a door long blocked up, to what had been her own apartments. And in this phantasm Podmore would recognize not the ghost of a deceased sister visiting her brother on his death-bed, but an old man's reverie, shared telepathically by a grandchild playing on the staircase near his room. Where the connection between percipient and ostensible agent was merely local and temporary, the hypothesis of image-transference might seem less tenable. Yet even here Podmore would seek living intermediaries. A stranger to the Château de Prangins, for instance, would not be aware of Voltaire's one-time occupancy of a particular room, but this fact of local history might well exercise the minds of residents when a stranger was installed there. Certain narratives indeed (assuming their complete reliability) posed exceptional difficulties. But 'until either the theory of telepathy from the living has been proved inadequate to the facts, or the limits of its operation have been explored and defined', we are not justified in 'invoking *post-mortem* agency'— any more than in concluding 'that the possibility of such agency is disproved. The only legitimate conclusion from such premises is the practical one, that more evidence is required.'[247]

How then, applying Podmore's criteria, are the six manifestations of my illustrative group to be explained? The young lady of the first case (the longest, most fully documented, and most complicated of those quoted by Podmore), being no less suggestible but more pictorially imaginative than Affery Flintwich, translates the noises which preoccupy her into the recurrent spectacle of a woman in black. But in the five other cases (none of which is included in Podmore's survey) the phenomena may readily be accounted for as the product of telepathy between living persons. The brother in Australia, the servant possessed of his master's suit, the clergyman-experimenter, each living, each with varying degrees of conscious effort directing his thought towards a percipient, the maltreated child yearning (one presumes) for his kindly governess, are obviously the agents of their own psychic manifestations. The agent in the Boston case, however, is not the husband who died thirty-five years ago, but the wife, to all appearances unconscious, whose failing brain is occupied with memories of him. It is not a ghost, a *revenant*, that the nurse sees, but the image of her patient's thought.

There is an unmistakable tone of reproach in 'A Defence of Phantasms of the Dead', with which in January 1890 Myers answered his colleague's challenge. Podmore handled the theory of telepathy with a speculative freedom which the evidence so far accumulated did not justify. In *Phantasms of the Living*, certainly, a connection had been traced between experimental thought-transference and phantasmal appearances of the dying. Myers himself, however, would not on this basis infer that 'all these complex phenomena are merely varieties of the special phenomenon with which it was convenient to begin our inquiry;—but rather that a mixed multitude of obscure phenomena can now be seen to have a certain kinship'. In the evidence for post-mortem apparitions collected since 1886 he found 'no rational halting-place' between experimental thought-transference and 'apparitions generated by men long dead'; but his theory, misrepresented by Podmore as a belief in 'survival' and communications from the dead, was, more comprehensively, 'that the individualised energy which generates veridical phantasms is not coeval with the body. . . . [I]t may have pre-existed, and it may survive.' One thing, from the evidence, seemed clear: whatever the energy may be that generates these phantasms, of the living as of the dead, it is not dependent on 'the physiological activity of the brain', since 'the "agent," at the moment of the apparition, was often asleep, or fainting, or even in a state of coma'. 'It follows,' says Myers, 'that the presumption commonly urged against the conscious mind's continuance after bodily decay loses much of its force when we are considering this new-found form of mental energy,—so much less manifestly dependent upon bodily states.'[248]

To deal seriatim with Podmore's arguments would admittedly have been tedious: Myers selects a few points only for discussion. A mythopœic tendency to be allowed for? Certainly: that only makes for the genuineness of most post-mortem apparitions, 'flavourless' or 'odd' or lacking in apparent motive as most of them are. Relatively few veridical cases among them? Of course; but 'to found a negative argument upon the small number of cases yet encountered which point to man's continuance is rash indeed;—as rash as it was to argue against man's *antiquity* when only a few batches of flint implements had yet been discovered'. Podmore objects that dead animals cannot be the agents of their own phantasmal appearances? 'We are agreed that a phantasmal figure need not be directly generated by a mind or entity precisely resembling itself;' and in any case phantasms of animals, alive or dead, are difficult to explain. Next, a percipient's liability to subjective hallucination might improve, not (as Podmore inferred) weaken, the 'veridicality' of a particular case—it might indicate 'a predisposition or sensitiveness to *veridical* hallucinations'. As to the hypotheses favoured by Podmore: that of latency was admissible and to some extent useful, but not those of collective and of transferred hallucinations. Myers acknowledges that he had himself, in his paper of March 1889, advanced a precisely similar hypothesis of transfer; but that particular transfer had been, as one may say, only a little one, whereas Podmore's grossly outraged the probabilities. 'In the present state of our telepathic evidence we must avoid postulating sudden irregular extensions of this little-known power.'[249]

Here Myers abandons Podmore and the detailed consideration of evidence, to engage in the free-ranging speculation more congenial to him. We must assume 'that the vast majority of the effects produced by the unseen world upon our own are not definitely recognised by our intelligence'; and that 'the perception of certain psychical influences may be . . . an innate capacity which from its practical uselessness has never yet been fostered by the race, and which consequently reaches its higher grades only in a few chance individuals'. 'The great majority of psychical influences' will be unobserved, or when observed mere 'vague, inchoate sounds or sights'; and these vague phenomena, which so far have little evidential value, must not meanwhile be used 'to *discredit* those distincter phenomena' of which they form an integral part. There is need for a complete, factual record, both of the rudimentary phenomena mentioned and of the phenomena which distinguish insane and merely subjective from veridical hallucinations. We have, moreover, to allow for another factor which may diminish the intelligibility of 'post-mortem phantasms', and that is the '*local attraction*' which often seems to affect them: if we admit the influence of locality on such phantasms, contemporary human witness may be expected to validate only a very small minority. Myers goes on to distinguish five stages of psychic phenomena—hypnotic suggestion, telepathic experiments, spontaneous telepathy during life, phantasms at death, and phantasms after death—and finds that at each stage the manifestations take one of three forms—sensory hallucinations, emotional and motor impulses, and definite intellectual messages. At the third and subsequent stages, 'actual apparitions' become the predominant form; but the two other classes persist, and Myers considers that at the fifth stage it is the class of 'definite verbal messages' which offers the strongest presumption of post-mortem agency, and which therefore demands the closest attention: to illustrate its importance he presents five new cases, one of which, I have suggested, James drew upon in the story 'Sir Dominick Ferrand'. Myers's peroration, reviewing current attitudes to the problem of survival, and urging a disciplined boldness of enquiry, is as usual eloquent and somewhat impassioned.[250]

This whole performance, indeed, exhibits Myers at his most characteristic—one hardly knows which to admire more, the elasticity of his logic or the ease with which he changes his ground. And as characteristically Podmore eschews rhetoric, masses his evidence, and only occasionally permits himself a flash of rather sardonic humour. Here in fact we have, true to type, the enthusiast confronting the sceptic, the only anomalous feature being that the two are joint secretaries of one and the same society. But it so happens that their opposing views are set forth in a volume which may have been James's introduction to the records of that society's deliberations—a volume of which beyond reasonable doubt he made repeated use in his fiction. It is this circumstance, over and above their general relevance to my enquiry, that has led me to deal at such length (if still inadequately) with these two papers. One may disregard, as James for his fictional purposes seems to have done, the merely human tensions which were released in this battle of the phantasms. What is more to the point is that here two authorities, deeply versed in psychic phenomena, give each his considered interpretation of phantasms of the dead; and what is directly to the point—each of these conflicting interpretations is based on the same narrative evidence. The evidence being imperfect, no decision on such phantasms is possible—judgment must remain in suspense; but as *idola specus*, whether naturalistic or spiritualistic, they may still have their champions. It is this double reading of narratives accepted as veridical which, as it were, *authorizes* James's ambiguous treatment of the supernatural in *The Turn of the Screw*. And we can now, I think, accurately distinguish the alternatives so dissembled.

ix

There was no danger, Myers thought, that his own arguments would pander to superstition—would delude with 'an unwarranted expectation of the immortality which man's heart desires'.

For this is *not* what men desire—this inferential, incomplete demonstration that in some fashion or other there is something which survives the tomb. What men want is the assurance of personal happiness after death; or if they cannot feel this, they wish at least for such half-belief as may enable them to dismiss such speculations altogether. They do not desire to know more about death, but to avoid thinking of what they know already. A man will tell you in the same breath that he trusts to enter upon eternal happiness when he dies, but that he would rather not discuss such depressing subjects. . . .

Our work, so far as I can tell, is mainly followed by readers of a very different type. There is an attitude of mind, becoming yearly commoner among educated men, which, although neither cynical nor pessimistic, yet regards the present without enthusiasm and the future without eagerness. There is an acquiescence in the life of earth, and a deep distrust of the unknown. With the advance of knowledge, with the quickening of imagination, a feeling almost new in the world has arisen,—a kind of shrinking from the magnitude of Fate. . . .

Such, as I observe, is the prevailing temper which our evidence has to meet. That evidence does not attract, it rather irritates many of the best minds of our age. . . . [And yet] it *is* evidence; and if any evidence there be, then neither can science continue to ignore the problem nor philosophy to assume the solution. What is needed is simply a dispassionate intellectual curiosity bent upon unravelling the indications of man's survival after earthly manhood with the same candid diligence which has so lately unravelled the indications of man's descent from the brute.

But given human intelligence, was a completely dispassionate enquiry even possible? Myers himself from constitutional endowment and emotional experience was a believer, seeking evidence to support his belief. 'I am—as you surely know [he told William James]—no more than an insatiable lover of life & love, to whose earthly existence a kind of unity is given by his passionate effort to project his life & love beyond the tomb. This is not ethical, but organic.' As early as 1883 he had begun publishing first drafts of the material ultimately to be incorporated in his *magnum opus*—the posthumously issued *Human Personality and its Survival of Bodily Death* (1903). By the time of his duel with Podmore the mediumistic communications of Mrs. Piper had already furnished 'evidence' he judged to be conclusive. He was now armed in his belief, and increasingly found weapons to his hand.[251]

Podmore's bent was scientific, and his involvement in matters psychical —from 1875 to 1880 as a Spiritualist, but from its foundation in 1882 as an officer of the Society for Psychical Research—expressed a concern for their psychological rather than their metaphysical implications. A parallel concern was Socialism: Podmore was a foundation member of the Fabian Society, and his one publication outside the psychical field (his 1906 biography of the philanthropist Robert Owen) allowed him to combine both interests in a study wholly sympathetic. His publications within this field —seven books in addition to his articles and reports for the Society—reveal from first to last the one constant attitude. 'The question' is 'one of evidence. The task before us is the patient analysis of the existing evidence, and the attempt, preferably by direct experiment, to acquire new evidence on the subject.' There are some as yet inexplicable, but no demonstrably supernatural phenomena; that there are in operation supernatural agencies remains so far 'not proven'; but 'there is a superstition of incredulity' as inhibiting as its antithesis, the 'resolute credulity' named by Myers, is dangerous—one must preserve an open, if a vigilant mind. So, with careful tolerance, Podmore ends his *magnum opus, Modern Spiritualism: A History and a Criticism* (1902)—his scepticism only the more expert and comprehensive for his survey of three centuries' fraud, delusion, and honest bafflement in pursuit of the supernatural. Five minor works (the subject was obviously in vogue) are more or less simplified accounts of current psychical investigation and theory. Here he merely restates, with successive changes of illustration, the position reached in his argument of 1890 with Myers. The Miles–Ramsden correspondence of 1907 provides fresher instances of thought-transference than the Godfrey experiments of 1886, but telepathy between living minds is still his central theme. And whatever curiosity or hope beyond the scientific had at first impelled his search, he could in August 1900 write to the dying Sidgwick: 'I am not sure now that I very much care whether there is a personal, individual immortality. But I have at bottom some kind of inarticulate assurance that there is a unity and a purpose in the Cosmos: that our lives, our own conscious force, have some permanent value—and persist in some form after death.'[252]

Sidgwick himself remained the unwilling sceptic, finding his state of mind most truly expressed in the 'balanced, rhythmical fluctuation of moods' of Tennyson's *In Memoriam*. His farewell letters more than once echo its phrasing, but in a spirit closer to that of Arnold's 'Dover Beach': 'I hold on—or try to hold on—to duty and love; and through love to touch the larger hope.' Gurney had had no protracted leave-taking, and such personal testimony regarding 'survival' as may be gathered from his writings is of the nature of a *tertium quid* between affirmation and denial: 'the notion of personal continuance after death . . . exists as a doubt, but a doubt presenting itself to the majority in the positive form—not as "probably no" but as "possibly yes" '—in the key of hope not of resignation. Yet it was 'a fact' (so Myers in his eulogy declared) 'that Edmund Gurney had *not* a strong personal craving for a future life—had not even that kind of confidence in Providence, or in evolution, which leads most of us to take for granted that if that life exists, then for us and for the universe all must in the end be well'. William James, rounding off *The Varieties of Religious Experience* with a statement of his own philosophic position, was for the time being content to rest on Gurney's *tertium quid*: 'For practical life, at any rate, the *chance* of salvation is enough.' The most heavily charged of all theological terms is here used without doctrinal implication— James is speaking for a 'piecemeal supernaturalism' and a pluralistic universe.

The whole drift of my education goes to persuade me that the world of our present consciousness is only one out of many worlds of consciousness that exist, and that those other worlds must contain experiences which have a meaning for our life also; and that although in the main their experiences and those of this world keep discrete, yet the two become continuous at certain points, and higher energies filter in.

'Higher energies', 'the more characteristically divine facts'—'the over-belief on which I am ready to make my personal venture is that they exist': 'God is the natural appellation, for us Christians at least, for the supreme reality, so I will call this higher part of the universe by the name of God.' 'Pragmatic religion', one may think, readily assumes the attitudes of a more orthodox faith. Regarding psychical phenomena, William James to the end of his career maintained a scientist's caution: 'evidence' that to Myers gave assurance of personal survival to him indicated at the most 'supernormal knowledge'; but as an empirical philosopher intolerant only of systematic bounds, he could without any sense of incongruity acknowledge an intuitive belief. Confronted in 1904 by the direct questions, 'Do you believe in personal immortality?' and, 'If so, why?', he answered: 'Never keenly; but more strongly as I grow older. Because I am just getting fit to live.' Alas, as we have seen, notwithstanding all 'the forces of passion, of reason, of personality, that lived in [him]', when in obedience to his wishes his widow and his brother tried to communicate with him after death, there was no retrospective sign.[253]

In the last analysis, I think, Henry James was constitutionally more of the sceptic, more tough-minded perhaps, than his brother. From time to time he proclaimed his acceptance of William's philosophical views: 'I'm *with* you, all along the line,' he wrote in 1909, having read *A Pluralistic Universe* 'with enchantment, with pride, and almost with comprehension'. But this was rather a tribute to brotherly affection than acknowledgment of a craving-for-enlightenment satisfied. Such intellectual curiosity as he possessed was not, like his brother's, questing and aggressive, but passive and contemplative, directed not to general ideas and their mastery but to the scrutiny of particular cases—riddles of behaviour and social relationship each to be pondered for the interest of its subtlety rather than the importance of its solution. His artistic imagination was exerted within the range of his sensibility, not more and more widely on speculative flights but more and more intensely on the experience of consciousness. 'The question' of survival meanwhile 'took care of itself' for him. When in 1910 (no longer exposed to William's criticism nor overawed by his example) he himself ventures to philosophize, his argument, predictably encumbered with verbiage, is lit by flashes from his brother's thought—it represents, more loyally than Myers required of any phantasm, 'a dead man's memory or his dream'. But from it emerge both his own still-ardent love of 'living' and his persuasion that the cultivated consciousness (with a certainty measured by its effective cultivation) is the only pledge of immortality—it gives him 'the splendid illusion of doing something myself' towards the possibility. Many a creative artist has voiced the same hope, or defiance of fate, in terms considerably more arrogant; but in confrontation with this band of psychic researchers, his testimony places Henry James at an almost equal distance from Podmore (whose scepticism he shares, but not his indifference) and from Myers (whose desire for survival he can match without any of the accompanying faith).[254]

And that he is expressing no mere *ad hoc* conclusion, but one long ruminated, appears from a 'rough note' of January 1894, for a *donnée* (never fully utilized) belonging 'to the general group of themes of which *The Private Life* is a specimen'. The story was to deal with 'the drama, the tragedy, the general situation of disappointed ambition'. 'The idea of *death* both checked and caught me; for if on the one side it means the termination of the consciousness, it means on the other the beginning of the drama in any case in which the consciousness survives. In what cases *may* the consciousness be said to survive—so that the man is the spectator of his own tragedy?' James first decides on a self-betrayal of the kind Nick Dormer, in *The Tragic Muse*, avoids; but rejecting this situation as too 'thin', opts for his hero's 'real' death, half-way through the story: 'His verses, his poems, the things he has done for [his sacrificed first love], must play a part in the business.' The idea is taken up again, more than a year later: 'He himself, the man, must, *in* the tale, also materially die—die in the flesh as he had died long ago in the spirit, the *right* one. Then it is that his lost treasure revives most—no longer *contrarié* by his material existence, existence in his false self, his wrong one.' The fictional situation is used, in part, for 'The Way It Came' (1896); but not the underlying conception of death as the end of the story—which can be reread, as it were, but not added to. That grimly elegiac conception—all the more patently devoid of Christian hope for the fantasy of Christian observance with which James envelops it—had meanwhile been elaborated in 'The Altar of the Dead' (1895). And so expressed it stands (in the New York Edition) not as a companion piece, but like a manifesto at the head of James's group of supernatural tales. Sir Thomas Browne, who also meditated on the theme ('Our Fathers finde their graves in our short memories, and sadly tell us how we may be buried in our Survivors'), would at once have recognized, in that memorial blaze desperately illuminating 'the uncomfortable night of nothing', a reversion to 'old expectations' and a denial of the hope and evidence acknowledged by 'noble beleevers'. For Stransom, and for James, to be remembered was to survive, in the only way humanly possible: so long as the thought of them was kept by the living, the dead 'were saved better than faith or works could save them, saved for the warm world they had shrunk from dying to, for actuality, for continuity, for the certainty of human remembrance'. The dead, so cherished, 'had looks that remained, as great poets had quoted lines'. 'The idea,' James says in his

Preface (p. 241), 'had always, or from ever so far back, been there, not inter-fering with other conceits, yet at the same time not interfered with.'[255]

In January 1897, after a long silence, William James wrote to Myers: he sent New Year greetings, and made friendly enquiries about the great work on the subliminal consciousness. Myers responded at once, with characteris-tic effusiveness, and among other grateful memories associated with William James, recorded a meeting with his brother: 'I have had [two] pleasures lately connected with America. One, a delightful time with your brother at Aston Clinton, where in a long walk together I seemed to be allowed some-what nearer to him than heretofore.' Myers's second pleasure had been the appointment of Lyman Gage ('whom I really *loved* when at Chicago') to the Secretaryship of the Treasury, and this event can be precisely dated in January 1897. But 'lately' is a vague word, and since in this same letter the cast of Myers's gratitude extends to hospitalities of September 1893, the meeting at Aston Clinton may have occurred well before the New Year—though hardly early enough to account for the little touch of Myers in 'The Way It Came'. Neither Henry James's biographer, nor his hostess in her memoirs throws any light on the question; but whenever it took place, this *rapprochement* must have a bearing on his treatment of the supernatural in *The Turn of the Screw*. Edmund Gurney also had been an intimate of Cyril Flower's, and for both Myers and James, to revisit Aston Clinton was a nostalgic experience, evocative of a host of personal associations. If, how-ever, in prolonged conversation Myers found James less aloof than usual, one can infer, not that James relaxed anything of his scepticism, but that Myers was encouraged to discourse without restraint upon his ruling passion. Whatever psychical information James requested would now have been abundantly supplied; and he would have been reminded afresh not only of the fictional resources offered by the Society for Psychical Research, but also of the standing enigma presented by an alleged manifestation from the dead.[256]

Some chronological details will make the position clear. *PSPR* Volume VI had supplied a good many touches in James's fiction of 1891 and 1892, and not only in the 'ghostly tales'. Then, for over three years, he had published nothing on a supernatural theme, and only occasional *Notebook* entries (the record of Archbishop Benson's *donnée* in January 1895 and a first sketch for 'The Way It Came' in December 1895) show that his interest in such matters still persisted. But 'The Way It Came', as finally composed and published in May 1896, indicates (I have argued) a change of approach; and this can be most plausibly explained by James's acquaintance with what was in 1894, and till 1923 remained, the *last* authoritative word on spontaneously occurring psychical phenomena.[257] The prime object of the Census of Hallucinations had been to collect evidence of telepathy; but the Census Committee recognized the wider, psychological interest of the enquiry, and their Report, in *PSPR* Volume X, dealt concisely but comprehensively with the subject of hallucinations as a whole. With its two hundred new narrative illustrations, it constituted not merely a supplement, but also a synoptic guide to the much more copious but less systematically ordered material in *Phantasms of the Living*. And for Henry James this seems to have been an important consideration. *Phantasms of the Living* had been published five years before he resumed his composition of 'ghostly tales' in 1891; but although he may have looked into it earlier, it is not a source for any of his fiction before *The Turn of the Screw*. And the same is true of *PSPR* Volume VIII. In *The Turn of the Screw*, however, we find detail after detail traceable to *Phantasms of the Living* and to *PSPR* Volume VIII; *PSPR* Volume VI is put to more varied and more significant use than in 1891–92; and there are indications that the apparitional scheme has been checked against the Census Report.

Such a command of resources, in an area where James felt 'so alien', could result only from some external stimulus to his curiosity and interest, and this (as Myers's letter testifies) *was* in part supplied by the encounter at Aston Clinton. The ambience here, unless Myers grossly deceived himself, was one of sympathy and respect. But a few months later, matters psychical were brought very forcibly to the attention not only of Henry James, but of fashionable society and the newspaper-reading public generally, by an episode which threatened to reduce 'the whole business' to the level of farce. This was the investigation, on behalf of the Society for Psychical Research, of 'the alleged haunting of Ballechin House'. At this point, therefore, and close as we now are to Bly and its ghosts, a short detour is necessary.

x

Ballechin was a pleasant country-seat on the north bank of the Tay, some three miles above its junction with the Tummel. Dunkeld lay about eleven and Comrie about twenty-two miles to the south. The house, of moderate size for all its four storeys, had been built in 1806, and in the 1880s a wing of four rooms had been added. It was, therefore, a modern house, 'cheerful, sunny, convenient, healthy', and its modernity was emphasized by its plumbing: it had a hot-water system, and 'set basins' in all the main bedrooms. It had a large, central stair-well, lighted by a glass cupola; its walls were very thick, their thickness 'exaggerated by wood casing which everywhere [gave] a hollow sound on percussion'; its floors joists, however, were less substantial, 'for the floors vibrate[d] on the smallest provocation'. 'It follows,' to quote the same contemporary description, 'that the house [was] one huge sounding board.' In these combined facts of structure and site (near the Highland fault) lay the explanation for any number, variety, or intensity of intermittent 'audile phenomena'. But the latter, it seems, had not achieved any notoriety until, in 1892, they were reported to the Marquis of Bute, who from 1890 had been a vice-president of the Society for Psychical Research. In January 1897, at Lord Bute's suggestion and at his expense, Lieut.-Colonel Taylor, a Spiritualist as well as a member of the SPR, took a four months' lease ('with shooting and fishing') of Ballechin House. And since neither Colonel Taylor nor, apparently, any officer of the Society was immediately able to visit Ballechin, 'Miss X.', volunteering her services, was asked to take charge of the investigation—to instal herself and the necessary staff of servants in Ballechin House, and to invite as guests any persons who might to her judgment be reliable observers.[258]

The choice of investigator was less daring than it might at first appear. The Society's expert on poltergeists and allied matters was Frank Podmore, who had himself conducted as many as four such enquiries (beginning with the 'Worksop' case in 1883) and who had just published, in the twelfth and latest volume of *Proceedings*, a critical account of the eleven cases investigated and of certain others reported, up to 1896. But Podmore was a Civil Servant, and could not have spent weeks at a stretch in Perthshire; so that Colonel Taylor, retired and at leisure, and himself a practised investigator of such phenomena, was a fairly obvious second choice. Neither of these veterans, however, could match Miss X.'s precocious celebrity. Towards the end of 1891, the journalistic riches gone to waste (as he considered) in the Society's *Proceedings*, had been discovered, and promptly salvaged, by W. T. Stead: in the process, he had made the acquaintance of Miss X., then aged twenty-six, and already a psychicist of international repute. This 'perfectly self-possessed' young lady, with her position 'in Society' and her 'first-class education', so impressed him that, under her guidance, he began psychic experimentation on his own account, and then, enthusiastic at his success, launched a new quarterly, a psychical *Review of Reviews*, with Miss X. as his co-editor. *Borderland* ran from July 1893 to October 1897, and Miss X. in number after number displayed her learning and her varied experience in the psychical field. Haunted houses were frequently discussed, and Miss X.'s personal investigation, in June 1896, of 'Silverton Abbey' with its noises and its rumoured apparition, was a fitting preparation for her rôle at Ballechin. The 'Silverton' enquiry failed either to explain the noises or to raise the ghost; but her report of it was so circumstantial and so coolly judicial in tone that her readers might well believe its prolongation, for the 'month or two' she thought desirable, would have brought full enlightenment. After all, a mere two nights had been enough for her to receive powerful 'intuitive impressions', and (with some aid from local gossip) to detect a maleficent *living* influence, telepathically conveyed. One can appreciate the force of Myers's 'urgent' invitation to her: 'If you don't get phenomena,' he wrote, 'probably no one will.' This questionable compliment may in part reflect dissatisfaction with Podmore's sceptical habit and his standard, 'psychological' interpretation of poltergeist cases—the 'naughty little girl' formula; but it also indicates that the Ballechin case had not been presented to the Society as one of merely 'audile phenomena'. On the contrary, from its first reporting to the Marquis of Bute, it was sophisticated by psychical additions which had nothing to do with Ballechin House itself, but everything with Father H——, S.J., who reported them. He had stayed at Ballechin to hold a retreat for some nuns, and when he complained of the noises, the owner (so he claimed) had suggested that these might represent the efforts of his Protestant uncle, from whom he had inherited the estate, to obtain prayers for the repose of his soul. Father H—— had merely asperged his rooms and recited the prayer *Visita quæsumus*, and had himself seen only one vision—of a crucifix; but 'expectancy' was now roused, and would in due course be satisfied. For not only had Father H——'s account of the phenomena invested them with darkly traditional, ghostly terrors: his awed repetition of it, aided by Lord Bute's enquiries, had (one may infer) given a new impetus to local gossip about the deceased uncle—the 'wicked Major', who was suspected of an immoral relationship with his housekeeper, who had certainly kept fourteen dogs, and who had once imprudently told his gardener that if the work were neglected after his death 'his soul would go into a mole and haunt the garden and him too'. At any rate Lord Bute was now able to record, as Ballechin legend, pious visions and awful monitions never before mentioned in connection with the Ballechin noises; and as suitable adjuncts to the latter, a resourceful lady could in a magazine article evoke three quite unrelated, but unmistakably Gothic spectres.[259]

Miss X. thus entered on her rôle in the belief that here was not just a series of extraordinary and terrifying noises to be investigated, and if possible explained, but a case of alleged 'haunting', in which, once the 'audile phenomena' were established as genuine (that is, actually occurring and not illusory, and not the product either of demonstrably natural forces or of mischievous human agency), they must be assumed to be supernatural, when all that remained would be to suggest (tentatively, of course) a plausible psychic origin. The first requirement, therefore, was to induce a 'normal' attitude of mind, the state of quiet receptivity which, as she had personally discovered, was most favourable to psychic manifestations. So, all through those inclement months of winter and early spring at Ballechin (from 3 February to 14 May 1897), the semblance of a country-house party was kept up. Successive guests met at breakfast to report disturbed nights. When the weather prevented outdoor recreation, they spent their days in efforts to reproduce the disturbing sounds, in exploring and measuring every part of the house, or in making journal records of their impressions. They returned from twilight walks down the snowy glen to describe phantasms they had seen—a young nun entreating, an older laywoman admonishing, audibly if not intelligibly. And in the evening they sat by the drawing-room fire to play card games ('such as "Old Maid" and "Muggins" '), to talk over experiences and theories, or to make trial of the crystal or the Ouija board. The names 'Ishbel' and 'Marget' spelt out by the latter set a fascinating problem of identification. And there were other diversions: one guest had a vision of a black-robed figure, later identified as Father H—— himself; the most remarkable of numerous phantoms seen by Miss X. was the ghost of a black spaniel, presumably that owned by the 'wicked Major'. Psychical intimations seem to have reached their height with the visit of a Roman Catholic bishop and two priests: during their celebration of Mass the two spectres of the glen were emboldened to appear outside the windows of the house. On the other hand, after repeated aspergings of the rooms, the noises ceased, and ten days later, with the expiration of the tenancy, so did all opportunity for better observation.[260]

It must not be supposed that Miss X. lacked support for her conduct of affairs. Colonel Taylor spent five weeks at Ballechin (from 10 February to 16 March); during Miss X.'s three weeks' absence in April, both Myers and Lodge (accompanied by a Trinity College friend and a non-professional medium) were present for over a week; and Lord Bute, who throughout the tenancy kept in touch with developments by letter, came for the forty-eight hours preceding her return. Regrettably, it may seem, neither Podmore nor the Sidgwicks visited Ballechin, but even their rationality would have been powerless against the devout credulity encouraged by Lord Bute: by force of personality, as well as rank and wealth, that remarkable man would inevitably dominate the project he had set on foot. He did not need proof, he believed that this country-house was assailed by the forces of evil—to be repulsed only by the rites of Holy Church. But in fact both he and Myers, an enthusiast of a different persuasion, were influenced less by the noises (which during their stay were not obtrusive), than by the subjective impressions they themselves received (of presences, of 'violent hatred and hostility' and the like), and by the rather dubious visual manifestations reported to them. Miss X. herself, it is true, became fairly sure that these latter were telepathically communicated by a living agent—a false accretion, so to speak, to the original mystery. In the matter of 'experiment and investigation' she and her recruits, lacking better direction, had to proceed 'on ordinary common-sense lines': they had 'left the scientific part of the inquiry' to Lodge, among all thirty-four visitors to Ballechin the only professional scientist. And Lodge, being mainly concerned with the revelations of the medium, did little for scientific objectivity. He found 'nothing to investigate on the physical side':

There has been nothing capable of being photographed. The sounds are objective though not impressive. . . . I have seen nothing to suggest electricity or magnetism, or any of the ordinary physical agents in connection with the disturbances; but the noises are so momentary and infrequent, that they give no real scope for continued observation.

But the noises had not always been so insignificant, while the lease of Ballechin had provided a quite exceptional opportunity for systematic continuance of observation, and this, with Colonel Taylor and Miss X. as his deputies, Lodge could surely have arranged.[261]

Scientific advice had been available, however, and the obstinate neglect of it is one of the more puzzling features of the case. Long before the tenancy Sir William Huggins, the astronomer, had advised recording the sounds by means of a phonograph: the owner had refused to do so, but nothing prevented the tenants from using what apparatus they pleased. Again, only in the last days of the tenancy do we hear of a seismograph being employed—and then the two instruments surreptitiously imported by a guest 'recorded nothing'. Another belated visitor, Sir James Crichton-Browne, made the obvious suggestion that Miss X. should consult England's leading seismologist, John Milne: she did so, on 13 May, and his reply two days later made it clear that *all* the noises she described were most probably of seismic origin: 'Such sounds I have often heard, and the air waves, if not the earth waves, can be mechanically recorded.' But by then the tenancy was at an end, and the owner refused to extend it.[262]

Meanwhile, in spite of Miss X.'s assumption that her guests, being ladies and gentlemen, would, unasked, keep silence about their experiences, the Ballechin investigation had for months past been the subject of London gossip. And the house had not been three weeks vacated when on 8 June an unsigned article, 'On the Trail of a Ghost', appeared in *The Times*. The anonymous correspondent was easily identifiable: he had been one of a party of three headed by Sir James Crichton-Browne, the alienist, who (at his own request) had been entertained at Ballechin during the week-end of 8–10 May. Whatever had motivated the visit, the object of the article was plainly to discredit the Society for Psychical Research. The whole management of the enquiry and the methods of observation employed were, not unjustifiably, ridiculed; the reported spectres, the allegations against the 'wicked Major', and the implied connection of both with his successors' ordeal by noise, were treated with equal, and again not unjustifiable, derision. The writer gave full details of the tenancy arrangement, along with a description of the house and its location, and his account was the more damaging because in so many particulars it was strictly accurate. He had himself been one of the guests, had interrogated other guests, as well as the temporary household staff and the permanent employees at Ballechin, had consulted the local minister, and had gone to Perth to interview the family lawyer and the estate agent. Since, during his visit, the noises were largely intermitted, he could reasonably explain those he himself heard on a familiar, domestic basis—as the result of stoves cooling, water-pipes clanking, or servants moving about in adjacent passages and rooms. His irresponsibility appeared when he discussed the much more extraordinary sounds reported to him: either they were imaginary or they were the work of practical jokers. In fact, 'younger members of the H. family', who had held the tenancy for the 1896 shooting, were probably the culprits, and to continue their mischief had 'made a confidant of some one about the estate, who amuses himself by occasionally—it is only occasionally that the more remarkable noises are said to be heard—repeating their tricks'. But this was not his only libel. He professed to be moved by indignation at the 'appreciable injury' done by the SPR to the owners of Ballechin, yet his own article had a depreciatory effect much more extensive; he published the anecdotes of the 'wicked major' at the same time as, by implication, he criticized Miss X.'s 'impressive recital' of them; and in one breath declared that 'the story of a haunted history of 20 years rests upon nothing but anonymous rumour' and that a member of the family had endorsed it: 'I was, indeed, shown some admissions made under pressure of cross-examination by the widow of the late proprietor, who died in 1895.' But the full animus of the writer came out in his peroration:

Without attempting to judge individuals, it must be said that an experience like the present intensifies the suspicion and disgust which close contact with the S.P.R. always tends to excite. I am well aware that among its members are many men of eminence, ability, and unquestionable honesty. So on the direction of many a dubious company we may find the names of men of honour and integrity. Men do not sufficiently consider the responsibility which they incur, financially or morally, when they lend the sanction of their names to proceedings which they do not control and perhaps never inquire into. Seen at all close the methods of the Society for Psychical Research are extremely repulsive. What it calls evidence is unsifted gossip always reckless and often malignant; what it calls investigation would provoke contempt in Bedlam itself; and what it calls discrimination is too often the selection from gossip, all worthless, of those portions which fit best into the theory it happens to be advocating. As for its treatment of the degraded beings whom it calls 'sensitives' and 'mediums,' the epileptics, the neurotics, the *crétins*, and the tricksters from whom it pretends to draw spiritual insight— that is a system of moral vivisection more cruel and degrading than the worst practices ever laid at the door of physiologists.

The mere fact that *The Times* published so virulent an attack shows both the interest of its readers in the supernatural, and the antagonism faced by the SPR. The result was such as editors dream of: instant rejoinders, and an ensuing controversy prolonged from June to November. For the present-day reader, not the least interesting feature is that most of the correspondents seem to be at cross purposes.[263]

The owner, from his address in Paris, was not the first to reply, but when he did so, it was to repudiate the SPR entirely. He had believed his tenant to be a Colonel Taylor: 'I had no idea I was letting Ballechin to Lord Bute and the Psychical Society, and would never have done so had I known. . . . As to the stories contained in the article, they are without foundation.' From the dower-house at Ballechin, his mother, indignant at having been 'dragged into publicity . . . as "having made admissions under pressure of cross-examination"', also denied knowledge of the tenants' real quality: 'In my intercourse with them I spoke as one lady to another, never imagining that my private conversations were going to be used for purposes carefully concealed from me—a deceit I resent deeply.' The estate agents, protesting their complete innocence, wrote to put in as evidence the whole correspondence relating to the tenancy: Lord Bute and the 'society calling itself the Psychical Research Society' had never been mentioned. One after another friends and relatives of the owners wrote to protest Ballechin's freedom from both ghosts and troublesome noises, and to defend the 'Major's' reputation: 'Local gossip is not safe to go upon in country districts, whether in Scotland or England. . . . Eccentric to some extent he was, but it is a calumny to talk of him as the "wicked major".' The Earl of Onslow, writing from Clandon as a brother-landlord and fellow-victim of psychical 'researches', wished 'there were some means of making this society responsible in hard cash for the effects of the light-headed nonsense by which they depreciate other people's property'.[264]

'Mr. H.' wrote to 'deny most emphatically' the charge of practical joking levelled at his family. Nevertheless, throughout their stay at Ballechin, there had been 'extraordinary noises' which had at last forced them to surrender the tenancy two months early. As soon as they arrived they learned that the house was supposed to be haunted. Mr. H., however, not believing in ghosts, and persuaded that 'the very remarkable noises heard' were attributable to 'the hot-water pipes and the peculiar way in which the house is built', did his best to discourage such rumours; 'but I am afraid I was not always successful'. Miss X., incidentally, was later able to cite the evidence of a number of Mr. H.'s guests at Ballechin, and these all testified to the extraordinary violence, variety, and erratic dispersal of the noises heard, but none of them reported *seeing* anything. John Macdonald, previously employed as butler by the owner, wrote that he had never heard any unaccountable noises at Ballechin, and 'would have no hesitation in sleeping or staying in the house alone'. Harold Sanders, butler to Mr. H., wrote at great length to describe the alarming sounds, and the movements of bed and bed-clothes by which he and others had repeatedly been disturbed: 'One night I remember five gentlemen meeting at the top of the stairs, in their night-suits, some with sticks or pokers, one had a revolver, vowing vengeance on the disturbers of their sleep.'[265]

Miss X., perhaps less mollified by the acknowledgment that she made 'an admirable and charming hostess' than irate at the corollary that, *being* a lady and the hostess, she was 'unfit' to carry out the Ballechin investigation, was the first to challenge the anonymous correspondent. And she did so, not on the score of his illiberal prejudice, nor his misrepresentation of fact, nor his denigration of individuals and of the SPR collectively, but solely for his transgression of that social code, applicable it seems to matters psychical as well as amatory, the first article of which enjoins, 'Thou shalt name no names.' All her invited guests came to Ballechin 'on the distinct understanding that we were bound in honour and courtesy to the owners of the house not to reveal its identity'; and this 'principle of reticence' would have been observed in the official report of the case: she could only express her 'unbounded astonishment' and her 'deep regret at such violation of hospitality'. In short, as plainly as if Miss X. had stated it in words, the anonymous correspondent was declared to be an underbred cad, and psychical research to be the domain of ladies and gentlemen—governed by the rules of polite behaviour, not the requirements of the law-court or the laboratory. The cad was unabashed: through an editorial footnote he protested that 'no such understanding was so much as hinted at to him', and that before his visit 'the name of the house was known to many people in London'—a statement promptly corroborated from Torquay: 'the name of the house in Scotland and the names of the proposed visitors were known in London as early as March and were spoken of without reserve'. Other writers took issue with Miss X. and the Society on the 'principle of reticence'. One asked, 'Can anything be more useless or more absurd than an inquiry in which names of persons and places are omitted from the depositions? . . . Such proceedings are the caricature of a legal inquiry and the parody of a scientific investigation. The S.P.R. cannot have the remotest idea of the legal or scientific meaning and value of evidence.' Another described a meeting of the Society where 'the audience was treated to a complex ghost story of supposed especial importance' in which *all* particulars, not only local and personal names but even the substance of the ghostly communication, were suppressed: 'of what profit or interest was it to know that a nameless lady (whose veracity we had no possibility of testing) saw a nameless ghost in a nameless house, who sent her to a nameless village to set to rights unmentionable family affairs? . . . No one can doubt the usefulness of some branches of work done by it, but, in order to invite scientific attention, the society should eliminate root and branch such childish methods.' Members of the Society would at once recognize the case in question: it had, like the Ballechin case, been reported by the Marquis of Bute, and was included by Myers, with all its obfuscations intact, in Volume XI (1895) of the Society's *Proceedings*. Anyone acquainted with it would doubt not so much the percipient's 'veracity' as her sanity, and question even more the judgment and reliability of her sponsors. Well-informed readers of *The Times* might be trusted to draw the obvious inference.[266]

Chivalry, to be sure, was not entirely dead. In one letter, if only one, Miss X. and the Society were vigorously defended against premature and superficial criticism. 'Caution amounting to scepticism' marked the work of the SPR, as any reader of *Phantasms of the Living* must admit, while in the opinion

of 'a real man of science', Professor Oliver Lodge, Mr. Myers's 'unifying
and synthetic scheme' would ultimately be regarded as 'equal in merit to
any orthodox scientific work of the present age'. Miss X. was 'known to the
literary world, and to society in general as possessing in a high degree perception of the psychical order, together with a sensitive accuracy in register-
ing such impressions, comparable to that of a fine scientific instrument, and as
maintaining with regard to the sources of such impressions a thoroughly
agnostic attitude'. Persons of discrimination would await *her* version of the
Ballechin phenomena: 'The worst mood in presence of a new branch of
science, is that of ignorant contempt.'[267]

And there were others, neither students of the Society's publications nor
friends of its members, the Samaritans of the correspondence column, who
wrote to offer from their own experience a choice of solutions to the Ballechin mystery. In an Oxfordshire house, a tangle of forgotten bell-wires
beneath an attic floor had turned one particular room into a ghost chamber:
'The wires were adjusted, the chinks and crannies closed up, the ghost was
laid, and the haunted room has been comfortably occupied ever since.' The
purchaser of an Esher house found himself the owner of a haunted attic:
there and nowhere else were heard, in the dead of any but not every night,
Ballechin-like sounds of a blow, of a heavy fall, of hurried movement and of
muffled wailing, and the necessary ghost duly appeared. A hole below the
eaves and four bats' nests under the roof explained the sounds, and reflections in a mirror explained the ghost. Readers of an earlier letter would
recall that the maligned Major had rid Ballechin of a similar looking-glass
phantom. From Normandy came a letter telling how an underground spring
'affected in its flow by the state of the tide' produced intermittent 'ghostly
sounds' in the staircase of the house built above it: 'the staircase acted as the
sounding board of a piano, increasing the volume of the noise'. 'A Late
Guest at Ballechin', writing with less benevolent intention, conjectured that
any sounds really heard there might possibly 'be explained by earth tremors
(Ballechin is only 20 miles from Comrie, the chief centre of seismic disturbance in Scotland)'. And John Milne, amplifying the advice previously
given to Miss X., added his authority to the suggestion:

For years past this part of Perthshire has been well known as the hotbed for
British earthquakes. Between 1852 and 1890 no less than 465 shocks have been
noted there, out of which number 430 are claimed by Comrie. Many of these have
been accompanied by sounds, and often, as is common in earthquake countries
and as I can testify from considerable personal experience, sounds may be heard
and no movement can be either felt or recorded by an ordinary seismograph.
. . . [B]ecause such sounds do not travel far from their origin, they might be heard
at an isolated house in the country and nowhere else.

He gave advice on the choice and installation of a suitable recording instrument, and concluded: 'The Society for Psychical Research when on bogey-

hunting expeditions' might, with the aid of such apparatus, both 'lay home-made ghosts' and 'furnish materials of value to all who are interested in seismic research'. The polymath Andrew Lang, in his rôle of psychical expert, also had a contribution to make. Writing in qualified support of John Milne, he first cited an eighteenth-century parallel to the Ballechin noises, and then queried the hypothesis he seemed to endorse: how to explain seismically the fact that at Hinton Ampner in 1769, as at Epworth and now at Ballechin, the sounds were not uniformly audible to listeners? And with that air of intellectual condescension by now familiar to the SPR (which he had not yet joined) he presented himself as mediator and adviser in the Ballechin affair:

As I understand the Psychical Researchers, they interpret such local sounds (if, that is, no more vulgar origin can be found) as perhaps purely hallucinatory, not as real noises at all, still less as necessarily caused by 'spirits.' Thus a proper examination should either demonstrate an ordinary cause or causes, or the existence of seismic echoes, or should raise, in the last resort, a kind of presumption that the ear as well as the eye may be the victim of 'collective hallucinations,' which was Coleridge's theory.[268]

It is noteworthy that among these champions of science and common sense, scornful of ghosts as they all are, only one disparages the reported phenomena: the Ballechin investigators may need guidance, but they have a real, and an interesting problem. Only Sir James Crichton-Browne, imperfectly disguised as 'A Late Guest at Ballechin', is so prejudiced against the researchers that he refuses to take any of their evidence seriously. His letters, and indeed his whole conduct in the affair, present a curious blend of the scientific rationalist's impulse to clear away other people's mysteries, and the medicine-man's jealous defence of his own. The SPR were a band of amateurs trespassing on ground safe only for experts. That in the Ballechin case they were acting under the direct patronage of Lothair may have sharpened Sir James's resentment, but Myers was the enemy in chief. With his unguided excursions into fields where professional training and practical experience were indispensable, with his rhapsodical language, his rash hypotheses, and worst of all his cultivation of bogus 'sensitives' and trance mediums, Myers must have seemed a truly dangerous charlatan. Moreover, fifteen years before, he had been concerned in those 'thought-transference' demonstrations of which (unknown as yet to the general public) Sir James had helped to expose the fraudulence. Even after twenty-five years the recollection of 'the last scene of all, or passage-at-arms' was still vivid:

Mr. Myers, standing in front of the fireplace, said: 'It must be allowed that this demonstration has been a total failure, and I attribute that to the offensive incredulity of Dr. Crichton-Browne.' To which I rejoined: 'I hope I always will show offensive incredulity when I find myself in the presence of patent imposture.'[269]

Sir James, therefore, can have needed little persuasion to intervene at Ballechin. According to his own, not altogether trustworthy account,[270] written thirty-five years after the event, it was Sir William Huggins who 'begged' him to do so—to 'inquire into the matter from a scientific point of view'; and after prolonged negotiations, he 'agreed', 'stipulating that [he] should have an absolutely free hand in any observations [he] might wish to make and in reporting them'. So, in his first letter to *The Times*, Sir James brushed aside Miss X.'s genteel reproof: he had visited Ballechin as a scientific observer, free of any conditions, only to discover that there was nothing for him to observe—'I heard no sough of the supernatural and saw no glimmer of a ghost.' What did strike him was the ineptitude of the whole proceeding: 'Unscreened evidence of improbable phenomena had been collected in heaps, but the simplest and most obvious tests had not been applied. The residents and visitors, it seemed to me, had been sitting there all the time, agape for wonders, straining on the limits of audition, and fomenting one another's superstitions. . . .' Miss X. herself 'had evidently an open mind' for she 'offered us every facility for our investigations' and readily adopted suggestions: 'I regret to learn that there was no time to put these in practice.' As for the 'occult phenomena' described to him, most could be explained as 'practical joking, hallucination, and fraud', and for the rest a 'simple natural cause' might be inferred. Meanwhile Sir James awaited the official report—not, he gathered, likely to be unanimous, for 'with reference to the Ballechin revelations' it appeared that the Society was 'a household divided against itself'.

Miss X., retorting, stretched the 'principle of reticence' to its limits:

I entirely agree with the distinguished physician who in your columns to-day so justly deprecates secrecy in matters of scientific interest. I believe, however, that it is no part of medical etiquette in sharing experience of a 'case' to publish the name and address of the patient in the *Lancet*, nor have I hitherto found it necessary to request my visitors to refrain from 'making copy' of the conversations (in this case not always accurately remembered) of their fellow-guests.

Sir James, still pseudonymous, replied with undiminished vigour but some failure of logic. Closely examined, the points he made told against himself. No doubt it was essential for a *Lancet* contributor to identify himself; but neither Sir James nor his protégé had done so, while SPR reports always named the investigators concerned. And on any estimate, psychical or natural, the Ballechin phenomena could not reasonably be compared to an outbreak of disease, publication of which demanded 'the fullest particulars as to the locality and the other observers'. Besides, what would Sir James have had to say if another physician had demanded access to an investigation he himself was conducting, and then, before Sir James's report could be presented, publicly denounced his whole procedure? For if (as he maintained) he was not a guest, since he 'had no previous acquaintance' with his hostess, Sir James was not an 'invited investigator' either, but a self-imposed inquisitor, who, because of his professional standing, was over-trustingly deferred to and consulted during his brief visit. Miss X., it seems, had confided to him that Myers, having organized seances at Ballechin, now wished to treat as evidence the revelations of the medium, and these she herself could not accept: would Sir James give his opinion? Whether he did so, does not appear; but both here and in his former letter, he betrayed her confidence by publicizing her disagreement with Myers. In case his first allusion had been too guarded, he amplified it in his second letter, and by so doing advertised his effective responsibility for the *Times* article. Mr. Callender Ross might conceivably have taken the same view and favoured the same arguments as Sir James without benefit of coaching; he might by nature have been Sir James's equal for thick-skinned indifference to others' rights and feelings; but he could not, unless Sir James told him, have known of the Ballechin seances, of their quality, or of Myers's intention with regard to them; and without this special knowledge he would not have shaped as he did his concluding attack on the SPR. Miss X.'s indignation was justifiable.[271]

Myers's reaction was less so. He did not spring to Miss X.'s defence: his reply to the anonymous correspondent was to disown the whole Ballechin enterprise. Somewhat disingenuously, he professed to find in the article a suggestion 'that some statement has been made on behalf of the Society for Psychical Research with regard to the house' in question:

This, however, is not the case; and as a misleading impression may be created, I must ask you to allow me space to state that I visited Ballechin, representing that society, before your Correspondent's visit, and decided that there was no such evidence as could justify us in giving the results of the inquiry a place in our 'Proceedings.' I had already communicated this judgment to Lord Bute, to the council of the society, and to Professor Sidgwick, the editor of our 'Proceedings,' and it had been agreed to act upon it.

In vindication of the Society's methods and activities he appealed to the twelve volumes of its *Proceedings*: 'any definite criticism upon any matter contained therein' would be met 'with respectful attention'.[272]

This assumption of authority on Myers's part was instantly rebuked by 'one of the witnesses' at Ballechin: the complete report, of which Myers had seen (and, incidentally, endorsed) only a small part, had not yet been submitted to the SPR Council—the Honorary Secretary was taking too much upon himself. Myers ignored this charge, but wrote again, in his loftiest vein, to answer Sir James and the assailants of the 'principle of reticence'. The charge of inept observation was summarily disposed of. The Society had often discussed ways of testing allegedly psychic phenomena: 'But it would have been pedantic to apply such tests—e.g. tests for "seismic disturbance" to the few noises which Professor Lodge and I heard at Ballechin.' As to 'reticence', the Society observed no such 'principle': 'the extreme desirability of public attestation' was constantly urged upon informants, but in default of it (and anonymity might be variously inspired, as the *Times* correspondence showed) 'a signed attestation received privately' had to be accepted. Nor did the Society aim at uniformity of opinion: it merely desired that the phenomena on which an opinion was based 'should be investigated in a serious and careful spirit'. As to the publication of evidence, caution had always been the Society's rule, even when the investigation had been 'wholly under its own management (which was not the case at Ballechin)', and so far only one case had been judged to meet its requirements—standards of 'evidential value' had to be maintained, and, obviously, the final decision on eligibility for publication must 'be left with those who are responsible for the management of the society'. To anyone directly, or like Sir James indirectly, acquainted with the history of the Ballechin seances, this last statement amounted at least to *suggestio falsi*; but Myers left Henry Sidgwick to deal with the accusation in Sir James's second letter. Briefly and (it is plain) reluctantly, Sidgwick testified that 'some time previous' to the meeting on 28 May of the SPR Council, Myers had given him an unfavourable report of the Ballechin investigation, and as editor, he himself agreed 'that the results were not such as to justify publication in our *Proceedings*'. Myers had stolen a march on his critics, Miss X. included, and he might be thought to flaunt his advantage when in a third letter, asserting the Society's innocence in the matter of Clandon House, he assured Lord Onslow ('by the way') that the SPR was not 'a party to the renting of Ballechin-house': in fact, 'most of my friends (and I myself)' really deserved not the censure of owners and tenants but testimonials as fantasy-dispellers—'so often has it proved true, as the poet has it—

> "That when the glum Researchers come
> Those brutes of bogeys go."'[273]

If Myers had set out to damage his own and the Society's reputation he could not have done so more effectively than by these exchanges. Only members of the Society would care whether or not he had the right to act as its spokesman; and (despite Sir James's efforts at enlightenment) only a few of the actual participants would realize the degree of his involvement in the Ballechin case; but any plain-dealing reader of *The Times* could detect his sophistries. Of course the Society, having accepted Lord Bute's offer, was 'a party to the renting' of Ballechin; of course the Society, having deputed certain of its members for the task, was responsible for the investigation. The charges regarding Ballechin were not that an investigation was uncalled-for, but that this had been surreptitiously entered on and had then been ineptly conducted. Myers by ignoring it tacitly admitted the first charge (he and the Society, it appeared, condoned underhand dealings), and his answer to the second revealed his total incomprehension of scientific method. If systematic tests were to be held 'pedantic' in such a case, what on earth did the Society's claims as an investigating body amount to? Glanvill or the Wesleys or Dr. Johnson could have done as well—even Major Moor of Bealings could scarcely have done worse. Yet the motives governing Myers's ill-judged policy are easy to grasp. To him the Ballechin experiment was merely the latest chapter in a history of disappointment and wasted effort. As we have seen, in his endeavour to formulate a theory of survival, he had long been concerned with the possible effects of 'local attraction' on post-mortem phantasms. 'Haunted houses', especially those where the record of phenomena extended beyond mere poltergeist activity, might supply evidence of great importance for such a theory, and their investigation had been assigned to one of the earliest-formed committees of the SPR. After 1884, however, this committee had been allowed to lapse—not because reports of haunted houses were lacking, but because of the practical difficulty of substantiating them. Where a fully authenticated, convincing report was received and stood up to investigation, it was a matter for congratulation to the whole inner circle of the SPR. As Myers in his letter remarked, one such case, and only one, had so far occurred: Mrs. Sidgwick took preliminary note of it in her paper of April 1885 on the evidence for phantasms of the dead, and in 1892, more than seven years after it had first been reported, following continued observations by the residents and repeated visits and enquiries by Myers himself, the chief percipient's detailed record was printed in Volume VIII of the *Proceedings*. This was the now-celebrated 'Morton' case. But failing satisfactory verification, not necessarily on so elaborate a scale, to publish a case was to invite disaster. The SPR had taken this risk in the very first (1882) volume of its *Proceedings*, with its account of 'Mr. X. Z.'s' haunted house, and some three years later had been obliged to retract the whole story: 'Mr. X. Z.', on whose unsupported testimony they relied, had (not withstanding his 'reputation' and his 'considerable intellectual distinction') told a pack of lies. When therefore the authenticity of the Ballechin case—spectres, noises, and all—was publicly challenged, Myers's reaction was instantaneous: regardless of general obligations or specific undertakings, without warning either to Colonel Taylor or to Miss X., Ballechin and its phenomena must be repudiated. As late as 23 April, Myers himself had arranged with Miss X. a date for the formal presentation of the Ballechin evidence to the Society; but business engagements were trifles weighed against the credit and continued functioning of that Society, on which (so Myers believed) the greatest of all issues, the proof of immortality, might depend. As William James could have told Miss X., Myers was a fanatic, and fanatics pressing to their ends are reckless of means and immune to scruples.[274]

But Miss X. had come to an end of her patience. Her letter of 16 June, taking Sir James to task, began with the announcement that 'further material' on Ballechin would shortly be published in the *Nineteenth Century*, and in the August number her article, 'Psychical Research and an Alleged

"Haunted" House', duly appeared. As the title conveys, she aimed at more than a narrative of the Ballechin investigation: the first half of her article summarizes SPR activities from 1882 on. Some such exposition might be thought necessary to justify by precedent the Society's intervention at Ballechin; but Miss X.'s purpose was very different. One has to bear in mind that the public statements of Callender Ross and of Myers had made her position extremely awkward. According to Myers she had not, at Ballechin, been the fully accredited agent of the Society (whose attitude to publicity she misrepresented), and Myers himself, its authorized representative, had anticipated Callender Ross in rejecting the evidence she offered: for the procedure and the inferences ridiculed (and Myers seemed to imply, justly ridiculed) in *The Times*, Miss X., not the Society, was responsible. Thus assailed by unbelievers from without, and betrayed by the recreant Myers from within, Miss X. could no longer hold Ballechin, but she could, and did, first hang the traitor over the battlements and then, using the enemy's own approaches, contrive a fighting escape for herself and her supporters. The first section of her article is therefore a thinly-veiled denunciation, satirical in tone, of Myers's influence on psychical research. Up to 1890 (she notes) apart from the study of hypnotism, the Society had been mainly concerned with spontaneous phenomena. But from 1890 onwards, the trance communications of Mrs. Piper, 'occupying two entire numbers of the *Proceedings*', 'Mr. Myers's brilliant exposition of his hypothesis of Subliminal Consciousness', and 'the phenomena of the high-priest of Spiritualism, Mr. Stainton Moses' had become the main subjects of interest —'the cult of hysteria and "induced" states on the one hand, and the belief in the suspension of the laws of matter, as commonly received, on the other'.

The mechanism of Séances with their trances and paid mediums . . . had been felt hitherto to be contrary to the genius of the Society for Psychical Research, and to all our manners and customs for eight years. But now we began to 'level up,' or 'level down,' as the case may be, and we acquired a medium of our very own. Certainly Mrs. Piper, in her secondary personality of Dr. Phinuit, was very startling.   Sludge begins
    At your entreaty with your dearest dead.

There follows a description of Mrs. Piper entranced: one remembers, from *PSPR* Volume VI, that Miss X. had taken part in three sittings with Mrs. Piper during the latter's visit to England, and that Myers regarded these sittings as 'perhaps the most successful and convincing of the whole series'.

One was told that the heavy preliminary sigh, the convulsed countenance, the gnashing teeth, the writhing body, the clenched hands were 'purely automatic,' but they were none the less horrible for that. Even more horrible was the change of personality; the evil expression, the loud voice, the coarse speech, the shrewd cunning of 'Dr. Phinuit.' Those who heard him 'at his best,' discoursing most volubly of one's private affairs, of facts, as far as one can tell, unknown to any living person, could not but acknowledge that here indeed were problems which even all our learning as to multiplex personalities and thought transference and automatism failed to explain. If we admit the 'psychic' hypothesis at all, if we feel that such deterioration of personality denotes anything more than a change in brain matter or nervous force, ought we not to ask ourselves how far we have a right to express our problems, however interesting, in terms of human souls, to work our sums in addition and subtraction in induced suffering and unconscious sacrifice?

In terms reminiscent of the contemporary vivisection debate, Miss X. concludes that the mediumistic trance is indefensible even for the purpose of psychic research: 'if the subject of our inquiry demands the handling of the uncleanliness of hysteria, the induction of morbid conditions of mind and body, surely, in the name (to invoke none more sacred) of the dignity of human life, let us restrain our prurient curiosity, and leave the morbid secrets of nature to the physician and the alienist whose lawful concern they are!'[275]

And errors of omission as well as commission were chargeable against the Society. Take the matter of 'haunted' houses. These ('unless we accept Mr. Podmore's theory of telepathic infection') have at least the advantage that their phenomena 'do not depend upon the observers', nor do they require any 'machinery of trances and automatism', so that 'although some persons seem to be more "sensitive" to such phenomena than others, we are not limited to the evidence of the "Mediumistic" and the Morbid'. Yet although the Society early recognized the challenge of alleged hauntings, these were never more than perfunctorily dealt with by its special committee: 'At the end of a few months only, they practically dismissed a subject which, if considered at all, required years of patient research.' Individual members of the Society, it is true, had been more persistent: Miss X. mentions with approval the enquiries of Colonel Taylor and of Podmore, with whose 'naughty girl' explanation she is in agreement—'the phenomena of hysteria are legion!' But these efforts aside, the only record of a haunted house admitted since 1890 to the *Proceedings*, was 'an elaborate story' based 'on the evidence of two or three ladies, two servants, a charwoman, and a little boy. No proper journal was kept, and the Society for Psychical Research investigators came upon the scene when all was practically over.' Even thus travestied, the 'Morton' case is easily recognizable—as is the implied contrast with Myers's treatment of Miss X. And sharply denouncing the Society's prejudiced, superficial, unresourceful conduct of such enquiries, Miss X. proceeds to account for her stewardship at Ballechin.[276]

It is a spirited, if not wholly convincing performance. There are no petty recriminations, no personalities: two disdainful sentences are enough to characterize the *Times* article, that 'strange medley of fact and fancy', and

Miss X. demonstrates her fidelity to principle by never once naming the house, the owners, or (apart from Taylor, Lodge, and Myers) any of the visitors. Conversely, there are neither retractions nor apologies: to justify herself, it is implied, Miss X. need only rehearse the facts of the case. So she does—with vigour, with some humour, and with a profusion of 'statistics': both observers, with the dates and length of their stay, and phenomena, with the tests applied, are zealously enumerated and classified. Even the best statistics are rather less overwhelming in written than in spoken argument, and unimpressionable readers might question the relevance of many of the details so ostentatiously assembled. These sceptics would at once note Miss X.'s hedging on the subject of 'visual phenomena'. She classifies them, and asserts their corroboration by independent witnesses, of whom disarmingly she admits to being the chief, but she refuses any description.

Whatever may be the personal convictions of the witnesses, it is especially difficult to make such experiences in any degree evidential, and they must always rest, to some extent, upon the personal veracity of the seer. Poor Sludge's climax of imposture was 'I'm ready to believe my very self.' I, on the other hand, one of the witnesses to all these visual phenomena, and to others since my earliest childhood, never believe myself under such circumstances at all, until my impression is corroborated by others, or unless there is some independent coincidence in fact. I know my own mental habit, that of an intensely vivid visualiser, and I am, perhaps morbidly, alive to all possibilities of expectation, and suggestion, and thought transference, and subconscious memory and observation. It would be necessary to enter into circumstances too minute for the present occasion were I to attempt to describe these occurrences with any sort of detail, and I therefore prefer merely to mention them in passing.

Miss X. in short claims privilege over the selection of evidence, very much as she does in the matter of names: she will argue the Ballechin case on noises alone. Sceptics would again object that by classifying certain of these, without qualification, as 'footsteps' and 'voices' she begs the question of 'haunting'. They would note further that the passage quoted from her Ballechin journal, and intended (one assumes) to prove her methodical superiority to observers such as Miss 'Morton', suggests not so much an excerpt from a scientific report as a chapter from a Wilkie Collins novel. Yet again, in a Victorian lady they would excuse even total ignorance of acoustic theory, but they might nevertheless be surprised that Miss X. had not better practical acquaintance with the vagaries of sound transmission. And if, having read Harold Sanders's letter, they surmised (correctly) that, during Miss X.'s occupancy also, 'vibrations' were felt as well as heard, bedsteads violently shaken and so on, they might wonder why the word 'earthquake' never insinuated itself into the deliberations at Ballechin, and why Miss X. in this article treats Professor Milne's explanation so coolly: 'It was even conceivable that as we were well within a marked earthquake district, the sounds themselves might be due to slight seismic disturbance.' But when at this point Miss X. declares that the Ballechin noises should for the present be accepted as inexplicable mysteries of Nature, when, as if in conclusion from this, she insists that valid (as distinct from spurious) psychic phenomena should not be profaned by investigation, their only wonder would be that she joined the SPR at all. Miss X., clearly, is a superlative example of feminine intuition, which, when elevated to psychic awareness in a lady both 'awfully clever' and (even on hostile testimony) 'nice', it is impossible to convict of error. As a psychical adept Miss X. is as jealous of her faculty and its exercise as Crichton-Browne of the alienist's domain—and indeed she often seems to share his views. For like the fanatic, but to his distress psychically insensitive Myers, she has little regard for consistency, and lacking his inventiveness, does not scruple to appropriate an enemy's arguments.[277]

Miss X.'s article, if it does nothing to clarify, at least adds psychological interest to the Ballechin mystery, but unless the three August letters already quoted were written in response to her confession of bafflement, no reference whatever was made to it in *The Times*. During September and October the correspondence lapsed, but in November a series of three letters provided a mocking epilogue to the affair. 'C. B.' wrote to clear Ballechin of ghostly aspersions: over a three months' tenancy just concluded neither family, servants, nor guests were 'disturbed by noises of any kind: in fact, I never slept in a quieter or more comfortable house'. 'An Earnest Inquirer' professed to be troubled by the implications of C. B.'s experience: did it prove that seismic disturbances as well as bogles were non-existent 'in Athol at any rate? Or would it not be fair to say that what is sauce for the seismic goose is sauce for the psychic gander?' 'A Cynical Observer' retorted that there was no proof of seismic origin for the Ballechin noises: they began and ended with the occupancy of certain interested persons, 'and when upon the withdrawal of these persons the house relapses into the quiet it had enjoyed for half a century before their advent—then I think the commonsense inference is very obvious'. And so the Ballechin case rested, until, more than a year later, it was reopened by Miss X. and the Marquis of Bute in collaboration. Their publication of 1899, designed to justify the enquiry on psychical grounds, instead exposed its contradictions and absurdities more thoroughly and more amusingly than Callender Ross had been able to do.[278]

What then (to justify so lengthy a report of it) is the connection between this faintly ridiculous episode, this fiasco of psychical research, and *The Turn of the Screw*? I have discussed a number of impulses and influences which (it seems to me) contributed to the finished work as we have it: here is something different—the 'happening' which (again, as I think) finally triggered the whole series of creative reactions. Many years before, in a privately recorded fragment of autobiography, James had observed: 'A single word from outside often moves one (moves *me* at least) more than the same word infinitely multiplied as a simple voice from within.' In June 1897, the month of Jubilee, and for James of novel-reading, such an external prompting (Myers might have called it 'guidance') was supplied by his morning newspaper. Very often James's knowledge and consequent use of a potential 'source' are arguable as probabilities only; but he could not possibly avoid the Ballechin case, served up to him almost daily for the best part of a month. No doubt he was aware of the gossip circulating in London 'as early as March'; he may even, through his contact with Myers, have been in possession of 'facts of the case' not generally accessible; but the June bombardment in *The Times*, sustained by volleys from both sides of the Channel, and if not from Land's End to John O'Groats at least from Torquay to Perth, was inescapable. Even *Punch* was driven to humorous complaint. And *Punch* also, in its 'Booking-Office' review of not-too-exacting literature, had a June phenomenon to recommend 'to all who enjoy the very weirdest of weird tales'—Bram Stoker's *Dracula*. Henry James could never have been tempted to so lurid an essay in Gothic fantasy, nor did the success of this 'ingenious romance' put its author on the best-selling level of Hall Caine or Marie Corelli, but its appearance was an opportune reminder of the market value of supernatural horror. And again opportunely, on 10 June (the date of Myers's first letter) *The Times* in 'Books of the Week' chanced to indicate a means of exploiting this which lay to James's hand. A review of two new books on the Brontës ('Despite Mr. Shorter's recent work we have not yet done with books about the Brontës') referred to 'the question of Charlotte's love tragedy—her affection for her Brussels teacher, M. Héger'. Here juxtaposed, an associative train ready to be fired, were two current preoccupations of the reading public—ghosts and the Brontës, more particularly Charlotte Brontë as her own heroine. A Brontë setting could provide acceptable distancing for a theme of only too topical interest; through a Brontë heroine Archbishop Benson's *donnée* could be used to suggest (obliquely, delicately, to informed and discriminating, not 'merely witless' readers) a vexed question of 1897. It might slyly convey other less amiable suggestions, too, and allow its author not merely to profit by a vogue, but also to requite a number of affronts to himself and offences against Art. It was on 26 June, one remembers, that Shaw delivered his criticism of Sarah Bernhardt's *Lorenzaccio*.[279]

But James was not yet free to undertake a new literary venture, and could wait (as the result shows he did) for Miss X.'s promised elucidation of the Ballechin affair. And reading her article, as he would have done, after the initial attack by Callender Ross and the ensuing dispute in *The Times*, one can see why the indications of her 'Record' in *PSPR* VI should have seemed so appropriate to the governess-narrator in *The Turn of the Screw*. The article appealed to James's memory of his own 1890 experience, when, as William's deputy, he had read to the assembled SPR an account of Mrs. Piper's trance performances. Remembering also 'the "Kate Walsh" freak', he would have every sympathy with Miss X. in her distress at 'Phinuit's' intimate knowledge of 'private affairs, of facts, as far as one can tell, unknown to any living person'—although in William's brother curiosity might have the protection of stronger nerves, so that 'interest' (as he was to say), rather than disgust like hers, would be his reaction to 'the medium and the trance'. Given this sympathetic predisposition, James could very easily regard 'Miss X.', not of course the lady 'known to the literary world and to society', as just another mediating 'consciousness'—like Laura Wing, like Fleda Vetch—an almost fictional character herself in a fantastic, near-fictional situation. She was not the model he needed for his governess, but inevitably her personality and the circumstances displaying it were present to his imagination as he composed his new story, and in their 'veridical' singularity provided a touchstone of the actual for his fiction.[280]

At a number of points, indeed, 'Miss X.' seems to have interposed between Jane Eyre and our governess. She was not, it is true, as youthful as either of these, but she was young enough to feel she must assure her readers that three ladies 'came in succession to act as chaperon' at Ballechin. And there, as directionless as if 'in a great drifting ship', she, like our governess, 'was, strangely, at the helm' (p. 19). She, too, might look back 'with amazement' at 'the situation [she] accepted' (p. 27). Lothair at fifty, though still un- doubtedly 'gallant and splendid', could not quite match the fascination of the governess's Harley Street patron, but something of the charm operated, when, after his generous provision for the tenancy, 'not a person could be found to take the smallest trouble in the matter': 'with some feeling of in- dignation, and at considerable personal inconvenience, I offered my services as a *pis aller*. . . .' Like our governess's, her acceptance of responsibility was 'a kind of favour, an obligation he should gratefully incur' (p. 9). The scene of her duties, too, had the cheerful aspect and modern comfort of Bly; and the manner in which she was informed of its disadvantages a little suggests that in which our governess learned of Miles's unacceptability at school (pp. 20–21): 'I had avoided learning anything as to the alleged phenomena, and broke the seal of the packet of statements by earlier witnesses in the presence of a second person twenty-four hours after our arrival.' None of the Ballechin phenomena was in the least applicable to James's story, but as their observer and still more as their recorder, Miss X. offered a number of traits by which a ghost-seer might be not too solemnly characterized. There is, naturally, much more ample self-revelation in Miss X.'s personal 'Record', and most of the details utilized by James come from this source. But it is the Ballechin case and its violations of decorum that excite her rigidly Victorian, ultra- Brontëan sense of propriety, of class distinctions and class obligation. Jane Eyre could at need be 'pressed into her service' by Mrs. Fairfax, and far from resenting her subordination was 'as active and gay as anybody' (xvii, 193–94). At Ballechin, once ' "experiences" among the servants' were reported, Miss X. 'lived in terror, much worse than that of ghosts, of the unanimous resignation of the household; and the distribution of the house- work among the guests was a standing joke. Happily it never came to that;

the servants . . . soon accepted the mental standpoint of the dining-room, and behaved in a rational manner.' But only after rigorous examination, such as Miss X. never dreamed of imposing on her guests, was their testimony admissible. James's governess for the most part ignores the 'household' of which she is nominally in charge, and in her 'really great loneliness' (p. 11) makes a friend and confidante of Mrs. Grose; on the latter's departure, however, she becomes 'very grand and very dry' and with a touch of Miss X.'s *hauteur* lets it be known that she is 'quite remarkably firm' (pp. 151–52). But it is Quint who provokes her most decided expression of class consciousness; and it is Miss X.'s denunciation of the *Times* correspondent, in his behaviour (like Shaw, another journalist) not merely in his demeanour (like James Taylor) so blatantly no gentleman, exhibiting his crudity moreover in a supernatural context, that is the immediate precedent here. And in the article also, much more explicitly than in the earlier 'Record', for Miss X. now writes with the spontaneous vehemence of indignation, there emerges the habit of speech which James's quick ear has at once caught as the distinctive idiom of her type. 'To use the schoolboy formula, a good many will take their dying oath who won't bet sixpence'; ' "ghosts", like others unconventionalised, refuse to come up to time'; 'he could give points to a Scotland Yard detective'; '[poachers] don't waste shot over rabbits—nothing so sportsmanlike'; 'three [other gentlemen] came on purpose to defend us from possible "humbug" '. And contrasting with this breezy, careless, *almost* slangy assurance—which *seems*, at any rate, her natural tone—is Miss X.'s occasional awkward pomposity of phrase, when with some uncertainty she puts on the scientist: the term 'haunted' 'used generically can only be applied . . . to a house in which there occur . . . phenomena . . . assumed to be of super-normal origin'; 'as our unit of thought, for the moment, is the reasonable person . . .'; 'the phenomena recorded in the journal may be dichotomised as (1) audile, (2) visual'. In the style of James's governess, as we have remarked, there is a similar contrast of slanginess and grandiloquence.[281]

Miss X., therefore, as she declared herself over Ballechin, made a significant contribution to James's story, and it was her August article—so provocatively at odds with the impression created by Myers (in his writings and doubtless also at Aston Clinton), comparatively so favourable to the dissentient Podmore, yet ultimately asserting only her distrust, as a 'witness', of all hasty theorizing—that, one must conclude, induced him to turn (in some cases, return) to the SPR publications already noted. And these, it has to be observed, among his many contributory 'sources' are the only works which, to be reflected as they are in *The Turn of the Screw*, need have been 'consulted' expressly to that end. If Frederic Harrison in 1895–96 or Shorter in the winter of 1896–97 did not inspire its reperusal, James's recollection of his main source, *Jane Eyre*, may have been refreshed during his June orgy of novel-reading. But *Jane Eyre* is one of the novels every 'bookworm' devours in childhood, and novels so read, as James read *David Copperfield* for instance, often take so firm a hold on the imagination that, especially where a memory of such tenacity is in question, it may be unnecessary to assume even this degree of premeditation.

At all events, by September 1897 the Ballechin episode had effectively coloured James's conception of his *donnée*. And that he was not merely aware of this, but willing that his readers should perceive a connection, too, is shown by the name he chose for his fictional setting. English 'Bly' and Gaelic 'Ballechin' are not formal equivalents, but as place names they express an identical intention: each designates the *locus amoenus*, the 'pleasant' abode in which one is happy to dwell.[282] One often has to acknowledge a strange unanimity between Life and Art, but it is hard to believe that such coincidence of verbal irony should be the work of chance. Anyone like Myers, however, who had been closely and painfully involved in the affair, would without any such hint discern, or at least suspect, a connection. Was this the burden of his enquiry in 1898? Had James's new fiction, dealing at such unprecedented length with a subject near to Myers's heart, some reference to certain recent, dubiously psychic experiences? We have only James's disclaimer in reply:

I'm afraid I don't quite *understand* the principal question you put to me about 'The Turn of the Screw.' . . . I am afraid I have on some former occasions rather awkwardly signified to you that I somehow can't pretend to give any coherent account of my small inventions 'after the fact.' There they are—the fruit, at best, of a very imperfect ingenuity and with all the imperfections thereof on their heads. The one thing and another that are questionable and ambiguous in them I mostly take to be conditions of their having got themselves pushed through at all. The *T. of the S.* is a very mechanical matter, I honestly think. . . .[283]

Or, as he phrases it in the *Preface*, 'a piece of ingenuity pure and simple, of cold artistic calculation' (p. 172). Understanding now more fully what he means, one has to agree: this is no lucky *ébauche*, no random sally of genius, but a miniature masterpiece of intricate design, like a baroque jewel or a Fabergé ornament—not art of the highest seriousness, and not, emphatically not (the protest seems to underlie every word of his answer to Myers) a bodying forth of deep personal concern over the question of survival. The 'ambiguity' which seems to have troubled Myers, and which by pleading guilty to James evades discussing, which indeed clouds every unresolved problem, in *The Turn of the Screw* faithfully reproduces that created round every alleged ghostly manifestation by the dispute of Myers and Podmore.

xi

'So there we are,' at Bly, with our two rival psychicists to urge each his own solution of the mystery. What, on their showing, are the alternatives offered?

Considering first that suggested by Myers, we do not, it must be insisted, imply any belief on the author's part in spirit return: all that is entailed is a temporary suspension of disbelief, an impersonation, as it were, of a spiritist in the interests of art. On Myers's interpretation, the rationale of the manifestations in *The Turn of the Screw* will be very close to that presumed for the 'Morton' case, with the 'Record' of which in *PSPR* Volume VIII James must have acquainted himself, and for the investigation of which Myers himself had been responsible. The details accessible to James[284] and applicable to his story may be very briefly summarized. On the direct and independent, signed evidence of six witnesses, the house in question was frequented over a period of several years by the phantasm of a tall woman in widow's weeds, the face always concealed, as if she were crying, by a handkerchief held in the right hand. This phantasm was seen by daylight or half light or bright gaslight, outside or inside the house, stationary or in movement from one floor or one room to another, and sometimes for as long as half an hour at a stretch; when it appeared on an upper landing a distinctive light footstep was audible. The widow with whom the apparition was provisionally identified had died in 1878, but for more than two years before her death had been living in another town. Her remains, however, were brought back for interment in a churchyard near her former home, which she had not revisited in life. The recorded appearances (although hearsay evidence of earlier date was collected) first took place in 1882, occurred frequently from 1884 to 1886, up to which time the figure 'was so solid and life-like that it was often mistaken for a real person', then became rarer and less distinct, and ceased entirely after 1889. It is noteworthy that despite the large number of witnesses (among them two small boys) certain members of the family, including the father and the mother, never saw the figure, although the mother sometimes heard the noises, as of a poltergeist, which in the later stages tended to replace the visual phenomena.

Here then we have the warrant for Miss Jessel's repeated ghostly appearances in a former abode remote from the scene of her death, and the suggestion, one may think, both for her garb and for her grief. But the most remarkable feature of an altogether exceptional case was the behaviour of the chief percipient and narrator, Miss Rose 'Morton'. This young lady (in 1882 aged nineteen) was, it is obvious, a 'sensitive' after Miss X.'s pattern—on one occasion her impression of the phantasm together with her own image was transmitted clairvoyantly to a distant friend with whom she was *en rapport*—but she was also a medical student, with 'a scientific training', and showed herself an intrepid and resourceful investigator. She *proved* the immateriality of the figure which she nevertheless repeatedly followed and addressed. The figure, she reported, would often pause and seem about to speak, but never did so. Here in general is the warrant for our governess's boldness and persistence in confrontation or pursuit of what she is convinced are spirits of the dead. In particular Miss Rose 'Morton's' first recorded experience, of June 1882, may be thought to have suggested the introduction to our governess's third encounter with Quint. The governess, it will be recalled, had sat up late reading *Amelia*. Her attention was suddenly drawn to the door of her room, and she was reminded of the sounds of movement about the house that had disturbed her first night at Bly.

I laid down my book, rose to my feet and, taking a candle, went straight out of the room and, from the passage, on which my light made little impression, noiselessly closed and locked the door. . . . I went straight along the lobby, holding my candle high, till I came within sight of the tall window that presided over the great turn of the staircase. . . . My candle, under a bold flourish, went out. . . . (pp. 76–77)

Miss 'Morton' reports:

I had gone up to my room, but was not yet in bed, when I heard someone at the door, and went to it, thinking it might be my mother. On opening the door, I saw no one; but on going a few steps along the passage, I saw the figure of a tall lady, dressed in black, standing at the head of the stairs. After a few moments she descended the stairs, and I followed for a short distance, feeling curious what it could be. I had only a small piece of candle, and it suddenly burnt itself out; and being unable to see more, I went back to my room. ('Record of a Haunted House', p. 313)

Now Miss Morton, like the rest of the witnesses and the SPR investigator, Myers, himself, was persuaded that on the occasions recorded, by means unexplained and for reasons which could only be conjectured, some emanation from the dead, if not in the traditional sense 'a spirit', had been manifested. If the evidence as a whole is accepted (and to reject it, mass deception of unparalleled extent and inconceivable motivation would have to be assumed) it is difficult to see what other conclusion could be reached. James's governess was similarly persuaded, and if her conviction carries weight, the conclusion in the Bly case must be similar also. But certain objections have to be met. At Bly only the governess *testifies* to seeing the phantasms. Mrs. Grose.accepts the governess's testimony on the grounds, which to a thorough-going sceptic would seem irrelevant, that the girl has become 'really shocking' and the boy has purloined a letter (pp. 147–50): she herself never goes back on her massively honest assertion of the day before

—'nobody's there' (p. 139). The girl perhaps dishonestly at the lakeside ('I see nobody. I see nothing. I never *have*.') and the boy with patent honesty at the window severally deny percipience (pp. 139, 168). If, therefore, we believe James's story to be that manifestations of the dead occurred which only the governess saw, we must (with Myers's blessing) be prepared to accept both the theory of latency—since Quint and Miss Jessel had died months before—and the possibility that the governess (like the black nurse in the Barbados case) was 'intercepting' visual communications which did not reach Miles and Flora, the intended percipients. We may, of course, brutalize our version by assuming that the children were lying—in which case no 'interception' need be postulated.

James, however, has presented his story in such a way that we may just as logically use Podmore's theory to interpret it. And to me this alternative (involving 'thought transference, or 'telepathy', between living persons only) seems preferable, if only because it automatically saves everyone's credit: it rescues the author from the imputation either of naïve superstition or of fraudulent dealing with his reader, and it warrants the governess both sane and benevolent. Has James himself shown any such preference? Since, of all the apparitions he calls in aid from SPR narratives, only the 'Morton' ghost defies Podmore's interpretation, and since he has obviously paid special attention to Gurney's account of 'telepathic hallucinations',[285] the answer must be: 'Yes, in his selection of details; but in his development of the story he carefully holds the balance even.' Let us interpret *The Turn of the Screw* according to Podmore, and see how his theory fits the evidence of the text.

The governess, like Miss X., is a sensitive. Given favourable conditions, she might find herself the agent or the percipient of a telepathic communication; independently of normal information or expectation, she might become aware of events past or events to come; she might have the faculty of 'seeing' things distant or things hidden. She will in any case be exceptionally responsive to the persons with whom she associates, will instinctively react to their moods, and even at times intuit their unspoken thoughts. But in her 'small, smothered life' hitherto, none of these potentialities has been developed— or at least her narrative gives no intimation whatever to that effect. And abruptly she is transported to a situation in which for 'the first time' she knows 'space and air and freedom, all the music of summer and all the mystery of nature' (p. 28). And so, in spite of her first sense of 'uneasiness' (p. 16), of 'slight oppression' (p. 18), in spite of her dismay at the boy's expulsion from his school, all her reserves are swept away and forgotten in, as she says, 'a passion of tenderness' (p. 26). She loves the children: she doesn't consciously suspect them of any vicious tendency, let alone any wrongdoing. And then the apparitions begin.

Here we have a sensitive, relaxed, happy, 'off her guard' as she says herself (p. 28)—the most receptive state imaginable, as Miss X. has testified.

And because of the growth of her love and concern for the children, she suddenly (like the nurse in the Boston case) becomes aware of what is obsessing their minds: the memories of whatever illicit satisfactions Quint and Miss Jessel have taught them to need, and the images of those fascinating purveyors of evil who are physically lost to them. Her unconscious clairvoyant faculty shapes these impressions into visual images[286] before her conscious mind has begun to take account of them. At first, and it is an important testimony to her honesty, she is merely puzzled and curious—so there is a strange man at Bly? And being, like Catherine Morland, a reader of Mrs. Radcliffe's Gothic romances, she wonders if there can be 'a "secret" at Bly—a mystery of Udolpho or an insane, an unmentionable relative kept in unsuspected confinement' (p. 34).[287] But once Mrs. Grose, from her description, has identified the man she sees, then immediately, because of her own romantic reading and of her childhood circumstances, her conscious mind interprets this figure, and the phantasm of a woman that next appears, as 'ghosts'. How else should she interpret them? Her 'eccentric' father's sermons need not have been very unorthodox to include references to guardian angels, good and bad spirits, clouds of witnesses, or miraculous appearances; and (as Charlotte Brontë's history indicates) in the vicarage kitchen and nursery, village superstitions and tales of local hauntings will have been staple entertainment. Bred up as she has been, inexperienced as she is, she knows intuitively that the children are endangered by the apparitions, but her rationalizing intelligence misinterprets these as evil spirits returned to entice the children into danger, not as emanations from the children's own minds. Consequently she misinterprets her own rôle: 'I was a screen—I was to stand before them. The more I saw, the less they would' (p. 54). Her duty she thinks, with a desperate innocence, is to interpose herself physically between the children and—ghosts. And since they may as yet be quite ignorant of the fiendish presences menacing them, she says nothing to her charges, only waits and watches for the all-revealing incident which never occurs. Never once does she convict Miles and Flora of seeing the phantasms which every now and then rise up before her. But the more vigilant she becomes, the more anxious, the more tense, the more excited— the more she allows the children to perceive that she is aware of their past evil associations (for these, it is to be remembered, have never been in doubt) and their present evil bent of mind and habits (whatever these may amount to), the less her love is free to help and release them. She is no longer the spontaneously affectionate, happy, normal young girl they have, with a return of affection, accepted. Her love now becomes an extra burden for these small, precociously excited, and in the case of the boy at least, outlawed creatures. And when in the final, climactic scenes (with Flora, by the lake and with Miles, at the window) she is impelled to declare the presence of a 'ghost', when, that is, to the children's ears she jabbers of 'seeing' things that aren't there, she reveals *herself* as their enemy—to the girl a hatefully, insupportably censorious accuser (p. 144), to the boy a torturing 'devil' (p. 168). In fact, she kills Miles on the spot, with mingled excitement, fright, rage, and despair, because she convinces him that Peter Quint is actually present—that she can *see* Peter Quint whom he needs, if not loves, and that he cannot.

The Turn of the Screw on this interpretation is, in effect, a 'moral mystery' —an undidactic fable of the conflict of appearances and the underlying reality, of the difficulty of understanding other people even when, as here, the contents of their minds are paraded visibly before one—a somewhat dubious privilege, luckily vouchsafed to few. The governess is a good young woman: she cannot compass, accept, and ignore evil. If, as well as good, she were merely intelligent, or if she were good and merely ignorant and un-suspecting as Mrs. Grose is, she could act, perhaps, to redeem. But she has this fatal 'psychic' faculty whose operation she completely misunderstands, and with her goodness and her intelligence she acts to destroy. 'Acting', however, is almost always dangerous when it is directed to interference with another's mind and character. And the evangelizing attitude of mind which determines that souls must be saved, characters straightened, minds puri-fied 'at any cost', is already poised for destruction, not redemption. Whatever young Miles had done, it surely did not merit death.

I come back to the author with whose influence on James I began— Nathaniel Hawthorne. This is exactly the 'moral' of Hawthorne's stories, 'Rappaccini's Daughter' and 'The Birthmark', and it is of the same order as the moral of 'Young Goodman Brown'. Rappaccini's daughter, who lives and flourishes with poison in her veins, dies of the antidote; in 'The Birth-mark' Georgiana's husband, idolizing her beauty, causes her death in trying to clear it of one tiny flaw. Young Goodman Brown, having seen, or dreamed, or fancied he saw his respected elders, his young wife, and himself engaged in an unholy rite, can never again 'credit' anyone's truth or virtue, can never share in the joy of life again. And this, as Henry James the elder was never tired of insisting, is every creature's divinely bestowed birthright—inde-feasible, as Stevenson's Highlander wonderingly remarked, even in creatures uncanny and sure of damnation. In his fiction, we all agree, James never preaches; but the unconfessed persuasion, the *arrière-pensée*, 'the truth', it may be, 'at the back of the head' has a way of obtruding itself, willy-nilly— and we should not be disconcerted if, in this 'wanton little Tale', 'another turn of the screw of ordinary human virtue' gives it an equivocal twist. Thus wryly emergent, it has more than a touch of likeness to *Dipsychus* and its epilogue, but not a fleck of the transcendental whitewash with which Emerson, so usefully for American ambition, gives a face of promise to social evils.[288] For the 'moral' of our story (if one can with any safety apply this heavy and uncompromising term to an *amusette* so intricate and so nicely balanced) would seem to run somewhat as follows. Virtue is rela-tive not absolute; the better is the enemy of the good; don't try forcibly to eradicate the darling vice which may be someone's root of life; don't strip anyone of the cloak of respect we all need to tolerate one another. Human beings can't be, shouldn't want to be, or want others to be, perfect. We have all heard of redeeming virtues: there are perhaps redeeming vices too—'and the Lord forgie us!', says Andie Dale. [289]

Notes

To avoid repetition of references, a general acknowledgment is here made to Leon Edel and Dan H. Laurence, *A Bibliography of Henry James*, 2nd ed., rev. (London: Hart-Davis, 1961). In all questions relating to the periodical or book publication of work by Henry James, this bibliography is the prime authority.

1   John Macmillan Brown (1846–1935) was a foundation professor of Canterbury University College in 1875, and retained the chair of English until 1895. From 1879 he had been a member of the Senate, and in 1916 became Vice Chancellor, of the University of New Zealand, of which he was Chancellor from 1923 until his death. Professor Macmillan Brown is commemorated by an annual lecture series, delivered in rotation at the Universities of Canterbury, Otago, Victoria, and Auckland.

2   The text used throughout this discussion is that of the first English edition: Henry James, *The Two Magics: The Turn of the Screw*, *Covering End* (London: William Heinemann, 1898).

3   The text of the *Prefaces* used throughout this discussion is that of *The Art of the Novel: Critical Prefaces* by Henry James, with an Introduction by R. P. Blackmur (New York: Scribner, 1934).

4   Leslie A. Fiedler, *Love and Death in the American Novel* (New York: Criterion Books, 1960), pp. 122–23.

5   George Stransom, in 'The Altar of the Dead', quoted from Vol. IX of *The Complete Tales of Henry James*, ed. Leon Edel (London: Hart-Davis, 1962–64), p. 238.

6   Leon Edel, ed., *The Ghostly Tales of Henry James* (New Brunswick: Rutgers Univ. Press, 1948), p. 26.

7   C. Hartley Grattan, *The Three Jameses*, *A Family of Minds: Henry James Sr.*, *William James*, *Henry James*, 2nd ed. (New York: New York Univ. Press, 1962), p. 53. The account of Henry James Sr. given here is summarized from Book II of this work.

8   In her Introduction to Emanuel Swedenborg, *The True Christian Religion* (London: Dent, 1933).

9   *Notes of a Son and Brother*, Ch. vi, especially pp. 330–41, in *Henry James: Autobiography . . .*, ed. F. W. Dupee (London: W. H. Allen, 1956).

10 *Heaven and its Wonders and Hell, from Things Heard and Seen: A translation of De Caelo et ejus Mirabilibus, et de Inferno ex Auditis et Visis*, by Emanuel Swedenborg, rev. ed. (London: Swedenborg Society, 1958). References are to numbered subdivisions, not to pages.

11 *A Boy's Town* [1890], in *Selected Writings of William Dean Howells*, ed. Henry Steele Commager (New York: Random House, 1950), pp. 718, 722–23.

12 *A Small Boy and Others*, in *Henry James: Autobiography*, pp. 196–97.

Edward White Benson

on holiday in Rome, 1855; and as
Archbishop of Canterbury, 1883

William James in 1894

Edmund Gurney

F. W. H. Myers

Frank Podmore

Four pioneers of psychical research

13 The large drapery and fancy goods establishment of Howell and James in Lower Regent Street was a familiar feature of the West End till past the turn of the century. Thanks to W. S. Gilbert's verses in *Patience* (first staged on 23 April 1881), the firm became a symbol of stolid conservatism in matters of taste, as opposed to the 'greenery yallery' aestheticism sponsored by the Grosvenor Gallery in Bond Street from 1877 to 1890.

14 Quentin Anderson, *The American Henry James* (1957; rpt. London: Calder, 1958).

15 *Heaven and Hell*, 76.

16 *Heaven and Hell*, 450.

17 *Arcana Cœlestia* ... from the Latin of Emanuel Swedenborg, II (London: Swedenborg Society, 1901), 1635, 1637, and 1639.

18 *Heaven and Hell*, 553.

19 William James, review of *Human Personality and its Survival of Bodily Death*, by F. W. H. Myers, rpt. from *Proceedings of the Society for Psychical Research*, XVIII (1903), in *William James on Psychical Research*, ed. G. Murphy and R. O. Ballou (1960; rpt. London: Chatto and Windus, 1961), p. 233; William James, 'Final Impressions of a Psychical Researcher', in *Memories and Studies* (London: Longmans, 1911), pp. 191, 196, 201–05: this article was first published as 'Confidences of a Psychical Researcher' in the *American Magazine*, October 1909.

20 R. H. C. (A. R. Orage), *Readers and Writers, 1917–1921* (London: Allen and Unwin, 1922), p. 23.

21 Henry James, ' "Is there a Life after Death?" ', in *In After Days, Thoughts on the Future Life* (New York: Harper, 1910), rpt. in F. O. Matthiessen, *The James Family* ... (New York: Knopf, 1948), p. 606.

22 F. O. Matthiessen and Kenneth B. Murdock, edd., *The Notebooks of Henry James* (New York: Braziller, 1955), pp. 178–79.

23 William Lyon Phelps, *Autobiography with Letters* (New York: Oxford Univ. Press, 1939), p. 551.

24 'Recent Novels', *The Times*, 28 December 1898, p. 10, col. 4.

25 Percy Lubbock, ed., *The Letters of Henry James* (London: Macmillan, 1920), I, 304–05.

26 Quoted, on the authority of Henry Dwight Sedgwick, in *The Legend of the Master*, ed. S. Nowell-Smith (London: Constable, 1947), p. 48.

27 See Edmund Wilson, 'The Ambiguity of Henry James', in *The Triple Thinkers* (London: Lehmann, 1952), p. 95.

28 Oscar Cargill ('*The Turn of the Screw* and Alice James', *PMLA*, LXXVIII [1963], 238–49) suggests that Douglas is named after the 'noble Scot' who is Hotspur's ally in *Henry IV Part I*. It is barely possible, for reasons which I examine later, that James had this play in mind as he wrote *The Turn of the Screw*; but if Shakespeare's Douglas *is* evoked here, it is surely as the ally of the visionary Owen Glendower.

29 Mrs. Grose, after a night in charge of Flora, declares that the governess's 'idea's the right one'. Since yesterday, she herself has '*heard* ... from that child—horrors!' Some at least of the 'horrors' include abuse of the governess, 'beyond everything, for a young lady'. The day before, Mrs. Grose could not accept the possibility of 'such doings', now she says, 'I believe' (pp. 147–49).

30 I cite some examples from the text:
1. The governess, discussing the news of Miles's expulsion with Mrs. Grose, turns to see Flora, whom she has left at a task in the schoolroom, watching them from the open door (p. 22).
2. Once the identity of the male apparition has been established, the governess is struck by the oddity of Miles's silence with regard to Quint: 'And you tell me they were "great friends"?' (p. 50).
3. When Flora at her own request has been taken to play by the lake, and the governess becomes convinced that they are both under ghostly scrutiny, the child, instead of giving 'some sudden innocent sign either of interest or of alarm', falls uncharacteristically silent, and appears to be absorbed in a new game (p. 57).
4. The governess notes with approval that the children are 'extraordinarily at one'; but 'sometimes . . . I perhaps came across traces of little understandings between them by which one of them should keep me occupied while the other slipped away' (p. 75).
5. Miles, in atonement, it seems, for his recalcitrance the previous day, offers 'for half an hour' to play to the governess (p. 127). Meanwhile Flora has slipped away, rowed across the lake, and hidden in the copse (pp. 131–34).

31 'The Words of the Host to the Physician and the Pardoner', *Canterbury Tales*, VI (C), 293–96. The governess, in the full tide of her admiration for her charges, is aware of their vulnerability: 'They had the bloom of health and happiness; and yet, as if I had been in charge of a pair of little grandees, of princes of the blood, for whom everything, to be right, would have to be enclosed and protected, the only form that, in my fancy, the after-years could take for them was that of a romantic, a really royal extension of the garden and the park' (pp. 28–29).

32 Letter to Henry James (17 January 1909), urging him to rewrite his play *The Saloon*, in *The Complete Plays of Henry James*, ed. Leon Edel (London: Hart-Davis, 1949), p. 643.

33 An example of the 'trust' James inspired is recorded by Mrs. Humphry Ward, *A Writer's Recollections*, 2nd ed. (London: Collins, 1919), p. 194; and an example of the 'terror' by Muriel Draper, *Music at Midnight* (London: Heinemann, 1929), pp. 87–88.

34 Leon Edel, *Henry James: The Treacherous Years, 1895–1901* (London: Hart-Davis, 1969), pp. 191–203.

35 William James, writing to his wife (29 July 1889), says that his brother, in spite of a veneer of alien manners, remains 'the same dear old, good, innocent and at bottom very powerless-feeling Harry' (Henry James, ed., *The Letters of William James* [Boston: Atlantic Monthly, 1920], I, 288). But a sibling's judgment, however privileged, is not necessarily endorsed by the victim.

36 William James and most of Boston recognized Miss Birdseye in *The Bostonians* as the fictional equivalent of Miss Peabody (letter of Henry James, Lubbock, I, 115–18); most critics see traits of Alice James in Rose Muniment of *The Princess Casamassima*; Vernon Lee, in her story 'Lady Tal' (1892) presents an expatriate American novelist, 'a kind of Henry James', who considers 'intellectual vivisection a praiseworthy employment' (*Vanitas: Polite Stories*, 2nd ed. [London: John Lane, 1911], pp. 64, 111); Maud Elliott, daughter of Julia Ward Howe, records that although 'Henry James was often my mother's escort' and 'later in life we became fast friends', as a girl 'I rather avoided talking with him, fancying that he was "studying" me for copy' (*Three Generations* [London: John Lane, 1925], pp. 140–41).

37 Alice James records (17 June 1891), 'H[enry], by the way, has embedded in his pages
many pearls fallen from my lips, which he steals in the most unblushing way, saying,
simply, that he knew they had been said by the family, so it did not matter' (Leon
Edel, ed., *The Diary of Alice James* [London: Hart-Davis, 1965], p. 212).

38 Harold C. Goddard, 'A Pre-Freudian Reading of *The Turn of the Screw*', *Nineteenth-
Century Fiction*, XII (1957), 1–36.

39 Ezra Pound, 'Henry James', *The Little Review*, August 1918, rpt. in *Literary Essays
of Ezra Pound*, ed. T. S. Eliot (London: Faber, 1954), p. 326.

40 Edmund Wilson, 'The Ambiguity of Henry James', *Hound and Horn*, VII (1934),
385–406, rpt. in *The Triple Thinkers*, 2nd rev. ed. (London: Lehmann, 1952), pp.
89–128. The many fallacies in Wilson's interpretation of the story have long been
fully, but it seems vainly, exposed. A. J. A. Waldock, 'Mr. Edmund Wilson and
The Turn of the Screw', and R. B. Heilman, 'The Freudian Reading of *The Turn of
the Screw*', *Modern Language Notes*, LXII (1947), 331–34 and 433–45 respectively;
Oliver Evans, 'James's Air of Evil: "The Turn of the Screw"', *Partisan Review*,
XVI (1949), 175–87; Kathleen Fitzpatrick, 'Notes on Henry James and *The Turn of
the Screw*', *Meanjin*, IX (1950), 275–78, argue convincingly from the text in refutation of the Freudian theory. Some of the points raised are dealt with, briefly, on pp.
22–23 below.

41 The possibility was first suggested by Oscar Cargill, in 'Henry James as Freudian
Pioneer', *Chicago Review*, X (1956), 13–29, rpt. in *A Casebook on Henry James's "The
Turn of the Screw"*, ed. Gerald Willen (New York: Crowell, 1960), pp. 223–38.

42 Ralph Barton Perry, *The Thought and Character of William James* (Boston: Little
Brown, 1935), II, 169. The eight lectures were never published or even written out,
only notes for them being preserved; but it is of course possible that ideas developed
in them had formed the subject of earlier discussions.

43 Josef Breuer and Sigmund Freud, *Studies on Hysteria*, Vol. II of *The Complete
Psychological Works of Sigmund Freud*, trans. James Strachey, Anna Freud, Alix
Strachey, and Alan Tyson (London: Hogarth Press, 1955), pp. 53, 56, 72, 78, 126
et passim.

44 *Heaven and Hell*, 527.

45 Henry James, *Hawthorne* (1879; rpt. Ithaca: Cornell Univ. Press, 1956), pp. 49–51.

46 'He is as solitary in the history of the novel as Shakespeare in the history of poetry.'
—Graham Greene, 'Henry James' in *The English Novelists . . .*, ed. Derek Verschoyle
(London: Chatto and Windus, 1936), p. 228.

47 *Notebooks*, p. 178.

48 This link with *A Midsummer Night's Dream* has been noted by Leon Edel, *The
Ghostly Tales of Henry James*, p. 432.

49 There is another connection also. Joseph Sheridan Le Fanu was a Swedenborgian,
and one is tempted to think that this partly explains both his interest and his 'authority' in dealing with the supernatural themes recurrent in his books. Oddly enough,
in *Uncle Silas*, Swedenborgians are presented in a most unfavourable, not to say
villainous, light.

50 *Eminent Persons: Biographies reprinted from* The Times, III (London: Macmillan, 1893), 118 (obituary notice, 22 March 1883).

51 *The Law Times Reports* . . ., XL, NS, March–August 1879, 445–53.

52 A neat comment on the case is made by J. M. Robertson, *A History of Freethought in the Nineteenth Century* (London: Watts, 1929), I, 300: 'Secured the custody of her children [in fact, of her daughter only] under a marital deed of separation, she was deprived of it at law (1879) on her avowal of Neo-Malthusian and atheistic opinions, with the result that her influence as a propagandist was immensely increased.'

53 Annie Besant, *Death—And After?*, Theosophical Manuals No. 3, 7th. ed. (Madras: Theosophical Publishing House, 1968), pp. 39–42.

54 Ernest Weekley, *Jack and Jill: A Study in Our Christian Names*, 2nd. ed., rev. (London: Murray, 1948), pp. 77–78.

55 In the 1893 edition of *The Private Life*, James ends his story 'Owen Wingrave' (1892) with the sentence, 'He looked like a young soldier on a battle-field.' In the New York Edition the sentence reads, 'He was all the young soldier on the gained field.'

56 E. Ekwall, *The Concise Oxford Dictionary of English Place Names*, 4th. ed. (Oxford: Clarendon Press, 1960), p. 50, *s.v.* Blythe.
    James's use of the name may well have been prompted by the holiday he had spent in Suffolk during most of August and the first days of September 1897. He was staying near American cousins in Dunwich (Edel, *Henry James: The Treacherous Years*, pp. 178–83), and from there made excursions by bicycle to Woodbridge, Aldeburgh, Westleton, and 'as far inland as [he had] time to go', as he tells us in the article 'Old Suffolk' (dated 31 August 1897) which he wrote for *Harper's Weekly*. Even if he never succeeded in visiting the church at Blundeston, his map would tell him that to reach it he must pass (on the main road north) through Blythburgh, on the tidal river Blyth. Nearby, on the riverside, was the village of Blyford—to acquaint him with the alternative spelling.

57 The text cited is that of Henry Fielding, *Amelia*, 3 vols. (Oxford: Blackwell, 1926).

58 P. H. Reaney, *A Dictionary of British Surnames* (London: Routledge, 1958), p. 146, *s.v.* Griffin, Griffen. What may have influenced James in naming both Douglas and Griffin is the fact that *Henry IV Part I* had been lavishly staged as recently as the summer of 1896: it had been the matinée attraction of Beerbohm Tree's last season at the Haymarket. Cargill, however, in 'The Turn of the Screw and Alice James', pp. 239–40, equates James's Griffin with the heraldic gryphon. He does not link either Douglas or Griffin with James's mention of *Amelia*, being concerned only to demonstrate (p. 248) the governess's morbid self-identification with Fielding's heroine.

59 Henry James Jr., *Transatlantic Sketches* (Boston: Osgood, 1875, reissued Houghton Mifflin), p. 26. Edel, *The Ghostly Tales of Henry James*, p. 433, quotes the passage from *English Hours* (1905).

60 *Notebooks*, pp. 198, 208.

61 The formulae of reminder are varied: e.g. 'I remember', pp. 14, 31, 40, 73, 87, 105; 'I recall', p. 50; 'I recollect', p. 15; 'I am as sure to-day as I was sure then', p. 96; 'So I see her still', p. 114; 'I suppose I now read into our situation a clearness it couldn't have had at the time', p. 160; 'They are in my ears still', p. 168; etc.

62 Donald P. Costello, 'The Structure of *The Turn of the Screw*', *Modern Language Notes*, LXXV (1960), 312–21.

63 Costello, p. 317: 'Before the next sequence [No. 10, in Ch. xviii] begins there is an incident which is not foretold, is not interpreted, and has no plan resulting from it. It is the isolated incident of the "extraordinary blast and chill". . . . The interpretation of this mystifying scene is left to the imagination of the reader.'

64 J. Sheridan Le Fanu, *The Cock and Anchor* [1845], ed. H. van Thal (London: Cassell, 1967), pp. 189–91. The first publication was anonymous: *The Cock and Anchor, being a chronicle of Old Dublin City*, 3 vols. (Dublin: Curry, 1845). It was republished as *Morley Court. Being a chronicle of Old Dublin City. By the author of 'Uncle Silas'* (London: 1873); and again, under the author's name, as *The Cock and Anchor: A Novel* (London: Downey, 1895).

James's continuing interest in Le Fanu is attested by his story 'The Liar' (first published in the *Century Magazine*, May–June 1888). Oliver Lyon, invited to Stayes to paint the portrait of its owner, when conducted to his room first, according to his custom, looked 'at the books on the shelf and the prints on the walls. . . . There was the customary novel of Mr Le Fanu, for the bedside; the ideal reading in a country house for the hours after midnight. Oliver Lyon could scarcely forbear beginning it while he buttoned his shirt.' The story itself carries hints of James's acquaintance with *The Cock and Anchor* (read, probably, in the 1873 edition): the 'very agreeable' master of the house, Sir David Ashmore, 'proud of his age but ashamed of his infirmities', recalls the similarly aged, invalid, and picturesque, but malignant Sir Richard *Ash*woode, of *Morley* Court, while the painter's name echoes that of the heroine's 'good' uncle, Oliver French. Incidentally, the heroine of *The Cock and Anchor* is rescued by a compassionate serving-maid named Flora Guy. A number of circumstances may have helped to keep alive James's memory of the book. W. R. Le Fanu in his reminiscences praised this first novel as one of his brother's best (*Seventy Years of Irish Life* . . . [London: Arnold, 1893, rpt. 1914], p. 150): James would almost certainly have read William Le Fanu's 'first and only book', which ran through three impressions from November 1893 to January 1894, and was reprinted in November 1896. And non-musical as he was, on 6 March 1896 James took a friend to hear Charles Villiers Stanford's opera *Shamus O'Brien*, the libretto of which was founded on Sheridan Le Fanu's ballad, quoted in full by his brother (Elizabeth Robins, *Theatre and Friendship* [London: Cape, 1932, rpt. 1934], p. 182).

65 The references to Ibsen quoted in this passage occur in three reviews written during the years 1891 to 1897. In order of citation, the sources are: 'Ibsen's New Play' [*The Master Builder*], *Pall Mall Gazette*, February 1893, rpt. as Part II of 'Henrik Ibsen' in *Essays in London and Elsewhere* (London: Osgood McIlvaine, 1893), p. 261; 'On the Occasion of *Hedda Gabler*', *New Review*, June 1891, rpt. as Part I of 'Henrik Ibsen' in *Essays in London and Elsewhere*, p. 252; review of *John Gabriel Borkman* [newly translated by William Archer and others, but not yet produced] in 'London', dated 15 January 1897, *Harper's Weekly*, XLI (1897), 6 February, 134; 'On the Occasion of *Hedda Gabler*' in *Essays in London and Elsewhere*, p. 249.

66 Letter to Elizabeth Robins, 22 November 1894, in *Theatre and Friendship*, p. 157. It is worth noting here that the first London production of *The Lady from the Sea* was on 11 May 1891, and that of *Little Eyolf* on 23 November 1896. James mentioned the latter production in his London letter (dated 1 January 1897) for *Harper's Weekly*, XLI (1897), 23 January, 78. The first English translation of *The Lady from the Sea* was Eleanor Marx-Aveling's, published by Unwin in 1889 with an introduction by Edmund Gosse; subsequent translations, by Clara Bell and Mrs. F. E. Archer respectively, appeared in Vol. II of *The Prose Dramas of Henrik Ibsen*, ed. Edmund Gosse (New York and London: Lovell, 1890), and Vol. V of *Ibsen's Prose Dramas*, ed. William Archer (London: Walter Scott, 1890–91). The first English translation of *Little Eyolf* was William Archer's, published by Heinemann in 1894. But, as he

notes in his review of *John Gabriel Borkman*, James might also consult French or German versions.

67 Edel, *Henry James: The Treacherous Years*, p. 193.

68 'I think it is a most wonderful, lurid, poisonous little tale, like an Elizabethan tragedy. I am greatly impressed by it. James is developing, but he will never arrive at passion, I fear.'—Letter to Robert Ross, [? 12 January 1899], in *The Letters of Oscar Wilde*, ed. Rupert Hart-Davis (London: Hart-Davis, 1962), p. 776.

69 Henrik Ibsen, *Little Eyolf: a play in three acts*, trans. William Archer (London: Heinemann, 1894, rpt. 1897), I, pp. 25–28. All quotations are from the text of this edition.

70 Henrik Ibsen, *The Lady from the Sea: play in five acts*, trans. Mrs. F. E. Archer, in Vol. V [1891] of *Ibsen's Prose Dramas*, ed. William Archer (London: Walter Scott, 1890–91), II, pp. 166–67. All quotations are from the text of this edition.

71 Letter to Henry James, 22 October 1905, on the subject of *The Golden Bowl*, Perry, I, 424.

72 Flora, surprised at the window, answers the governess's question as if it 'were as irrelevant, or at any rate as impersonal, as Mrs. Marcet or nine-times-nine' (p. 81). Mrs. Jane Marcet's first publication, *Conversations on Chemistry . . .*, appeared in 1806, but she was still the Victorian governess's stand-by in the 1870s. Hers were the first elementary scientific textbooks, but she dealt also with language, English history, and (an innovation) political economy.

73 Leon Edel, *Henry James: The Untried Years, 1843–1870* (London: Hart-Davis, 1953), p. 294, and *Henry James: The Conquest of London, 1870–1881* (New York: Lippincott, 1962), p. 333; *The Middle Years*, ed. Dupee, p. 562.

74 Lubbock, II, 211, 413, 501.

75 Frederic Harrison, *Studies in Early Victorian Literature* (London: Arnold, 1895). The text used here is that of the third (1901) edition.

    These studies appeared originally in *The Forum* in 1894 and 1895, and some of them were also reprinted as separate booklets: e.g. *Charlotte Brontë's Place in Literature* (London: Arnold, 1895) reproduced Harrison's article bearing the same title in *The Forum* for March 1895. Whether or not James saw the original article, he may well have seen, or been informed of, the laudatory notice in the *Review of Reviews* for 15 April 1895 (XI, 361, col. 1): 'Much the best paper in the *Forum*, from a literary point of view, is Mr. Frederic Harrison's brilliant essay on Charlotte Brontë's place in literature. Mr. Harrison is very enthusiastic about "Jane Eyre" '—Harrison's evaluation of the novel is then summarized. The volume of *Studies* was not published until November 1895; but this reference in the April number of the *Review of Reviews*, that vade-mecum for the harassed reader of the nineties, would provide exactly the stimulus required both to bring *Jane Eyre* to James's mind (as I suggest below) in the spring of 1895, and to induce his reading of Harrison's volume later. When a work by one of his friends appeared serially, James's habit (so he declared) was to wait for its production in book form—as he adjured his friends to do in his own case—so that he is perhaps unlikely to have read the Brontë essay before its publication in the collected *Studies*. But Harrison had been discussing the early Victorian writers in such numbers, over so many months, so confidently, and to such acclaim (by the *Review of Reviews*, for instance), that the 'advance publicity' alone would have ensured that James read it then.

76 *Notebooks*, pp. 199, 251.

77 'On the Occasion of *Hedda Gabler*', *Essays in London and Elsewhere*, p. 257.

78 James notes, ambivalently, 'the ugly interior on which his curtain inexorably rises and which, to be honest, I like for the queer associations it has taught us to respect; the hideous carpet and wall-paper and curtains (one may answer for them), the conspicuous stove, the lonely centre-table, the "lamps with green shades," as in the sumptuous first act of *The Wild Duck*, the pervasive air of small interests and standards, the sign of limited local life.'—ibid., pp. 249–50.

79 *Notebooks*, pp. 137, 216, 248.

80 'But this is so far from being a book to dismiss in a phrase that its fulness of suggestion bore, to my perception, on the very fact that the decisive word about the unhappy family it commemorates has still to be written. It gives us afresh the image of how much their unhappiness was the making of their fame. In the presence of that sore stress on the one hand, and of a sounder measure, on the other, than we had as yet been able to take of some matters that it is important to disengage from the glamour of pathos, we receive a forcible lesson on the art of not confounding things. It is very true that the lesson may well leave a reader wondering whether, especially as regards Charlotte, a yet happier thought than to try to utter the decisive word be not perhaps to let silence, still more decisively, descend. The danger of course is that silence won't!'—*Harper's Weekly*, XLI (6 February), 135.

James repeats this judgment, more forcefully and at greater length, in his lecture, *The Lesson of Balzac*, delivered on 12 January 1905 to the Contemporary Club of Philadelphia: 'If these things[*Jane Eyre* and *Wuthering Heights*] were "stories", as we say, and stories of a lively interest, the medium from which they sprang was above all in itself a story, such a story as has fairly elbowed out the rights of appreciation. . . . Literature is an objective, a projected result; it is life that is the unconscious, the agitated, the struggling, floundering cause. But the fashion has been, in looking at the Brontës, so to confound the cause with the result that we cease to know, in the presence of such ecstasies, what we have hold of or what we are talking about. They represent, the ecstasies, the high-water mark of sentimental judgment'—Leon Edel, ed., *The House of Fiction* . . . (London: Hart-Davis, 1957), pp. 63–64.

It may be observed that 'ecstasies' better describes the impassioned laudation by Swinburne in *A Note on Charlotte Brontë* (1877) than the warmest praise to which Harrison commits himself. But the memory of a critical extravagance twenty years old, even if embittered by Swinburne's vilification of George Eliot and (in 1887) of Whitman, and refreshed (in 1894) by a new edition of the *Note*, can scarcely have provoked James's riposte to *Jane Eyre* in 1897. Harrison's advocacy was 'noticeable' where that of Swinburne, 'as hysterical and vociferous as usual', could be ignored. In fact, after January 1877 and his review of the pamphlet attacking Carlyle, James *had* ignored everything Swinburne wrote.

81 Clement K. Shorter, *Charlotte Brontë and her Circle* (London: Hodder and Stoughton, 1896), pp. 275, 276, 403; 33; 58, 259 and note; 381; 309; 314, 316, 317 (letters of 5, 9, and 23 April 1851).

82 Mrs. Humphry Ward, op. cit., pp. 315–16 (James's stay at Levens Hall); W. S. Peterson, 'Henry James on *Jane Eyre*', TLS, 30 July 1971, pp. 919–20 (Mrs. Ward's rendering of James's Brontë criticism); Henry James, 'London Letter', *Harper's Weekly*, XLI (1897, 31 July), 754.

83 The governess is twenty when she goes to Bly (p. 9); her reported experiences there have occurred 'long before' the time she meets Douglas (p. 6), who is ten years younger

than she is (p. 5), and as an undergraduate would be aged from eighteen to twenty. The Bly episode has therefore occurred about ten years before the meeting, which, as another guest notes, has taken place 'forty years' (p. 7) before Douglas reads the story to the company. The story published in 1898 is, we are told, a transcript of the governess's manuscript 'made much later' than the reading (p. 8). James, therefore, asks us to accept the events of the story as occurring more than fifty years before 1898.

84   Hamilton Ellis, *British Railway History ... 1839–1876* (London: Allen and Unwin, 1954), pp. 89–91.

85   John Copeland, *Roads and their Traffic 1750–1850* (Newton Abbot: David and Charles, 1968), pp. 100–01, cites an 1822 list of coaches leaving London for the eastern counties from which it appears that travellers to Colchester had a choice of two 'post coaches' for the six-hour journey, as well, presumably, as the chance of a place on the through coaches to Ipswich, Yarmouth, and Norwich. During the thirties and early forties the coaching firms kept in business by supplementing the growing railway services, e.g. by meeting trains at stations and by carrying passengers on to destinations not yet served by rail: Copeland, pp. 186–90, cites details from local newspapers, e.g. *The Essex Standard*.

86   James Elmes, *Metropolitan Improvements; or London in the Nineteenth Century ...* (London: Jones, 1829), pp. 14–16.

87   G. E. Mitton, *Hampstead and Marylebone*, in the series *The Fascination of London*, ed. Sir Walter Besant (London: Black, 1902), pp. 70–71, 82, 98–100 etc.

88   Charles Dickens, *Little Dorrit*, Book I, opening of Ch. xxi 'Mr. Merdle's Complaint'.

89   E. S. Turner, *Call the Doctor: a social history of medical men* (London: Joseph, 1958), p. 208; and cf. p. 309—'According to the *Medical Directory*'s last count of plates [in 1957, presumably] there were 960 consultants operating there, as against some 800 in 1948.' It must in justice be noted that there was, and is, a legitimate reason for the migration in the proximity of large hospitals, e.g. the Middlesex, in Mortimer Street.

90   I note, without suggesting any influence here, that Augustus Hare, a sceptic in such matters, tells of a visit (in 1866) to a lady who 'talked incessantly for three hours, chiefly of spirits'. One of her anecdotes concerned a child possessed by evil spirits: 'Why, the poor little thing used to struggle for hours. It used to describe the devils it saw. They were of different kinds. Sometimes it would say, "Oh, it's only one of the innocent blackies," and then it would shriek when it thought it saw a red devil come. It was the red devils that did all the mischief.'—Augustus J. C. Hare, *The Story of My Life*, III (London: George Allen, 1896), 104–05. A very ancient and widespread popular tradition holds red hair to be the badge of evil, and thus proper to murderers and traitors (cf. *Cain-coloured*, *Judas-coloured*, *OED*, *s.vv.* Cain[2] and Judas). According to Montague Summers (*The Vampire, his Kith and Kin* [1928, rpt. New York: University Books, 1960], p. 183) in parts of the Balkans red hair is, or was, also believed to be the distinguishing mark of certain vampires, 'the foulest of the foul'. The 'bushy reddish hair and beard' of Ibsen's Stranger (*The Lady from the Sea*, Act III, p. 178) is thus doubly appropriate, as symbolizing both a murderer and an evil demon, a troll.

91   Charlotte Brontë, *Jane Eyre: an autobiography* (London: Oxford Univ. Press, 1933, rpt. 1964), p. 211 (Ch. xvii). All subsequent citations (by chapter and page number) are from the text of this, *The World's Classics*, edition.
      Hitherto *Jane Eyre* has been acknowledged only as offering a general parallel to

the situation in *The Turn of the Screw* (Edel, *The Ghostly Tales of Henry James*, p. 431; *Henry James: The Treacherous Years*, p. 195; Rolande Ballorain, 'The Turn of The Screw: L'Adulte et l'enfant, ou les deux regards', *Études Anglaises*, XXII (1969), 254–55), or as a source of isolated 'borrowings' (Cargill, '*The Turn of the Screw* and Alice James', p. 243).

92 It is significant that Lucy Snowe, of *Villette*, is 'abroad', alone and not far from destitution, before she accepts employment as a children's nurse, and then is rapidly promoted to class teacher.

93 Cf. Jane Eyre's reverie in the gallery at Thornfield (xii, 127) and that of the governess in the garden at Bly (p. 30); Jane's new content at Thornfield (xv, 173; xxiii, 302) and that of the governess at Bly (pp. 28–29); Jane's attempts at a common-sense assessment of her relationship to her employer (xv, 179; xvii, 192, 208) and the governess's alternate hopes of pleasing and fear of ridicule (pp. 94–95, 102); Jane's self-reproach and admission of weakness (xxvii, 387; xxxi, 434) and the governess's scorn of her own irresolution (pp. 109, 151); etc.

94 With such passages in *Jane Eyre* as iv, 41; x, 103; xv, 115, 171; xxii, 294 cf. *The Turn of the Screw* pp. 22–23, 27, 63, 65, 73, 80, 89, 123, 134, 163.

95 *The Story of My Life*, I (1896), 105–09, 111–12, 186–88 etc. Like many other anecdotes related of Aunt Esther, the hanging of the child's cat (p. 186) seems to argue a complication of moral disorders for which religiosity alone can hardly be the full explanation.

96 The discussion of Quint's appearance (pp. 46–47) has been criticized on this score. What the governess takes for granted, and therefore does not mention, is the genteel superstition (firmly established in Victorian stage convention) that features too regularly 'handsome' and clothes over 'smart' for the occasion are an infallible mark of the ill-bred cad and bounder. But while Mrs. Grose, with the aesthetic innocence of her class, accepts Quint as 'handsome', she is as expert as the governess in the unwritten sumptuary laws of Victorian England: certain stuffs and styles are 'too fine' for wear by a servant—so worn, they must be either cast-offs, or, as in this case, stolen. The sartorial niceties of class consciousness are frequently discussed in *Jane Eyre*: there is a sardonic relish in James's allusion to them here.

97 Jane Eyre quotes Shakespeare and Milton frequently, but also on occasion Pope, Thomson, Goldsmith, Johnson, Cowper, Burns, Scott, Coleridge, Byron, Moore, and Campbell; her childhood reading (e.g. of *The Arabian Nights*, *The Pilgrim's Progress*, and *Gulliver's Travels*) supplies many allusions; but the Scriptures are her mainstay, providing scores of references.

98 Flora's lack of self-consciousness reminds the governess of 'the deep, sweet serenity indeed of one of Raphael's holy infants' (p. 17); the children are 'unpunishable', 'like the cherubs of the anecdote, who had—morally, at any rate—nothing to whack!' (p. 37); though Quint and Miss Jessel 'were not angels, they "passed", as the French say' (p. 101). There are the occasional pious ejaculations (pp. 85, 148); but even the expression of piety may have an unorthodox ring: 'Well, my eyes *were* sealed, it appeared, at present—a consummation for which it seemed blasphemous not to thank God. There was, alas, a difficulty about that: I would have thanked him with all my soul had I not had in a proportionate measure this conviction of the secret of my pupils' (p. 99).

99 This (p. 127) is a reference to I Samuel xvi. 23: 'And it came to pass, when the evil spirit from God was upon Saul, that David took an harp, and played with his hand:

so Saul was refreshed, and was well, and the evil spirit departed from him.' The scriptural metaphor of 'girding the loins' is applied to Mrs. Grose's efforts to 'meet' the governess's theory (p. 143). But although at least three texts might fit the case (Proverbs xxxi. 17; Luke xii. 35; I Peter i. 13), it is unlikely that James intends a specific allusion here, any more than he does by the accidentally appropriate description of the housekeeper's room (p. 114) as 'all swept and garnished', which a writer such as Charlotte Brontë could not have used without a memory of the 'unclean spirits' of Matthew xii. 43–45 or Luke xi. 24–26. In James's use these phrases are mere *clichés*: 'a girding of loins', for example, occurs as part of a metaphor unnecessarily mixed in his London letter of 15 January 1897 to *Harper's Weekly*.

100 *Jane Eyre*, ix, 92–94; cf. *The Turn of the Screw*, pp. 120–23: 'I marked the coolness of his firm little hand. . . . there was light enough to show how he smiled up at me from his pillow. . . . His clear, listening face, framed in its smooth whiteness, made him for the minute as appealing as some wistful patient in a children's hospital. . . . He gave . . . like a convalescent slightly fatigued, a languid shake of his head. . . . My face was close to his. . . .'

101 See *Jane Eyre*, i, 3; xiii, 147; xv, 179; xxvi, 356–57.

102 'The narrative is supposed to be written, many years ago, by another governess, who had developed Mr. James's style, down to an occasional Americanism' (*The Times*, loc. cit.). James himself might be thought to underline the American connection: recording, as it were in his own person, Douglas's introduction to the story, ' "Well then," I said, "just sit right down and begin" ' (p. 4). But the English of today is so permeated with American idiom that the traces in the governess's narrative are no longer obvious. In any case the expressions censured by nineteenth-century critics are often mere English colloquialisms: for instance, 'a kind of' (e.g. 'a kind of comforting pledge', p. 18) and 'a sort of' (e.g. 'a sort of passion of tenderness', p. 26), both frequently used by James, are as old as Shakespeare and Defoe.

103 The governess's favourite pejoratives are 'dreadful/dreadfully', 'horrible/horribly', 'awful/awfully', and 'monstrous'; but she also uses 'hideous', 'ugly', 'queer', 'terrible', 'horrid', and exceptionally, a few less conventional terms: 'the particular deadly view' (p. 70); 'grievous fancies' and 'odious memories' (p. 72); 'my vile predecessor' (p. 112). With most of these terms, and especially with those in most common use, such as 'dreadful', the reader has to be alert to a possible shift of intention from light irony ('my dreadful boldness of mind', p. 69) to serious, literal description ('things terrible and unguessable and that sprang from dreadful passages of intercourse in the past', p. 101). It is no doubt appropriate that to the governess's highly-developed aesthetic sense the physical signs of distress (pallor, tears, etc.) should appear simply as 'ugly': 'the ugly signs [of tears]' (p. 65); 'how ugly and queer I looked' (p. 105). But so used, the word unavoidably gathers its darker connotations of 'evil' and 'menacing'. And one word of the governess's especially invites misinterpretation: she speaks of 'the strange steps of my obsession' (p. 99) and 'my endless obsession' (p. 119), using the word quite correctly in the sense of persistent harassment (literally 'siege') from without by evil spirits. But in twentieth-century usage the word is applied almost exclusively to the harassment from within of a persistent notion, or *idée fixe*. The difficulty of the governess's situation is in fact epitomized in the ambiguity of this one word. The grieving irony of her allusions to the final rout of Quint, followed as it is by the death of Miles—'success' (p. 163), 'triumph' (p. 164), 'victory' (pp. 165, 167), 'the loss I was so proud of' (p. 168)—offers less excuse for misinterpretation.

  The governess's colloquialisms are sometimes emphasized by inverted commas: so ' "game" ' (p. 36), ' "caught" it' (p. 37), ' "kicked out" ' (p. 74), ' "had" me'

(p. 88); but there is not always this self-consciousness in their use: 'It was plump . . . in the middle of my very hour' (pp. 29–30); 'my scrappy retirements' (p. 38); ' "Yes, you're getting on" ' (p. 105). Occasionally, and the intention may be humorous, these expressions are rather oddly misapplied: 'I cropped up in another place' (p. 24); 'I say courage because I was beyond all doubt already far gone' (p. 40). The governess's joke about cherubs (p. 37) and her glance at Flora standing barefooted 'in so much of her candour and so little of her nightgown' (p. 79) are indications that life at Bly may have been less constantly oppressive than some readers suppose.

104 In the following list, references to *Jane Eyre* (by chapter and page) precede page references to *The Turn of the Screw*: the rookery (xi, 115, 124; xii, 130 cf. pp. 15, 31); the park (xi, 115, 124 cf. pp. 38, 40); the position of the church (xi, 115, 124 cf. pp. 38, 111); the crenellated parapet (xi, 115, 124 cf. pp. 19, 30–33); the windowed front (xi, 114–15; xxxvi, 514 cf. p. 14); the gallery (xi, 113–14 *et passim* cf. pp. 77, 81, 83, 119); the staircase (xi, 112–13, 114 cf. p. 77); the unused, 'chilly' rooms (xi, 121 cf. p. 84); the remote, 'antique' parts of the house (xi, 122–23 *et passim* cf. p. 19).

105 Jane Eyre, welcomed by Mrs. Fairfax, thinks 'She treats me like a visitor. . . .' (xi, 111); the 'great looking-glass' in the red-room at Gateshead had mirrored Jane in a crisis of childhood terror (ii, 9–10, 13); Mrs. Fairfax shows Jane the house and takes her up to the leads, to which she frequently returns (xi, 122–24; xii, 127); Jane Eyre makes the first day's lessons easy and brief (xi, 120); strange laughter, stranger 'murmurs', and stealthy movements are heard outside her room by night (xv, 174–75); after her first meeting with Mr. Rochester, Jane 'lingered at the gates' and 'on the lawn' and 'paced backwards and forwards on the pavement' till the sky was dark and the moon high (xii, 136–37); 'there was a mystery at Thornfield' (xvii, 195); Mrs. Fairfax changes the subject (xi, 125; xiii, 150); Jane questions Grace Poole (xvi, 180–83); there are no ghosts at Thornfield (xi, 123); servants' gossip is discouraged (xvii, 195, 215); Adèle's 'simplicity, gay prattle, and efforts to please' (xii, 126); the 'plantation' at Gateshead makes a winter setting for Jane's childish misery (iv, 39); a sheet of ice covers the sloping lane when Mr. Rochester returns to Thornfield—his horse falls, and he is slightly injured (xii, 130–32); Jane makes her decision to escape from Thornfield and does so instantly, with the minimum of preparation and without farewells (xxvii, 385).

106 On the occasion of Mr. Rochester's house-party the piano is removed from the library, which has in his absence served as the schoolroom (xi, 120), to the drawing-room (xvii, 199); and here Jane's rival, Miss Ingram, performs on it, 'rattling away' and accompanying Mr. Rochester's singing 'in spirited style' (xvii, 212–14). Later, during their 'month of courtship', 'the master' plays and sings for Jane; 'for he could play as well as sing' (xxiv, 325).

107 Bessie's singing is a 'lively delight' to Jane as a child, but in her state of 'morbid suffering' the plaintive ballads bring uncontrollable tears (iii, 19). And Jane finds that music and song, far from being a calming diversion as she had hoped, merely kindle Mr. Rochester's ardour (xxiv, 327).

108 Alice Meynell, 'The Unready', *Pall Mall Gazette*, 4 November 1896, rpt. in *Ceres' Runaway and other Essays* (London: Constable, 1909; rpt. Freeport, N.Y.: Books for Libraries Press, 1967), pp. 123–24.

109 Corresponding passages in Mrs. Meynell's essays are: childish beauty and 'temperament'—'Children in Midwinter' in *The Children*, pp. 21, 25–26; 'The Child of Tumult' in *Ceres' Runaway . . .*, pp. 127–28; cf. for boyish independence, 'The Boy'

in *The Children*, pp. 72–75; the diversionary gesture—'Out of Town' in *The Children*, p. 38; pleasure in 'twice-told tales' and repetitive games—'The Unready' in *Ceres' Runaway* . . ., pp. 122–23; the sense of remoteness in time and space—'The Illusion of Historic Time' in *The Colour of Life* . . ., pp. 89, 92–94; the stimulus of darkness— 'Out of Town' and 'Under the Early Stars' in *The Children*, pp. 44–45. Perhaps the most illuminating of these correspondences is the one cited from 'Out of Town' (*The Children*, p. 38): 'Being afraid of dogs this little girl of four years old has all kinds of dodges to disguise her fear, which she has evidently resolved to keep to herself. She will set up a sudden song to distract attention from the fact that she is placing herself out of the dog's way, and she will pretend to turn to gather a flower, while she watches the creature out of sight.' Compare with this 'Flora, a short way off, stood before us on the grass and smiled as if her performance was now complete. The next thing she did, however, was to stoop straight down and pluck—quite as it if were all she was there for—a big, ugly spray of withered fern. I instantly became sure she had just come out of the copse' (p. 134). James has taken Mrs. Meynell's special case as a general precedent for the depiction of childish duplicity: Flora's inconsequential action and the unhesitating certainty with which (both here and in the early passage by the lake, p. 57) the governess interprets it as a subterfuge are thus, on Mrs. Meynell's authority, warrant for the presence of an inimical third party, of which both the governess and the child are aware, but of which the child pretends ignorance.

Thanks in some degree to the enthusiastic praise of Coventry Patmore and of Meredith, Mrs. Meynell's reputation as an essayist stood high in the nineties, and the subtlety of her child studies was especially admired. As A. K. Tuell notes (in *Mrs. Meynell and her Literary Generation* [New York: Dutton, 1925], p. 139), the *Pall Mall Gazette* claimed: 'It may almost be said of Mrs. Meynell that she has newly created the child in literature. . . . Hers may almost be called the "new child".' How far can we assume Henry James to have been familiar with this section of her work? Most of her essays on children originally appeared from 1894 to 1898 among her weekly contributions to the *Pall Mall Gazette*. Eighteen were reprinted in *The Children* (London: John Lane, 1896). One, 'The Illusion of Historic Time', was included in *The Colour of Life, and other Essays on Things Seen and Heard* (London: John Lane, 1896). 'The Unready' and 'The Child of Tumult', which appeared in the *Pall Mall Gazette* for 4 November 1896 and 20 October 1897 respectively (Tuell, p. 268), were not reprinted until 1909. Meredith, in a letter to Mrs. Meynell of 31 May 1896, writes: 'My book of "The Rhythm" will be flying to-morrow to Henry James, who was here yesterday, and earned the gift by his appreciation of the contents. I could not let him have it until another was on its way to fill the vacancy' (*Letters of George Meredith*, ed. W. M. Meredith [London: Constable, 1912], II, 483). But while it is thus certain that by mid 1896 James knew the pieces collected in *The Rhythm of Life and other Essays* (London: Elkin Mathews and John Lane, 1893), which he had not before possessed, both the phrasing of Meredith's remarks and his own reference, in his London letter, to *The Children* as a book 'not so much of yesterday as of the day before,' suggest a familiarity with Mrs. Meynell's work in its original, journalistic form, which its brevity no less than its excellence would fully explain.

110 Dan H. Laurence, ed., *Bernard Shaw, Collected Letters 1874–1897* (London: Reinhardt, 1965), pp. 107; 623, 660 (letters to Ellen Terry, 6 April and 21 September 1896); Frank Harris, *Bernard Shaw* . . . (London: Gollancz, 1931), p. 30; Barbara Drake and Margaret I. Cole, edd., *Our Partnership, by Beatrice Webb* (London: Longmans, 1948), p. 38; Wilfrid Scawen Blunt, *My Diaries* . . . (London: Secker, n.d.), II, 136. The most comprehensive group of photographs is that reproduced by Stanley Weintraub in *Shaw: An Autobiography, 1856–1898* (London: Reinhardt,

1970). The Newcombe portrait is reproduced as frontispiece to *Platform and Pulpit : Bernard Shaw*, ed. Dan H. Laurence (London: Hart-Davis, 1962).

111 Letters concerning James's play *The Saloon* were interchanged in 1909, and are reproduced by Edel in *The Complete Plays of Henry James*, pp. 642–47; Shaw's reference to a conversation with Henry James occurs in *Sixteen Self Sketches* (London: Constable, 1949), XIV, 'Biographers' Blunders Corrected', pp. 80–81: Shaw gives no indication in this sketch (dated 1947–48) of the circumstances in which the conversation took place.

There has never been any suggestion, by the biographers of either James or Shaw, that the two might have been earlier and better acquainted than either has taken the trouble to state. Yet, as Edel notes (*Henry James : The Conquest of London*, p. 275), one of James's first letters home, after his arrival in London at the end of 1876, tells of his meeting, at the home of Sir William Power (son of the actor, Tyrone Power, and a friend of James's relatives, the Emmets), 'a curious and interesting specimen of a wondrous type—the London female literary hack.' This lady was Mrs. Cashel Hoey, Shaw's first cousin. She was a most industrious hack, producing, between 1865 and 1896, some dozen three-volume novels, besides a multitude of short stories and translations. She was also a familiar figure, both as guest and as hostess, in London society of the time: kindly as well as loquacious, it appears, something of a busybody and a wirepuller. When Elizabeth Robins first came to London (in 1888), Mrs. Cashel Hoey exerted herself to provide introductions; on one occasion she lent the young actress ten pounds (Elizabeth Robins, *Both Sides of the Curtain* [London: Heinemann, 1940], pp. 23, 42, 129, 188 etc.). It was Mrs. Cashel Hoey's introduction which in 1879 procured for Shaw a berth with the Edison Telephone Company (Bernard Shaw, Preface to *Immaturity* [London: Constable, 1930, rpt. 1950], p. xxxvi). Shaw does not mention attending his cousin's receptions, or being introduced by her to houses she visited (that of Sir William Power, for instance), but he does admit to having received, and on occasion accepted, invitations to dinner-parties, soirées, and the like (Preface to *Immaturity*, pp. xxvi–xxviii; xli–xlii; Preface to *The Irrational Knot* [London: Constable, 1931, rpt. 1950], pp. xi–xii). On such occasions—'As it never occurred to me to conceal my opinions any more than my nationality, and as I had, besides, an unpleasant trick of contradicting everyone from whom I thought I could learn anything in order to draw him out and enable me to pick his brains, I think I must have impressed many amiable persons as an extremely disagreeable and undesirable young man.' Was the gregarious, the polite and conversable Mr. Henry James Jr. among the persons so antagonized? It seems more than likely.

112 See the references to Paul Muniment in *The Princess Casamassima*, Chapters 7, 14, 15, 21 etc. Hesketh Pearson (*Bernard Shaw: His Life and Personality* [London: Methuen, 1961], p. 79) quotes the opening of Shaw's first reported public speech, delivered in January 1885, in which he bracketed shareholders and landlords with burglars.

113 Harris, *Bernard Shaw*, pp. 115–17; Clarence Rook, 'George Bernard Shaw', *The Chap-Book*, V (1896), 533–34; Bernard Shaw, *Our Theatres in the Nineties* (London: Constable, 1932, rpt. 1948), II, 43, 47; Bernard Shaw, Preface to *The Irrational Knot*, p. xi; Bernard Shaw, *London Music in 1888–89 [sic] as heard by Corno di Bassetto . . .* (London: Constable, 1937, rpt. 1950), p. 350. It is worth noting that on 1 May 1896 *The Chap-Book* carried Henry James's story 'The Way It Came', and in 1897, serially from 15 January to 1 August, the novel *What Maisie Knew*.

114 Laurence, *Letters 1874–1897*, pp. 106, 115, 139, 634 (stage appearances; the programme for the Socialist League production of *Alone* is reproduced facing p. 115),

372 ('I have spent so much time at rehearsal [of *Widowers' Houses*] that I am stark ruined': letter of 14 December 1892), 423 (rehearsing *Arms and the Man*: letter to 'Raina', 16 April 1894), 787 (rehearsing *Candida* for provincial tour: note of 21 July 1897), 778 (disowns responsibility for the Carson production of *The Man of Destiny* 1–3 July, which was not rehearsed: letter to Ellen Terry, 2 July 1897); Shaw, Preface to *The Irrational Knot*, p. xix; Weintraub, p. 301, n. 16; *The Sketch*, 25 April 1894, p. 673, full-page illustration subtitled 'Mr. George Bernard Shaw at the rehearsal of his play at the Avenue Theatre, drawn by J. Bernard Partridge (Bernard Gould).' Bernard Gould played Sergius in the 1894 production of *Arms and the Man*. Shaw, in the *Saturday Review* for 2 May 1896 (*Our Theatres in the Nineties*, II, 117) wrote: 'I once elaborately explained to Mr. Gould a part of which I was myself the author. He paid me the closest attention; retired to ponder my utterances; and presently returned with a perfectly accurate and highly characteristic drawing of me, which I shall probably never live down.'

115 Laurence, *Letters 1874–1897*, pp. 266 ('flavor of brimstone': letter to E. D. Girdlestone, 26 September 1890), 175 ('known as Socialist': letter to the proprietor of an American journal, 18 August 1887), 262 (lecture tour: letter to Jules Magny, 12 September 1890), 109 (article on Anarchism: letter to Henry Seymour, 5 January 1885, and Laurence's note); Bernard Shaw, 'How I became a Public Speaker', in *Sixteen Self Sketches*, p. 59; Bernard Shaw, 'The Ideal of Citizenship' (address delivered at the Progressive League Demonstration, 11 October 1909), in *Platform and Pulpit*, pp. 74–75 (reference to Autonomie Club); G. Bernard Shaw, *The Fabian Society: its Early History*, Fabian Tract No. 41 (London: Fabian Society, 1892), p. 3; Bernard Shaw, *The Impossibilities of Anarchism*, Fabian Tract No. 45 (London: Fabian Society, 1893).

116 Laurence, *Letters 1874–1897*, p. 801 (letter to Ellen Terry, 8 September 1897). Mrs. Webb's fondness for the term 'sprite' is exemplified in a diary entry of 8 May 1897: '[Shaw] is a good-natured agreeable sprite of a man—an intellectual cricket on the hearth, always chirping brilliant paradox, sharp-witted observation and friendly comments. Whether I like him, admire him or despise him most I do not know.'— Janet Dunbar, *Mrs. G. B. S.: A Biographical Portrait of Charlotte Shaw* (London: Harrap, 1963), p. 143; in an entry of 21 May 1916, where she refers to G. B. S. as 'the intellectual sprite at play with the life and death of a poor human [Roger Casement]'—Margaret I. Cole, ed., *Beatrice Webb's Diaries 1912–1924* (London: Longmans, 1952), p. 63; and in an entry of 23 June 1926: '[G. B. S.] is just the same dear friend and somewhat sobered but still brilliant sprite that used to stay with us at The Argoed over thirty years ago.'—Margaret Cole, ed., *Beatrice Webb's Diaries 1924–1932* (London: Longmans, 1956), p. 104.

117 St. John Ervine, *Bernard Shaw, His Life, Work and Friends* (London: Constable, 1956), pp. 130–32, 144–47, 151–68, 170–73; Weintraub, pp. 138–43, 164–71, 261, 267; Kitty Muggeridge and Ruth Adam, *Beatrice Webb, A Life, 1858–1943* (London: Secker and Warburg, 1967, rpt. 1968), p. 141; H. G. Farmer, *Bernard Shaw's Sister and her Friends . . .* (Leiden: Brill, 1959), pp. 140–41 (letter of Lucy Shaw to Janey Crichton, 24 July [?1901]).

Widowers' Houses was published as No. 1 in the Independent Theatre Series, ed. J. T. Grein (London: Henry, 1893); it was republished in *Plays: Pleasant and Unpleasant*, 2 vols. (London: Grant Richards, 1898), along with all the other plays completed by the end of 1897, except *The Devil's Disciple*, which was first published in *Three Plays for Puritans* (London: Grant Richards, 1901). As he notes in his letters, Shaw frequently sent his plays for reading, or himself read them, before production, both to actor-managers and to friends. *The Philanderer*, for instance, was read by

Shaw to Charles Wyndham in June 1894 (*Letters 1874–1897*, p. 444); it was read by
Alexander in December 1894 (p. 473), in March 1895 both by Yorke Stephens in
Brighton and by Richard Mansfield in America, where Tree also saw it (pp. 487, 489,
503); from the Fabian holiday retreat at Saxmundham Shaw wrote to Ellen Terry
in August 1896 that 'in the evenings they make me read plays to them', one being
The Philanderer which 'quite disgusted me' (p. 644); Ellen Terry, reading it the
following December, declared it was 'perfectly wonderful' (p. 711); and Charles
Hawtrey in January 1897 sent for it to read (p. 716). *The Philanderer*, however, was not
staged until 1905. *Candida*, *The Man of Destiny*, and *You Never Can Tell* were
similarly bandied about.

118 St. John Ervine, *Bernard Shaw*, p. 138; Bernard Shaw, *Sixteen Self Sketches*, XIV,
pp. 80–81; Shorter, *Charlotte Brontë and her Circle*, p. 313 (stricture on Harriet
Martineau, 1851).

119 The details of Shaw's early literary career have been assembled mainly from the
biographies of St. John Ervine and Hesketh Pearson, Laurence's annotated edition
of the *Collected Letters 1874–1897*, and Allardyce Nicoll's *A History of Late Nineteenth Century Drama 1850–1900*. Part of Stevenson's letter to Archer, who had sent
him a copy of *Cashel Byron's Profession*, is printed by Colvin in *The Letters of Robert
Louis Stevenson* (London: Methuen, 1899, rpt. 1901), II, 92–93; Shaw, in his Preface to the 1901 edition of *Cashel Byron's Profession*, supplies the portion omitted,
from which it appears that Stevenson thought 'Henry James or some kindred author,
badly assimilated' accounted for one fifth of Shaw's literary method in 1882.

120 Laurence, *Letters 1874–1897*, pp. 463 (letter to Henry Arthur Jones, 2 December
1894), 625 (letter to Janet Achurch, 14 April 1896); Beatrice Webb, *Our Partnership*,
p. 312 (diary entry of 5 October 1905). Details of Shaw's education in music and art
are given in 'George Bernard Shaw', *The Chap-Book*, V (1896), 532; *Sixteen Self
Sketches*, XII; the Preface to *London Music in 1888–89*.

121 Laurence, *Letters 1874–1897*, pp. 464 (letter to R. Golding Bright, 2 December
1894), 424 ('the Bulgarian admiral who gave me the local color': letter to C. T. H.
Helmsley, 17 April 1894), 716 (copy of 'Fonblanque' received: letter to Charlotte
Payne-Townshend, 7 January 1897), 36 (letter to Dr. J. Kingston Barton, 29 November 1880); G. Bernard Shaw, 'A Dramatic Realist to his Critics', *New Review*, XI
(1894), 61–65, 67–68 (Lord Wolseley, General Porter, 'an officer who served in the
Franco-Prussian war', and General Marbot cited).

122 Edith Wharton, *A Backward Glance* (New York: Appleton, 1934), pp. 183–84; report
on a visit to Paris by Corno di Bassetto, *The Star*, 11 April 1890, in *London Music
1888–89*, pp. 345, 347; *Our Theatres in the Nineties*, I, 154–62, 76–77; II, 248–56;
III, 174–75.

123 Mary Anderson de Navarro, *A Few More Memories* (London: Hutchinson, 1936),
p. 47 (cf. for James's interest in the performance, Muriel Draper, *Music at Midnight*,
pp. 90–92); *Notebooks*, p. 97; *The Portrait of a Lady*, Ch. 28 (1883: Lord Warburton
'thought [Miss Archer] looked excited . . .'; 1908: 'It struck [Lord Warburton] that
Miss Archer, had, in operatic conditions, a radiance, even a slight exaltation . . .'),
Ch. 18 (1883: 'She was playing something of Beethoven's [1908: Schubert's]—Isabel
knew not what, but she recognised Beethoven [1908: but recognised Schubert] . . .');
G. Bernard Shaw, 'The Religion of the Pianoforte', *Fortnightly Review*, NS LV
(1894), 255–66.

124 G. Bernard Shaw, 'On Going to Church', *The Savoy*, I (1896), 13–28; *Letters 1874–
1897*, pp. 308–12 (tour of Italy: letter to William Morris, 23 September 1891), 454

(note to letter of 17 September 1894), 633 (letter to Elbert Hubbard, 15 June 1896, and note); Graham Greene, 'Henry James: the Religious Aspect', in *The Lost Childhood and other essays* (London: Eyre and Spottiswoode, 1951), pp. 34–35.

125 '*Arms and the Man*, at the Avenue', *The Sketch*, 25 April 1894, p. 672; Edel, *Diary of Alice James*, p. 64; Bernard Shaw, *Music in London 1890–94* (London: Constable, 1932, rpt. 1949–50), I, 168, 212; III, 241–42; *Our Theatres in the Nineties*, II, 85–91.

126 The details of James's association with Elizabeth Robins are derived from her book *Theatre and Friendship*, especially pp. 25–54, 175–90, 215–17.

127 Shaw, *The Irrational Knot*, p. xix (use of Lord translation and debt to Archer); Laurence, *Letters 1874–1897*, pp. 126 (note on Shaw's projected translation of *Peer Gynt*, 1888), 213 (note on Shaw's review of *A Doll's House*, 1889); Shaw, *London Music in 1888–89*, pp. 148–51 (report of the *Doll's House* dinner at the Novelty Theatre on Sunday 16 June 1889); Bernard Shaw, *The Quintessence of Ibsenism* in *Major Critical Essays: The Quintessence of Ibsenism, The Perfect Wagnerite, The Sanity of Art* (London: Constable, 1932, rpt. 1948), pp. 11–12 (Preface, June 1891, to the first edition), 13–90; E. J. West, ed., *Shaw on Theatre* (New York: Hill and Wang, 1958), pp. 1–18 (Appendix to the first edition of *The Quintessence of Ibsenism*); Edmund Gosse, 'Henrik Ibsen' (Parts I, 1873 and II, 1889) in *Northern Studies* (London: Walter Scott, [1890]), pp. 38–104; Henry James, 'On the Occasion of *Hedda Gabler*', *New Review*, IV (1891, June), 519–30; Henry James, 'The Science of Criticism, I', *New Review*, IV (1891, May), 398–402 (Parts II and III of this symposium were contributed by Andrew Lang and Edmund Gosse respectively); William Archer, '*The Quintessence of Ibsenism*: An Open Letter to George Bernard Shaw', *New Review*, V (1891, November), 463–69.

128 Laurence, *Letters 1874–1897*, pp. 287 (Elizabeth Robins as Mrs. Linden: letter to Charles Charrington, 30 March 1891), 291–92 (Martha Bernick and Hedda Gabler: letter to Elizabeth Robins, 20 April 1891), 314 (*Denise*: letter to Elizabeth Robins, 19 October 1891), 379–81 (advice after the 'interview': letter to Elizabeth Robins, 5 February 1893), 397 (the hansom cab: letter to Elizabeth Robins, 5 June 1893), 708 (letter to Elizabeth Robins, 1 December 1896); Elizabeth Robins, *Ibsen and the Actress* (London: Hogarth Press, 1928), p. 35; *Our Theatres in the Nineties*, III, 126–27.

129 Laurence, *Letters 1874–1897*, p. 473 ('[Alexander] asked me to let him read [*The Philanderer*]. . . . He said he wanted a play, because neither Jones nor Pinero were ready. He meant ready to step in on the failure of Henry James's play; but naturally he did not say so.'—letter to William Archer, 28 December 1894); Lubbock, I, 234 (letter to William James, 9 January 1895); Edel, *Henry James: The Treacherous Years*, pp. 79–80; *Our Theatres in the Nineties*, I, 6–7, 192–95; Henry James, '*Hours of Exercise in the Alps*', unsigned review, *Atlantic Monthly*, XXVIII (1871), 634–36; Henry James, '*Daniel Deronda*: A Conversation', *Atlantic Monthly*, XXXVI (1876), 685, 694.

130 Lubbock, I, 238 (letter to W. D. Howells, 22 January 1895); *Notebooks*, pp. 171, 173–74 (*The Wings of the Dove*), 225 (*The Ambassadors*), 130 (*The Golden Bowl*); Henry James, 'On the Death of Dumas the Younger', *New Review*, XIV (1896, March), 297, 301, and cf. p. 295 'The whole undertaking of such a writer as Dumas is, according to his light, to carry reflection as far as it will stretch—to study, and study thoroughly, the bad cases' with the passage as I have quoted it from the 1914 version (rpt. in *Henry James: The Scenic Art . . .*, ed. Allen Wade [London: Hart-Davis, 1949], p. 269).

131 Henry James, 'London Letters', *Harper's Weekly*, XLI (1897), 639–40, 834; 946; 135, 315, 563, 754, 834. The Jubilee is discussed in letters dated 1 June and 31 July; the book reviews referred to occur in letters dated 15 January, 3 March, 5 May, 1 July and 31 July.

132 *Harper's Weekly*, XLI (1897), 78 (letter dated 1 January: Watts), 183 (1 February: Leighton, Madox Brown), 563 (5 May: Madox Brown, Millais, Sargent, and others), 640 (1 June: Whistler, Sargent); *Our Theatres in the Nineties*, III, 70–75.

133 *Harper's Weekly*, XLI (1897), 78 (*Richard III*, Ibsen); *Our Theatres in the Nineties*, II, 285–92 ('Richard Himself Again').

134 *Harper's Weekly*, XLI (1897), 78 (*Little Eyolf*), 134 (letter dated 15 January: *John Gabriel Borkman*); George Bernard Shaw, 'Ibsen's New Play', *The Academy*, 16 January 1897, pp. 67–68; *Our Theatres in the Nineties*, II, 256–64 ('*Little Eyolf*'), 271–78 ('Ibsen Without Tears'); III, 122–29 ('John Gabriel Borkman').

135 *Harper's Weekly*, XLI (1897), 411 (letter dated 3 April); Lubbock, I, 234–35 (letter to William James, 9 January 1895); *Our Theatres in the Nineties*, III, 90–97.

136 Edel (*Henry James: The Treacherous Years*, p. 168) notes Fullerton's query, and quotes James's reply (1 March 1897); Edmund Gosse ('Henry James', in *Aspects and Impressions* [London: Cassell, 1922, rpt. 1928], pp. 60–61) records the incident connected with *Roderick Hudson*, concluding 'I inly resolved that not one word of question should ever escape my lips on this subject again.'

137 *The Academy*, 6 November 1897, p. 376 ('An Academy of Letters'); 13 November 1897, p. 402 (letter from G. Bernard Shaw); Henry James, 'George Du Maurier', *Harper's New Monthly Magazine*, XCV (1897), 594–609.

138 Edel, *Henry James: The Treacherous Years*, pp. 178–83, 186–88; Lubbock, I, 270 (letter to Mrs. William James, 1 December 1897); Henry Brewster, ed., 'Henry James: Fourteen Letters', *Botteghe Oscure*, XIX (Spring 1957) 193 (letter to Henry B. Brewster from Ford Castle, 6 October 1897); Christopher Hussey, 'Ford Castle, Northumberland', *Country Life*, 11, 18, and 25 January 1941, pp. 32–35, 56–60, 78–82; Augustus J. C. Hare, *The Story of Two Noble Lives . . .*, 3 vols. (London: George Allen, 1893). Ford Castle in 1852 did not appeal to Victorian taste: 'There is no sort of park, only some high trees, and a little bit of shrubbery beside a kitchen garden, but it might be made a very nice place. The house is amply large enough, the modern part very ugly, but, at a distance, you chiefly see the old towers, and very little expense would make it much better' (*Two Noble Lives*, I, 359). When, at the death of the Marquis of Waterford in 1859, Ford passed into the hands of his widow, she began the process of altering and restoring the building (1861–65), and extending the gardens and plantations, which continued until her death in 1891. To Hare, when he first visited it in 1861, Ford Castle seemed 'a sort of gothic castle of Otranto'; when he next saw it, in 1865, 'the gingerbread castle of Udolpho had marched back three centuries, and is now a grand massive building in the Audley End style, but with older towers' (*The Story of My Life*, II, 280; III, 10). In 1873 Lady Waterford wrote: 'I am making a new walk from the kitchen-garden to the new village, shutting in the upper pond (and any curious ducks I can get) for myself. . . . But as the pond is deep and dangerous, and a little boy fell through the ice there last week, I hope mine is not a very crying piece of tyranny' (*Two Noble Lives*, III, 317). Here is a tantalizing suggestion of an 'ornamental water' at Ford, but neither Hare nor Hussey mentions the pond, and one is forced to conclude that in any case a village pond would scarcely be of the dimensions required for the shallow lake at Bly. Apart from lawn and trees, the only other detail which recalls the surroundings of Bly is one mentioned by

Lady Waterford in 1886: the 'cawing of rooks (such a rookery here!)' (*Two Noble Lives*, III, 440). James, by the way, has given his tower an architectural feature which (if it is intentional) is an addition of his own: not one of the towers at Ford, ancient or modern, is machicolated, though all are crenellated. But the wording of the passages quoted from pp. 19 and 30 of *The Turn of the Screw* suggests that James regarded these terms as synonymous.

It is noteworthy that the Elizabethan Levens Hall, despite its 'grey lady', its towers, and James's preoccupation with *Jane Eyre* during his stay there, seems to have furnished not a single detail in the description of Bly.

139 Laurence, *Letters 1874–1897*, pp. 637 (note to letter of 4 August 1896), 653 (letter dated from Stratford St. Andrew, 16 September 1896, 'last day—leave tomorrow'); Henry James, 'Old Suffolk', *Harper's Weekly*, XLI (1897), 946 (dated from Dunwich, 31 August 1897).

140 Citations (by chapter and page number) are from Charles Dickens, *The Personal History of David Copperfield*, New Oxford Illustrated Dickens (London: Oxford Univ. Press, 1948 rpt. 1957). Edel, *The Ghostly Tales of Henry James*, pp. 431–32, mentions David Copperfield as one of several 'little boys, from life and literature, thronging the Jamesian consciousness'; he also refers to James's childhood enthusiasm for Dickens's novel, and his revival of interest in Dickens during his Suffolk holiday; but he does not mention any correspondences between *David Copperfield* and *The Turn of the Screw*, and apparently discounts the possibility of any influence.

141 *Harper's Weekly*, XLI (1897), 946; Hesketh Pearson, *Bernard Shaw*, p. 199.

142 *Harper's Weekly*, XLI (1897), 563 (letter dated 5 May 1897). The publication history of *L'Orme du mail*, together with the various identifications suggested for locality and characters, is given by Jean Levaillant, *Essai sur l'évolution intellectuelle d'Anatole France*, Les Aventures du Scepticisme (Paris: Armand Colin, 1965), pp. 441 ff. 'L'Evêché de Tourcoing' par Anatole France, *Yellow Book*, V (April 1895), 283–89, represents Ch. viii of *L'Orme du mail*: there are minor differences between the two texts, the most considerable being the omission from the latter of M. Guitrel's professions of compliance (p. 289). *A Little Tour in France* (Boston: Osgood, 1885 [1884]), first appeared serially under the title 'En Province' in the *Atlantic Monthly*, LII (1883, July–Nov.) and LIII (1884, February, April–May): Poitiers is the subject of Ch. xvii.

143 Anatole France, *L'Orme du mail* (Paris: Calmann-Lévy, n.d.), pp. 125–39 (Ch. ix), 159–76 (Ch. xi) deal with Mlle Deniseau; pp. 187–89, 208, 210 (Ch. xii), 276–90 (Ch. xv), 314–20 (Ch. xvi) deal with Mme veuve Houssieu. The second volume of *Histoire contemporaine*, *Le Mannequin d'osier*, published in the latter part of 1897, has no discernible relevance to James's story.

144 *Our Theatres in the Nineties*, III, 171–73 (*Lorenzaccio*); II, 248–51 (*Peer Gynt*); Lubbock, I, 8 (Perry recalls James's 1860 literary essays).

William and Charles Archer, *Peer Gynt*, *A Dramatic Poem*, *by Henrik Ibsen*, *Authorised Translation* (London: Walter Scott, [1892]), pp. 126 (IV. i), 83 (II. vi)—the lover; 129 (IV. i)—the self-taught man; 158 (IV. vi)—the prophet; 164 (IV. vii) —the musician; 1–7, 16–21 (I. i), 25–26 (I. ii), 46–47 (I. iii), 65–67 (II. iv) etc.—the fantast; 248 (V. vii)—the self-sufficient, never himself; 255–56 (V. viii)—the secret troll, living by the troll's motto 'To thyself be enough!'; 274 (V. x)—'I fear I was dead long before I died.'

Consecutive fifths intrude, e.g. in *London Music 1888–89*, p. 271; *Music in London*, I, 46, 68.

145 Lubbock, I, 286, 304, 308, 306.

146 Edel, *Henry James: The Treacherous Years*, p. 198.

147 Cf. James's comment in his essay of January 1897, 'She and He: Recent Documents' (*Yellow Book*, XII [1897], 15–38): 'The lovers are naked in the market-place and perform for the benefit of humanity. The matter with them, to the perception of the stupefied spectator, is that they entertained for each other every feeling in life but the feeling of respect. What the absence of that article may do for the passion of hate is apparently nothing to what it may do for the passion of love' (p. 25).

148 Lubbock, I, 277 (letter to Grace Norton, Christmas Day, 1897.) Had James also in mind an article in the *Revue des Deux Mondes* for 15 January 1897—'Les Jeunes criminels, l'École et la Presse', by Alfred Fouillée (CXXXIX, 417–49)? The author, discussing the growth of juvenile crime in France, its causes (chief among them, 'la littérature ordurière', whether of the yellow press or of yellowbacks) and possible correctives, mentions a case which lends some support to my view of the corruption practised at Bly. During the trial of a revolutionary at Lyons, 'un journal du parti' printed 'cette excitation adressée aux filles du peuple placées en service dans les maisons bourgeoises: "Vengez-vous en dépravant les enfans de vos maîtres."'

149 Edel, *Henry James: The Treacherous Years*, pp. 239–40, quotes with approval Edmund Wilson's description of this phase as 'a subsidence back into himself' (*The Triple Thinkers*, pp. 108–09).

150 The social rôle of the unmarried daughter—her right to develop her own talents, to train for an independent, 'useful' career, to choose her own friends and amusements; her duty within the family; the pros and cons of chaperonage—furnished matter for a running controversy in the periodicals of 1893–94. Mrs. Crackanthorpe's article 'The Revolt of the Daughters' (*Nineteenth Century*, XXXV [1894], 23–31) expressed a decidedly liberal view: 'The far-seeing mother will consent to sit a quiet and smiling spectator when her daughter ventures on small, or even comparatively big, social experiments' (p. 27). Lady Jeune (*Fortnightly Review*, NS LV [1894], 267–76) vehemently opposed Mrs. Crackanthorpe: it would be 'disastrous' to concede to girls 'the perfect freedom which marriage alone should give a woman' (p. 269). In Mrs. Frederic Harrison's sketch entitled 'Mothers and Daughters' (*Nineteenth Century*, XXXV [1894], 313–22) Madame des Deux Mondes and her English hostess discuss the problem, with a sympathetic tribute (which James would no doubt have approved) to the French ideal of 'une femme aimable'. In March 1894 the *Nineteenth Century* published a symposium on the subject ('The Revolt of the Daughters', *Nineteenth Century*, XXXV [1894], 424–50), in which Mrs. Crackanthorpe (reiterating her plea: 'It is high time that our daughters were trusted too' [p. 427]) and Mrs. Haweis (armed with precedents from America) for the enlightened mothers, and Kathleen Cuffe and Alys Pearsall Smith for the rebellious daughters together urged a new dispensation, of greater freedom and responsibility, for young unmarried women. Such discussions have clearly influenced James's choice of subject for *The Awkward Age*—first recorded in the *Notebooks* on 4 March 1895 (p. 192).

151 Edel, *Henry James: The Treacherous Years*, p. 237.

152 *Prefaces*, pp. 170, 175 (*The Turn of the Screw*); 73 (*The Princess Casamassima*). James has, it is clear, read *Wuthering Heights*, but this reference is the only detectable trace it has left on his own work.

153 The suggestion was made to me by my colleague Miss Margaret Edgcumbe, who is not, however, in any way responsible for my development of it or the conclusions here reached.

154 *Notes of a Son and Brother*, ed. Dupee, p. 481.

155 '*Home Sketches in France*, and Other Papers. By the late Mrs. Henry M. Field (New York: G. P. Putnam's Sons. 1875.)', *The Nation*, XX (1875), 400. The dates of Henry James's 1875 stay in New York and his departure for Europe are given by Edel, *Henry James: The Conquest of London*, pp. 181, 194, 199.

156 *Home Sketches in France* . . ., p. 20. This obituary was no doubt written by William Cullen Bryant. Others, as laudatory, appeared in the New York *Times* and *Tribune*; and the private letters of condolence, from a range of friends as diversified as the President of Cornell University, Mrs. Stowe, and the Countess of Minto (Henriette Deluzy's first pupil), express a genuine warmth of regard. The New York diarist, George Templeton Strong, recording Mrs. Field's death and her association with *l'affaire Praslin*, noted, 'I knew her at one time quite well, and she was universally liked, being uncommonly clever and cultivated' (A. Nevins and M. H. Thomas, edd., *The Diary of George Templeton Strong* [New York: Macmillan, 1952], IV, 553).

157 The *Illustrated London News*, for example, first reported the murder on 21 August; a detailed account, two and a half columns long, was given on 28 August; on 4 September a still more elaborate account, including quotations from the Duchess's letters, and illustrated by views of the Hôtel Sébastiani and plans of the murder chamber, occupied a total of four pages; brief supplementary notices appeared for a month thereafter, and the case was not finally dismissed till 27 November, with the announcement of Mlle Deluzy's release..

158 *Œuvres complètes de Gustave Flaubert: Correspondance, Nouvelle édition augmentée*, II (Paris: Conard, 1926), 36–37, 43, 47 (letters to Louise Colet, August–September 1847).

159 Armand Fouquier, *Causes célèbres de tous les peuples*, I (Paris: Lebrun, 1858), Cahier 3, 'De Praslin (1847)'; Pierre Larousse, *Grand dictionnaire universel du XIXe siècle*, XIII (Paris: 1875), 34–35.

160 Nathalia Wright ('Hawthorne and the Praslin Murder', *New England Quarterly*, XV [1942], 5–14) argues conclusively, from the text of *The Marble Faun* and from circumstantial evidence, that Hawthorne 'knew [Mlle Deluzy's] story, if indeed he did not actually meet her'. Miriam's choice, in her new life, of an artist's calling, and the detail (not mentioned by Professor Wright) that her shadower is a Capuchin friar, reminiscent of Mlle Deluzy's persecutor the Abbé Gallard, are of themselves sufficient to show that the echoes of the Praslin case are more than accidental.

161 Henry James, 'Nathaniel Hawthorne', *Library of the World's Best Literature*, ed. C. D. Warner and associate edd., XII (New York: Peale and Hill, 1897), 7053–61, rpt. *Henry James: The American Essays*, ed. Leon Edel (New York: Vintage Books, 1956), pp. 11–23.

162 Julian Hawthorne, *Nathaniel Hawthorne and his Wife*, a Biography (London: Chatto and Windus, 1885), II, 236. Cf. Edel, *Henry James: The Conquest of London*, p. 386.

163 The passages quoted are taken from the reports of Henriette Deluzy's various interrogations as reproduced by Fouquier ('De Praslin', pp. 6, col. 1; 7, col. 1; 11, col. 2) and in one instance by Albert Savine (*L'Assassinat de la Duchesse de Praslin d'après les Documents d'Archives et les Mémoires* [Paris: Michaud, 1908], pp. 182–83, cf. pp. 132, 144: the *juge d'instruction* queries the implication of Mlle Deluzy's references to the Château de Praslin); from Mlle Deluzy's *mémoire justificatif* (Savine, p. 61); and from a journal entry of the Duchess's dated 15 September 1842 (Fouquier,

'De Praslin', p. 21, col. 2). To a nineteenth-century enquirer all these sources were accessible in official publications of 1847.

164 As Professor Wright notes ('Hawthorne and the Praslin Murder', p. 13), a century's discussion of the crime has produced some changes in the estimate of its central figure, the victim. Nineteenth-century commentators noted 'le caractère un peu difficile de la duchesse, sa jalousie un peu ombrageuse' without assailing her moral character; but according to Savine she was a monster of unnatural vice, 'une monstrueuse détraquée' (p. 6). The most recent discussion of the case—Stanley Loomis, *A Crime of Passion* (New York: Lippincott, 1967)—gives the reader the benefit of these speculations without actually endorsing them. It must, however, be observed that Savine's allegations (pp. 20, 50–51, 71, 135–36), based as they are either on unreliable gossip or on ambiguous written statements, do not carry conviction.

165 Charlotte Brontë, *Jane Eyre*, ed. Jane Jack and Margaret Smith (Oxford: Clarendon Press, 1969), p. xiv; Hare, *The Story of My Life*, I, 245; unsigned article, '*Vanity Fair, Jane Eyre*, and Governesses', *Quarterly Review*, LXXXIV (1848, December), 154, 167, 174, 176: Shorter (p. 348) identifies the author as Miss Rigby, afterwards Lady Eastlake.

The colour of Mlle Deluzy's eyes is vouched for by the Duchess: in a letter to her husband she complains that on her return to Praslin (after a visit to her married daughter in Italy) she read 'dans votre air glacial, dédaigneux et mécontent, dans l'expression contrariée des regards de mes enfants, dans les petits yeux verts qui apparaissaient derrière votre épaule' the prospect of intolerable humiliations (Fouquier, 'De Praslin', p. 22, col. 1).

166 J. Barthélemy-Saint Hilaire, *M. Victor Cousin, sa vie et sa correspondance* (Paris: Alcan/Hachette, 1895), II, 410–14.

167 Victor Hugo, *Choses vues*, ed. Paul Meurice (Paris: Hetzel/Quantin, 1887), reissued, with supplementary material, in *Œuvres complètes de Victor Hugo*, as *Choses vues*, 2 vols. (Paris: Ollendorff, 1913).

168 Henry James, 'The Journal of the Brothers de Goncourt', *Fortnightly Review*, L (1888), 501–20, rpt. in *Essays in London and Elsewhere* (1893), pp. 195–232; Edmond et Jules de Goncourt, *Journal: mémoires de la vie littéraire, 1re série* (Paris: Charpentier, 1887–88, rpt., *édition définitive*, Paris: Flammarion/Fasquelle, 1935–36), III, 233–34.

169 Lubbock, I, 7–8 (notes by T. S. Perry); Barthélemy-Saint Hilaire, II, 413.

170 Henry James, '*Days near Rome*. By Augustus J. C. Hare . . .', *The Nation*, XX (1875), 229 (unsigned review); Henry James, '*Cities of Northern and Central Italy*. By Augustus J. C. Hare . . .', *The Nation*, XXII (1876), 325–26 (unsigned review); Hare, *The Story of My Life* (1900), IV, 481; V, 16 (James at Lord Houghton's); (1896), III, 19–21 (*l'affaire Praslin*). *Blackwood's* reviewer in December 1896 ('A Raid among Books', CLX, 833–38) despite 'some amusing anecdotes' found *The Story of My Life* a 'truculent performance', part snobbish and part 'vicious and venomous'. W. H. Mallock, however (*Memoirs of Life and Literature* [London: Chapman and Hall, 1920], 2nd ed., pp. 102–03), testifies to the eagerness with which fashionable society devoured its 'indiscretions'.

171 Edmond de Lignères, comte d'Alton-Shée, *Souvenirs de 1847 et de 1848, pour faire suite à* Mes Mémoires (Paris: Dreyfous, 1879), pp. 44–45, 50.

172 Larousse, *Grand dictionnaire universel du XIXe siècle*, XIII, 34, col. 3. Cf. *Choses vues*, I, 275: 'Dimanche 22 [août]. A l'heure qu'il est, on voit encore à la fenêtre de

Mlle de Luzzy, chez Mme Lemaire, rue du Harlay, dans la cour, le melon, le bouquet et le panier de fruits que le duc avait apportés de la campagne à Mlle de Luzzy, le soir même qui a précédé l'assassinat.'

173 Elmes, *Metropolitan Improvements* . . ., p. 15.

174 Fouquier, 'De Praslin', p. 7, col. 1.

175 'The Story in It' (1902), *Complete Tales of Henry James*, XI, 326.

176 *Jane Eyre*, xxxv, 508–09; xxxvii, 542–43. Mrs. Gaskell, in *The Life of Charlotte Brontë* . . ., 3rd ed., rev. (London: Smith, Elder and Co., 1857), II, 149, records: 'Some one conversing with her once objected, in my presence, to that part of "Jane Eyre" in which she hears Rochester's voice crying out to her in a great crisis of her life, he being many, many miles distant at the time. I do not know what incident was in Miss Brontë's recollection when she replied, in a low voice, drawing in her breath, "But it is a true thing; it really happened." '

177 In the following, necessarily incomplete list, authors are given in order of publication of their earliest work mentioned:

Charles Mackay, *Memoirs of Extraordinary Popular Delusions, and the Madness of Crowds*, 3 vols. (London: Routledge, 1841). A two-volume edition appeared in 1856, and was reprinted for the third time in 1892.

Mrs. Catherine Crowe, *The Night Side of Nature; or, Ghosts and Ghost Seers*, 2 vols. (London: Newby, 1848). Robert Dale Owen notes (*Footfalls* . . ., p. 4 n.) that this work 'reached its sixteenth thousand in 1854'. It went through at least nine editions, in England and America, before 1900; and was last reprinted in 1904 (from an edition of 1892) as one of a series of 'Half-Forgotten Books'.

Henry Christmas, ed., *The Phantom World: or, The Philosophy of Spirits, Apparitions, &c.*, by Augustine Calmet, 2 vols. (London: Bentley, 1850).

Robert Dale Owen, (1) *Footfalls on the Boundary of Another World, with Narrative Illustrations* (Philadelphia: Lippincott, 1859/London: Trübner, 1860). The sixth English edition ·of 1899 was 'reprinted from the tenth American edition, with emendations and additions by the author'.
(2) *The Debatable Land between This World and the Next, with Illustrative Narrations* (New York: Carleton/London: Trübner, 1871, rpt. 1872).

Frederick George Lee, (1) *Glimpses of the Supernatural. Being Facts, Records and Traditions relating to Dreams, Omens, Miraculous Occurrences, Apparitions, Wraiths, Warnings, Second-Sight, Witchcraft, Necromancy, etc.*, 2 vols. (London: Henry S. King, 1875).
(2) *More Glimpses of the World Unseen* (London: Chatto, 1878).
(3) *Glimpses in the Twilight: being Various Notes, Records and Examples of the Supernatural* (Edinburgh: Blackwood, 1885).
(4) *Sights and Shadows: being Examples of the Supernatural* (London: W. H. Allen, 1894, 2nd ed. 1895).

John H. Ingram, *The Haunted Homes and Family Traditions of Great Britain*, 2 series (London: W. H. Allen, 1884). An illustrated edition, at least the fourth, was published in 1890, and reprinted in 1929.

Thomas Firminger Thiselton-Dyer, *The Ghost World* (London: Ward and Downey, 1893).

Andrew Lang, *The Book of Dreams and Ghosts* (London: Longmans, 1897, reissued 1899).

Sabine Baring-Gould, *A Book of Ghosts* (London: Methuen, 1904).

178 Edward B. Tylor, *Primitive Culture* . . . (London: Murray, 1871, 3rd ed. 1891), I, 143–44. Podmore (*Modern Spiritualism*, I, 109) while regarding Swedenborg as the source, traced the doctrinal descent through the German Magnetists, Jung-Stilling and Kerner. It is perhaps significant that Keighley, 'the chief provincial centre of English Spiritualism' (ibid., II, 43 and note), also had its Swedenborgian New Church. But many Swedenborgians, including J. J. Garth Wilkinson and Henry James Sr., rejected the practice of Spiritualism as futile and dangerous.

179 Sophia Elizabeth De Morgan, *Memoir of Augustus De Morgan* (London: Longmans, 1882), pp. 206–08 (letter of De Morgan to the Rev. W. Heald, undated, but assigned by Mrs. De Morgan to 1849: detailed clairvoyant description by 'a little girl . . . mesmerised for epileptic fits' of the house 'about a mile' distant which De Morgan was visiting), 221–22 (letter of De Morgan to the Rev. W. Heald, July 1853: account of a seance with Mrs. Hayden); E. C. McAleer, ed., *Dearest Isa: Robert Browning's Letters to Isabella Blagden* (Austin: Univ. of Texas Press, 1951), p. 299 (letter of 19 June 1868: Arabel Barrett's dream of 19 July 1863 recorded by Browning 21 July 1863 and fulfilled by her death 11 June 1868); Charles Dickens, 'The Mortals in the House', Part I of *The Haunted House*, Extra Christmas Number 1859, *All the Year Round*, II (1859–60), and 'No. 1 Branch Line: The Signal-Man', Part IV of *Mugby Junction*, Extra Christmas Number 1866, *All the Year Round*, XVI (1866); 'Is it Possible?', *All the Year Round*, XVII (1866–67), 614–20 ('Note by the Conductor', p. 620, includes his premonitory dream of 'a lady in a bright red wrapper'); 'Mrs. M.', *All the Year Round*, XVIII (1867), 155–57 (introduced as 'a pendent to the paper . . . headed "Is it Possible?" . . . a simple narrative taken down in short-hand from the lips of the narrator. . . . As a statement at first hand of an appearance testified to by the narrator and corroborated by his wife, both living, it has seemed to me, while simply transcribing the notes, to possess an interest often wanting in more artistic stories of artificial manufacture.' Ingram (op. cit., pp. 367–75) quotes the story, with the observation that 'the transcriber is believed to have been Charles Dickens himself'). Under Dickens's editorship the treatment of spiritualistic activities is in general severely critical: e.g. 'The Ghost of the Cock Lane Ghost', *Household Words*, VI (1852–53), 217–23 (account of a seance with Mrs. M. B. Hayden); 'Rather a Strong Dose', *All the Year Round*, IX (1863), 84–87 (review of William Howitt's *The History of the Supernatural in all Ages and Nations* . . .) and 'The Martyr Medium', ibid., 133–36 (review of D. D. Home's *Incidents in My Life*, First Series) both by Dickens himself. There is usually an attempt to rationalize traditional ghost stories: e.g. George Hogarth, 'An Incident in the Life of Mad^lle Clairon', *Household Words*, I (1850), 15–19 (the ghostly cry explained as imposture by Mlle Clairon's maid) and the Conductor's diagnosis, in the 'Note' cited above, of Lady Beresford's case as a dream culminating in 'a stroke of local paralysis'.

180 A. C. Benson, *The Life of Edward White Benson, sometime Archbishop of Canterbury*, new ed., abridged (London: Macmillan, 1901), pp. xi, 37, 40. The young investigators, it seems, followed a procedure that was to become standard in such matters: they issued a 'circular' inviting the submission of 'ghostly' experiences—A. S. (Arthur Sidgwick) and E. M. S. (Eleanor M. Sidgwick), *Henry Sidgwick: A Memoir* (London: Macmillan, 1906), p. 43. This circular was printed in full by Robert Dale Owen as an appendix to his *Footfalls on the Boundary of Another World* (pp. 377–80 in English edition of 1899).

181 *Henry Sidgwick: A Memoir*, pp. 43–44, 52–55, 103–06, 160, 162, 165, 167–69, 171, 285 (Myers's resolve of 3 December 1869 quoted); Alan Gauld, *The Founders of Psychical Research* (London: Routledge and Kegan Paul, 1968), Chs. iv–vi.

182 Perry, I, 375 (letter to William James, 28 February [1877]); Edel, *Henry James: The Conquest of London*, p. 336; A. C. Benson, 'Henry James', *Cornhill Magazine*, NS XL (1916), 511.

183 Perry, I, 596 (letter to Mrs. Alice James, 16 December 1882: impression of Gurney), 609 (James's opinion of *The Power of Sound* quoted), 791 (letter to Josiah Royce, 8 May 1881: opinion of Sidgwick); II, 156 (James's interest in the non-normal), 163 (notation by James on letter from Myers, 12 January 1891); Oscar Browning, *Life of George Eliot* (London: Walter Scott, 1890), p. 116; Leslie Stephen, *George Eliot* (London: Macmillan, 1902), p. 191.

184 Edmund Gurney, Frederick W. H. Myers, and Frank Podmore, *Phantasms of the Living*, 2 vols. (London: Society for Psychical Research and Trübner, 1886); Perry, I, 599 (letter of Croom Robertson to William James, 13 August 1883); *Letters of William James*, I, 279–80 (letter to Henry James, 11 July 1888).

185 *Letters of William James*, I, 287 (letter to Mrs. Alice James, 29 July 1889); Edel, *Diary of Alice James*, pp. 25–26, 49–50, 58 (references to Mrs. Sidgwick), 52 (discussion of suicide apropos of Edmund Gurney), 65 (Henry James's report and comment); Perry, I, 610 (letter of Croom Robertson to William James, 8 September 1888).

186 Perry, I, 416–17 (letters of Henry and William James, 9 and 20 October, 7 November 1890); Lubbock, I, 248 (letter to A. C. Benson, 11 May [1895]); Edel, *Henry James: The Treacherous Years*, pp. 185, 342.

187 W. F. Barrett, Edmund Gurney, F. W. H. Myers, 'Thought-Reading', *Nineteenth Century*, XI (January–June 1882), 890–900; Edmund Gurney and F. W. H. Myers, 'Apparitions', *Nineteenth Century*, XV (January–June 1884), 791–815; Edmund Gurney and F. W. H. Myers, 'Visible Apparitions', *Nineteenth Century*, XVI (July–December 1884), 68–95, and note, 851–52, quoting letters of F. H. Balfour and Sir Edmund Hornby; A. Taylor Innes, 'Where are the Letters? A Cross-Examination of certain Phantasms', *Nineteenth Century*, XXII (July–December 1887), 174–94; Edmund Gurney, 'Letters on Phantasms. A Reply', *Nineteenth Century*, XXII (July–December 1887), 522–33; A. Taylor Innes, 'The Psychical Society's Ghosts: A Challenge Renewed', *Nineteenth Century*, XXX (July–December 1891), 764–76.

The 'census of hallucinations' was completed in time for the Second International Congress of Experimental Psychology of August 1892; the final report appeared in *PSPR*, X (1894), 25–422. The 'census question' answered by 17,000 informants was: 'Have you ever, when believing yourself to be completely awake, had a vivid impression of seeing or being touched by a living being or inanimate object, or of hearing a voice; which impression, so far as you could discover, was not due to any external physical cause?' (*PSPR*, X, 33). This, however, was merely an improved version of a question circulated (with three others on allied topics) to members and associates of the Society as early as 1882–83: 'Have you ever, when in good health and completely awake, had a distinct impression of seeing or being touched by a human being, or of hearing a voice or sound which suggested a human presence, when no one was there?' Among the explanations and instructions appended to these questions, it was stated: 'For our purpose it is, of course, essential to obtain a due proportion of *negative* answers; and with this object we have framed the two questions [on *Dreams* and *Hallucinations*] in such a manner as to require no answer but "*yes*" or "*no*"; and we are desirous of obtaining *a very large number* of such monosyllabic replies. . . . In any case where a vivid impression or dream *has coincided* with the real event, it is particularly requested that the person who has had this experience will send an independent account of it' (*PSPR*, I [1882–83], 304–05). Since the reader was invited to submit these two questions 'to 20, 50, 100, or more, trustworthy persons', the Society was, even so early, conducting a 'census' of a rough and ready kind, the replies to which furnished much of the material incorporated in *Phantasms of the Living*. And in addition Gurney had from 5,705 of these informants elicited replies which limited the experience to a period of twelve years—'since January 1, 1874'—thus providing him with utilizable 'statistics' both of frequency and of probability to combat the hypothesis of chance coincidence (*Phantasms of the Living*, II, 6 ff.).

188 *Letters of William James*, I, 267 (letter to Carl Stumpf, 6 February 1887); A. Taylor Innes, 'The Psychical Society's Ghosts: A Challenge Renewed', *Nineteenth Century*, XXX (July–December 1891), 766; Francis X. Roellinger, 'Psychical Research and "The Turn of the Screw"', *American Literature*, XX (1949), 401–12. From the extent of his citations, Professor Roellinger appears to consider that James was familiar with the whole range of the Society's reports, from 1882 to 1897, 'the most remarkable parallels with "The Turn of the Screw"' being presented by Volumes III, V, and VIII. The question is discussed in Appendix II below.

The policy of the Society with regard to its *Proceedings* was stated in Professor Balfour Stewart's Presidential Address at the General Meeting of 24 April 1885: 'since [the Society's] commencement it has issued seven parts of *Proceedings*, of which a total number exceeding 12,000 has been distributed to Members and others, placed in public libraries, sent for review, and sold through the ordinary channels' (*PSPR*, III [1885], 65).

189 Henry James, 'London', rpt. from *Century Magazine*, XXXVII (1888), in *Essays in London and Elsewhere* (1893), p. 17; Henry James, 'George Du Maurier', *Harper's New Monthly Magazine*, XCV (1897), p. 598: James had moved from his lodgings in Bolton Street, Piccadilly, to a leasehold flat at 34, De Vere Gardens, Kensington on 6 March 1886 (Leon Edel, *Henry James: The Middle Years, 1882–1895* [New York: Lippincott, 1962], p. 160; *PSPR*, VI (1889–90), 53–54, 60–62.

190 'A Record of Observations of Certain Phenomena of Trance', (5) Part III, by Professor William James, *PSPR*, VI (1889–90), 656; parenthetical note on Sitting No. 40, in (2) Part I of the 'Record', by Professor Oliver Lodge, ibid., 493; note on Sittings Nos. 70 and 71 in Appendix to (3) Part II of the 'Record', ibid., 645; Gauld, *The Founders of Psychical Research*, pp. 178–79 and notes: Dr. Gauld quotes at length from Mrs. Sidgwick's letter to Sir Oliver Lodge, 25 July 1915, and gives the passage I cite from a letter of F. W. H. Myers to William James, 28 February 1890; Edel, *Henry James: The Middle Years*, p. 297; Richard Hodgson, 'A Record of Observations of Certain Phenomena of Trance', *PSPR*, VIII (1892), 92–95 ('The "Kate Walsh" freak'); F. W. H. Myers, 'On Indications of Continued Terrene Knowledge on the part of Phantasms of the Dead', ibid., 206–08 (a series of five communications each signed 'Wilson Quint'). Myers introduces the series with this comment: 'Dr. Hodgson has interviewed Mr. Quint, and considers him a trustworthy witness. He has never asked money for the exercise of his powers.' Neither, of course, did Shaw, for his Fabian oratory. Professor Roellinger, in his article 'Psychical Research and "The Turn of the Screw"', notes *PSPR* Volume VIII as James's probable source for the name Quint; but cf. the discussion in Appendix II below.

191 'Sir Edmund Orme', *The Complete Tales of Henry James*, VIII (1963), 119–51.

192 Trevor H. Hall, *The Strange Case of Edmund Gurney* (London: Duckworth, 1964).
The evidence cited for the collusion of G. A. Smith and Douglas Blackburn in their
'thought-transference experiments' of 1882–83 for the SPR is convincing; but it is
less certain that G. A. Smith, after his appointment in 1883 as Gurney's assistant,
and in independence of Blackburn, continued in systematic trickery of the Society.
Dr. Gauld (op. cit., pp. 179–81), briefly reviewing Smith's case and Mr. Hall's
arguments, concludes that while Smith's integrity in some of the later experiments
might be questioned, his *reports* as a psychic investigator might be relied on; and that,
as to Gurney, while the shock of a friend's betrayal might drive him to suicide, the
discovery that his researches of the past six years had been compromised, would not.
This seems a just assessment of Gurney's moral quality. G. A. Smith, however, defies
even Mr. Hall's analysis: Mrs. Piper's Dr. Phinuit, who used the American idiom,
described him as 'a very smart young man' (*PSPR*, VI [1889–90], 623).

193 Gordon S. Haight, ed., *The George Eliot Letters* (London: Oxford Univ. Press, 1956),
V, 398 (letter of George Eliot to Mme Eugène Bodichon, 2 [August] 1877); Con-
stance Lady Battersea, *Reminiscences* (London: Macmillan, 1922, rpt. 1923), p. 206;
PSPR, V (1888–89), 575–76 (list of contributors to 'Edmund Gurney Library Fund');
Notebooks, pp. 9–10 (entry of January 1879: theme of 'Sir Edmund Orme').

194 'Owen Wingrave', *The Complete Tales of Henry James*, IX (1964), 13–51; *Notebooks*,
pp. 118–20 (entries of 26 March and 8 May 1892).

195 'Nona Vincent', *Complete Tales*, VIII, 153–87.

196 'The Private Life', *Complete Tales*, VIII, 189–227; 'The Third Person', *Complete
Tales*, XI (1964), 133–69; *Notebooks*, p. 110 (entry of 3 August 1891); F. W. H.
Myers, ' "Das Doppel-Ich" ', *PSPR*, VI (1889–90), 207–15.

197 'Sir Dominick Ferrand', *Complete Tales*, VIII, 343–405; *Notebooks*, pp. 117–18 (entry
of 26 March 1892), 109, 110, 119 (name lists); F. W. H. Myers, 'A Defence of
Phantasms of the Dead', *PSPR*, VI (1889–90), 353–55; ibid., 681 ('Bundy'). Several
other names used by James in his fiction during the nineties may have been primarily
suggested by their occurrence in *PSPR* VI: e.g., 'Wingrave' is taken from the *Notebooks* (p. 66), but the Christian name 'Owen' may well recall that 'honest' if sometimes 'grossly deceived' investigator of the supernatural, 'a man of the world and a
diplomatist;—in no way an absurd personage, but liked and esteemed in good society
in several countries', Robert Dale Owen, who is twice quoted by Myers (pp. 32–33,
54–55); the name of Mrs. Marden's daughter, 'Charlotte', occurs in three separate
cases (pp. 256, 293, 365); the name 'Douglas' occurs *passim* in the 'Notes of Séances
with D. D. Home' (pp. 98–127); in the second case cited by Myers among 'recognized apparitions' of the dead, 'Eliza Quinton' appears as the name of a housekeeper-
nurse in attendance on the decedent whom the phantasm had 'come to call' (p. 21).
'Quinton', a fairly common surname in England, occurs in the States less frequently
than 'Quint', which it would help to recall.

198 'The Way It Came', *Complete Tales*, IX, 371–401; *Notebooks*, pp. 231, 241–44
(entries of 21 December 1895 and 10 January 1896).

199 James's friendship with Stevenson was one of the most valued of his 'middle years',
but the personal contact was brief—from early in 1885 to August 1887, when the
Stevensons left England for good—and the ensuing correspondence, though maintained till Stevenson's death in December 1894, was an inadequate substitute. James's
friendship with Du Maurier dated from 1877 or 1878, and continued uninterruptedly
and on the easiest possible terms till the latter's death in October 1896.

200 R. L. Stevenson, 'The Genesis of *The Master of Ballantrae*', unfinished essay first published in the 'Edinburgh' ed. of the *Works*, XXI (1896, December), rpt. in the 'Swanston' ed., XVI (1912), 341–44; R. L. Stevenson, 'A Chapter on Dreams', *Scribner's Magazine*, III (1888), rpt. in *Across the Plains, with other Memories and Essays* (London: Chatto and Windus, 1892), and in the 'Swanston' ed., XVI, 177–89; Colvin, I, 210, 211 (letters to Colvin and to W. E. Henley, July 1881: 'The Merry Men'), II, 88 (letter to Colvin, 24 December 1887: 'the Master is all I know of the devil'), 99 (letter to James, March 1888: 'The elder brother is an INCUBUS'); Henry James, 'Robert Louis Stevenson', *Century Magazine*, XXXV (April 1888), rpt. in *Henry James and Robert Louis Stevenson: A Record of Friendship and Criticism*, ed. Janet Adam Smith (London: Hart-Davis, 1948), p. 158: in *Partial Portraits* (London: Macmillan, 1888), pp. 172–73, 'the author's talent for seeing the actual in the marvellous' is altered to 'the author's talent for seeing the familiar in the heroic'.

Stevenson is listed as an associate of the Society for Psychical Research in *PSPR*, IX (1893–94), 390, and X (1894), 450.

201 Lubbock, I, 218 (letter to George Du Maurier, [May 1894]); Dr. J. Milne Bramwell, 'James Braid; his Work and Writings', *PSPR*, XII (1896–97), 134–35 (Jenny Lind's participation in an experiment of Dr. Braid's, quoted from an observer's account in the *Medical Times* for September 1847); *Phantasms of the Living*, I, 314–15 (simultaneous dreams)—further examples are given in I, 316–20, and II, 380–83; F. W. H. Myers, 'The Subliminal Consciousness, Ch. v, Sensory Automatism and Induced Hallucinations', *PSPR*, VIII (1892), 508–09 (retrocognitive scene); W. F. Barrett, 'Note on the Existence of a "Magnetic Sense" ', *PSPR*, II (1883–84), 56–60, cf. Lord Kelvin, *Popular Lectures and Addresses*, 2nd ed., I (London: Macmillan, 1891), 265–69; Henry James, 'George Du Maurier', *Harper's Weekly*, XXXVIII (1894), 342, and 'George Du Maurier', *Harper's New Monthly Magazine*, XCV (1897), 603, 606.

The examples given above are quoted, not as sources for Du Maurier's fantasies, but as typifying the marvels, of varying credibility, under current popular discussion during the nineties.

202 Colvin, II, 20 (letter to J. A. Symonds [Spring 1886]); Henry James, 'George Du Maurier', *Harper's New Monthly Magazine*, XCV (1897), 598; Henry James, 'The Letters of Robert Louis Stevenson', *North American Review*, CLXX (1900), rpt. in *Notes on Novelists* (London: Dent, 1914) and in *Henry James and Robert Louis Stevenson . . .*, ed. Janet Adam Smith, p. 251.

203 Lubbock, I, 286–87 (letter to Arthur Benson, 11 March 1898: 'But à propos, precisely, of the ghostly and ghastly, I have a little confession to make to you that has been on my conscience these three months and that I hope will excite in your generous breast nothing but tender memories and friendly sympathies. . . . [P]lease think of the *doing* of the thing on my part as having sprung from that kind old evening at Addington—quite gruesomely as my unbridled imagination caused me to see the inevitable development of the subject'); E. C. Gaskell, *The Life of Charlotte Brontë*, 3rd ed., rev., II, 161–62.

Lambeth Palace kept in touch with the Society for Psychical Research from its foundation: Mrs. Benson (Henry Sidgwick's sister) is listed as an associate till December 1890 and thereafter as a member.

204 Benson, pp. 4–9; 26. A passage in the Archbishop's diary for 15 September 1887 describes a railway journey through Yorkshire, and includes this reminiscence: 'Dear Skipton with its sweet and holy memories of five years old, and fifteen, and eighteen! Could now just see the castle where I spent such magic hours with my old aunt, over the abominable mills and railway sheds. . . .' (Benson, p. 315).

205 F. W. H. Myers, 'On Recognised Apparitions occurring More than a Year after Death', *PSPR*, VI, 26 (duration); *Phantasms of the Living*, II, 531 (duration); 'Report on the Census of Hallucinations', *PSPR*, X, 120, 83, 378, 380 (percipients' statements regarding health and anxiety); 168–70 (assessment of effects of anxiety); 33 (SPR stipulation regarding persons to be included in Census).

The supplementary questions addressed to any person answering 'yes' to the Census question (cf. note 187 above) were:

'1. Please state what you saw or heard or felt, and give the place, date and hour of the experience as nearly as you can.

'2. How were you occupied at the time, and were you out of health or in grief or anxiety? What was your age?

'3. Was the impression that of some one whom you were in the habit of seeing, and do you know what he or she was doing at the time?

'4. Were there other persons present with you at the time, and if so did they in any way share the experience?

'5. Please state whether you have had such an experience more than once, and if so give particulars of the different occasions.

'6. Any notes taken at the time, or other information about the experiences will be gratefully received' (*PSPR*, X, 404).

206 *Phantasms of the Living*, I, 483–84; *PSPR*, X, 85–87 ('Sense of Presence'); William James, *The Principles of Psychology* (New York: Holt, 1890), II, 322–24 (e.g. 'The phenomenon would seem to be due to a pure *conception* becoming saturated with the sort of stinging urgency which ordinarily only sensations bring'); 'A Record of Telepathic and other Experiences. By the Author of "A Record of Recent Experiments in Crystal Vision"', *PSPR*, VI, 358–97.

207 Thomas Barkworth, 'Duplex Personality. An Essay on the Analogy between Hypnotic Phenomena and Certain Experiences of the Normal Consciousness', *PSPR*, VI, 84–97.

208 F. W. H. Myers, 'The Subliminal Consciousness, Ch. v, Sensory Automatism and Induced Hallucinations', *PSPR*, VIII, 484. Details concerning Miss X.'s family were given by Mrs. Piper in Seance No. 25 during her English visit of 1889–90 (*PSPR*, VI, 630).

209 *PSPR*, VI, 370–71 ('at an evening entertainment' H. faints, and both she and Miss X., whose hand she takes, become aware of the same phantasm: 'a figure—standing a few feet distant, directly facing us and looking down at H.—which, not being in evening dress, could not be any of our fellow-guests'); 383 ('during the second lesson' Miss X. becomes aware of D.'s entering the church, 'though absolutely out of sight').

210 *PSPR*, X, 34 (age of persons questioned), 149 (age of percipients), 178–81 (noises creating expectancy), 171–73 (repose and abstraction favourable to hallucinations; effect of crystal-gazing; 62 per cent. of percipients alone), 86 (percipient on one occasion was reading Cicero, *De Senectute*, on another Thomson's *Laws of Thought*); *Phantasms of the Living*, I, 542 (percipient was reading 'a chapter on Chalk Streams in "Kingsley's Miscellanies"'), 533 (percipient was 'reading a book called "Mr. Verdant Green" . . . and . . . laughing heartily over some of its absurdities').

211 At the opening of the Grosvenor Gallery in May 1877, Richard Doyle exhibited a number of his spirit-populated landscapes, two of which depicted a White Lady haunting a bridge over a stream—a variant of the *dame blanche* who on any *lande* of Normandy might decoy the benighted traveller into a pond (J. Fleury, *Littérature orale de la Basse-Normandie* . . . [Paris: Maisonneuve et Cie, 1883], pp. 23, 26–27). These pictures were shown again in the posthumous (1885) exhibition of Doyle's

work at the Grosvenor Gallery; and were mentioned in a sympathetic article, 'The Pictures of Richard Doyle', in *Blackwood's Edinburgh Magazine*: 'The only sprite (according to Doyle) that has ever evinced a steady purpose, is one clad in white, who makes it her business to haunt a particular bridge. . . . This sprite has evidently suffered some great wrong, most likely from a male sprite. . . .' (CXXXVII, [1885, April], 485). Doyle's White Lady receives more serious mention in Moncure D. Conway's *Demonology and Devil-Lore*, 2nd ed. (London: Chatto and Windus, 1880), I, 203: 'She is of a sisterhood which passes by hardly perceptible gradations into others, elsewhere described—the creations of Illusion and Night. She is not altogether one of these, however, but a type of more direct danger—the peril of fords, torrents, thickets, marshes, and treacherous pools, which may seem shallow, but are deep.'

212 *The Story of My Life*, IV (1900), 202–03 (part of a diary entry of 24 June 1874). Hare's informant was a Captain Fisher, an amateur of the supernatural, it appears: it was his zeal, or inventiveness, which supplied the narrative (quoted by Hare, ibid., pp. 203–08) of Croglin Grange, Cumberland and its vampire—a 'prodigy' which even Montague Summers found hard to swallow. James cannot, of course, by September 1897 have read Hare's account of Mrs. Hungerford's banshee, but he may have heard the story related. He twice made holiday visits of some weeks' duration to Ireland: in July 1891 and in March 1895 (Edel, *Henry James: The Middle Years*, pp. 294–95 and *Henry James: The Treacherous Years*, pp. 108–13).

213 *PSPR*, X (1894), 332–33 (in 'Report on the Census of Hallucinations, Ch. xvi: Premonitions and Local Apparitions').

214 Augustus Hare (*The Story of My Life*, IV, 286–87), under the date 12 December 1874, records being told 'from personal knowledge' by the Hungarian Countess Bathyany, then resident in England, of the appearance of a ghost to Lord Grey and his son-in-law, Sir Charles Wood, as they 'were walking on the ramparts of Carlisle': 'a man passed them, returned, passed them again, and then disappeared in front of them over the parapet, where there was really no means of exit. There was a red scarf round his throat.' Both men were struck by his likeness to Sir Samuel Romilly, who 'at that moment' [in the afternoon, therefore, of 2 November 1818] 'had cut his throat in a distant part of England' [actually at his London house in Russell Square]. The story bears all the marks of a fabrication after the fact—not that this would restrict its currency. If it had ever been related to James, it might have been recalled to his memory by the extremely plausible ghost story of the South-West Pacific quoted by Myers in *PSPR*, VI, 55–57, from the first-hand account of Romilly's great-grandson. But even if James had, in sympathy with Byron and Shelley, held a biased opinion of Romilly, the latter could never have inspired the portrait of Quint.

215 In his *Book of Dreams and Ghosts* Lang quotes thirteen cases from the SPR *Proceedings* and another seven from *Phantasms of the Living*; but only one of these, the well-known 'Morton' case, includes a standard feature (the woman in black) utilized by James.

216 *Impressions of luminosity* are recorded in *PSPR*, VI, 26, 59, 60, 61, 244, 253, 289, 293; *PL* (i.e. *Phantasms of the Living*), II, 176, 181, 183, 215, 611, 622. A general discussion appears in *PL*, I, 550–51. *Impressions of cold* are recorded in *PL*, I, 210, 319, 527; II, 37, 122, 150, 350, 500, 618; and cf. II, xxii, additional note to p. 37, where J. Russell Lowell is cited to the effect that his 'frequent hallucinations of vision' were 'ushered in (he believes invariably) by a feeling of *marked chill*. . . .'

The examples of standard psychical effects cited here, and in the following notes, are (with one exception—see note 224 below) taken from the three sources James must, on the evidence, be conceded to have used (*PSPR*, VI; *PSPR*, VIII; and *Phantasms of the Living*), and from *PSPR*, X—James's use of which is probable but less conclusively demonstrable. Similar effects are recorded in almost every volume of the SPR *Proceedings*, as well as in independent publications.

217 *Phantasm looks in at a closed window*: *PSPR*, VIII, 317; X, 189–90; *PL*, I, 523, 525; II, 90, 143, 244–45, 496. Occasionally *phantasm appears framed, as it were, by a half-open window*: *PL*, II, 527, 532.

218 *Percipient on, or at head of staircase 1. sees phantasm ascending*: *PL*, II, 85, 520, 582; *2. sees phantasm on upper landing*: *PSPR*, VI, 270; VIII, 313, 315; *PL*, II, 60, 178; *3. sees phantasm descending*: *PSPR*, VIII, 313, 315, 324, 325; *PL*, I, 218; II, 538, 603; *4. sees phantasm on lower floor*: *PSPR*, VI, 22–23; VIII, 314, 321, 326; *PL*, I, 569.

219 *Phantasm has its back turned to the percipient*: *PL*, I, 207–08, 427, 433, 513, 517; II, 201, 541.

220 *Phantasm is seen from the waist up*: *PSPR*, VIII, 227, 236; X, 190; *PL*, II, 213, 530, 597, 608.

221 *Phantasm peers round edge of door, etc.*: *PSPR*, VI, 58, 260. *Hand of phantasm is specially noted*: *PSPR*, VI, 265; VIII, 224; *PL*, I, 416; II, 202.

222 *Percipient notes some particularity in the clothing of an unknown phantasm, which permits later identification*: *PSPR*, VI, 22–23, 53–54, 375; *PL*, I, 214–16; II, 256. *Where the phantasm is known, some unfamiliar detail of the clothing may later prove the genuine nature of the appearance*: *PSPR*, X, 218–19, 237; *PL*, II, 89, 91, 93, 94–95, 626.

223 *Complete Tales*, IX, 382, 392.

224 The most striking instance of a ghost seen successively in different clothing is recorded in *PSPR*, V, 445–47: on one occasion the ghost 'wore a black cap with a flower or red bow at the side, a black dress, black mittens, and a white neckerchief, edged with lace, folded cornerways and fastened with a brooch', on another 'was attired in a lavender dress', the dead woman's servant, who had identified the phantasm from the first description, saying of the second, 'she never wore the same twice running'.

225 'Of the class of *repeated* hallucinations representing the same person, we have about five presentable records' (*PL*, II, 78). The five examples are recorded pp. 78–90, the agent in one of these observing, 'In the course of my life I have been accused four times of appearing to people' (p. 83). Repeated appearances of phantasms of the dead are recorded in *PSPR*, VI, 55–57, 60–63, 251–55, 256–69, 270–76, 276–82, 300, 371; VIII, 311–32 ('Record of a Haunted House', by Miss R. C. Morton); X, 387–91.

226 *Phantasm of woman is clad in black*: *PSPR*, VI, 249, 254; VIII, 236, 313–29 (the 'Morton' case); X, 192, 212, 354; *PL*, I, 213, 220; II, 85, 178, 204, 417. In most of these cases, the black dress represents the actual, identifiable clothing of the agent; but in II, 417 the 'widow's dress complete' was symbolic and anticipatory; in *PSPR*, VI, 254 the phantasm, 'a tall woman's figure dressed in black', if not a mere subjective response to expectancy, was a conventional rendering of the experience, for the first percipient of the same phantasm (VI, 251) described it as 'the figure of a woman apparently about fifty, dark hair and eyes, a red dress and a mob cap'.

227 *General impression of unrecognized phantasm recalls to the percipient some independent impression normally received*: *PSPR*, X, 284–86; *PL*, II, 208–09. The only occurrence

of the 'borrowed clothes' motif I have noted is *PL*, I, 542–44 (the fourth case of the group cited in Section vii below).

228 *Hat or cap worn by phantasm is either the chief means of identification, or is conspicuous among the identifying marks*: *PSPR*, VI, 22–23; X, 133; *PL*, I, 210; II, 89, 92–93, 247–48, 502. *Phantasm is bare-headed, and this detail aids verification*: *PSPR*, X, 271–72; *PL*, II, 94. A traditional ghost story may be improved by crowning the phantasm with a hat of noticeable pattern: e.g. one of the percipients in the celebrated Wynyard ghost story is made to exclaim, 'The fellow has got a devilish good hat, I wish I had it' (*PL*, II, 260); and the apocryphal 'Cator' ghost is validated by its wearing 'one of our modern [chimney-]pot hats' several years before these came into use (*PL*, I, 151–52). An unidentified phantasm comes up to a house 'dressed in a dark blue over-coat—somewhat shabby—and with a flat-topped felt hat', but seen immediately afterwards seated in the drawing-room, it 'had, of course, no hat on' (*PL*, II, 199–200). With this well-conducted phantasm may be compared the top-hatted figure that intrudes upon a musical soirée (*PL*, II, 201–02). 'The top part of the head' and the broad-brimmed 'tall hat' alone may be sufficient identifying marks when, in a familiar locality, some obstruction prevents the complete view of a recognized phantasm (*PL*, II, 71).

229 Professor Roellinger makes this point in his article 'Psychical Research and "The Turn of the Screw" ', citing the same passages from the *Preface* (pp. 169, 174); but he gives a different explanation of James's attitude: 'The Preface was written many years after the story was first published, and James might well have been replying to a criticism that he had failed to adhere to scientific accounts of the nature of apparitions and hallucinations. With his characteristic air of deprecation he stresses the point that he had no intention of making his apparitions "correct," and dwells upon the differences rather than the similarities between his ghosts and those of the reports. . . . For James and his contemporary readers, steeped in the lore of psychical research, the significant point about his ghosts was that they were departures from the usually inartistic and meaningless apparitions of scientific investigation.' But James's retraction goes much farther than this, as I attempt to show.

230 *Phantasms of the Living*, I, 546.

231 The plan of the New York Edition (discussed by Leon Edel in 'The Architecture of Henry James's "New York Edition" ', *New England Quarterly*, XXIV [1951], 169–78) had to be modified owing to the inordinate length of six of the novels. As a result James had in certain cases to regroup his short stories, and to 'dismember' prefaces already written (Edel, *Henry James: The Master, 1901–1916* [New York: Lippincott, 1972], p. 339). Volume XVII, it seems, but not Volume XII was affected by this rearrangement.

232 Henry James, 'The Art of Fiction', *Longman's Magazine*, IV (1884, September), rpt. in *Partial Portraits*, pp. 388, 403.

233 R. L. Stevenson, 'A Humble Remonstrance', *Longman's Magazine*, V (1884, December), rpt. in *Memories and Portraits* (London: Chatto and Windus, 1887, rpt. in 'Swanston' ed., IX, 1911), 152–55, 155–56.

234 Trevor H. Hall, *The Strange Case of Edmund Gurney*, pp. 109–11 (criticism by Dr. H. B. Donkin), 111–15 (supporting criticism by Sir James Crichton-Browne), 137–39 (confession by Douglas Blackburn).

235 Case 1: *PSPR*, VI, 255–70;
   Case 2: *PSPR*, VIII, 229–31;

Case 3: *PL*, I, 540–42;

Case 4: *PL*, I, 542–44—Mrs. Bolland's unsigned article 'What Was It?' (*All the Year Round*, NS XXI, 1878 [31 August], 209–12) makes it clear, as Gurney's summary does not, that Ramsay's expressed gratitude and devotion, in response to her kindness, constituted a strong emotional link between him and the percipient. Gurney also omits Mrs. Bolland's acknowledgment of Victorian class distinctions: 'All very well, you will say, but don't tell me you can mistake your man-servant for an equal, and stand up to receive him as a visitor!';

Case 5: *PL*, I, lxxxi–iv;

Case 6: *PL*, II, 570—The light footsteps of the 'Morton' ghost, heard on the upper landing outside bedroom doors, are often referred to (*PSPR*, VIII, 315, 316).

236 Frank Podmore, *Apparitions and Thought-Transference: An Examination of the Evidence for Telepathy* (London: Walter Scott, 1894), pp. 228–30; *Studies in Psychical Research* (London: Kegan Paul, 1897), pp. 249–51.

237 Podmore devotes Chapter vi to a 'general criticism of the evidence for spontaneous thought-transference' and among the 'errors' which have to be allowed for enumerates 'errors of narration': 'Of much greater importance than errors of observation or inference are those due to defects either in narration or memory. Deliberate deception amongst educated persons is no doubt comparatively rare, though it would perhaps be unwise to hold out any pecuniary inducement for the production of evidence. But there are those, like Colonel Capadose in Mr. Henry James' story *The Liar*, who tell ghost stories for art's sake, and on a slender basis of fact build up a large superstructure of fiction' (pp. 149–50). See also note 257 below.

238 Camille Flammarion, *Uranie*, Illustrations de Bieler, Gambard et Myrbach (Paris: C. Marpon et E. Flammarion, 1889). The second and third editions of 1891 and 1893 added Bayard, Falero, and Riou to the list of illustrators. Two separate English translations, using the original illustrations, appeared in 1890 and 1891. The Godfrey case was one of four cited by Flammarion from *Phantasms of the Living*.

239 Professor Roellinger notes: 'A remarkable feature of the story, stressed in the prologue, is that the percipients are children; although rare in fiction, it is common in the reports, ten such cases appearing in the first three volumes.'

240 *PSPR*, VIII, 226; 231–32. The following cases from *Phantasms of the Living* also offer correspondences with Griffin's story. In Case No. 345 (II, 235–36) a boy of seven came running from his room into that of his aunt with the announcement that he had just seen his father, and, refusing to return to his bed, was put by the aunt into her own, where he fell asleep. Some hours later the aunt herself was roused from sleep to see the form of her brother, then in Hong Kong, and was terrified by the apparition. In Case No. 657 (II, 610–11) a girl of eleven, in bed with her mother, shared the latter's vision of her dying grandfather, and was terrified; the mother, however, recognizing the figure, was not.

241 William Crookes, 'Notes of Séances with D. D. Home', *PSPR*, VI, 120–21. Flowers are perhaps the most common apports at spiritualistic seances. For example, at a Boston seance of 25 June 1867 attended by Robert Dale Owen, the 'apparition' 'dropped into [his] hand what proved to be a white rose'; and at Kate Fox's seances not only does the manifestation 'Estelle' wear decorations of roses and violets, but flowers ('a red rose with green leaves and forget-me-nots', 'a pink rose-bud with green leaves') may also be deposited, later to 'melt away' (*The Debatable Land between This World and the Next*, pp. 478, 489, 493–94). It may be worth noting that, as revealed by 'Dr. Phinuit' to the medium Mrs. Piper, 'delicate pink roses' were

...Marquis of Bute,
...ctor of the
...rsity of St. Andrews

Leaders of the Ballechin investigation

Miss X., otherwise
Miss Ada M. Goodrich-Freer,
in 1894

Ballechin House photographed by Miss X.

UPPER: *The south front and gardens with members of Miss X.'s house party in the foreground.* LOWER: *From the south-east, showing the new wing*

associated with the sensitive, Miss X. (' "You have them about you, spiritually as well as physically" '), and Myers's report adds, 'Miss X. has on a certain day in every month a present of delicate pink roses. She frequently has hallucinatory visions of flowers' (*PSPR*, VI, 629).

242 *Faust, eine Tragödie, 2. Teil*, 11699 ff. James is unlikely either to have read the fifteenth-century *Castle of Perseverance*, where Belial is routed by the Virtues armed with roses, or to have been familiar with the Christian symbolism of the rose on which the motif is based.

243 *Phantasms of the Living*, II, 61–62. Cf. II, 256; and II, 613 (Case 660).

244 'On Apparitions occurring soon after Death', by the late Edmund Gurney, completed by F. W. H. Myers, *PSPR*, V (1888–89), 403–485. The paper read by Gurney to the Society on 28 January 1888 (including the passage quoted, p. 404) extends to p. 426.

245 F. W. H. Myers, 'On Recognised Apparitions occurring More than a Year after Death', *PSPR*, VI (1889–90), 13–65. References are to pp. 13, 15, 34, 46, 47, 63.

246 F. Podmore, 'Phantasms of the Dead from Another Point of View', *PSPR*, VI, 229–313 (under the date 29 November 1889). References are to pp. 229–230, 231, 232 (passage quoted).

247 Ibid., pp. 283–86, 290–93, 297–301 (Podmore's discussion, *inter alia*, of Mme de Gilibert's experience—Case III cited by Myers [*PSPR*, VI, 22–23]; and of the apparition at the Château de Prangins—Myers's Case XI [ibid., pp. 53–54]), 307–08. It is noteworthy that the psychical prepotency of the *dying* is accepted even by Podmore. Otherwise (one might suppose) in Myers's Case III a more likely 'agent' than the dying Earl of Egremont would have been the 'superior servant' Garland who acted as his nurse. 'All the grandchildren were very fond of Garland, who spoilt us all.' It was Garland of whom the percipient had been in search when the phantasm appeared, and who, when told of it, 'seemed vexed at first, and ended by scolding me'. Garland's attitude clearly implied that she recognized the phantasm: had she, during her absence at dinner in the steward's room, been discussing (or merely thinking about) the late Lady Carnarvon?

248 F. W. H. Myers, 'A Defence of Phantasms of the Dead', *PSPR*, VI, 314–57 (under the date 31 January 1890). References are to pp. 318, 319, 320–21.

249 Ibid., pp. 321–28.

250 Ibid., pp. 329–57. Specific references are to pp. 329, 330, 331, 332–33, 333–37. Myers's fourth case, possibly used by James, appears on pp. 353–55.

251 Ibid., pp. 338–40; Gauld, *The Founders of Psychical Research*, p. 327 (passage quoted from letter of F. W. H. Myers to William James, 3 January 1894).

252 Gauld, op. cit., p. 316 (passage quoted from letter of Frank Podmore to Henry Sidgwick, 27 August 1900).
Podmore collaborated in the preparation of material for *Phantasms of the Living*. His independent publications, in addition to the two books cited in note 236 above, were: *Modern Spiritualism: A History and a Criticism*, 2 vols. (London: Methuen, 1902); *Robert Owen: A Biography* . . ., 2 vols. (London: Hutchinson, 1906); *The Naturalisation of the Supernatural* (New York and London: Putnam, 1908); *Mesmerism and Christian Science: A Short History of Mental Healing* (London: Methuen, 1909); *The Newer Spiritualism* (London, Leipsic: Unwin, 1910); *Telepathic Hallucinations: The New View of Ghosts*, XXth Century Science Series (Halifax: Milner, n.d.).

The Godfrey case of 1886 must be one of the best publicized of telepathic experiments: following its first appearance in *Phantasms of the Living* it has been quoted by Flammarion (1889—), Podmore (1894, 1897, 1908), Myers (1903), and most recently Professor C. D. Broad, in *Lectures on Psychical Research* . . . (London: Routledge, 1962), pp. 149–51.

253 *Henry Sidgwick: A Memoir*, pp. 468, 587 (letter to F. W. H. Myers, 24 May 1900: cf. his letter of 29 May to H. G. Dakyns—'It is through human love that I try to touch the Divine and "faintly trust the larger hope." '); Edmund Gurney, 'The Controversy of Life', in *Tertium Quid: Chapters on Various Disputed Questions* (London: Kegan Paul, Trench and Co., 1887), I, 147–48 (cf. the conclusion, p. 99, of the essay ' "Natural Religion" ': 'It must suffice to suggest that, as addressed to the majority of mankind, the keynote of the one gospel [Natural Religion] is Resignation, and of the other [Supernaturalism], Hope.'); F. W. H. Myers, 'The Work of Edmund Gurney in Experimental Psychology', *PSPR*, V (1888–89), 364; William James, *The Varieties of Religious Experience: A Study in Human Nature* . . . (1902; rpt. London: Longmans, 1952), pp. 507, 509, 516; William James, *Memories and Studies*, p. 200; *Letters of William James*, II, 214 (answers to questionnaire on the subject of religious belief); Henry James, 'Is there a Life after Death?', in *The James Family* . . ., p. 607.

254 Perry, I, 428 (letter to William James, 18 July 1909); Henry James, 'Is there a Life after Death?', *The James Family* . . ., pp. 609, 614.

255 *Notebooks*, pp. 143–44 (entry of 9 January 1894), 184 (entry of 5 February 1895); 'The Altar of the Dead', *Complete Tales*, IX, pp. 237, 267. In Volume XVII of the New York Edition 'The Altar of the Dead' is followed by 'The Beast in the Jungle', and James in his *Preface* (pp. 245–46) says that this order results from his desire 'to place, so far as possible, like with like'. It may be that the likeness James has in mind extends no farther than the autobiographical link Professor Edel has established between these two tales, and in that case (the fictional situations in the two being so different) the import of the statement would have been, intentionally, private and inaccessible to the contemporary reader. Such a *cachotterie* would not be uncharacteristic of James, but a more straightforward interpretation offers itself. 'The Beast in the Jungle' is *like* 'The Altar of the Dead' in that it defines the human limits of human fulfilment: there occurs neither supernatural enhancement nor supernatural extension of 'living'. On this view, James would seem to have introduced his ghostly tales with a double notification of scepticism.

256 Perry, II, 165–66 (letter of William James to F. W. H. Myers, 19 January 1897), 166–67 (Myers's reply to James, 3 February 1897).

257 It must be allowed that an equally systematic and authoritative, though admittedly *ex parte* discussion, covering the whole range of psychic phenomena and supported by over one hundred examples, was supplied by Podmore's *Apparitions and Thought-Transference*, published in September 1894. Since its examples are all drawn from SPR records, this work could, equally with the SPR volumes I specify, have provided James with a number of the standard details, as well as at least one striking illustration (the Godfrey experiment), utilized in *The Turn of the Screw*. But it would account for relatively few of the parallels there noted, and for none of those in the earlier tales. At the most, therefore, it can have furnished James (one would think, unnecessarily) with a supplement to *PSPR* Volume X. Did Myers at Aston Clinton perhaps recommend, or disparage, his colleague's book?

In 1923 Mrs. Henry Sidgwick published 'Phantasms of the Living: An Examination and Analysis of Telepathy between Living Persons printed in the "Journal" of the Society for Psychical Research since the Publication of the Book "Phantasms of the Living" by Gurney, Myers, and Podmore, in 1886' (*PSPR*, XXXIII [1923], 23–429). This paper is, however, comparable to *Phantasms of the Living* and the Census Report only in its classification and analysis of a large number of cases (139 quoted, 52 described), here arbitrarily limited to those recorded within five years of the experience. There is very little and (if one excludes the not highly illuminating substitution of 'transfusion' for 'transmission' as a description of 'the normal type of telepathic process') nothing new in the way of theoretical discussion.

258 I have used three contemporary sources of information about the Ballechin episode:
1. An article, 'from a correspondent', entitled 'On the Trail of a Ghost', *The Times*, 8 June 1897, p. 10, cols. 3–5; and a series of letters in response published in *The Times* from 9 June to 8 November 1897.
2. A. Goodrich-Freer ('Miss X.'), 'Psychical Research and an Alleged "Haunted" House', *Nineteenth Century*, XLII (August 1897), 217–34.
3. A. Goodrich-Freer (Miss X) and John, Marquess of Bute, K.T., edd., *The Alleged Haunting of B—— House, including a Journal kept during the Tenancy of Colonel Lemesurier Taylor* (London: George Redway, 1899).
   The details I give concerning Ballechin House and its tenancy are quoted from *The Times* article and from *The Alleged Haunting* . . ., pp. 9, 79, 82, 91, 93–94, and frontispiece (floor plans of house).

259 F. Whyte, *The Life of W. T. Stead* (London: Cape, 1925), II, 36–38 (letter to Myers September 1891, concerning material used in *Real Ghost Stories* . . . and *More Ghost Stories* . . ., Christmas and New Year's Numbers, *Review of Reviews*, IV [July–December 1891] and V [January–June 1892], revised and reissued as *Real Ghost Stories* . . . [London: Bell, 1897]; letter to a friend, September 1891, describing Miss X.); Miss X., 'Haunted Houses Up to Date: Silverton Abbey and Some Others', *Borderland*, III (1896), 284–96; *The Alleged Haunting* . . ., pp. 9–22, 30, 32, 34–35, 38–39, 68, 82, 96 (I have been unable to trace 'Mrs. G.'s' magazine article, quoted pp. 64–68).
   Miss X. is first listed as a member of the SPR in May 1889, and her first contribution to the *Proceedings*, 'Recent Experiments in Crystal-vision' (*PSPR*, V, 486–521), was read at the thirty-second General Meeting of the Society that year: it won favourable comment from both Janet and Dessoir. 'A Record of Telepathic and Other Experiences' (*PSPR*, VI, 358–97) has already been discussed (see pp. 147–50 above). At the General Meeting in June 1894 Miss X. read a paper on 'The Apparent Sources of Supernormal Experiences', published with slightly altered title in *PSPR*, XI (1895), 114–44. From the autumn of 1894 she was engaged, for the SPR, on an enquiry into second sight in the Highlands; but her papers on this subject and one on 'Some Recent Experiences, apparently Supernormal', read at the December meetings 1894–96, were published in *Borderland*, not in the *Proceedings*. Her paper entitled 'A Passing Note on a Haunted House', read to the Society on 29 January 1897 (*PSPR*, XII, 337) and published in *Borderland*, IV (1897), 167–69, dealt with Clandon House, Surrey, the property of the Earl of Onslow. Some years earlier, on behalf of the SPR and at Lord Bute's suggestion, Miss X., assisted by Mr. Bidder, Q.C., had collected and examined evidence for the 'haunting'. She herself visited Clandon House, and saw the ghost.

260 'Journal kept during a Visit to B—— House', *The Alleged Haunting* . . ., pp. 91–215. 'We drove, bicycled, walked, tobogganed, as circumstances permitted; there was fishing and shooting for those who liked killing things, there was a wealth of wild life on the hills and by the river for those who liked to see them alive. We made excursions, archaeologised, botanised: in the evening we played games, we made music, we danced' ('Psychical Research and an Alleged "Haunted" House', p. 226).

According to the letters published by the estate agents, Colonel Taylor's lease ran from 18 January to 15 May 1897. The last guest, it seems, departed on 14 May, but Miss X. remained 'to wind up household affairs' till 19 May (ibid., p. 225).

261 *The Alleged Haunting* . . ., pp. 113, 152, 189, 191–92, 200–01; 'Psychical Research and an Alleged "Haunted" House', pp. 225, 233.

262 *The Alleged Haunting* . . ., pp. 15–16, 219–23.

263 Ibid., pp. 215–18; *The Times*, 8 June 1897, p. 10, cols. 3–5. Thirty-five years later Sir James disclosed the anonymous correspondent's identity: he was 'Mr. Callender Ross, a member of the staff of *The Times*' (*The Doctor's After Thoughts* [London: Benn, 1932], p. 176).

264 *The Times*, 14 June 1897, p. 6, col. 4 (letter from J. M. S. Steuart, the owner); 18 June, p. 6, col. 6 (letter from Caroline Steuart); 16 June, p. 9, col. 6 and 19 June, p. 10, col. 2 (letters from estate agents); 21 June, p. 4, col. 6 (letter from J. A. Menzies, M.D., friend of the Major); 23 June, p. 21, col. 1 (letters from family friend and relative); 19 June, p. 10, col. 1 (letter from Lord Onslow). Dr. Menzies protested that the Major was not 'a rigid Presbyterian' as alleged by *The Times* correspondent, but 'an Anglican, and his grandfather, by the mother's side, if I am not mistaken, was an English Archbishop'. Dr. Menzies evidently did not regard the Major's threat to his gardener (recorded in this letter) as an expression of serious belief.

265 *The Times*, 12 June 1897, p. 11, col. 1 (letter from John Macdonald); 14 June, p. 6, col. 4 (letter from H.); 21 June, p. 4, cols. 5–6 (letter from Harold Sanders)—cf. *The Alleged Haunting* . . ., pp. 56–71 (testimony of Mr. H.'s guests).

266 *The Times*, 9 June 1897, p. 6, col. 3 (letter from X.); 12 June, p. 11, col. 1 (letters from Teresa Musgrave, Torquay; and H. R.); 14 June, p. 6, col. 4 (letter from L. E. B.: the case referred to in this letter is quoted by Myers as an apparent instance of 'unseen *protection* or *guidance*', pp. 547–59 in 'The Subliminal Self', Chs. viii and ix, 'The Relation of Supernormal Phenomena to Time—Retrocognition' and 'Precognition', *PSPR*, XI [1895], 334–593).

267 *The Times*, 10 June 1897, p. 4, col. 6 (letter from '*Tenez-le-Droit*').

268 *The Times*, 25 August 1897, p. 4, col. 6; 16 August, p. 6, col. 5; 27 August, p. 8, col. 3 (letters concerning houses in Oxfordshire, Surrey, and Normandy respectively); 12 June, p. 11, col. 1 (letter from 'A Late Guest at Ballechin'); 21 June, p. 4, col. 6 (letter from John Milne); 24 June, p. 10, col. 6 (letter from Andrew Lang).
 Up to this date Lang's only direct contributions to the activities of the SPR had been a paper on 'Cock Lane and Common Sense' read at the General Meeting of 26 January 1894, and one on 'The Voices of Jeanne d'Arc' read on 17 May 1895 and printed in *PSPR*, XI (1895), 198–212; but reviews of his essay on 'Comparative Psychical Research' and his edition of Kirk's *Secret Commonwealth* in *PSPR*, IX (1893–94), 367–69, of the miscellany *Cock Lane and Common Sense* in *PSPR*, X (1894), 423–26, and, in *PSPR*, XIII (1897–98), 616–18, of *The Book of Dreams and Ghosts*, published in September 1897, note with a certain irritation both his tendency to rebuke the Society 'for ignorance of the history of our own subject' and his free use of the material they published.

269 The 'thought-transference' experiments in question were those conducted by the Society in December 1882 and January and April 1883 with Douglas Blackburn as agent and G. A. Smith as percipient (*PSPR*, I [1882–83], 161–215). The demonstration attended by Crichton-Browne was probably that 'omitted from the series . . . as having been rendered nugatory through accidental circumstances which

were calculated to exercise, and obviously did exercise, a distracting effect on Mr. Blackburn's mind' (p. 162, note). Crichton-Browne wrote an account of the proceedings in a letter to the *Westminster Gazette* of 29 January 1908 (quoted here from Hall, op. cit., p. 114); and this account he repeated, with minor variations, in *The Doctor's Second Thoughts* (London: Benn, 1931), pp. 58–64.

270 'A Haunted House', in *The Doctor's After Thoughts*, pp. 175–84. This account seems to be pieced together from recollections, from *The Times* article, and from *The Alleged Haunting* . . . .

271 *The Times*, 16 June 1897, p. 9, col. 6 (letter from X.); 18 June, p. 6, col. 6 (letter from 'A Late Guest at Ballechin'). Concerning the medium's revelations, Miss X. later noted: 'These remarkable disclosures included, among other details, the murder of a Roman Catholic family chaplain, at a period when the S——s were and had long been Presbyterian, the suicide of one of the family who is still living, and the throwing, by persons in mediaeval costume, of the corpse of an infant, over a bridge, which is quite new, into a stream which until lately ran underground' (*The Alleged Haunting* . . ., p. 199 n.).

272 *The Times*, 10 June 1897, p. 4, col. 6 (letter from 'Frederic W. H. Myers, Hon. Sec. of the Society for Psychical Research').

273 *The Times*, 12 June 1897, p. 11, col. 1 (letter from 'One of the Witnesses'); 15 June, p. 12, col. 6 (letter from 'Frederic W. H. Myers, Hon. Sec. of the Society for Psychical Research'); 19 June, p. 10, cols. 1–2 (letter from Henry Sidgwick); 22 June, p. 14, col. 4 (letter from Frederic W. H. Myers): Myers denies, not the SPR's investigation of the Clandon 'haunting', but its responsibility for the publicity complained of.

274 Mrs. H. Sidgwick, 'Notes on the Evidence, collected by the Society, for Phantasms of the Dead', *PSPR*, III (1885), 69–150 (The 'Morton' case is noted on p. 117; Mrs. Sidgwick throws doubt on the 'X.Z.' case, pp. 100–01); Miss R. C. Morton, 'Record of a Haunted House', *PSPR*, VIII (1892), 311–32; 'First Report of the Committee on Haunted Houses', *PSPR*, I (1882–83), 101–15 (The 'X. Z.' case is reported, pp. 105–08); Edmund Gurney, 'Retractations and Alterations of View', SPR *Journal*, 1885 (August), p. 3, quoted by Hall, op. cit., pp. 69–70 (a detailed refutation of 'X. Z.'s' account); *The Alleged Haunting* . . ., pp. 193–94 (Myers and Miss X. discuss a date for the presentation of the Ballechin evidence to the Society).

275 'A Record of Observations of Certain Phenomena of Trance', Appendix to (3) Part II, (*PSPR*, VI [1889–90], 629: comment on sittings of Miss X. with Mrs. Piper, Nos. 24, 25, and 26); 'Psychical Research and an Alleged "Haunted" House', pp. 219–23.

276 Ibid., pp. 223–24.

277 Ibid., pp. 225–34. The 'tests' described by Miss X. were improvised attempts to reproduce the sounds heard, which therefore must have been assumed to originate within the house and by human agency, at the same time as practical considerations ruled out the latter. The potentialities of the 'unprotected [bell-]wires and water pipes' mentioned seem to have been altogether neglected. Miss X. apparently believed that when the pipes of a hot-water system were not conducting hot water, they were unable to conduct sound either: 'If the correspondents who solve everything as "hot-water pipes" knew the tone in which a patient maid can murmur "the seventh can I've brought up from the kitchen, miss," we should hear less positive statements on that subject' (p. 233). An external source was conceived only in terms of the cry of birds, or the sound of trains, yet Miss X. knew that a stream recently bridged had

'until lately run underground'. The only mention of this stream as a possible source for the noises occurs in Sir James Crichton-Browne's 1932 reminiscences.

Apropos of borrowed arguments, one may note, e.g. that Miss X.'s rejection of the term 'psychical research' as implying prejudgment of the issue under investigation (p. 217), and her insistence on the necessity for 'lengthened inquiry, an entire familiarity . . . with all normal phenomena. . . .' (p. 224), convert accusations by Callender Ross and Crichton-Browne; her suggestion of the term 'super-normal' to replace 'supernatural' (p. 217), and her passing allusion to 'a widely diffused primal instinct, lost or held in abeyance in a changed environment' (p. 220), echo observations by Myers (*PSPR*, XII, 174 and VI, 330).

278 *The Times*, 2 November 1897, p. 6, col. 3 (letter from C. B.); 6 November, p. 9, col. 5 (letter from 'An Earnest Inquirer'); 8 November, p. 6, col. 4 (letter from 'A Cynical Observer').

279 *Notebooks*, p. 27 (autobiographical memoranda recorded in Boston, November 1881); *The Times*, 10 June 1897, p. 11, col. 3 (review of *The Brontës: Fact and Fiction* and *The Brontë Homeland: or, Misrepresentations Rectified*, in 'Books of the Week'); *Punch, or the London Charivari*, 26 June 1897, p. 327 (review of *Dracula*, in 'Our Booking-Office'); ibid., 3 July 1897, p. 332, ' "The Chap with the Raps" ': An elderly ghost explains to a young one how he became possessed of 'this desirable residence'. When he discovered that the presence of himself and his friends, especially that of a 'slightly vulgar' 'chap who woke them up with raps', was 'driving away possible tenants' from 'the very best parts of town', he applied to a firm of 'eminent estate agents and auctioneers' and arranged for a transfer to a house where ghostly occupancy 'hurts no one, because the estate is in Chancery'.

> 'I see. And what has become of the chap with the raps?'
> 'Well, I scarcely know; but from what I see in the papers, I fancy *he* must be the originator of that immense correspondence, "On the Trail of a Ghost." '
> 'And will he keep in the papers long?'
> 'I should think so,' I replied. 'For such a fellow is the right man in the right place in the silly season.'

280 One cannot imagine that at this date James would recall more of his brother's paper than its general drift and certain substantive details. But, to take one example, Miss X.'s statement concerning visual phenomena, quoted above, is in striking conformity, both critical and verbal, with that of William James on mediumistic communications: 'The medium showed a most startling intimacy with this family's affairs, talking of many matters known to no one outside, and which gossip could not possibly have conveyed to her ears. The details would prove nothing to the reader, unless printed *in extenso*, with full notes by the sitters. It reverts, after all, to personal conviction' (*PSPR*, VI, 653).

281 That Lord Bute was indeed 'gratefully' conscious of his indebtedness to Miss X. is shown by the phrasing of a passage quoted, in *The Alleged Haunting* . . ., from his letters to her on the subject of Ballechin: 'December 20th. [1896] . . . I am afraid I shall encroach even further upon your kindness. Myers has all the papers, but I fancy you would rather know as little as possible, so as not to be influenced by expectation. It is no case of roughing it. B—— House is, I believe, a luxurious country house, ample, though not too large, in a beautiful neighbourhood . . .' (pp. 86–87). The quotations illustrative of Miss X.'s situation, assumptions, etc., are taken from her article, pp. 227; 225; 231; 226; 218, 223, 224, 231, 232 (colloquialisms); 217, 229 (pretentious jargon). The term 'audile' seems to have been coined by French psychologists: it occurs in A. T. Myers's report of the 1889 International Congress of

Experimental Psychology (*PSPR*, VI [1890], 173), which was probably Miss X.'s source. 'Audile phenomena' is used as a standard descriptive phrase in *The Alleged Haunting . . .*, pp. 234, 245–49.

282 I take 'Ballechin' to be the contracted popular rendering, simplified in spelling, but still phonetically recognizable, of the ancient Gaelic *Baile-aigidh-chaein*, 'town (or stead, or home) of the pleasant, lovely face (or aspect)'. As to the likelihood that James knew of this etymology—is it possible that 'the name of the house' could recur in London gossip over a period of three months (so that in June the *Times* correspondent felt obliged to indicate its correct pronunciation) without there being repeated discussion of its meaning?

283 Lubbock, I, 307–08 (letter to F. W. H. Myers, 19 December 1898).

284 The only printed source at this date was 'Record of a Haunted House', by Miss R. C. Morton, *PSPR*, VIII (1892), 311–32, where the 'principle of reticence' is firmly adhered to; but James, through his acquaintance with Myers, may have had additional information. The house in question was 'Garden Reach', Cheltenham, and the tenant was a Captain Despard, whose eldest unmarried daughter, Miss Rose Despard, recorded the case. The haunting phantasm was taken to be that of Mrs. Imogen Swinhoe, second wife and (from 1876) widow of the original owner of the house. She had died at Clifton. In his summarized account (op. cit., pp. 197–98), Dr. Gauld observes: 'It is without doubt the most curious case of its kind ever printed.'

285 Ch. xii, 'The Development of Telepathic Hallucinations', *Phantasms of the Living*, I, 519–73. Of the six cases I have noted as unquestionably supplying details used in *The Turn of the Screw*, Nos. 3 and 4 occur in this chapter.

286 Gurney argues that in most cases the percept has been supplied by the percipient's mind. 'But . . . there is a converse type, where the dress or aspect includes features which equally clearly could *not* be supplied by the percipient's mind. . . . If, then, the phantasmal appearance includes [such features] . . . we must here admit that a ready-made concrete image, and not a mere idea, has been transferred from one to the other' (ibid., pp. 554–55).

287 This is a standard motif in Gothic romances, as in traditional and invented ghost stories; but James's reader is inevitably reminded of *Jane Eyre*. This strange *doppelgänger* effect, with two Jane Eyres momentarily in confrontation, seems designed, as if in playful bravado, at once to obtrude and to negate the suggestion of a pastiche.

288 James nowhere, that I recall, expresses an opinion of Clough or his poetry; but he has a good deal to say of Emerson and his 'ripe unconsciousness of evil': 'He knows the nature of man and the long tradition of its dangers; but we feel that whereas he can put his finger on the remedies, lying for the most part, as they do, in the deep recesses of virtue, of the spirit, he has only a kind of hearsay, uninformed acquaintance with the disorders' ('Emerson', in *Partial Portraits*, pp. 7–8). The passage I have in mind, from 'Considerations by the Way', Ch. vii of *The Conduct of Life*, in which Emerson elaborates the maxim that 'the first lesson of history is the good of evil', is a typical expression of his innocent optimism.

289 In 'Another Reading of *The Turn of the Screw*' (*Modern Language Notes*, LVI [1941], 196–202), Nathan Bryllion Fagin uses, and I think misinterprets, the same parallels from Hawthorne to define a harsher if more orthodox moral. 'The Birthmark', in particular, unmistakably condemns the ruthless perfectionist.

APPENDIX I

James's Revision of *The Turn of the Screw* for the New York Edition

James, we know, imposed more or less (sometimes considerably less) extensive revisions on the text of his works to prepare them for the New York Edition of 1907–09. I am not aware who first suggested that these revisions might, with regard to the stories and their characters, indicate a change of attitude from that in which they were first conceived. But as far as *The Turn of the Screw* is concerned, this suggestion was given authoritative expression by Leon Edel in his edition of *The Ghostly Tales of Henry James*, p. 434, and again in *The Psychological Novel: 1900–1950* (London: Hart-Davis, 1955), p. 45. I quote:

The evidence of what James sought to do with his governess is to be found in the revisions which he made for the New York Edition. If there is speculation as to what James's 'conscious intentions' were, we can find a concrete answer here. The word 'perceived' as used by her is invariably altered to *felt*. 'I now recollect . . .' is changed to 'I now feel . . .' and 'it appeared to me . . .' to 'it struck me. . . .' In another instance 'Mrs. Grose appeared to me' becomes 'Mrs. Grose affected me. . . .' In each case—and they are relatively numerous—we note the determination to alter the nature of the governess' testimony from that of a report of things observed, perceived, recalled, to things *felt*.

But we have one significant clue to the author's 'blanks.' In his revision of the story for the New York Edition he altered his text again and again to put the story into the realm of the governess's feelings. Where he had her say originally 'I saw' or 'I believed' he often substituted 'I felt.'

Thus impressively sponsored, the contention is now, it seems, accepted as a fact of James's literary history, and is in its turn subject to elaboration and extension. Thomas M. Cranfill and Robert L. Clark Jr., for example, in *An Anatomy of* The Turn of the Screw (Austin: Univ. of Texas Press, 1965), Ch. ii, after noting many of James's revisions as stylistically intended, proceed (p. 18):

Analyzing James's revisions, Leon Edel noticed in his edition of *The Ghostly Tales* that the changes betrayed James's determination 'to alter the nature of the governess' testimony from that of a report of things observed, perceived, recalled, to things *felt*.' Edel arrived at the conclusion that the tale is primarily a record of feeling. We could not agree more heartily. Our own study of the text validates Edel's findings, gives us a wholesome respect for James's prefatory remark, and leads us to believe that the master meant precisely what he said when he spoke of 'felt' trouble.

Here are a few illustrations of how James reinforced this already conspicuous tone. He changed 'I perceived' to 'I felt' (twice), 'I now reflect' to 'I now feel,' and 'Mrs. Grose appeared to me' to 'Mrs. Grose affected me.' These in addition to the scores of passages in which the governess had already confided her feelings in the 1898 version. The result is unmistakable.

Robert Kimbrough, in his edition of *The Turn of the Screw* (New York: Norton, 1966), p. 91, states that, through his revisions in the 1908 text

James seemed intent on shifting the center of attention away from the details of action observed by the governess to the reactions felt by the governess. By removing commas . . . he came closer to approximating the stream of her consciousness. . . . By increasing the use of the possessive pronoun 'my' and by replacing verbs of perception and thought with those of feeling and intuition . . . James draws us intimately into the course of her narrative. The effect is more vital and vivid than that created by either of the earlier versions.

This is the critical equivalent of a process familiar to historians under the name applied to it years ago by the late Professor Rait: it is a 'chain of error', and it breaks at any and every point when tested by the facts. James's known habit of composition from February 1897 onwards and the texts themselves supply these facts: I speak, of course, of the first authoritative text, the 1898 Heinemann edition (for James always begged critical immunity for the serial, magazine printing of his work), and the text of the 1908 New York Edition. All we need to do is to consult Miss Bosanquet's testimony, and to collate the two texts. Now Cranfill and Clark observe that 'such drudgery as collation' is in general left 'to the pedant' (p. 16), but they do not say that their own 'study' is based on a 'collation', and the term may in any case be used to describe a comparison of selected passages only, and a 'spot check' of selected words. For the present enquiry, however, it is necessary to make *a complete, line by line collation* of the two texts. Having done so, I state categorically that, with a single exception, James's revisions in *The Turn of the Screw* not only were stylistic, and merely stylistic, in intention but also, as regards character and incident, effect no change whatever in the impression conveyed to the reader. The single exception occurs in Ch. xiii: 'the eccentric nature of my father' becomes 'the whimsical bent of my father', as if to guard against any possible suspicion of inherited madness in the governess. That any author should spend months over an improvement (as he considered it) in the mere *wording* of his novels and stories, is a procedure incomprehensible, it seems, to critics of the present day: in their eyes it requires the justification of an ulterior purpose. But to James (the French-trained, nineteenth-century artist) style was a matter of supreme importance, worth the utmost expense of time and ingenuity.

A fully detailed report of the stylistic changes James thought necessary in *The Turn of the Screw* would occupy too much space here, so that I shall attempt only to dispose of some current misapprehensions and to indicate the 'main lines' of the revision. In the latter attempt I shall be dealing, though I hope more systematically if as briefly, with material which has for the most part already been handled by Cranfill and Clark. In many cases the changes introduced by James, and their stylistic effect, have been noted, accurately, by these two scholars: my objection is not, in the main, to their evidence but to their principal induction from it—that, agreeably to their thesis, James by his 1908 revision intended to emphasize the 'effusive and nerve-wracked' governess's disqualification as a witness.

First, there is the ancillary matter of punctuation to be considered. The nineteenth-century printer, on both sides of the Atlantic, as a rule over-punctuated, so that, for example, a page of dialogue in a Victorian novel can be as uncomfortable to the eye as it is unnecessarily explicit. The French had, and still have, a better system of indicating dialogue, but this, like their method of printing dramatic works, was not agreeable to English readers. When James began to dictate instead of write his work, he had to *state* every mark of punctuation as it occurred (*teste* Miss Bosanquet), a process of extreme tedium which he increasingly alleviated by the most obvious means—the omission of as many of the commas with which Victorian convention peppered the page, as was consistent (sometimes, except to the author, barely consistent) with intelligibility. And since, in the New York Edition, James was determined to present a uniform image of maturity, the works, such as *The Turn of the Screw*, composed before full emancipation from the comma had been achieved, had all to be brought up to date in this matter of punctuation. The effect is to free the reader visually, but to impose on him instead an aural discipline: he must hear 'in his head' the sentences unroll and their cadence will assist his interpretation. The record of the 'stream of consciousness' is therefore unaffected, since the reader still has, mentally, to supply the grammatical checks and pauses formerly ensured by the printer. Moreover, commas once discarded, their chance insertion by an over-zealous compositor becomes a danger to be obviated—this is the point of James's letter quoted by Kimbrough (p. 89): 'It is vital that [Martin Secker] adhere to that authentic punctuation—to the last comma or rather, more essentially, no-comma.' The destruction of sense produced by disregarding this injunction is exemplified on page after page of our modern cheap editions.

One other typographical feature must be noted. In *The Turn of the Screw* James makes frequent use of italics, in narrative passages as well as dialogue. Here of course he is writing 'in character', since over-indulgence in italics is traditionally a woman's foible. But it can scarcely be maintained (as Cranfill and Clark, p. 17, appear to do) that the two versions differ significantly in this respect. In 1908 Douglas is made to say, 'That is she *had* been'; the governess says, 'I *have* it from you then'; Miles says, 'You'll have to *tell* him'; whereas on pp. 6, 51, and 122 of the 1898 version these words are not italicized. But on the other hand 'some of the company *he* kept' (p. 52) becomes in 1908 'some of the company he himself kept'.

Now let us test by the facts the generalizations of Professor Edel and others regarding verbal alterations in *The Turn of the Screw*. 'Perceived' is indeed altered to 'felt' in chs. i and xxi, but to 'noticed' in ch. x and to 'recognised' in ch. xxii; and it is retained unaltered in ch. ix. 'I now reflect [long after the episode, not 'recollect']' is altered to 'I now feel' in ch. xiii, but 'I recollect' in ch. i remains unaltered. 'It appeared to me' is altered to 'it struck me' in ch. xiv; but 'appeared [i.e. 'seemed']' is retained in chs. iv, xiii, and xxii. In ch. i 'the little girl who accompanied Mrs. Grose [not 'Mrs. Grose'] appeared to me' in 1898 and 'affected me' in 1908; but in ch. vii Mrs. Grose still 'appeared to assent to this' and in ch. xxi 'appeared . . . more reluctant', while Miles in ch. xxiv 'appeared now to be thinking' in 1908 as in 1898. On one occasion 'see' becomes 'know' (ch. xx) and on another 'saw' becomes 'knew' (ch. ix); but there are no instances of 'I saw' or 'I believed' becoming 'I felt', though 'I became sure' is altered to 'I felt sure' in ch. xix. On one occasion 'felt' becomes 'conceived' (ch. x); on another 'I found myself' becomes 'I knew myself' (ch. ix). 'It struck me' occurs fewer than a dozen times in the course of the story; but both 'I saw' (30 odd examples) and 'I felt' (40 odd examples) are very frequently used; and James's revision of the text makes virtually no change in these proportions.

But the evidence of isolated words changed or retained is not very persuasive, one way or the other. If there is indeed a shift in 'the nature of the governess' testimony' from 'seeing' to 'feeling', it must appear in her description of the alleged visitations. Here is the record, with every variation of wording in the 1898 and 1908 texts noted as it occurs.

Ch. iii —the first visitation: the man on the tower, 'as definite as a picture in a frame'—'So I saw him as I see the letters I form on this page.'

Ch. iv —the second visitation: the man at the window—'he was the same, and seen, this time, as he had been seen before'.

Ch. v —the report to Mrs. Grose of the two visitations: ' "Have you seen him before?" "Yes—once. On the old tower. . . . I saw him as I see you." '

Ch. vi —the third visitation: Miss Jessel at the lake. 'There was no ambiguity in anything; none whatever, at least, in the conviction I . . . found myself forming as to what I should see straight before me and across the lake as a consequence of raising my eyes. . . . Then I again shifted my eyes—I faced what I had to face.'

Ch. ix   —the fourth visitation: Quint on the stair—'the next instant, I saw that there was someone on the stair [1908: 'knew that there was a figure on the stair']. . . . I saw the figure disappear; . . . I definitely saw it turn. . . .'

Ch. x   —the fifth visitation: Miss Jessel on the stair. 'Looking down it from the top I once recognised the presence of a woman seated on one of the lower steps. . . .'

Ch. xv   —the sixth visitation: Miss Jessel in the schoolroom. 'Seated at my own table in the clear noonday light I saw a person. . . .'

Ch. xx   —the seventh visitation: Miss Jessel at the lake. 'Miss Jessel stood before us on the opposite bank. . . . This first vividness of vision and emotion were things of a few seconds, during which Mrs. Grose's dazed blink across to where I pointed struck me as a sovereign sign [1908: 'struck me as showing'] that she too at last saw. . . . I felt—I saw [1908: '*saw*']—my livid predecessor press, from her position, on my defeat. . . .'

Ch. xxiv—the eighth visitation: Quint at the window. 'Peter Quint had come into view. . . . It came to me . . . that the act would be, seeing and facing what I saw and faced, to keep the boy himself unaware. . . . I kept my eyes on the thing at the window and saw it move and shift its posture.'

In a single instance, in ch. ix, the operative verb is changed; but what has induced the change, it would seem, is merely James's regard for euphony—three sibilants in a row offended his ear. The change from 'sovereign sign' to 'showing' in ch. xx is a gain both in euphony and in ease of diction. These are the only verbal changes in the crucial passages cited. It must, I think, be admitted that throughout her narrative James has maintained the governess's testimony at one and the same pitch of visual intensity.

Kimbrough further suggests that in the 1908 version James increased 'the use of the possessive pronoun "my" ', so as to draw us 'intimately into the course of' the governess's narrative. Occasionally, it is true, when a phrase is recast (for one or other of the purposes to be discussed below) a personal, if not always a possessive, pronoun becomes necessary and is introduced; but equally often an existing pronoun becomes superfluous and is discarded. In ch. xvii, for example, 'my absolute conviction of his secret precocity . . . imposed him almost as an intellectual equal' becomes 'forced me to treat him as an intelligent equal'; but in ch. xv 'I had made up my mind I would fly' becomes 'I had made up my mind to cynical flight.' In ch. xx 'I had said . . . that she was not at these times a child, but an old, old woman, and that description of her. . . .' becomes 'and my description of her. . . .'; but in ch. xv 'I reeled straight back upon my resistance' becomes 'I reeled straight back upon resistance'. And why, if this theory of narrative 'intimacy' is correct, does James in the 1908 text more than once substitute a general for a personal expression of the governess's relation to her pupils and to Mrs. Grose? In ch. xiii, for example, 'my charges' twice becomes 'our young friends'; in ch. xv 'my little friend' becomes 'our young friend'; in ch. xvi 'the return of my pupils' becomes 'the return of the others'; in ch. vi 'guard the tranquillity of my companions [i.e. Mrs. Grose as well as the children]' becomes 'guard the tranquillity of the rest of the household'. James's recourse, in the late text, to that *cliché* of the omniscient author, 'our young friend(s', is surprising: a rational explanation here would be that he desired to thicken the period associations of his tale; but the probability is that this phrase, with others less noticeably incongruous, is merely part of the late-Jamesian idiom.

For the benefit of the 1908 edition James altered the wording of *The Turn of the Screw* in over three hundred separate instances—some dozen of which occur in the prefatory chapter. These alterations range from the abbreviation, replacement, insertion, or omission of a single word to the rearrangement or complete recasting of a phrase or sentence. They may be classified as follows:

Abbreviation of auxiliary verb in combination with pronoun or noun, or of negative in combination with auxiliary verb. This is already the rule in conversational passages, but it is more freely used in the 1908 text: e.g. in ch. v ' "What's he like?" ' and ' "Mr. Quint's dead." ' The significant increase, however, occurs in narrative passages: e.g. 'couldn't' (chs. xiii, xx); 'hadn't' (chs. i, viii, ix); 'shouldn't' (ch. viii, twice); 'wasn't' (chs. x, xx, xxii).

Changes in the interest of euphony. The repetition in too close succession of plosive or sibilant consonants, or of identical (or even like) syllables is frequently, but not invariably, eliminated: e.g. 'a wonder that in a few instants more became intense' is replaced by 'a wonder that in a few seconds more became intense' (ch. iii); 'to keep terms with so compromising a contract' becomes 'to keep terms with so stiff an agreement' (ch. vi); 'make me sit there for an hour in close, silent contact' becomes 'make me sit there for an hour in close mute contact' (ch. xv); 'In this position she produced an almost furious wail' becomes 'In this position she launched an almost furious wail' (ch. xx); 'I speedily perceived' becomes 'I quickly recognised' (ch. xxii). These are *sound* changes, not primarily designed to increase the force or clarity of an expression. At times the point of an observation or interchange is sacrificed: e.g. in ch. xxii Miles asks, ' "Did Bly disagree with her so terribly suddenly?" ' and this is altered to ' "so terribly all at once?" ', with the result that the governess's reply, ' "Not so suddenly as you might think" ', becomes less sharply pertinent.

Simplification of expression. The formal connective 'that' (for noun or relative clause) is often avoided: e.g. 'saw that the drawn curtains were unstirred' becomes 'saw the drawn curtains unstirred' (ch. xvii); 'I had so perfectly expected that the return of my pupils would be marked' becomes 'expected the return of the others to be marked' (ch. xvi); 'the more or less noise that at the moment we might be engaged in making' becomes 'the more or less noise we at the moment might be engaged in making' (ch. xiii). The simplification may consist in the removal of an otiose word (e.g. in ch. xxii 'precisely' is omitted from 'It was precisely, in short, by just clutching the helm. . . .' and 'outside of the window of which' becomes 'outside the window of which'); in the substitution of a familiar for a pedantic word (e.g. 'informant' for 'interlocutress' in ch. vi. and 'conclusions' for 'inductions' in ch. xiii), or of a colloquially easy for a stilted phrase (e.g. in ch. viii 'It was a dreadfully austere enquiry. . . .' becomes 'It was a straight question enough. . . .'; in ch. xi 'than a signal more resonant' becomes 'than any noisier process'; in ch. xiii 'could not have been so successfully effected' becomes 'couldn't have been made successful'). A mixed metaphor may be freed of its incongruous element (e.g. in ch. i 'my fortitude mounted afresh and . . . encountered a reprieve that was probably but a proof of the point to which it had sunk' becomes 'my fortitude revived and . . . took a flight that etc.'). A clumsily verbose statement may be reworded: e.g. in ch. xix 'The pond, oblong in shape, had a width so scant compared to its length, that, with its ends out of view, it might have been taken for a scant river' becomes 'This expanse, oblong in shape, was so narrow compared to its length, that etc.'; in ch. xx 'this was a stroke that somehow converted the little girl herself into the very presence that could make me quail' becomes 'this was a stroke that somehow converted the little girl herself into a figure portentous'.

Alteration of word order. These changes, often trivial, seem in general to be prompted by considerations of rhythm, although they may also be designed to give more prominence to an adverb or adverbial phrase. The thrusting of an adverb between a noun or pronoun and its verb becomes an obsessive mannerism only in James's latest writing, and he does not obtrude it in *The Turn of the Screw*. Here the rearrangement usually makes for a tighter construction: e.g. 'for I was rooted as deeply as I was shaken' becomes 'since I was as deeply rooted as shaken' (ch. iv); 'with which, in these days, I overscored their full hours' becomes 'with which I in these days overscored etc.' (ch. ix); 'noise that at the moment we might be engaged in making' becomes 'noise we at the moment might be etc.' (ch. xiii); 'I had lived, by this time, too long among wonders' becomes 'I had by this time lived etc.' (ch. xix). In the following case, the gain from reuniting a broken main clause may be thought to outweigh the merely grammatical ambiguity which results: ' "No more. . . ." I shrieked, as I tried to press him [Miles] against me, to my visitant [Quint]' becomes 'I shrieked to my visitant as I tried to press him against me' (ch. xxiv).

Replacement of a colourless or imprecise expression by one more evocative or more accurate. For example, 'I couldn't have borne the business alone' becomes 'I couldn't have borne the strain alone' (ch. xi); 'their instructress' becomes 'their deputy-guardian' (ch. xi)—the apparent self-reliance, not the ignorance, of the children is in question; 'they're steeped in their vision of the dead restored' becomes 'the dead restored to them' (ch. xii); 'through any deepened exhilaration', a contradiction in terms, becomes 'through any intensified mirth' (ch. xiii); 'driven from school' becomes 'expelled from school' (ch. xxii). Revisions of this type applied to expressions of the governess's own actions and feelings have been seized on (e.g. by Cranfill and Clark, p. 18) as evidence of James's intention to emphasize her emotional instability. But where they are not James's correction of some inaccuracy, such changes are more justifiably ascribed to his desire to keep at a consistent level the picturesqueness which (as I argue in Chapter V above) he has made a distinctive feature of her style. In ch. xv, for example, 'I might easily put an end to my predicament' becomes 'I might easily put an end to my ordeal', not because 'ordeal' is the more emotional term, but because, while the governess can at any moment cease to submit herself to the test of her difficult situation, or 'predicament', she cannot end the situation itself—although, in an alternative and equally euphonious revision, she might escape from it. In the same chapter, 'I made, in my bewilderment, for the schoolroom' becomes 'I made, in my turmoil, for the schoolroom.' The governess is not bewildered—she has been arguing the pros and cons of departure at some length; but she cannot make up her mind: she is swayed by contrary impulses, she is 'in a turmoil' of indecision. The increase, not very conspicuous, in the already large number of colloquialisms, and some additional, rather affectedly 'literary' words, may also be explained as confirming, or enhancing, the governess's typical picturesqueness of expression: e.g. 'in retrospect' becomes 'in raking it all over' (ch. vi); 'turn my back and retreat' becomes 'turn my back and bolt' (ch. xv); 'the exposure of my society' becomes 'the exposure of sticking to me' (ch. xix); 'watching' becomes 'vigils' (ch. x); 'proof' becomes 'gage' (ch. xv).

Consequential changes. Any substitution or addition of a word or phrase, whatever the purpose may be, entails the risk of introducing new stylistic blemishes (faults of euphony, repetitions), so that one change may necessitate another. For example, in ch. xxi James alters 'promptly' to 'at once', only to find that his sentence ends with 'once more', which has therefore to become 'afresh'. In the first paragraph of ch. xxiv, for reasons of euphony, he alters 'My sense of how he received this. . . .' to 'My grasp of how he received this. . . .' and then, three sentences further on, is impelled to change 'recovered her grasp of the *act*' to 'recovered her command of the *act*'.

An attempt, not always successful, to clarify an imperfectly verbalized image or a notion ambiguously expressed. For example, in ch. xxii 'Mightn't one, to reach his mind, risk the stretch of an angular arm over his character?' becomes 'Mightn't one, to reach his mind, risk the stretch of a stiff arm across his character?'. All James intends, as the next sentence shows, is the comparison of a forcing of confidence (a use of 'shock tactics', as we have learned to say) with a breach of table manners: 'It was as if, when we were face to face in the dining-room, [Miles] had literally shown me the way'—his own 'table manner' being so precociously refined. But neither version expresses this homely image appropriately enough to be instantly clear. Again, in ch. xx rephrasing gives a surface definition to a more than usually nebulous observation of the governess's: 'I saw . . . so much of him that it was as if it were more than it had ever been' becomes 'I saw . . . so much of him that it fairly measured more than it had ever measured.' The context allows us to interpret 'it' as 'Miles's behaviour' and 'measured' as 'indicated' or 'suggested' [troubling, or evil, preoccupations], but the sentence remains obscure. And in ch. x altering 'by almost sitting on her to hold her hand' to 'by almost sitting on her for the retention of her hand' does nothing at all to explain, to suspicious critics, the innocence of the nursery situation, to which James's laconic phrase 'by almost sitting on her' has given the air of some perverse cruelty. Flora's bed is low and narrow, Flora's arm is very short, yet 'Hold my hand!' she demands, and until she falls asleep the governess has to remain sitting crouched over her at the bedside. Again, in ch. xi the governess, leading Miles back to his room after his moonlight escapade, reflects that *this* time he will find it difficult to invent a plausible excuse. She goes on: 'It was a sharp trap for the inscrutable! He couldn't play any longer at innocence; so how the deuce would he get out of it?' What she means, presumably, is that successfully as Miles has so far evaded explanations, he is now caught, and will *have* to explain; but her remark is undeniably cryptic. In the 1908 text, however, obscurity is compounded: 'It was a sharp trap for any game hitherto successful. He could play no longer at perfect propriety, nor could he pretend to it; so how the deuce would he get out of the scrape?' Has James revived the dead metaphor of 'trap'—is 'game' the hunted animal —why then keep the expression 'play at'? Could the most infatuated devotee of the 1908 text claim this as an improvement?

But indeed there is no question that many of James's alterations are unnecessary, or inept, or both, and that they may justly be described as the perfectionist's obsessional tinkering with his work. Certain favourite words, by 1908 almost Jamesian trade marks, are introduced into contexts already adequately served: e.g. 'I . . . found myself doubtful again' becomes 'I . . . found all my doubts bristle again' (ch. i); 'the poor woman groaned' becomes 'the poor woman wailed' (ch. viii) and 'cried and sobbed' becomes 'cried and wailed' (ch. xx). What conceivable gain is there in altering 'melancholy' to 'dreary' (ch. i); 'half replaced' to 'half-displaced' [when a 'restored' building is the subject] (ch. i); 'the affair' to 'the business' (ch. ix); 'I used to say to myself' to 'I used to wonder', and then, a few lines below, 'I remember wondering' to 'I remember asking' (ch. ix); 'I fancy my smile was pale' to 'I imagine my smile was pale' (ch. xxiii)? And is ease or accuracy or picturesqueness served by replacing 'without a concession, an admission, of her eyes' [Flora merely *looks* her hatred] by 'without an expressional concession or admission' (ch. xx)? But there is no doubt whatever that it is James of the third phase, the multiplier of words, who amplifies 'no history' into 'nothing to call even an infinitesimal history' (ch. iv); who expands 'everything . . . would have to be enclosed and protected' into 'everything . . . would have to be fenced about and ordered and arranged' (ch. iii); who replaces the clumsy 'I encountered her on the ground of a probability that. . . .' by the lengthier clumsiness of 'I closed with her cordially on the article of the likelihood that. . . .' (ch. viii); who is not content with 'I should have found the trace' but must add, still equivocally, 'should have felt the wound and the dishonour [if Miles had ever been "chastised"]' (ch. iv). Only at that late and garrulous stage could James have marred the perfection of 'The rooks stopped cawing in the golden sky and the friendly hour lost, for the minute, all its voice' (ch. iii): 'the unspeakable minute', insists the text of 1908.

The Question of Sources

Quellenforschung used to be an honourable, and obligatory, critical pursuit; 'source-hunting' is now a term of critical disparagement, if not abuse. And yet in some cases (and that of Henry James pre-eminently) a knowledge of his sources is indispensable for a correct appraisal of the author's intention. But if we accept this as an article of critical faith, we need also to be strict in our application of it. What must be our criteria for admitting not merely the general 'influence' of an admired author (Turgenev, say, in James's case) but the possibility that a certain work, or body of factual data, has supplied a plot, a character, a situation, a method of treatment, or even a single effect in a given novel or story of James? What, in short, constitutes *for James* a source? The personal limitation has to be noted; for the only universally operative restriction is the mechanical one of priority in time—accessibility is variously conditioned.

The writer's intellectual habit is all-important. What facts were to Shaw subjective impressions were to James: he would never laboriously accumulate data out of which to construct a novel or a play. It was one thing to visit Millbank Prison, it would have been quite impossibly another to hunt up details of anarchist plots in the newspaper room of the British Museum: recollections of actualities (of things and persons seen and studied with unusual intentness), memories of an extraordinary catholicity of books (not to mention articles and 'news items') read and inwardly digested, were in his possession already and continually being replenished. 'My notes,' as he tells us in his Preface to *The Princess Casamassima*, 'were exactly my gathered impressions and stirred perceptions, the deposit in my working imagination of all my visual and all my constructive sense of London. . . . I recall pulling no wires, knocking at no closed doors, applying for no "authentic" information; but I recall also on the other hand the practice of never missing an opportunity to add a drop, however small, to the bucket of my impressions or to renew my sense of being able to dip into it' (pp. 76–77). His private *Notebooks* testify to the truth of this, for what they record is not a succession of facts and references (the name lists are the only material answering at all to this description) but first the seminal *donnée* and next the play of James's own creative imagination about it. What has stimulated that play, what has gone into the 'bucket of impressions' is surely the critic's legitimate concern—most of all, perhaps, where the contribution is literary in origin. For although, as Professor Edel truly observes (in his Introduction to *Henry James: A Collection of Critical Essays* [Englewood Cliffs, N.J.: Prentice Hall, 1963], p. 9) James's imagination was 'saturated with literature', we cannot therefore argue either that 'all the writings of the past . . . provided the soil for his own work' or that in consequence literary influences are of negligible importance for the student of it. The claim sometimes made for James, of familiarity with the Greek and Latin classics, is ill-founded: the worn classical tags and allusions (such as the vague 'Olympian' suggestions in his story 'The Velvet Glove') which he very occasionally employs prove, if anything, the contrary. One need only turn to a nineteenth-century writer who is also a classical scholar (F. W. H. Myers, for instance) to grasp the very different effect such familiarity produces. James read omnivorously, it is true, but in modern literature, and there for the most part novels, plays, biography and memoirs, and criticism: he himself never owned to a line of verse, and after his early reviewing days seems to have read little poetry. Still, even from these reaches of literature he might fill a very deep bucket, and what he dips out of it nourishes his own creations as certainly as any draught from his reservoir of personal memories. But the selectivity of taste which operated in his reading also affected his use of it.

It is not necessarily what James has most admired in his reading that finds reflection in his work. Any number of fortuitous circumstances, not to mention the counter-suggestibility so strongly developed in him, might ensure that one remembrance was utilized and another neglected. For example, he rated all the Brontës low as artists, but in *The Turn of the Screw*, for the combination of reasons I have adduced, he made extensive use of *Jane Eyre*, while ignoring *Villette* (which indeed contained little to his purpose) and *Wuthering Heights*, which he certainly read and which might be thought more potent in ghostly suggestion.

And since *Wuthering Heights* has in fact been proposed as a source for James's story (see Oscar Cargill, *Towards a Pluralistic Criticism* [Carbondale: Southern Illinois Univ. Press, 1965], p. 116), it is perhaps necessary to insist on the lack of correspondence between these two works. James's carefully decorated 'horror' is as far removed as any supernatural effect could well be from the immediacy of violence which is the prime characteristic of *Wuthering Heights*. None of Emily Brontë's characters bears the faintest resemblance to James's: it would take a high degree of critical perversity to see in the friendly, somewhat bovine Mrs. Grose anything approaching the irrepressibly loquacious and indomitably contriving Nelly Dean—whose North Country brusqueness and peasant toughness are even more of a contrast to the strained conscientiousness and sensitivity of James's governess. And the framing devices, alleged as points of resemblance, are in reality quite different. James's immediate spokesman vouches for the narrator, but has no responsibility whatever for the tale, which, itself at one remove from actuality, encloses an experience unassailably remote. Lockwood, however, is joint narrator with Nelly Dean of a continuing action in which he himself participates: quoted dates and successive generations notwithstanding, the reader has no sense of perspective in *Wuthering Heights*—the effect is one of crowding actuality.

What then of a story which, from every consideration of accessibility, and from one or two specific points of resemblance in the text, we may safely accept as influenced in part by *Wuthering Heights*—Mrs. Gaskell's 'The Old Nurse's Story'? Has this in succession, as Miss Miriam Allott suggests (in *Notes and Queries*, NS 8, March 1961, pp. 101–02), influenced *The Turn of the Screw*?

Mrs. Gaskell's story first appeared in the 1852 Extra Christmas Number of *Household Words* (pp. 11–20), when James was nine years old and is unlikely to have had access to it; but it was several times republished: in collections of 1855, 1865, and 1888, and possibly in others I have not traced. Of all these collections, that of 1855 is the one James is most likely to have seen. By July 1855 the second of the James family's pilgrimages to Europe had begun, and it is highly probable that *Lizzie Leigh and Other Tales* was among Henry James's reading in that year of adolescent sickness and convalescence. In 1866 his unsigned review of Mrs. Gaskell's *Wives and Daughters* appeared in *The Nation* (II, 246–47): he expresses a very high opinion of Mrs. Gaskell's 'genius' (for 'it *was* genius' though 'so little of an intellectual matter') as displayed both in this posthumously-issued novel and in *Cranford*, 'manifestly destined in its modest way to become a classic', while he notes the deficiencies of her *Life of Charlotte Brontë*, 'readable and delightful' as it is; but he makes no reference to any of the collections of tales. He never mentions Mrs. Gaskell again until he comes in 1903 to write his account of *William Wetmore Story and his Friends*, and there he introduces her as 'Mrs. Gaskell, the author of "Cranford," "Sylvia's Lovers," "Wives and Daughters," admirable things which time has consecrated' (I, 352). James had obviously never re-read a line of Mrs. Gaskell's; and equally obviously, even in the 1860s he attached no importance to the ghostly tales and costume pieces she hastily and sometimes awkwardly worked up for various magazines. I note that A. B. Hopkins (in *Elizabeth Gaskell: Her Life and Work* [London: Lehmann, 1952], p. 113) describes 'The Old Nurse's Story' as 'one of Mrs. Gaskell's finest achievements in the field of psychic suggestion'. Granted that it is not the worst of its kind she produced, it is nevertheless overloaded with such a medley of Gothic devices that 'terror' is neutralized, and the violence borrowed from *Wuthering Heights* loses all its impact. And there is (I should say) no question that Dickens's objection to the climax was both psychically and artistically valid: a ghostly spectacle, enhanced by sound effects both ghostly and real, is heard and witnessed by four persons, including one of the participants in the original drama, who, nearing eighty, not only views herself but is viewed by the rest as her own portrait of sixty years before come to life (gown, hat, and all). This is simultaneously having and eating not one cake but several. Gloomy house, shadowing trees, moonlight and snow, darkness and howling wind—none of these, despite the narrator's insistence, carries any suggestion of unease to the reader; neither characters nor situations are convincing. Plainly, Mrs. Gaskell's heart was not in it: she was busy with her novel *Ruth*—'The Old Nurse's Story', useful as a pot-boiler, must have been an exasperating interruption. It is impossible to believe that James, even in the days of his earliest literary experiments, even in those of his boyhood reading, admired such a story; but if one concedes that he *may* have utilized details from an undistinguished tale he *may* have read, what are the correspondent features?

Miss Allott notes as the chief of these 'the governess's struggle for Miles . . . and [the nurse] Hester's for Rosamund' in the final scene of each story. The child, appealing to 'cruel, wicked Hester' to let her join the ghost-child, 'was almost convulsed by her efforts to get away; but I held her tighter and tighter, till I feared I should do her a hurt; but rather that than let her go towards those terrible phantoms' (pp. 19–20). With this we are to compare the governess's 'drawing [Miles] close' (p. 162) at Quint's first appearance, and at the second (for she does not, as Miss Allott states, continuously 'hold on to him') trying in vain 'to press him against [her]' (p. 167), until he utters his last, despairing cry, ' "Peter Quint—you devil! . . . *Where?*" ' (p. 168), when 'I caught him, yes, I held him—it may be imagined with what a passion; but at the end of a minute I began to feel what it truly was that I held' (p. 169). But the two situations are comparable only in part. The child Rosamund, who suffers no harm, is struggling to get to phantoms which she, the nurse, and the two other women present can both see and hear; Miles is straining to see, and trying to force the governess ('he was at me in a white rage', she says) to tell him *where* he may see, the phantom visible to her but invisible to him. The governess catches and holds Miles only when he falls. The tale therefore concludes with a death tableau remarkably like that of 'The Pupil' (1891): '[Mrs. Moreen] caught him ardently in her arms. . . . The boy made no protest, and the next instant his mother, still holding him, sprang up with her face convulsed and with the terrified cry "Help, help! he's going, he's gone!" ' . . . [Pemberton] pulled him half out of his mother's hands, and for a moment, while they held him together, they looked, in their dismay, into each other's eyes.' And one remembers the sick child Dolcino in 'The Author of "Beltraffio" ' (1884): Dolcino, called by his father, 'struggled in the maternal embrace, but he was too tightly held, and after two or three fruitless efforts he suddenly turned round and buried his head deep in his mother's lap'; and of the fatal crisis it is reported, 'She held him in her arms—she pressed him to her breast, not to see him.' What we have in all three cases, surely, is the Jamesian rendering (intensity of emotion conveyed with economy of description) of the Victorian set piece 'mortal sickness/death of a child'. And in literature, if not in actual fact, Victorian children, not merely infants, as often died resting on the mother's lap and clasped in her arms, as in their beds. Not the thrill of the supernatural, not, conceivably, any memory of Mrs. Gaskell's story, but the pathos of death in childhood dominates the ending of *The Turn of the Screw*.

'Other similarities' are noted by Miss Allott 'in the prowling of the phantoms outside the house in the moonlight' (but only the child phantom 'prowls', the mother remains 'weeping and crying' under the holly trees, while in James's story it is Miles, not Quint, who 'prowls' the moonlit garden) and 'in the fact that one of them is a ravaged female figure, a "lady", passionate in life and now doomed and wretched'—but the lord's daughter clandestinely married to a 'foreign gentleman', a consummate musician (even if he is said to have 'got such a hold over the old lord') is scarcely comparable to the governess seduced by the valet (however confidential a servant he may have been). 'Finally,' we are told, '*The Turn of the Screw*, like Mrs. Gaskell's story, is supposed to be a Christmas entertainment.' But so were all ghost stories—the 'Christmas Number' is their natural setting, as it was, in fact, for two earlier ghost stories by James.

Agreement on 'likenesses', whether physical or literary, is notoriously hard to arrive at; but to me the most striking correspondence between Mrs. Gaskell's story and *The Turn of the Screw* would seem to lie in nurse Hester's search for the missing Rosamund, of the 'large blue eyes', and the governess's for the missing blue-eyed Flora—first through the house, then outside it, up the hill in the one case, round the lake in the other—a November search for both children, but by daylight for Flora and by moonlight for Rosamund. And one remembers how, on the occasion of Flora's first midnight escapade, the governess says, 'I must have gripped my little girl with a spasm that, wonderfully, she submitted to without a cry or a sign of fright' (p. 80). That phrase, 'my little girl', used only once besides of Flora (p. 16), is the one by which Rosamund always refers to the ghost-child. Is the latter blended with Flora in James's mind? The implications of such a fusion would be decidedly curious. As for Miles, his only share in Mrs. Gaskell's Christmas fantasy would seem (to me) to be his leaving the house to wander in the moonlight—his intention, according to the governess, although not by his own admission, being to meet Quint.

In sum, then, complete or imperfect, important or trivial as they may appear to different readers, there *are* undoubted resemblances between the two stories. With these particular stories, however, such resemblances need not indicate a source relationship—they may be entirely coincidental. For these are not merely ghost stories, but stories of similarly functioning ghosts. There are (for the story-teller's use) monitory but benevolent ghosts, such as Sir Edmund Orme, and there are malevolent ghosts; and these latter may on challenge destroy, as Owen Wingrave found, or they may attempt to lure their living prey to physical death and possibly spiritual damnation as well. In both *The Turn of the Screw* and 'The Old Nurse's Story' we have

malevolent luring ghosts whose quarry is a child—I am of course here ignoring the subtleties of James's story and the confusions and excrescences
of Mrs. Gaskell's. Now the prime object of ghosts bent on enticing children
to destruction must be to get them away from their appointed guardians,
and this separation is most easily effected by luring them out of doors. Moreover the literary demands of picturesqueness and 'terror', no less than the
known predilections of ghosts, combine to make stormy nights, or nights of
moonlight and black shadows, the settings most favoured for these attempts.
So 'moonlight prowling' and stormy nights resonant with ghostly suggestion
are commonplaces of the whole genre, as the ever-watchful guardian and the
elusive child are of the sub-class.

But we have also to remember that both our authors have drawn very
freely on one and the same source, and that in so doing their invention may
well have been stimulated to similar expedients. For Miss Allott ignores a
novel which equally with *Wuthering Heights* has contributed to Mrs. Gaskell's story—*Jane Eyre*. It is *Jane Eyre*, not *Wuthering Heights*, that has
produced Furnivall Manor House, with its many-windowed front, its broad
gallery and great stair, its family portraits, its mysteriously disused suite of
rooms, its 'grand' hall with the bronze chandelier and (oddly located) the
billiard table. Mrs. Gaskell unwittingly betrays her dependence on *Jane
Eyre* when in mid career the servant Agnes becomes 'Bessy' and retails local
superstitions. And there is one curious, if trifling, correspondence. The child
Jane Eyre, on a miserable day of 'black frost' at Gateshead, 'covered [her]
head and arms with the skirt of [her] frock' and went out to walk in the
'plantation' (iv, 39): so nurse Hester, 'throwing the skirt of [her] gown over
[her] head for a cloak' (p. 15), ran out to look for the child Rosamund on the
snowy hillside by the holly trees. By contrast, the only specific points derived from *Wuthering Heights* are the sweeping boughs of the trees that dar-
ken the windows (pp. 12–13) and the child phantom's battering at the window
to be let in (p. 17). The ruined organ that plays of itself on windy nights,
the father equally obsessed by music and by pride of rank, the proud and
jealous sisters and their love for the same foreign musician, their portraits,
the sinister holly trees, the final burst of ghostly *son et lumière*—these come
neither from *Jane Eyre* nor from *Wuthering Heights*.

James derived the theme of luring spirits, each with a child victim, from
Archbishop Benson's anecdote; Mrs. Gaskell's source for the theme has not
been identified. It may be pertinent, in this connection, to remember that as
a child and youth Edward White Benson frequently visited Yorkshire relatives, including his cousins the Sidgwicks of Stonegappe (where he might
even have been present when, in 1839, 'the volume [or, the stone] was flung'
at governess Charlotte Brontë); and that the same Yorkshire ghost tale may
have been related both to him and to Mrs. Gaskell. *Her* informant might
possibly have been Charlotte Brontë herself, fascinated as she was all her
life by the supernatural. But in any case this common theme, however

derived, and the Brontëan infusion of emotion in the picturesque are sufficient to account for any resemblances between 'The Old Nurse's Story' and *The Turn of the Screw*—the dissimilarity of which, in any comparison genuinely literary, is what chiefly strikes the candid reader. In these circumstances, one requires some positive indication that James *knew* Mrs. Gaskell's story—that if he read it in youth he remembered it vividly forty years on (as he did *David Copperfield*), or that in 1897 some accident brought Mrs. Gaskell once more to his attention (as it did Charlotte Brontë). In June 1897, he has told us, he read 'a succession of novels': would *Mary Barton and other Tales* (1888) have been among the number? It seems more than doubtful.

A similar caveat applies to a novel which offers incidental correspondences quite as striking as those furnished thematically by Mrs. Gaskell—Mrs. Henry Wood's *The Master of Greylands*, first published in 1873. Here, set in rural England of the old coaching days, we have the story of a disputed inheritance which involves, centrally, murder and its detection, against a background of smuggling camouflaged by a sham haunting, and which (to cope with this and the three romantic sub-plots) employs a cast of some two dozen mainly conventional but clearly differentiated personages, at least nine of whom play major rôles and all of whom have speaking parts. An essential *ficelle* is supplied by a pretty, fair-haired, but 'indulged, selfish, ill-bred girl of twelve, sufficiently forward in some things for one twice her age' (p. 21), who is given to outbursts of evil temper and abuse of her would-be teachers (for instance, ' "You ill-natured, wicked, interfering dromedary!" ' [p. 129]), and who has already defeated three governesses. Her name is Flora, and a manservant in the same household is named Miles. In one passage their names are coupled: the true heir has arrived from France to claim his patrimony—' "Who was the young man?" "Flora described him as wearing a coat trimmed with fur; and Miles thought he spoke with a foreign accent," replied [Flora's mother], deviating unconsciously from the question' (p. 58). Next, the young French wife of the now-vanished heir arrives with her sick child, incognita, to search for her husband; and on her first night at the inn receives a supernatural intimation of his death: a wild storm rises 'without apparent warning'.

A blast of wind shook the white dimity curtain, drawn before the casement, and she turned to it with a shiver. What did this angry storm mean? . . .

'If the spirits of the dead are permitted to haunt the air, as some believe, it may be that *his* spirit is here now, seeking to hold commune with mine; calling upon me to avenge him. . . .'

As though to encourage the singular fancy, . . . a rushing blast wilder than any that had gone before swept past the house at the moment and died away in a wild and melancholy moan. The casement shook as though some unhappy spirit were indeed craving admission: and the poor young lady, in some irrepressible access of courage, born of desperation, drew aside the curtain and looked forth.

No, no; nothing there but the wind. . . .

The little child stirred in bed and threw out her arms. Her mother let fall the window curtain and softly approached her. . . . [She is thirsty, and is given a 'cup of herb tea'.] Before her mother had replaced [the cup] . . . and returned to her, her pretty face was on the pillow again, her eyes were closing. (pp. 152–53)

The young wife, in virtue of her excellent French, is engaged as Flora's governess, and one night, armed with a skeleton key, rummages a bureau to discover proof of her husband's fate:

Flora was fast asleep in her room in the front corridor, . . . for she had been in to see, and had taken the precaution of turning the key on the child for safety: it would not do to be interrupted by *her*. Yet another minute she stood listening, candle in hand. Then, swiftly crossing the corridor, she stole into the study through the double doors.

The further convolutions and final unravelling of the Greylands mystery invite no comparison with James's story, but the parallels already noted are undeniably close. Are they evidence of a source relationship? I would say that the clearest indications appear in James's treatment of Flora. In the 'storm' episodes what we have to allow for, probably, is both authors' familiarity with the same original—Sheridan Le Fanu's *The Cock and Anchor*. Mrs. Wood, unlike James, records no acquaintance with Le Fanu or his book, but her freak storm is an obvious importation. At most, one would think, a recollection of the sick child has added 'a touch of picture' to James's midnight scene.

Even accepting all the correspondences, however, we are left with the question: when can James have read the book? The possibilities are more narrowly defined than in the case of 'The Old Nurse's Story'. During 1873, the year of publication, he was still on his travels, immersed in his experience of Europe. During the years 1874–76, when *Roderick Hudson* and *The American* were in the making, his enforced, journalistic reading and his current literary enthusiasms would between them have excluded such a novel as *The Master of Greylands*. My guess would be that in 1877, his thoughts already turning to the production of the really 'big' novel, which should make his fortune, he applied himself to study the technique of the best-seller. Mrs. Wood's sales were already reckoned not in thousands, but in millions; and James, no doubt with a contempt to equal Meredith's, must long since have read *East Lynne* (1861–62), the most enduringly popular of all her books. *The Master of Greylands* was in comparison unsuccessful—by 1921, as tallied in the Macmillan edition from which I quote, only 80,000 copies had been printed—but it was completely typical of her method. What at first took James's attention, however, so as to divert him from his major purpose, was the romantic sub-plot involving the brother of the murdered heir. He is a charming young man, a French-speaking cosmopolite, an amateur painter, competent enough to have supported himself through years of roving, and as well as establishing his claim to the inheritance, he courts and wins his modestly beautiful, 'put-upon' cousin-by-marriage. His own sister-in-law, by the way, is named Charlotte. This is half the plot and probably the initial suggestion for *The Europeans*, so utterly different in its total effect. But there is no disputing the antecedents of Felix Young—even to the family likeness. The murdered elder brother had been 'a slight, active man of some eight-and-twenty years, under middle height, with a fresh, pleasant, handsome face, and bright dark eyes' (pp. 31–32); the younger was a 'tall, slender' man 'of perhaps some six-and-twenty years. He was very good-looking; with a fair, attractive face, blue eyes, and light wavy hair that took a tinge of gold in the sunlight' (p. 265). Felix Young is 'eight-and-twenty years old' and has 'a short, slight, well-made figure'; he is also (with that mixture of traits characteristic of families) 'fair-haired, clear-faced, witty-looking', with 'a warm blue eye'.

The projected 'big' novel, however, was not so long delayed as to escape all the effects of James's enquiry. It would be absurd to claim that Isabel's rejection of Goodwood and return to Osmond were inspired by Mrs. Wood's heroine Mary Ursula, who refuses marriage with the man she still loves in order to keep faith with the sisterhood she has undertaken to lead. Yet the moral justification is the same in both cases, even though James stops short of expressing it: Mrs. Wood quotes her 'warning verse' (Luke, ix. 62) with pietistic unction. Influence in minor details is easier to accept. Mrs. Wood, although she frequently asserts her disbelief in ghosts, is equally emphatic concerning the validity of signs and portents, dreams and visions; and she deals largely in symbolic breakages: 'At that moment a sound, as of some frail thing broken, was heard. . . . The Dresden vase lay on the hearth, shivered. . . . "Oh, papa! How did it happen?" "My dear, I swept it off with my elbow: I am very sorry," said Mr. Peter Castlemaine' (p. 59). It looks as though both Isabel's ghostly summons in Ch. 55, so heavily prepared for in Ch. 5, and the motif (in Ch. 49) of the delicate cracked cup which Osmond nearly lets fall, were best-selling devices hopefully applied to *The Portrait of a Lady*. And in that case not merely *The Turn of the Screw* but even *The Golden Bowl*, with its ponderously fragile successor to Madame Merle's cracked cup, may show the impress of Mrs. Henry Wood. Since it is unbelievable that, in June 1897, James should feel any inducement to reread a novel, by his standards, so devoid of art as *The Master of Greylands*, the correspondences traceable in *The Turn of the Screw* must be rooted in memories at least twenty years old. 'A good story', one may concede, has a vitality independent of literary merit: it remains viable just so long as the 'fictive world' it portrays remains intelligible. How long its suggestiveness for art persists in memory, is another matter.

But if caution is necessary in dealing with possible literary sources, one has to be even more guarded in ascribing to James a knowledge of scientific works. 'Accessibility' in this case, as many critics fail to note, is limited by more considerations than date or linguistic medium. For instance, as far as date or language is concerned, James *could* have read Breuer's and Freud's *Studien über Hysterie* in 1895; but unless William James or Frederic Myers (by letter or in conversation) specifically directed his attention to it, he would never have been aware of the book's existence, nor, probably, of its authors'. And if he *did* chance to hear of it, would he have read it? Cargill's reasoning here ('*The Turn of the Screw* and Alice James', p. 247) seems to me in the last degree implausible. Is it likely that after the painful termination of Alice James's illness, the burden of which and of her long invalidism had fallen heavily on the brother in England, Henry James should feel impelled to satisfy a 'continuing interest in his sister's case' by reading scientific treatises on hysteria? Such an interest and such reading might be expected of William, the professional psychologist; maintained by Henry, they would argue either a morbidly brooding grief or a coldly impersonal, 'scientific' curiosity—tendencies equally foreign to his temperament and incompatible with the known facts of his busy and sociable life. Even in 1895, that relatively unproductive year, he was neither solitary nor idle.

Cranfill and Clark (*An Anatomy of* The Turn of the Screw, pp. 36–37) add another link to this particular chain of error. 'James,' they argue, 'inevitably gained a personal, sometimes intimate knowledge of his sister Alice's mental illness with its attendant delusions and fantasies. His interest in these could scarcely have expired with her death in 1892.' So, as well as consulting Breuer and Freud, James must have 'prepared himself for his task' of writing *The Turn of the Screw* by reading Edmund Parish's *Hallucinations and Illusions: a Study of the Fallacies of Perception* (London: Walter Scott, 1897), first because 'Parish was a disciple of' William James, 'whom he often quotes', and secondly because this book was a London publication of 1897, and thus 'the last word on the subject'. A number of absurdities are combined in Cranfill's and Clark's hypothesis. The book in question was not published till July 1897; James was then still busy with *What Maisie Knew* and his *Harper's* letters, but he was also partially 'on vacation' in Bournemouth; and August, with a visit to Torquay as brief interlude to rustication in Suffolk, was even more of a holiday month. Is it suggested that in September or later, with his attention divided between Lamb House and the actual composition of his new story, James at the eleventh hour decided to lay a thoroughly scientific foundation for his ghosts? Or are we to suppose that for those evenings he spent in retreat from cousinly sociability at Dunwich, or from Norris's music at Torquay, he had armed himself with the English translation of a Munich professor's learned treatise on sensory delusions—a work which from its 'multitude of references' provided 'by far the most complete bibliography of the subject in existence'? Such was the SPR reviewer's estimate, in 1895 (*PSPR*, XI, 162–71), of Herr Edmund Parish's *Ueber die Trugwahrnehmung* (*Hallucination und Illusion*) . . . (Leipzig:

Abel, 1894). For the book was not in 1897 a new one, although for the English translation material from a later pamphlet (*Zur Kritik des Telepathischen Beweis Materiels*, 1897) was worked in. Nor would its author have tolerated the label of 'disciple' to William James, whom he quotes (not always with approval) as only one among many writers on the problems under discussion. Parish's own treatise was, in fact, one of numerous critical evaluations of the data which psychological experimentation (notably in France and in Germany) was currently producing in abundance, and like his fellow *savants* Parish had a thesis to maintain and another to demolish. He held that under various pathological and physiological conditions, including sleep and hypnosis, 'dissociation of consciousness' caused by obstruction of nervous impulses, and 'enforced association' caused by their diversion from the higher nerve centres explained both illusions and hallucinations; and this contention he supported by a variety of evidence, much of it supplied by the English Society for Psychical Research, whose theory of telepathy he was at pains to refute.

Cranfill and Clark not only ignore the scope and intention of Parish's work, but also, perhaps unintentionally, misrepresent the very small portion (Ch. iii, pp. 83–99) which they summarize:

He states that hallucinations most frequently attack women fifteen to thirty years of age, who experience more than half of all such seizures during this period, and that the lustrum from twenty to twenty-five yields the highest percentage of all. James's governess is twenty. (Alice James's first violent attacks of hysteria occurred, incidentally, when she was nearing twenty.) Parish's investigation of the causes of hallucinations also turns one's thoughts toward Bly. He lists 1) morbid emotional states, 2) a state of mental or physical exhaustion, 3) vivid expectation, and 4) the hypnogenic tendency of prolonged reading. (p. 37)

Actually, combining results independently reached in America, France, and Germany with those arrived at by the English Committee, Parish estimates that in the Census of Hallucinations a percentage of 14·56 among the women, but only 9·75 among the men, owned to having such experiences; and he computes that 52 per cent of the hallucinations reported in the English Census [sex not here distinguished] occurred 'between 15 and 30 years of age': 'The lustrum from 20 to 25 yields the highest percentage of all—over 21 per cent.; while after that their frequency diminishes in a regular curve' (pp. 83–84). Again, while the four 'causes of hallucinations' selected roughly correspond to factors noted by Parish (e.g. for 'morbid emotional states' read 'nervous disturbances, such as grief or anxiety', pp. 95–96), they have been given a new order and emphasis. It is, incidentally, surprising that critics who number the governess's 'seizures' and who also regard Parish's book as a source have not quoted the following passage:

In a few cases the informants state that they fainted from terror or shock at the apparition. Such communications remind us so forcibly of the hallucinations of the epileptic and hystero-epileptic aura, that we can hardly resist the conclusion that they occurred in a semi-conscious state, possibly of very short duration, preceding a state of complete unconsciousness. (pp. 99–100)

Can the reason be that for 'seizures' 1 to 6, during which the governess *may* have experienced what Parish would call a temporary 'dissociation of consciousness', James provides no indication of a subsequent fainting-fit, and that 'seizure 7', the second apparition by the lake, following which the governess *may* have fainted, is attended by marked activity and volubility on her part?

But the really extraordinary feature of their citation is that they ignore Parish's own acknowledgment (p. 82 and note) of the source from which his data are chiefly drawn—the 'Census Report' in Volume X of the SPR *Proceedings*. If, as seems probable, Henry James used *PSPR* Volume X, he *might* have seen the announcement (p. 401) of Parish's work in its original, German version, which he *could* therefore have consulted. All the leading psychical investigators, English and American, no doubt read both Parish's treatise of 1894 and his pamphlet of 1897—Myers and Podmore certainly did so, as William James must have done. They had to know their enemy; for they were all in some degree committed to the theory of telepathy Parish was attacking. But why should Henry James so occupy himself? The only material treated by Parish which Cranfill and Clark judge relevant to *The Turn of the Screw* was already under his hand—and presented, one may observe, in a form incomparably more lively and suggestive. The summarized examples, especially those from the Munich collection, with which Parish replaces the SPR narratives, efficiently (in the Teutonic manner) 'repel delight'.

Cranfill and Clark, like Cargill earlier, seem not to appreciate what Henry James's reading of such works as Parish's would imply—a preoccupation with highly specialized psychological problems in their laboratory aspects, and an interest in following explanatory clues through years, and tomes, of controversy. But of such an absorbing interest there is no trace in James's works, in his letters, or in his 'legend', and to be plain, there was no intellectual basis (of native scientific ability or acquired knowledge) on which such an interest could be sustained. 'There are diversities of gifts,' and Henry James did not covet those of his brother William: indeed, he was to an exceptional degree conscious of the proper limits of his art and its exercise. An 'intelligent interest' in 'questions of the day', as discussed among friends or as argued in newspapers and literary periodicals, might furnish material for easy speculation on the phenomena of mediumship, say, or hypnotism, or 'thought transference', from which (perhaps) might come hints for a tale. To play the scientist or the philosopher himself, by systematic reading in such fields, would have been the most useless and laughable of pretensions. To pursue even one specific 'enquiry' in this way would certainly never have occurred to him. For supposing his mind to have been 'caught' by a scientific problem—a physiological difficulty posed by hallucinations, for example— his impulse would surely have been to consult the family authority on the subject: to turn to his presentation copy of *The Principles of Psychology*— those 'great volumes' which, he had told William, he would 'save up' and imbibe at his leisure 'like sips of sherbet'. And supposing further that, in his unwonted thirst for information, he found the treatment of hallucinations in this work too cursory, would he conscientiously 'follow up' William's recommendations for additional reading—to James Sully's *Illusions*, for instance, by 1895 in its fourth edition, or to what William considered 'the most important thing on the subject from the point of view of theory', Myers's article of 1889 on the Daemon of Socrates? Would he not rather appeal to William directly, or to Myers, if the occasion presented itself, and there make an end?

I do not, of course, suggest that James lacked the capacity for intensive reading: he would 'prepare himself' for a major critical review (such as his essay on Dumas *fils*) in just this fashion. He would 'steep himself' till he was 'saturated', even in so familiar a body of work, and only then feel he had command of all the impressions it could yield. But he would not 'prepare himself' for a fictional evocation of ghosts by 'studying' the latest scientific theories of hallucinations. His brother's works, which thoroughly or not Henry James certainly read, those by Gurney and by Myers which he may have read, had an attraction for him quite independent of their scientific or philosophical purport, and such reading, the product of spontaneous, personal interest, might well find some reflection in his own work. But the studies of Breuer and Freud or Parish are as irrelevant to *The Turn of the Screw*, or any other of James's ghostly tales, as treatises on cancer or tuberculosis would be to *The Wings of the Dove*.

A problem different from either of the foregoing is posed by the records of the Society for Psychical Research, which are neither literature, philosophy, nor science, but an olio of all three. For the present-day reader, at least, the narratives, boring as William James found them, have an antiquarian interest comparable to that of the private diaries and letters of the same bygone age, while the speculative discussions based on them continually surprise by their modernity of outlook and expression. But the contemporaries of Myers and Gurney (whether merely curious, or sceptical, or hot for spiritual certainty) turned to these records for psychical information only— would in fact, as Sidgwick realized, be suspicious of literary graces. Since, whatever his practical aim of the moment, Henry James remained the creative artist, it might happen that as well as the typical, authentic detail (the staircase haunting, the phantasm seen only in part, and so on) he gathered some overtone of suggestion, some 'touch of picture' which would be applied in his own work. But, curiosity once satisfied, he can have had only the one overt, professional object in any subsequent consultation of these volumes—if indeed he did not rely solely on the memory of his first impressions. And from how many of the twelve volumes issued between 1882 and 1898 can we assume these impressions to have been derived?

Professor Roellinger, in his article on 'Psychical Research and "The Turn of the Screw" ', does not raise the question; but, from the parallels he quotes, he seems to assume James's familiarity with the whole range. The three cases he cites as particularly relevant to *The Turn of the Screw* all come from *PSPR*, III (1885): the appearance to three children of the figure of an old lady, who always '*looked* a great deal', in various rooms and frequently on the stairs (pp. 126–27); the repeated appearances to a governess, 'who kept a diary for many years', to five of her girl pupils, and to their mother of a woman 'dressed in black, with a large white collar or kerchief, very dark hair, and pale face', seen in various parts of the house, but most frequently on the stairs and in the hall (pp. 119–22); the appearance to various servants, to a grown-up daughter of the house, to a young child, and to a visiting nurse of 'a pale woman in black', 'with an evil face' according to some witnesses, with a dislocated neck according to others, seen on the stairs and in various rooms (pp. 122–26). Professor Roellinger also cites the identification of a ghost from an exact description of the clothes worn (*PSPR*, V [1888–89], 446], and another percipient's awareness on one occasion 'of being watched', and on two other occasions of feeling 'an icy wind blowing' through the room (*PSPR*, III, 116). It is strange that he disregards the case immediately preceding this last: here a percipient records her awareness more than once 'that there was a woman in the room, but I could not look up till she had gone. . . . Her face seemed in darkness, and yet I *could* see it. You will laugh, because it was all at my back. I am curious to know if anyone will believe in a *non*-seeing sight. I saw her in the back of my head; my face was to the wall. I felt I *could* not move' (*PSPR*, III, 114–15). This is an even closer parallel than the one chosen by Professor Roellinger to the governess's certainty 'without direct vision' of Miss Jessel's 'presence' at the lakeside (pp. 55–57), and as an illustration is more striking, if only because the experience has been intellectualized in the governess's manner. But in each of Professor Roellinger's cases, the correspondence he stresses is provided by some standard feature recurrent in narrative after psychical narrative, while the distinctive features which characterize the occurrence and make it memorable are not reflected in *The Turn of the Screw*. What he has demonstrated is James's familiarity with the stock items of the *materia psychica*, not the precise combinations James has drawn upon for his own use. We cannot say 'Here and nowhere else is James's authority for such and such details', as we are (I think) safe in doing when Voltaire and Beaupré and Orme, found in a single volume of the Society's *Proceedings*, turn up with apparent inconsequence in James's own work, and when not only the familiar 'woman in black', but also details peculiar to the narratives of Miss X. and of Mlle Julie Marchand appear with cumulative effect in *The Turn of the Screw*. Here (to use a favourite image of Gurney's) we have, not dependent links in an evidential chain, but independently corroborative sticks of evidence which massed together are unbreakable. James's text, therefore, by itself proves his familiarity with *PSPR* Volume VI, but as well we have the strong presumption of his interest in and possession of the volume.

As regards *PSPR* Volume VIII the textual evidence is less plentiful, and the circumstantial evidence depends to some extent on our acceptance of that for Volume VI; yet again the combination of factors is strong enough to warrant our declaring Volume VIII to be one of James's sources. It must, however, be noted that the one detail selected by Professor Roellinger, telling as it is—the occurrence in this volume of the name 'Quint'—would not in isolation be conclusive. 'Quint' is a very rare surname indeed in Great Britain, but though still uncommon, it is considerably less rare in the United States and Canada, where, not surprisingly in view of its French origin, it occurs chiefly along the eastern seaboard (in New England, especially Boston, and New York) and in Montreal. It was not recorded by James in his *Notebooks* precisely because it was *not* strange to him. No doubt, encountering it in Volume VIII, he would be struck by its appropriateness to his purposes; but, as I have argued in Chapter VI, v above, his choice of 'Peter Quint' to name the 'evil valet' of *The Turn of the Screw* was determined by quite other considerations than its sound. This in itself (*pace* Professor Roellinger) is not suggestive of anything more repulsive or dangerous than briskness and sharpness, rattle and snap; and these would be its connotations for the reader had the hero of *The Reverberator*, for example, been named 'Quint' instead of 'Flack'. Immediately preceding Wilson Quint's testimony in Volume VIII is that of Amos Crum, and apart altogether from its connotations in American slang, the latter monosyllable (if the onomatopœia were to be narrowly phonetic) is much more unpleasantly suggestive. But James was never, I think, primarily concerned with the sound of the names he chose for his characters: what counted was their symbolic value, or the associations, chiefly literary, they brought into play. Those responsive to the vocables 'Peter Quint' have nothing to do with Wilson, savings-bank clerk of Everett, Mass., for all his supernatural pretensions; and a one-time resident of New York and Boston would not *need* his signature as intermediary suggestion, even though to meet it, five times repeated, might stimulate the associative process. When, however, besides the name 'Quint', we find in *PSPR* Volume VIII two narratives reminiscent of Griffin's ghost story, a case in which the bare-headed, red-bearded, phantasmal intruder is unknown to the percipient, and the complete record of the 'Morton' case, we have to acknowledge another unbreakable bundle of significant details.

The evidence for James's use of *PSPR* Volume X is much less strong.

Here again the quoted narratives exemplify many of the customary features in the psychic repertory—the woman in black, the appearance at a window, and so on. But of some two hundred reported experiences, only one—the Irish idyll I have noted in Chapter VIII, vi above—offers, in its atypical setting, the possible source of a descriptive detail in *The Turn of the Screw*. A further indication, to my mind, is given by the disclaimers and qualifications James from time to time insinuates into the governess's report—such as the mention of her anxiety over family troubles (p. 38), or the hints of a state of expectancy caused initially by strange noises (pp. 16, 76)—which, as their designed effect, add the note (the very keynote of the Census Report) of cautious dubiety to the testimony of experience, but also, whether intentionally or not, suggest conformity to prescription. The Census Report as it were codifies the rules of the apparitional game, and in an impressive number of details (as is shown by the passage I quote in Chapter VIII, vi above) the behaviour of James's phantasms strictly accords with the rules. Yet these, after all, could be inferred from a reading of even a few narratives. On the other hand the contact with Myers at Aston Clinton offers a certain presumption in favour of James's direct consultation, on Myers's advice, of the important psychical dossier made available in *PSPR* Volume X. But definite, incontrovertible evidence is lacking: the case must be regarded as 'not proven'. Other readers might be more, or less, impressed by such hints of a source-relationship, enhanced or dulled as such correspondences always are by subjective associations.

Indeed, the hazards of source-identification are nowhere better exemplified than in this third category, the records of psychical phenomena. It is to be remembered that the Society for Psychical Research itself, counting only *Phantasms of the Living* and the annual *Proceedings*, had by 1894 published well over one thousand separate narratives of experience, in sampling which the critical palate, unlike the wine-taster's, soon fails to discriminate. In fact, the SPR records, appropriately enough considering their theme, are more often than not sources of illusory correspondences and deceptive echoes: what, on a first reading, vividly recalls a motif in some ghostly tale on a second or third proves nothing like. As an example, I offer a passage from one of these narratives, which, if the identification is accepted, would show that Professor Roellinger is right and I am wrong: that, to a limited degree at least, *PSPR* Volume V *did* provide a source for Henry James. The narrator is one of two lady friends, occupying rented lodgings in a widow's house:

One evening, we had been sitting up reading rather later than usual, and did not rise to retire until within a few minutes to 12 o'clock. We went upstairs together, I being perhaps a couple of steps behind my friend, when, on reaching the topmost step, I felt something suddenly slip behind me from an unoccupied room to the left of the stairs. Thinking it must be imagination, no one being in the house except the widow and servant, who occupied rooms on another landing. I did not speak to my friend, who turned off to a room on the right, but walked quickly into my own room which faced the staircase, still feeling as though a tall figure were behind and bending over me. I turned on the gas, struck a light and was in the act of applying it, when I felt a heavy grasp on my arm of a hand minus the middle finger. Upon this I uttered a loud cry, which brought my friend, the widow lady, and the servant girl into the room, to inquire the cause of my alarm. The two latter turned very pale on hearing the story. The house was thoroughly searched, but nothing was discovered. (p. 464)

Afterwards it was learned that the widow's late husband 'had lost the middle finger of his right hand', or, as the friend reports the matter, the 'late husband of the landlady had only three fingers on the one hand'. Did Henry James once read this passage, and recalling it in 1906, after a lapse of perhaps ten perhaps nearer twenty years, use the detail of the missing fingers to characterize Spencer Brydon's double? Or did he, on his return to America in 1904, *observe* just such a maimed personification of Success?

There remains one persistent ghost of a source which it may be as well to lay. Thirty years ago it was suggested (R. L. Wolff, 'The Genesis of "The Turn of the Screw" ', *American Literature*, XIII [1941], 1–8) that James's conception of Bly and its setting had been inspired by a full-page illustration in the 1891 Christmas Number of *Black and White*—the same number of the same magazine in which 'Sir Edmund Orme' appeared. From his disapproving mention of it in the *Preface* to Volume XVII of the New York Edition, we know that James saw his story in its magazine format, and he had only to turn thirty pages to see also 'The Haunted House', engraved by C. Streller from a drawing by T. Griffiths. If he did, what were the details that *could* so have impressed him as to be reproduced in *The Turn of the Screw*? In fact, only the presence of two children, boy and girl, and a 'lake'. The children do not live in the house, which is seemingly derelict: as the girl's basket of wildflowers suggests, they are making their twilight way home from play in the woods, on the edge of which this desirable residence had been erected. There is, if not a 'tower', a turret, but only the ghost of a steeplejack could haunt its pepper-pot roof. There is also a quite irrelevant glassed conservatory, which, with the conglomeration of styles, might indicate that the house was built during the railway boom and abandoned after the crash of 1848. Alternatively, the single lighted window, and the white-shrouded figure dimly visible through it, might belong to some congener of Mr. Mopes, whose domain (one remembers) in its 'mist of home-brewed marvel and romance' could also boast 'its ruined water'—'a slimy pond'.

Now James does on occasion use a picture, an individual identifiable picture, or else the characteristic *œuvre* of a specified artist, as motif in his fiction. He takes pains to tell us when he does so, or he would quite lose his effect, which is both subtle and important. Thus in 'The Diary of a Man of Fifty', Andrea del Sarto and Raphael's 'Madonna of the Chair' are invoked to suggest on the one hand trouble of mind and on the other unrealized domestic bliss; the Bronzino portrait in *The Wings of the Dove* is an intimation of death to Milly Theale and the reader; a landscape by Lambinet interprets for Strether the actuality of the French countryside. Who, even in James's own day, would unassisted conjure up Lambinet as the genius of the scene that beguiles his hero? And who, enjoying this aid, can miss the special limitation of vision which James has imposed on his aging *revenant*? But granting a special tolerance on James's part for the work of certain illustrators (Abbey, Boughton, Du Maurier, Parsons, for instance), so long as they did not meddle with the reader's conception of his own stories, what was there to appeal to him (if it caught his eye at all) in the reproduction of a commonplace 'pictorial anecdote' by the undistinguished landscape painter Tom Griffiths? The 'acres of canvas' yearly exhibited at Burlington House often included some work by Griffiths, but never anything to win a mention from James. Yet (we are to suppose) this particular banality haunted his imagination for six years to produce, unacknowledged, one detail of setting in *The Turn of the Screw*.

Here is a fallacy of the same kind as the identification of James's governess with Freud's patient, Miss Lucy R., on the grounds that each had two pupils and was in love with her employer. In this case, somewhat recalling the comparisons between Macedon and Monmouth, there is a lake in the picture, and there is a lake at Bly. I do not think this degree of resemblance would ever have appeared significant, even to a commentator unfamiliar with the English scene, if James had not, in his letters to Myers and Waldstein, described his subject as 'merely *pictorial*' and his own primary intention as that 'always, of the artist, the *painter*'. But if James's statement that his governess 'has "authority"' can be misinterpreted to mean that she is authoritarian, one should not be surprised at the assumption that for the appropriate treatment of a 'pictorial' subject he must have been indebted to an actual picture.

Index

Numbers in roman type refer to pages; numbers in *italic* refer to notes. In general, recipients of letters quoted (other than those from Henry and William James), editors of texts used, and authors of books or critical articles referred to, together with the modern periodicals in which these latter appear, are cited in the relevant notes, but are not indexed.